Multicultural Education of Children and Adolescents

by

LEROY G. BARUTH
Appalachian State University

and

M. LEE MANNING
Columbia College of South Carolin

To daughters Katey, Kelly, and Seana, and wife, Carmella, for their continuing example of the benefits of living in a diverse society

LGB

To my family: My wife Marianne, my children Jennifer and Michael, and the children's grandmothers, Margaret and Annie

MLM

Series Editorial Assistant: Carol L. Chernaik
Editorial-Production Service: Benchmark Productions
Cover Administrator: Linda Dickinson
Cover Designer: Suzanne Harbison
Manufacturing Buyer: Louise Richardson

Copyright © 1992 by Allyn and Bacon
A Division of Simon & Schuster, Inc.
160 Gould Street
Needham Heights, MA 02194

Library of Congress Cataloging-in-Publication Data

Baruth, Leroy G.
    Multicultural education of children and adolescents / by Leroy G.
Baruth and M. Lee Manning.
        p.   cm.
    Includes bibliographical references (p.   ) and index.
    ISBN 0-205-13410-6
        1. Intercultural education—United States.   2. Indians of North
American—Education.   3. Afro-American children—Education.   4. Asian
Americans—Education.   5. Hispanic American children—Education.
I. Manning, M. Lee.   II. Title.
LC1099.3.B37   1992
370.19'341—dc20   91-22985
                                                                              CIP

Printed in the United States of America
    10 9 8 7 6 5 4 3 2   97 96 95 94 93 92

Brief Contents

Part I   Understanding Culture and Ethnicity In a   1
Pluralistic Nation

Chapter 1   Our Increasingly Multicultural Society   1

Part II   Understanding Culturally Diverse Learners   29

Chapter 2   Understanding Native-American Children and   29
Adolescents

Chapter 3   Understanding African-American Children and   58
Adolescents

Chapter 4   Understanding Asian-American Children and   87
Adolescents

Chapter 5   Understanding Hispanic-American Children and   114
Adolescents

Part III   Understanding Multicultural Education: 145
Curriculum and Teaching Concerns

Chapter 6   Multicultural Education   145

Chapter 7   Curricular Efforts   167

Chapter 8   Instructional Practices   196

Chapter 9   Individual and Cultural Differences   226

Chapter 10   Culturally Diverse Parents and Families   252

Chapter 11   Administrators and Special School Personnel   286

Part IV   Understanding the Future of Multicultural   318
Education

Chapter 12   Multicultural Education in the 21st Century: 318
Unresolved Issues, Prospects, Challenges

Contents

Part I   **Understanding Culture and Ethnicity In a Pluralistic Nation**   1

Chapter 1 An Increasingly Multicultural Society   1

Overview   2

An Increasing Multicultural Society   2
Historical Perspectives: The Melting Pot Ideology   2   Contemporary
Perspective: The Salad Bowl Ideology   2

Children and Adolescents in an Increasingly Multicultural
Society   5
Culturally Different Populations   5   The Selection of Cultures for
this Text: A Rationale   9

Understanding Diversity   9
Culture   9   Race   10   Ethnicity   11   Socioeconomic   12   Gender
13   Individual   15

Challenges In a Culturally Diverse Society   15
Forming a Perspective on Culture: Deficits, Differences, and
Mismatches   15   Understanding and Reducing
Racism   18   Understanding and Clarifying
Stereotypes   20   Understanding and Helping Children and
Adolescents Develop   20   Positive Individual and Cultural
Identities   20

Multicultural Education: The School's Response to Diversity   22
Emergence of Multicultural Education   22   Definition and
Rationales   23   A Brief Historical Overview   24

Summing Up   26

Suggested Learning Activities   27

Expanding Your Horizons: Suggested Journal Readings and
Books   27

Part II   **Understanding Culturally Diverse Learners**   29

Chapter 2 Understanding Native-American Children and Adolescents   29

Overview   30

The Native-American People   30
Origins   30   Native-Americans Today   30

Stereotyping of Native-American Children and Adolescents   32

Native-American Children and Adolescents 33
Cultural Characteristics 33 Socioeconomic
Status 37 Families 38 Religion 40 Language 41 Cultural
Comparisons: Native-American and Anglo-American Children and
Adolescents 42

Native-American Learners in the School 43
Educators' Understanding Native-American Learners and Their
Culture 43 Developmental Theory: Children and
Adolescents 47 Achievement Level 47 Language
Problems 48 Learning Styles: Cultural Considerations 49 School
Practices Impeding Native-Americans' Progress 51 Promoting
Positive Self-Concepts and Cultural Identities 51 Cultural Portrait:
John—A Native-American Learner 53 How John's Teacher Can
Respond 54

Summing Up 54

Suggested Learning Activities 55

Expanding Your Horizons: Additional Journal Readings and
Books 56

Expanding Your Students' Horizons: Appropriate Native-American
Books for Children and Adolescents 56

Chapter 3 Understanding African-American Children and Adolescents 58

Introduction 58

The African-American People 59
Origins 59 African-Americans Today 60

Stereotyping of African-American Children and Adolescents 62

African-American Children and Adolescents 63
Cultural Characteristics 63 Socioeconomic
Status 67 Families 68 Religion 70 Language 71 Cultural
Comparisons: African-American and Anglo-American Children and
Adolescents 72

African-American Learners in the School 72
Educators' Understanding African-American Learners and Their
Culture 72 Developmental Theory: Children and
Adolescents 73 Achievement Level 74 Language
Problems 76 Learning Styles: Cultural Considerations 78 School
Practices Impeding African-Americans' Progress 78 Promoting
Positive Self-Concepts and Cultural Identities 81 Cultural Portrait:
Paul—An African-American Learner 83 How Paul's Teacher Can
Respond 83

Summing Up 84

Suggested Learning Activities 85

Expanding Your Horizons: Additional Journal Readings and
Books 85

Expanding Your Students' Horizons: Appropriate African-
American Books for Children and Adolescents 86

Chapter 4   Understanding Asian-American Children and Adolescents   87

Introduction   88

The Asian-American People   88
Origins   88   Asian-Americans Today   88

Stereotyping of Asian-American Children and Adolescents   91

Asian-American Children and Adolescents   91
Cultural Characteristics   94   Socioeconomic
Status   95   Families   96   Religion   98   Language   98   Cultural
Comparisons: Asian-American and Anglo-American Children and
Adolescents   100

Asian-American Learners in the School   100
Educators' Understanding Asian-American Learners and Their
Culture   100   Developmental Theory: Children and
Adolescents   103   Achievement Level   103   Language
Problems   104   Learning Styles: Cultural
Considerations   105   School Practices Impeding Asian-Americans'
Progress   106   Promoting Positive Self-Concepts and Cultural
Identities   108   Cultural Portrait: Mina—An Asian-American
Learner   109   How Mina's Teacher Can Respond   110

Summing Up   111

Suggested Learning Activities   111

Expanding Your Horizons: Additional Journal Readings and
Books   112

Expanding Your Students' Horizons: Appropriate Asian-American
Books for Children and Adolescents   113

Chapter 5   Understanding Hispanic-American Children and Adolescents   114

Introduction   115

The Hispanic-American People   115
Origins   115   Hispanic-Americans Today   116

Stereotyping of Hispanic-American Children and
Adolescents   118

Hispanic-American Children and Adolescents   119
Cultural Characteristics   120   Socioeconomic Status   122   Families
124   Religion   126   Language   126   Cultural Comparisons:
Hispanic-American and Anglo-American Children and Adolescents
128

Hispanic-American Learners in the School   128
Educators' Understanding Hispanic-American Learners and Their
Culture   129   Developmental Theory: Children and
Adolescents   130   Achievement Level   131   Language
Problems   132   Learning Styles: Cultural
Considerations   135   School Practices Impeding Hispanic-Americans'
Progress   137   Promoting Positive Self-Concepts and Cultural

Identities 139   Cultural Portrait: Carlos—An Hispanic-American
Learner 141   How Carlos' Teacher Can Respond 142

Summing Up 142

Suggested Learning Activities 143

Expanding Your Horizons: Additional Journal Readings and
Books 143

Expanding Your Students' Horizons: Appropriate Hispanic-
American Books for Children and Adolescents 143

**Part III   Understanding Multicultural Education: Curriculum
and Teaching Concerns   145**

Chapter 6   Multicultural Education   145

Introduction 145

Multicultural Education for Culturally Pluralistic Schools 147
The Need for Understanding and Appreciating Cultural
Diversity 147   Emergence of Multicultural
Education 00   Definitions and Purposes 00   A Brief Historical
Overview 00

Responsive Multicultural Education Programs
Concepts 00   Goals 00   Assumptions 00   Principles 00
Interdisciplinary Approaches 00   Attitudes 00

Challenges Facing Educators Designing Multicultural Education
Programs 155
Changing Attitudes in the United
States 155   Ethnocentrism 155   Developing Positive Multicultural
Identities 157   Racism 159   Stereotypes, Prejudices, and
Generalizations 160   Myths and Realities 162   Understanding
Cultures and the Learner's Individual Culture 162

Controversial Issues In Multicultural Education 163

Summing Up 164

Suggested Learning Activities 165

Expanding Your Horizons: Additional Journal Readings and
Books 166

Chapter 7   Curricular Efforts   167

Overview 167

Toward A School Curriculum Respecting and Promoting Cultural
Diversity 169
The Illusion of Change and Progress 169   Responding to Racism,
Discrimination, Ethnocentrism, and Stereotype 170

Planning and Implementing a Multicultural Education
Curriculum 173
Emphasis on Across-the-Curriculum 173   Reform

Efforts   175   The Hidden Curriculum   177   The Multicultural
Curriculum Respecting Cultural Diversity   178

Other Selected Curricular Approaches and Models
Teaching the Exceptional and Culturally Different   00   Human
Relations   00   Single Group Studies   00   Education That is
Multicultural and Social Reconstructionist   00

Extending the Multicultural Education Curriculum   189
Parental and Community Involvement   189   Extracurricular
Activities   191

The Language of the Curriculum and the School
Environment   192

Summing Up   193

Suggested Learning Activities   194

Expanding Your Horizons: Additional Journal Readings and
Books   195

Chapter 8   Instructional Practices   **196**

Overview   197

Teaching and Learning Contexts: Learners' Individual and Cultural
Differences   198
Valuing Objective Perceptions of All Learners   198   Recognizing and
Accepting Diversity: Culture, Ethnicity, Social Class, and
Religion   199

Teaching and Learning Contexts: Characteristics of Multiethnic/
Multicultural Educators   199
Knowledge   200   Attitudes   201   Skills   201   Teacher Self-
Evaluation   202

Teaching and Learning Contexts: Organization and Instruction—
Cultural Considerations   204
Practices Contributing to Exclusivity   204   Ability
Grouping   205   Cooperative Learning   206   Language
Differences   210

Activities   211

Teaching and Learning Contexts: The School Environment   214
Working Toward a Multicultural School
Environment   214   Promoting Positive Self-Concepts and Cultural
Identities   216   Making Faculty/Staff Diverse: Cultural, Ethnic, and
Racial Backgrounds   217

Teaching and Learning Contexts: Cultural Perspectives   218
Socioeconomic and Class Differences   218   The Role of Parents and
Families   221   Learner Evaluation   222

Summing Up   223

Suggested Learning Activities   224

Expanding Your Horizons: Additional Journal Readings and
Books   224

Chapter 9   Individual and Cultural Differences   226

Overview   227

The Reality of Individual and Cultural Diversity   228
Recognizing the Influence of Diversity on Teaching and Learning   228   Developing Positive Orientations Toward Diversity   229

Recognizing Individual and Cultural Diversities and Their Influence on Learning   229
Achievement, Intelligence, and Cognitive Processes   229   Self-Concept   231   Gender   231   Developmental Levels and Cognitive Readiness   232   Beliefs, Attitudes, and Values   232   Motivation   234   Socioeconomic Class   236   Exceptionalities   237

Celebrating and Responding to Cultural Diversities   244
Recognizing the Effects of Cultural Diversity   244   Building Cultural Identities   245   Learning Styles   246   Activities: Celebrating, Understanding, Appreciating, and Learning   00

Summing Up   249

Suggested Learning Activities   250

Expanding Your Horizons: Additional Journal Readings and Books   250

Chapter 10   Culturally Diverse Parents and Families   252

Overview   253

Involving and Educating Parents of Culturally Diverse Learners   254
Defining the Issue   254   Reasons for Parent Involvement and Education   255   Understanding Both Immediate and Extended Families   256   Reasons Parents Might Resist Teachers' Efforts   256   Understanding Cultural Diversity: Native-, African-, Asian-, and Hispanic-American Parents and Families   260   Differences in Parents, Families, and Homes   261

Parent and Family Involvement   263
Essential Elements of Effective Parent Involvement Programs   263   Five Major Types of Parent Involvement   265   Understanding Culturally Diverse Parents and Families   266   Visiting Parents and Families in the Home   268   Communication   269   Involving Parents and Families as Volunteers   271

Parent/Teacher Conferences   272

Parent Advisory Councils   273

Parent and Family Education   276
Defining Parent Education   276   Rationale for Parent Education Programs   276   Understanding Special Needs of Culturally Diverse Parents and Families   277   Formats of Parent Education Programs   278   Helping Parents Understand Child and Adolescent Development   278   Helping Parents Understand School Expectations and Parents' Roles   280

Summing Up 283

Suggested Learning Activities 284

Expanding Your Horizons: Additional Journal Readings and
Books 284

**Chapter 11   Administrators and Special
                School Personnel**   **286**

Overview 287

Administrators, Faculty, and Staff: Toward Total School
Efforts 288
Cultural/Ethnic/Racial Composition of Administration, Faculty, and
Staff 00   Commitment to Multicultural Education Emphasis at All
Levels 00

Administrators 289
Roles in the Multicultural Education Program 289   From the
Perspective of Classroom Educators: Working With
Administrators 292   Evaluation of the Administrator's Efforts and
Commitment 293

Special Educators 294
Roles in the Multicultural Education Program 294   From the
Perspective of Classroom Educators: Working With Special
Educators 298   Evaluation of the Special Educator's Efforts and
Commitment 300

Librarians/Media Specialists 301
Roles in the Multicultural Education Program 301   From the
Perspective of Classroom Educators: Working With Librarians/Media
Specialists 303   Evaluation of the Librarian/Media Specialist's
Efforts and Commitment 304

Counselors 305
Roles in the Multicultural Education Program 305   From the
Perspective of Classroom Educators: Working With
Counselors 308   Evaluation of the Counselor's Efforts and
Commitment 310

Communication Disorder Specialists 311
Roles in the Multicultural Education Program 311   From the
Perspective of Classroom Educators: Working With Communication
Disorder Specialists 313   Evaluation of the Communication Disorder
Specialist's Efforts and Commitment 315

Summing Up 315

Suggested Learning Activities 316

Expanding Your Horizons: Additional Journal Readings and
Books 317

**Part IV   Understanding the Future of
               Multicultural Education**   **318**

Chapter 12 Multicultural Education in the 21st Century: Unresolved Issues, Prospects, Challenges 318

Overview 319

Issue: Multicultural Education as a Concept 320
Differing Definitions of Multicultural Education 320 Multicultural Education's Lack of Acceptance 320 Differences Between Stated Ideals and Practice 321 Approaches to Race, Class, and Gender 322

Issue: Racism, Discrimination, and Injustices 322
Progress 322 Lingering Racism and Discrimination 322 Goals for the U.S. Society 324

Issue: Blaiming the Victim 325
Locus of Responsibility 325 More Humanistic Perspectives 326

Issue: Testing and Assessment 326
Arguments Supporting Standardized Tests 00 Arguments Critical of Standardized Tests 00 Culture and Testing 00

Issue: Language and Communication 328
Dialects 328 Bilingual Education 329 English as a Second Language 330 Nonverbal Communication 331

Issue: Accepting Professional Responsibilities 331
For Being Qualified and Committed 331 For Ensuring that Multicultural Emphasis Permeates All Areas of the Curriculum and the School Environment 333 For Involving Parents, Families and the Community In Multicultural Efforts 333

Summing Up 334

Suggested Learning Activities 335

Expanding Your Horizons: Suggested Journal Readings and Books 335

Epilogue Multicultural Education in the 21st Century: Unresolved Issues, Prospects, Challenges 337

Overview 00

A Changing U.S. Society 337
Increasing Cultural Diversity 337 Increasing Knowledge Base of Cultural Diversity 338 Increasing Need for Awareness and Acceptance of Cultural Backgrounds 338

Multicultural Education 339
A Rationale 339 Lingering Questions 339 Growing Acceptance: Present and Future 340

The Future 341
Professionally Trained Educators 341 Comprehensive Multicultural Education Programs 341 Personal and Professional Commitment 342

Summing Up 342

Preface

First and foremost, *Multicultural Education of Children and Adolescents* is based on the premise that culturally diverse groups enrich the United States and that a better understanding of people and their differences leads to higher levels of acceptance and respect for all people. This book is being published at a time when all demographic projections indicate that the number of culturally diverse people in the United States will increase during the 1990s and the twenty-first century. High birthrates among some culturally diverse groups, increasing numbers of Spanish-speaking people, and the recent influxes of immigrants from Southeast Asia will increase the cultural diversity of the United States and will challenge its people to accept and respect all people regardless of cultural, ethnic, racial, socioeconomic, gender, or religious differences.

At one time during the nation's history, the melting pot served to erase differences and to acculturate or "melt" cultural differences. In essence, the culturally diverse person was supposed to forsake cherished and traditional cultural values and adopt "American values," probably those of the middle-class Anglo-American population. This concept viewed differences as wrong or inferior, and promoted wholesale giving up of cultural heritages. Realistically, for any number of reasons, the melting pot did not work—people had difficulty giving up cultural characteristics, or they lived in enclaves where assimilation with the mainstream society was unnecessary. Likewise, some people chose to maintain their culture and to adopt American values, resulting in a "hyphenated" culture such as *Mexican-American*. Regardless of the reasons, the melting pot did not assimilate as some proposed, and the nation became a mixture of different peoples.

During the 1990s, serious questions continue to plague educators and other concerned people: Why is there an increase in racism? Since it has been nearly forty years since the landmark *Brown* decision, why are schools becoming more racist, and, in some cases, still segregated? Why do elementary and secondary schools address primarily the needs of middle-class Anglo learners and expect culturally diverse learners to adjust or fall behind? Why is diversity feared? Why does a culturally diverse person threaten another's well-being? Why are victims often blamed for their problems? These questions defy easy answers and provide evidence that many people believe that differences are negatives in need of eradication.

Rather than provoking anger or causing fear, differences in values, customs, and traditions should be celebrated and considered to be a means of enriching the United States' society. The authors do not claim that the people who perceive differences as enriching will eliminate racism and acts of violence; however, celebrating differences is a first step, especially if efforts focus upon children and adolescents who will lead the nation during the twenty-first century. Considering differences to be positives and enriching, however, will be only a beginning. Significant change will take more comprehensive and deliberate efforts.

The School's Role

Elementary and secondary schools can play a major role in efforts to teach acceptance and respect for cultural diversity. The schools, in fact, are logical places to begin steps to instill feelings of acceptance for all people, regardless of diversity. Schools, however, must do more than pay lip service—the curriculum must reflect diversity, and learning materials must show culturally diverse people in positive and meaningful roles. The authors believe wholeheartedly that multicultural education efforts should be a total school approach, rather than a unit or "Multicultural Education Week" approach. While teaching about "multiculturalism" is an admirable concept, schools should also *model* acceptance and respect for cultural diversity. Schools that teach about cultural differences and celebrate diversity, yet whose actions indicate racism or a lack of respect, fail in their multicultural efforts.

The Authors' Purpose in Writing the Text

The authors wrote *Multicultural Education of Children and Adolescents* to provide pre-service and in-service educators with a knowledge of the four most prevalent culturally diverse groups and to show the components of responsive multicultural education programs. The text staunchly maintains throughout all chapters that multicultural education programs should be a total school effort, that is, that administrators, special educators, counselors, and speech correctionists have vital roles in the multicultural education program. Similarly, the authors believe that multicultural efforts should be comprehensive. The curriculum, instructional strategies, materials, environment, and school practices should reflect multiculturalism and should show a genuine respect for all forms of diversity.

The Four Cultural Groups in the Text

After careful consideration and reflection upon the increasing cultural diversity of the United States, the authors decided to focus on only four groups of people: Native-Americans, African-Americans, Asian-Americans, and Hispanic-Americans. These groups will be the most populous during the 1990s and, in all likelihood, will continue to be the most populous groups in elementary and secondary schools. Choosing only four groups does not negate the importance of other cultures. The authors' hope and expectation is that learning about diversity in these four cultures will motivate readers to explore the values, customs, and traditions of other cultures.

Organization of the Text

Multicultural Education of Children and Adolescents is divided into four parts and twelve chapters. Part I documents the increasing cultural diversity of the United States, looks at selected types of diversity, and introduces multicultural education as a concept. Part II provides a cultural portrait of children and adolescents in the Native-, African-, Asian-, and Hispanic-American cultures. Part III focuses on multicultural education and suggests aspects to be considered when planning and implementing programs that teach acceptance and respect for cultural diversity. Part IV shows issues that will continue to challenge educators in the twenty-first century.

PEDAGOGICAL FEATURES

Pedagogical features of *Multicultural Education of Children and Adolescents* include:

CULTURE QUIZZES, located at the beginning of each chapter, provide an interesting means of showing readers how much they already know and also provide an indication of the content addressed in the chapter.

CASE STUDIES, which are appropriately arranged throughout the text to show how educators have addressed the topics under focus.

IMPLEMENTING RESEARCH, placed appropriately throughout all chapters, providing readers with research studies that focus on culturally diverse children and adolescents, and give practical suggestions for implementing the research. It is worth noting that, in an attempt to provide readers with a wide range of information and sources, research is defined in its broadest sense.

CULTURAL COMPARISONS, located in Chapters 2, 3, 4, and 5, show differences between culturally diverse and Anglo-American learners. This feature provides readers with a succinct comparison of general cultural characteristics—not to imply any degree of worth and not to suggest that culturally diverse learners should acculturate toward middle-class Anglo-American learners.

SUGGESTED READINGS are located at the end of each chapter to provide readers with resources for further study and consideration.

USING CHILDREN'S LITERATURE, located in Chapters 2, 3, 4, and 5, provides titles and a brief annotation of developmentally appropriate children's and adolescents' literature that can be used to help learners better understand their cultural heritages.

FOR ADDITIONAL INFORMATION, located in Chapters 2, 3, 4, 5, and other selected chapters, provides names and addresses of organizations and groups that promote cultural diversity and that act as disseminators of information about the respective cultures.

ACTIVITIES are arranged throughout the text and are designed either to assist educators in understanding cultural diversity, or to help educators as they plan activities for multicultural education programs.

A Word of Caution

Any discussion focusing on characteristics of culturally diverse children and adolescents risks stereotyping and an overdependence on generalizations. The many intracultural, socioeconomic, geographic, generational, and individual differences among cultural groups contribute to their diversity and to the difficulty of describing individuals in the various cultures. While this text is based upon the most current and objective information, it still remains crucial for educators to understand individual children and adolescents within a culture through conscientious study and through first-hand contact. Failing to understand individuals and to consider crucial differences may result in assuming too much cultural homogeneity, e.g., all Hispanic cultural groups sharing identical values, problems, and cultural expectations or all Asian-Americans fitting the "model minority" label.

Acknowledgments

We want to thank Carolyn Dapo and Susanne Brown for their typing and other work on the manuscript as it developed from only a thought to the final manuscript. Their assistance is very much appreciated. Likewise, we want to thank Jane Tuttle and John Vassallo, reference librarians, for their fine work and assistance. Authors' only chance and hope for making a valuable contribution lies in the willingness of librarians who help authors locate information. We also want to thank the reviewers: Donald Whitmore, Texas Woman's University, Annabelle Hardt, Arizona State University, Jose Macias, the University of Utah, and our copyeditor, Sandra Moore.

Thank you also to Amy Pedersen at Benchmark Productions and Kurt Boschen at Shepard Poorman Communications.

LGB

MLM

1

An Increasingly Multicultural Society

Understanding the material and activities in this chapter will help the reader to

1. Understand the historical and contemporary perspectives toward cultural diversity, viz., the melting pot ideology and the salad bowl ideology, respectively.
2. Provide a demographic description of the culturally diverse populations presently increasing in the United States.
3. Explain concepts such as culture, ethnicity, race, socioeconomic status, and gender, and explain why understanding these concepts are important when working with culturally diverse children and adolescents.
4. Explicate perspectives toward cultural diversity such as cultural deficit, mismatch, and difference, and provide a rationale for adopting a positive and enriching perspective, e.g., the culturally different.
5. Explain how culturally diverse children and adolescents can be hurt by racism, discrimination, and stereotypes, and how elementary and secondary schools can provide a response.
6. Define multicultural education and provide a brief introduction of these programs.

7. Provide concrete evidence that the United States society is becoming increasingly culturally diverse, and explain the elementary
and secondary school roles in addressing the needs of culturally-
diverse learners.

OVERVIEW

The increasing cultural diversity of the United States challenges elementary
and secondary educators to understand differing values, customs, and traditions, and to provide responsive multicultural experiences for all learners.
The melting pot, once thought to be a means of erasing cultural differences,
obviously did not assimilate differences, and, in light of the richness brought
to a nation by diversity, should not be viewed as a means of achieving a just,
equal, and accepting society. Educators need a sound understanding of cultural, ethnic, racial, socioeconomic, gender, and individual differences, especially since the number of culturally diverse learners increases daily. Based
firmly on the belief that differences among people can enrich both the
United States and its schools, this chapter examines the cultural diversity of
the nation and suggests that many challenges can be addressed through
responsive multicultural education programs.

AN INCREASING MULTICULTURAL SOCIETY

Historical Perspective: The Melting Pot Ideology

Glazer and Moynihan (1970), in their book, *Beyond the Melting Pot*, proposed
that the melting pot metaphor employed to describe the cultural composition
of the United States did not, in reality, provide an accurate description. To
strengthen their point, Glazer and Moynihan explained how Jews, Italians,
and the Irish of New York City chose to retain their old-world heritages.
Similarly, other groups have also failed (or elected not to try) to forsake
cherished cultural characteristics in order to become "Americanized." Asians
and Hispanics are often reluctant to give up ethnic customs and traditions in
favor of middle-class American habits that might appear contrary to beliefs
taught early in life. African Americans have fought to overcome cultural
dominance and discrimination, and, through efforts such as the Civil Rights
Movement, have sought to understand and maintain their cultural heritage.
This need to recognize and respect individual differences and similarities
within cultures becomes clear when one considers the geographic, generational, and social class differences among the Native-, African-, Asian-, and
Hispanic-American cultures.

Contemporary Perspective: The Salad-Bowl Ideology

Although some cultural assimilation undoubtedly occurred as culturally
diverse people adopted Anglo-American customs and standards, generally

speaking, the melting pot idea began to adjust to a perspective of the United States society as a "salad bowl", wherein each group reflected its unique identity and its American experience (McCormick, 1984). The salad bowl perspective, whereby all people live together yet hold on to cultural backgrounds, is a more realistic and humane expectation for the United States to adopt. Whether arriving from Southeast Asia, from one of the many Spanish-speaking countries, or from one of the other many areas from which immigrants have landed, people should not be expected to forsake their cultural heritages and traditions. Admittedly, some degree of assimilation may be necessary for successful participation in this country, e.g., English skills that are necessary for coping with everyday life, and the job skills needed to find employment. Even with this degree of assimilation, however, culturally different people can still be allowed—or, indeed, encouraged—to hold on to cherished and time-honored cultural customs and traditions. While the melting pot ideology appeared to perceive differences as entities to be eradicated, the more enlightened salad bowl ideology views differences as personal characteristics that contribute to and enrich United States society.

CASE STUDY 1-1 examines how Mrs. Rowe helped the teachers in her school better understand that a salad-bowl perspective toward cultural diversity should take precedence over expecting learners to forsake their cultural backgrounds.

CASE STUDY 1-1: Toward a Salad-Bowl Perspective

It was relatively easy for Mrs. Rowe, a fourth grade teacher, to detect that the school expected learners to assimilate middle-class Anglo-American values and customs: Textbooks emphasized middle-class Anglo-American characters, while contributions of culturally-diverse groups were downplayed; teaching styles and instructional strategies addressed the needs of Anglo-American learners; all learners were expected to abide by the same rules and policies; the school environment did little to celebrate cultural diversity; and the administration, faculty, and staff showed little evidence that culturally diverse professionals had been sought. Culturally diverse learners who were unable or unwilling to adopt middle-class Anglo-American values suffered the consequences of lower achievement, poorer self-concepts, and a feeling of not belonging to the school.

Mrs. Rowe thought of ways to move the school toward a more "salad-bowl" perspective where culturally diverse learners could retain cherished cultural values, and where the school could address the needs of all learners. Mrs. Rowe sought the administration's advice and support. The administration then formed a committee consisting of Mrs. Rowe, a speech correctionist, a special educator, a guidance counselor, several regular classroom teachers, and several culturally diverse parents. The committee decided to take deliberate action to make the entire school more responsive to culturally diverse learners. Plans were made to examine all phases of the school: textbooks and other curricular materials, the overall curriculum, instructional strategies, the efforts of special school personnel, the school environment, and efforts designed to celebrate diversity. Mrs. Rowe and the committee realized the need to be realistic—changing the school would take time, commitment, and the efforts of all educators. Two crucial steps, however, had been reached. The school had realized the need for change, and the decision had been reached to take planned and deliberate action.

ACTIVITIES FOR EDUCATORS: Knowledge of Cultures

Directions: Match the culture with the characteristic by placing the appropriate letter before the culture.

a. Native-American

b. African-American

c. Asian-American

d. Hispanic-American

_____ 1. The culture is often stereotyped as the "model minority."

_____ 2. A member of this culture delivered the "I Have a Dream" speech in a Washington, DC, protest march.

_____ 3. This culture is experiencing rapid population growth, and may be the most populous culture during the early years of the twenty-first century.

_____ 4. A member of this culture pioneered processes for storing blood plasma, thus saving thousands of lives during World War II.

_____ 5. This culture has a deep respect and reverence for the earth and all living things—the earth must not be harmed.

_____ 6. A member of this culture was a computer executive and built a multibillion dollar company.

_____ 7. Population numbers of this culture include Aluets and Eskimos.

_____ 8. A member of this culture traveled through towns in the south documenting lynching after lynching.

_____ 9. Population numbers of this culture include Pacific Islanders, or, more specifically, Hawaiians, Somoans, and Guamanians.

_____ 10. Racism, discrimination, and injustice have hampered this culture's economic, social, and educational progress.

_____ 11. This culture currently outnumbers African-Americans in such cities as New York, Los Angeles, San Diego, and San Francisco.

_____ 12. Educators and other professionals must use extreme caution to avoid stereotyping this culture because considerable diversity exists among children and adolescents.

Answers: 1. c 2. b (Dr. Martin Luther King) 3. d 4. b (Dr. Charles Drew) 5. a 6. c (An Wang) 7. a 8. b (Ida B. Wells-Barnett) 9. c 10. abcd 11. d 12. abcd

CHILDREN AND ADOLESCENTS IN AN INCREASINGLY MULTICULTURAL SOCIETY

The Culturally Different: Demographics

Present trends and projections indicate that the present influx and growth of diverse ethnic groups will continue. Table 1-1 shows a breakdown of race and ethnic groups and documents in an increasing multicultural society: African-American, 29.9 million; Native American, 1.5 million; Asian American, 3.5 million; and Hispanic, 19.5 million (U.S. Bureau of the Census, 1980, 1988c; "Black population is growing", 1988).

Native-Americans
Whether called "Original Americans," "Native People," "American Indians," or "Native-Americans", census data reported the Native-American population to be approximately 1.5 million, or one-half percent of the total United States population (U.S. Bureau of the Census, 1980). Slightly more than half of the present-day Native-American population resides in urban and metropolitan areas. Numerous tribes have as few as five members, while some tribes may have only one surviving member (Trimble and Fleming, 1989). Approximately one-half of Native Americans in the United States resides on Native-American lands, while the other half lives outside the reservations in urban or other predominantly Anglo-American geographical areas (Axelson, 1985). States with the greatest population of Native-Americans include California, Oklahoma, Arizona, New Mexico, and Washington (*America's first*, 1989).

Of the federal reservations, the Navajo Nation Reservation is the largest, and has a population of more than 165,000. Other states with reservations with large land holdings include Oklahoma, South Dakota, Wyoming, Montana, Arizona, and California (U.S. Bureau of the Census 1988b).

**Table 1-1   Selected Multicultural Groups in the United States
Numbers (1,000)**

Groups, Subgroups and Populations[1]

Native-Americans	1.5 m
Various American tribes	
Aluets	
Eskimos[2]	
African-Americans	29.9 m
African	
West Indians	
Haitians[3]	
Asian-Americans and Pacific Islanders	3.5 m
Asian: Chinese, Pilipino[4], Japanese, Korean, Asian Indian, Vietnamese	
Pacific Islander: Hawaiian, Samoan, Guamanian[4]	
Hispanic-Americans	19.4 m
Mexican	
Puerto Ricans	
Cubans	
Central and South Americans[5]	

Notes and Sources:

(1) As defined by the U.S. Bureau of the Census (1980).

(2) U.S. Bureau of the Census. (1980) *Census of the population, Vol. 1,* General Population Characteristics.

(3) "Black population is growing", . . . *Census and You, 23(6),* 3.

(4) Some controversy exists as to whether Filipino or Pilipino should reflect the people of the Philippines. Although the U.S. Bureau of the Census uses the [f] sound, the authors have decided to adopt the [p] sound since the soft [f] sound does not exist in the Pilipino language (Axelson, 1985), and because most multicultural counseling texts give the [p] sound as the preferred spelling.

(5) U.S. Bureau of the Census Reports. (1988c). Series P-20, No. 431, *The Hispanic population in the United States; March 1988 (Advance Report),* U.S. Government Printing Office, Washington, DC.

African-Americans

Whether termed African-Americans, Black-Americans, Afro-Americans, Negro, or Colored, most Blacks can trace their origin to an area in western Africa. Torn away from their families and cherished cultural traditions, Africans first suffered from the bonds of slavery and then experienced (and, undoubtedly, still experience) legal, educational, and employment discrimination. IMPLEMENTING RESEARCH 1-1 looks at the increasing use of the term African-American.

IMPLEMENTING RESEARCH 1-1: The Term "African-American"

Gill (1990) maintained that the term "African-American" is gaining widespread support as a replacement for "Black" and "Black-American." Terms used to describe this group of people have been "colored", "Negro", and, more recently, "Black"; however, the term "African-American" better recognizes the cultural heritage with Africa. Supporters of the term have been Jesse Jackson; Coretta Scott King; former mayors Andrew Young of Atlanta, and Richard Hatcher of Gary, Indiana; Supreme Court Justice Thurgood Marshall; and Ramona Edelin, president of the National Urban League. Another argument for the term "African-American" is its similarity with terms describing other cultures, e.g., Asian-Americans, Native-Americans, and Hispanic-Americans. Gill also summarized research which showed that names, particularly African names, can have a positive influence on self-concept.

IMPLEMENTING THE RESEARCH:

1. Educators should recognize and use the term that a group thinks best describes their cultural and heritage backgrounds.
2. Educators should recognize that the term used to designate a group of people can show the person's degree of respect and acceptance for that cultural group.
3. Educators can contribute to positive individual and group self-concepts when appropriate titles are used.

Source: Gill, W. (1990). "African-American: What's in a name?" *Educational Leadership*, *48(1)*, 85.

The lives of most African-Americans have been characterized by a series of struggles and conflicts, beginning with their arrival on American soil. Civil revolts, the Civil Rights Movement of the 1950s and 1960s, and the efforts of such leaders as Dr. Martin Luther King Jr., have significantly improved the lives of African-Americans. However, African-Americans continue to experience covert forms of racism and discrimination that impede their progress in mainstream American society (Banks, 1987).

Asian-Americans
It is unrealistic to present all the diverse Asian groups currently living in the United States. Refugees from Southeast Asia often include Blue, White, and Striped Hmong; Chinese, Krom, and Mi Khmer Cambodians; Chinese Mien, Thai Dam, and Khmer Laotians; and Lowlander and Highlander Vietnamese. The many Asian groups have their own history and culture with many stratifications within each group (Kitano, 1989).

The 3.5 million Asian-Americans previously shown in Table 1-1 include the Chinese, Pilipino, Japanese, Korean, Asian Indian, and Vietnamese; and the Pacific Islanders of Hawaii, Samoa, and Guam. The number of Asian-Americans has increased from 1.4 million in 1970 to 3.5 million in 1980, an increase of 141 percent (Banks, 1987). Of the cities with populations of 250,000 or more, those with the greatest concentrations of Asian-Americans include Buffalo, Chicago, Honolulu County, Los Angeles, New York, and San Francisco (U.S. Bureau of the Census, 1980).

The recent influx of another group of Asian-Americans, the Southeast Asian people, has contributed to the diversity among the Asian cultures in the U.S. In 1975, as the Vietnam War ended, 130,000 refugees began arriving in the U.S. (Divoky, 1988). Three years later, a second wave of 650,000 Indochinese started their journey from rural and poor areas, to refugee camps, to the towns and cities of the United States (*The new whiz kids,* 1987). Originating in such locations as Vietnam, Cambodia, Laos, and Thailand, these people differ from the most populous groups, e. g., Japanese and Chinese; however, it is important to remember that the Southeast Asian people differ greatly from each other (West, 1983).

Hispanic-Americans

While Hispanics share many similarities such as history, ancestry, language, and traditions, each Hispanic subgroup has its own unique and distinguishing social and cultural practices (Casas & Vasquez, 1989). Educators should recognize the rapidly increasing Hispanic population, and should plan approriate activities to celebrate the wide range of diversity among Spanish-speaking populations.

The term "Hispanic" is a general title, and includes all people of Spanish origin and descent. The Hispanic geographic place of origin includes approximately 60% from Mexico, 14% from Puerto Rico, 8% from Central and South America, 6% from Cuba, and 12% from other Spanish-speaking countries (U. S. Bureau of the Census, 1988c, "Current population reports"; Series P-20, No. 431). The Hispanic group is a very large, young, and rapidly growing, highly diverse, group of people. Depending on geographic origins, Hispanics can be Caucasian, Mongoloid, Negroid, or various combinations of the races (Casas & Vasquez, 1989). The 1980 census reported 14.6 million Hispanics living in the United States in 1980, up from 9.1 million in 1970. In 1980, one of every sixteen people in the United States was of Hispanic origin. From 1980 to 1987, the Hispanic population increased by 34%, or about 5 million persons (U. S. Bureau of the Census, 1988c, "Current Population Reports"; Series P-20, No. 431).

If predictions become reality, Hispanics will outnumber African-Americans and people of any other single minority ethnic background. In fact, Hispanics currently outnumber African-Americans in cities such as New York, Los Angeles, San Diego, Phoenix, San Francisco, and Denver. In 1988, 55% of all Hispanic-Americans resided in two states—Texas and California (U.S. Bureau of the Census, 1988c; "Current population reports"; Series P-20, No. 431). The rapidly increasing Hispanic population is already altering mainstream American culture in such areas as language, employment, education, and the fine arts.

Activity:

Survey an elementary or secondary school in your area to determine its cultural composition. To what extent has each culture increased or decreased? Give several examples of how the school has responded to culturally diverse populations.

THE SELECTION OF CULTURES FOR THIS TEXT

Rationale

Several factors influenced the authors' decision to concentrate on the Native-, African-, Asian-, and Hispanic-American cultures. The first factor contributing to the selection of these four groups was the actual population numbers and the estimated growth increases of each group. All four cultures have shown significant growth and are expected to increase, either by an increased number of births or by immigration. The numbers are presently of a sufficient proportion that educators will likely encounter one or more of these cultural groups in elementary and secondary schools. Second, most research studies have focused on either Native-, African-, Asian-, or Hispanic-American groups. Third, realistically speaking, it is not feasible for a text to focus in any significant detail on more than four groups.

UNDERSTANDING DIVERSITY

Culture

Although considerable debate and controversy continue to rage over an accurate definition (Banks, 1987), culture includes institutions, language, values, religion, ideals, habits of thinking, artistic expressions, and patterns of social and interpersonal relationships (Lum, 1986, p. 46). Culture is an essential aspect of all people, and consists of the behavior patterns, symbols, institutions, values, and other components of society (Banks, 1987).

Even readers with only limited cognizance of culture and its many dimensions realize that culture has been defined in many ways (Lum, 1986, p. 46):

> . . . the way of life of a society, consisting of prescribed ways of behaving or norms of conduct, beliefs, values, and skills (Gordon, 1978).
> . . . people's characteristics, behavior, ideas, and values (Brislin, 1981).

. . . the sum total of life patterns passed on from generation to generation within a group of people (Hodge, Struckmann, & Trost, 1975).
. . . elements of a people's history, tradition, values, and social organization that become meaningful to participants in an encounter (Green, 1982).

Others have argued that culturally diverse people are influenced by at least five intermingling cultures. Rather than living in one culture, people live in five intermingling cultures (Vontress, 1986). Table 1-2 looks briefly at the five cultures of which all people are members (Vontress, 1986).

People referred to as bicultural have competencies and can operate successfully in two or more cultures. These people have mastered the knowledge of more than one culture, are able to function effectively in each culture, and actually feel comfortable in two cultures (Gollnick & Chinn, 1990). The bicultural individual also has a strong desire to function effectively in two cultures. The reasons for, and levels of, biculturalism may vary, e.g., some African-Americans learn to function effectively in the Anglo-American culture in an attempt to attain social and economic mobility during a formal working day. However, in their private lives, these individuals may be highly African-American and monocultural (Banks, 1988).

Race

Ashley Montagu (1974) calls race "man's most dangerous myth" (p. 3) and seriously questions the validity of the concept of race. In fact, he believes that the concept of race has been highly destructive in the history of mankind (Banks, 1987). Without doubt, educators are wise to use caution when categorizing clients into a particular racial group.

Although race refers to biological differences among people, the term has long been used to differentiate between groups of people. Society has generally recognized differences between the races (e.g., physical character-

Table 1-2 Five Intermingling Cultures

Universal—humans all over the world are biologically alike, e.g., males and females are capable of producing offspring and are capable of protecting and ensuring the survival of offspring.

Ecological—humans' location on earth determines how its members relate to the natural environment.

National—humans are characterized by aspects such as language, central governments, and world views.

Regional—humans tend to settle in a region, thereby creating cultures specific to an area.

Racio-ethnic—humans have distinct racial and ethnic differences; however, all people are a reflection of their racial and ethnic background.

istics or genetic origins), but these differences satisfy only the biological aspects and do not explain differences in social behavior (Pedersen, 1988). Anthropologists have experienced difficulty in structuring racial categories because of the wide variety of traits and characteristics shared by people, and the extensive differences among groups (Banks, 1987).

Gollnick and Chinn (1986) make several important points concerning race. First, despite the movements of large numbers of people from one geographical region to another, and the incidence of intermarriage across racial groups, the concept of race today still has a significant social meaning. Second, race contributes few insights to cultural understanding. Cultural groups defined by nationality, geography, language, and religion seldom correspond with racial categories—at least not to the extent necessary to provide culturally-relevant information. Hence, racial identity, in and of itself, does not reveal an individual's nationality, language, or religion. Third, difficulties experienced in characterizing the population of the United States in government reports exemplifies the confusion regarding race and ethnicity. For example, individuals may be asked to define themselves in terms of categories that are not mutually exclusive (e.g., White, Hispanic, or Jewish; an individual could belong to all three of these categories) (Gollnick & Chinn, 1986).

Ethnicity

Ethnicity, a dynamic and complex concept, refers to how members of a group perceive themselves, and how, in turn, they are perceived by others. Ethnicity is defined on the basis of national origin, religion, and/or race (Gordon, 1964). Attributes associated with ethnicity include: (a) A group image and sense of identity derived from contemporary cultural patterns (e.g., values, behaviors, beliefs, language) and a sense of history; (b) shared political and economic interests; and (c) membership that is involuntary, although individual identification with the group may be optional (Appleton, 1983; Banks, 1981). The extent to which individuals identify with a particular ethnic group varies considerably; many have two or more identities. When ethnic identification is strong, individuals maintain ethnic group values, beliefs, behaviors, perspectives, language, culture, and ways of thinking (Hernandez, 1989).

Other definitions illustrating these varying notions of ethnicity include (Lum, 1986, p. 42–43):

> . . . those who share a unique and social cultural heritage passed on from generation to generation and based on race, religion, and national identity (Mindel & Habenstein, 1981).
> . . . a commmunity of people within a larger society that is socially distinguished or set apart, by others and/or by itself, primarily on the basis of racial and/or cultural characteristics such as religion, language or tradition. The central factor is the notion of set-apartness with a distinctiveness based on either

physical or cultural attributes or both. Ethnicity applies to everyone; people differ in their sense of ethnic identity (Bennett, 1986).

. . . ethnic groups are frequently identified by distinctive patterns of family life, language, recreation, religion, and other customs that differentiate them from others (Banks, 1987).

It is important to emphasize that each individual simultaneously belongs to a socioeconomic class, a gender, and an ethnic group(s). Each also constructs a personal reality, which may be influenced and constrained by a person's ethnicity, class, or gender (Grant & Sleeter, 1986).

Social Class

Social class differences also play a significant role in determining how a person acts, lives, thinks, and relates to others. Differences in values between student and educator basically represent class differences, since many minority group children and adolescents come from the lower socioeconomic classes. These differences in values, attitudes, behaviors, and beliefs among the various socioeconomic groups warrant the professional's consideration when planning intervention (Atkinson, Morten, & Sue, 1989).

The educator coming from a middle- to upper-class background may experience difficulty when relating to the circumstances and hardships that often affect the client living in poverty. Low wages, unemployment, underemployment, little property ownership, no savings, lack of food reserves, and meeting the most basic needs on a day-to-day basis easily lead to feelings of helplessness, dependence, and inferiority (Sue, 1981).

CASE STUDY 1-2 looks at Mrs. Westbury's response when she decided that social class differences should be an integral aspect of the multicultural education program.

CASE STUDY 1-2: Social Class Differences

Mrs. Westbury, a middle school principal, looked at the proposed multicultural education program that was the work of a committee she had organized and on which she had served. Still, she thought, something is missing. We have covered all aspects—culture, ethnicity, race—or have we? Mrs. Westbury thought. Children and adolescents can be of a similar culture, yet can still be vastly different. For example, all African-Americans are not alike. Likewise, not all Hispanic-Americans are alike. What contributes to the differences?

Mrs. Westbury decided that social class resulted in vast differences among children and adolescents. The evidence clearly indicated that social class had to be addressed: Tremendous differences separate lower, middle, and upper classes. In fact, people of the lower classes, regardless of cultural backgrounds, might have more similarities than even people of the same culture.

After thinking through her proposal, Mrs. Westbury asked the committee to consider her thoughts. The evidence is clear, she explained. Social class affects many aspects of learning, e.g., assessment, overall achievement, attitudes and motivation, parent involvement and expectations, and even social acceptance. What should the school's response be? First, special efforts must focus on avoiding stereotyping, just like other forms of diversity. All lower class learners are not alike. Second, instructional approaches need to be considered, e.g., what practices are most effective, what type of curricular materials, and what organizational patterns to employ. There must be a special effort to avoid grouping all lower-class students together. Third, the previous educational experiences of students should be considered, and should provide the basis for future teaching and learning activities. Fourth, the administration needed to respond by informing the teachers, who were probably from middle-class backgrounds, about lower-class learners, and the effects of social class differences on academic achievement and social progress.

It is wise to remember that a person's social class sometimes is thought to indicate one's ambitions or motivation to achieve. However, it is a serious mistake to stereotype people according to social class, i.e., that the lower classes lack ambition, do not want to work, or improve their education status. It is not unreasonable to suggest that the lower-class families, whether Native-, African-, Asian-, or Hispanic-Americans, want to improve their social status in life, but meet with considerable frustration when faced with low education and high unemployment, all the conditions associated with poverty, and the racism and discrimination all-too-often prevalent in U.S. society.

Social class differences in some cases may be more pronounced than differences resulting from cultural diversity. For example, as social class differences separate members of the Anglo culture, a lower-class African-American may share more cultural commonalities with lower class Anglo-Americans than with middle- or upper-class African-Americans.

Gender

Gender can be defined as a term which describes differences in masculinity and femininity—the thoughts, feelings, and behavior that are identified as either male or female (Gollnick & Chinn, 1990). A text examining diversity would be remiss if it failed to address gender differences. While many similarities exist between males and females, differences also exist which educators should recognize, and to which they should offer an appropriate response. Likewise, in addition to addressing differences and similarities, educators should also seek to clarify stereotypic beliefs about males and females.

What are some differences between males and females?

1. Beginning at about ten years of age, girls excel at verbal tasks; beginning in early adolescence, boys excel at mathematical tasks; between ten and twelve, boys begin to excel on visual/spatial tasks.
2. Concerning socialization and affiliation, there are no differences between the sexes.
3. Concerning activity level, there are no differences between the sexes.
4. Beginning around age two, boys are more verbally and physically aggressive (Gollnick & Chinn, 1990).

Activity:

Make a list of school practices or education-related issues that might fail to address gender differences. Do you think educators are aware of how school practices and expectations might fail to recognize gender differences?

Stereotyping defines male and female roles in a narrow fashion, and defines behaviors for the two sexes as quite different from one another. Gender stereotypes are instilled and perpetuated by television, children's literature, and adult expectations of sex-specific behaviors of boys and girls. While some progress has been made toward more objective perceptions of sex and gender roles, some stereotypical images continue to impede the progress of females (and in many cases, males):

1. Males and females are too often portrayed in traditional and rigid roles, e.g., careers such as doctors and nurses, or men as breadwinners and women as housekeepers.
2. Magazines and newspaper sections are often directed at one audience, e.g., women's sections that include articles on fashion, food, and social events.
3. Textbooks often portray boys involved with important activities, while girls are playing with dolls and giving tea parties.
4. In print and nonprint media, men are found in about six times as many different occupations as women (Gollnick & Chinn, 1990).

While the negative results of gender stereotyping are too numerous to list, educators who are working to address children's and adolescents' diversity can readily see the importance of addressing gender concerns. The challenge in multicultural situations is actually two-fold: Educators, in their efforts to address diversity, must include not only gender differences and cultural differences, but also the intricate relationship between the two.

Individual

Children's and adolescents' individual differences are yet another form of diversity that educators need to understand so that they may plan appropriate educational experiences. It is an equally serious mistake to assume too much cultural homogeneity among learners—all Hispanic learners cannot be assumed to be alike simply because they share a Spanish-speaking background. Likewise, African-American learners vary tremendously according to socioeconomic backgrounds and geographical location.

For an objective and clear understanding of learners, several individual differences should be considered as educators plan teaching and learning experiences: Overall abilities, interests, intelligence, problem-solving abilities, critical thinking skills, motivation, previous academic backgrounds, and the ability to use English or the language in which instruction is most often provided, just to name a few. However, it is crucial to point out that individual differences must be considered from a cultural perspective, i.e., intelligence and motivation may vary with culture, and should not be viewed from a middle-class Anglo perspective.

Individual differences can be addressed in various ways: individualized instruction, cooperative learning, materials with varying difficulty levels, timed and untimed paces of study, and changing the purposes of learning, i.e., mastery, understanding, or application.

CHALLENGES IN A CULTURALLY DIVERSE SOCIETY

Understanding and Forming a Positive Perspective on Cultural Diversity

Educators and other professionals need to examine their perspectives toward diversity to determine whether diversity is perceived as a "cultural deficit" (an entity in need of change), a "cultural mismatch" (an entity causing culturally diverse learners to fail because their traits are not compatible with the United States school system), or whether diversity is perceived as "culturally different" (an entity which enriches the classroom and makes individuals unique). Rather than being just an academic question, educators' perception of diversity determines their philosophical beliefs toward learners and learning, and the actual instructional practices employed.

The Cultural Deficit Model

In the cultural deficit model, social scientists described the culturally different as "deprived", "disadavantanged", and "socially deprived" only because they demonstrated behavior different from middle-class values, language systems, and customs. Placing this situation in a class perspective, middle-class Anglo-Americans often assumed that other cultures did not seek to advance themselves because of a cultural deficit (Draguns, 1989).

Instead of attributing racial differences to genetics, blame shifts to cultural lifestyles or values. Frank Riessman's book, *The Culturally Deprived Child* (1962), spread the notion that, lacking middle class advantages such as education and books, formal language experiences contributed to less-than-desirable educational progress. In essence, this mode of thinking results in "blaming the victim", in which the individual is considered at fault for not being more successful (whether educationally, economically, socially, or whatever). The cultural deficit model has failed to address the implicit cultural biases that shaped negative perceptions and inhibited the understanding of the role of sociopolitical forces (Jenkins, 1982), and has been refuted and replaced by the "culturally different" model (Draguns, 1989).

The Cultural Mismatch Model

In contrast to the cultural deficit perspective, the cultural mismatch perspective assumes that cultures are inherently different, but not necessarily superior or inferior to each other. Educational achievement in some culturally diverse groups is thought to occur because their cultural traits do not match those of the dominant culture as reflected in schools. Thus, the educational performance of culturally diverse groups is related to the degree of congruence between group values and traits, and those of the educational system: The better the match, the greater the likelihood of academic success. Efforts to improve the performance of minority students are aimed at increasing the congruence between the schools and the various cultures (Hernandez, 1989).

CASE STUDY 1-3 looks at the opinions of one teacher toward diversity, and another teacher's attempts to promote the culturally different perspective.

CASE STUDY 1-3: The Importance of a Proper Perspective

Mrs. Williams overheard a conversation in the teacher's lounge: "Those minorities—I don't know what to do—are different and so difficult to change, so far behind, can't do so many things; they are just not suited for my classes." Mrs. Williams considered what she had heard, and thought about what she had learned in a recent multicultural education course. This is what is meant by the cultural deficit model, or cultural mismatches, she thought. Realizing such thinking could hurt students' chances of learning, she decided to speak with this teacher about her attitudes toward diversity.

Mrs. Williams met with the teacher and tried to make her aware of the dangers of harboring such perspectives. Believing that differences need to be eliminated or changed reveals negative attitudes toward diversity, which undoubtedly affects feelings toward culturally diverse learners. Likewise, expecting learners to change to meet the teacher's instructional strategies is in opposition to what is known about effective education. Achievement and behavior expectations can also be affected when the teacher expects poor behavior. Realistically speaking, Mrs. Williams knew the difficulty in changing such thinking toward diversity and attitudes toward people.

Mrs. Williams wondered how many other teachers in the school harbored such feelings toward cultural differences. She decided to design an informal assessment device to determine other teachers' perspectives, and to ask the principal if it were possible to arrange in-service activities designed to help teachers form an appropriate perspective toward diversity.

The Culturally Different Model

This model recognizes differences as strengths that are valuable and enriching to schools and society as a whole. Proponents of the culturally different model still believe that all children and adolescents need to learn mainstream cultural values and knowledge. Researchers have begun to establish a research base documenting that cultural differences in language and learning style are not deficiencies, and can be built upon to facilitate learning. A certain degree of cultural compatibility is needed as teachers and students become increasingly aware of each other's cultural differences, whether differences relate to home or school expectations. The situation for children or adolescents might be even more acute than for teachers, especially since learners must switch from home to school cultures, and vice versa. In any event, learners should not be condemned for their language or culture, and should be encouraged to retain and build upon these differences whenever possible (Sleeter & Grant, 1988).

The culturally different model, however, holds that all cultural groups have cognitive strengths that can be built upon to facilitate classroom learning. To provide the most effective educational experiences, educators must learn wherein the culturally different learners' strengths lie, and must capitalize upon them as a resource, rather than disregarding these differences or placing students in groups that imply denigration of their abilities (Sleeter & Grant, 1988).

Activity:

Visit an elementary or secondary school to learn about its school philosophy, grouping practices, curricular and library materials, and extracurricular activities. Do you think the school's practices and policies indicate an acceptance of a cultural deficit, mismatch, or different model? What are the implications of the model the school chooses?

Understanding and Reducing Racism

While race relations and attitudes toward diversity have undoubtedly improved in the United States, signs of racist behavior and racial unrest indicate that "racism is alive and well in the public schools" (Stover, 1990, p. 14). One does not have to look extensively for serious examples of racism:

> Three students brought to school a white doll dressed in a Ku Klux Klan robe and a black doll with a noose around its neck.
>
> Racial tensions sparked when several white students displayed Confederate flags during a black history program.
>
> Fights broke out between whites and Asian immigrants in a mostly white, affluent section.
>
> A racial crisis erupted when a white-majority school board voted along racial lines not to renew the contract of the city's first black superintendent (Stover, 1990).

Racism can have serious effects on children and adolescents. First, learners interpret the actions of others as discriminatory or racist. Second, they attribute the cause to the person behind the action, to themselves, to the social circumstances, or to some combination of the three. Third, they form conclusions about themselves and their self-worth, and make decisions about how they will react to future racist acts. Another overall effect of racism is that children and adolescents suffer lower achievement and self-concepts, apathy, and a poor perception of the future (Murray & Clark, 1990).

Children and adolescents perceive racism in the insensitive remarks of students, biased teachers, and skewed textbooks. For example, students have reported that name-calling by their white peers has had traumatic and emotional effects. Teachers often base perceptions on stereotypes, rather than getting to know individual, culturally-diverse students. Also, textbooks either misrepresent or omit content related to minority groups, especially positive acts and contributions.

Eight patterns of racism show up in school:

1. Hostile and insensitive acts—racial slurs, name-calling, assaults and physical violence, and graffiti.
2. Bias in the use of harsh sanctions—punishment is often harsher for minority students than for Anglo students.
3. Bias in giving active attention to students—teachers often fail to address both easy and hard questions to majority and minority students alike.
4. Bias in the selection of curriculum materials—classroom materials

often omit authentic symbols, models, and images of different cultures and lifestyles.

5. Inequality in the amount of instruction time—school assignments for minority students often are at the wrong level, and fail to provide a challenge.

6. Bias in attitudes toward students—administrators, teachers, and counselors may require more or less effort because of beliefs about students.

7. Failure to hire racial minority teachers and other school personnel at all levels—absence of, or only token hiring of, qualified racial minority staff members.

8. Denial of racist acts—school leaders often downplay the existence, gravity, or significance of racist acts (Murray & Clark, 1990).

IMPLEMENTING RESEARCH 1-2 looks at the new racism with which educators must deal, and provides several implications for educators.

IMPLEMENTING RESEARCH 1-2: The New Racism

Stover wrote that "hate and prejudice come in some new guises, but their manifestations are ugly as ever" (p. 14). Across the nation, public schools are experiencing an increase in racist acts, and some contend that schools are not doing enough to counter this new wave of racism. Stover provided a plethora of disturbing examples to document the new surge of racism affecting America. While fighting and other violent acts can be detected easily, other forms of racism might often go unnoticed, e.g., students segregating themselves when they sit down to eat, and students avoiding other races at social functions. There are even more subtle aspects, such as teachers forming perceptions of students' potential and future possibilities based on racial or stereotypical beliefs.

IMPLEMENTING THE RESEARCH:

_____ 1. Educators can adopt a firm policy of zero tolerance for racism in any form.

_____ 2. Educators can arrange positive social contacts between racial groups.

_____ 3. Educators can participate in in-service activities and opportunities for teachers and administrators.

Source: Stover, D. (1990). The new racism. *The American School Board Journal, 177(6)*, 14–18.

Understanding and Clarifying Stereotypes and Misperceptions

Lum (1986) defines stereotyping as "the prejudicial attitude of a person or group that superimposes on a total race, sex, or religion a generalization about behavioral characteristics" (p. 135). Stereotypes produce an overly general mental picture that usually results in a judgmental, negative, or positive image of a person or an entire culture. Recognizing that stereotypes all too often contribute to people being victims of racism, educators should seek to understand and respond appropriately to others' and their own beliefs about culturally different learners.

The major characteristics of stereotyping and stereotypes include (Axelson, 1985):

1. They are *pervasive*, in that most people have their own "pet" personality theories about the characteristics of others.
2. They tend to emphasize *differences* when applied to individuals or groups different from oneself, but emphasize *similarities* when applied to individuals or groups similar to oneself.
3. They tend to be *negative* when applied to characteristics of individuals and groups different from oneself or one's own group.
4. They tend to become *habitual* and *routinized* unless challenged.
5. *First impressions* are usually based on stereotypes.
6. *New stereotypes* will supplement or supplant existing stereotypes as conditions and experiences in the culture change.
7. Stereotyping and stereotypes *impair* the ability to assess others accurately, and can readily lead to misinterpretations (emphasis Axelson) (p. 374).

The dangers of stereotyping learners are all too clear: Believing that African-Americans misbehave and are slow learners; assigning Asian-Americans to higher ability groups because they are all "bright and motivated"; or expecting reading problems and misbehavior from Hispanic-Americans. While stereotyping is only briefly explained at this section, Chapters 2, 3, 4, and 5 on culturally-diverse children and adolescents have sections on stereotyping the respective cultures.

Understanding and Helping Children and Adolescents Develop Positive Individual and Cultural Identities

Another challenge for educators is to help children and adolescents develop positive individual and cultural identities. Santrock (1990) provided the following passage to show the importance of a positive identity, and how others can affect an individual's identity:

The Hopi Indians are a quiet, thoughtful people, who go to great lengths not to offend anyone. In a pueblo north of Albuquerque, a 12-year-old boy speaks: "I've been living in Albuquerque for a year. The Anglos I've met, they're different. I don't know why. In school, I drew a picture of my father's horse. One of the other kids wouldn't believe that it was ours. He said, 'You don't really own that horse.' I said, 'It's a horse my father rides, and I feed it every morning.' He said, 'I can ride a horse better than you, and I'd rather be a pilot.' I told him I never thought of being a pilot."

The 12-year-old Indian boy continues, "Anglo kids, they won't let you get away with anything. Tell them something, and fast as lightning and loud as thunder, they'll say, 'I'm better than you, so there!' My father says it's always been like that" (Santrock, 1990, p. 382).

Without doubt, educators can help culturally diverse learners to develop positive identities by providing positive images of all people, regardless of race, culture, ethnic backgrounds, or social class; teaching about the contributions of all groups; ensuring equal and fair treatment for all learners and their families; and celebrating cultural diversity through appropriate multicultural educational experiences for all students.

As IMPLEMENTING RESEARCH 1-3 indicates, Mendelberg (1986) feels that learners being considered in derogatory terms may be affected in their identity formation.

IMPLEMENTING RESEARCH 1-3: Identity Conflicts in Mexican-American Youth

Mendelberg's (1986) study focused on 20 Mexican-American adolescents (ages 16–18) whose families had origins in rural Texas, but who had later settled in an industrial, mid-sized city in the Midwest. Attempts were made to clarify the subjects' reactions to distortions and omissions, frequently presented by the mass media, of Mexican-Americans' past and present characteristics. Images, which affect adolescents' identity development, can take several forms: wetback, barbwired, or the funny dull Mexican. Conclusions offered by Mendelberg include: (1) Identification with members of outside groups, and with their own group, appears to be blocked for minority members; (2) observed symptoms included self-hate, self-blame, and aggression against oneself and against significant others; and (3) only a limited number of ideal images exist that can be explained by the Mexican American's migrant origin.

IMPLEMENTING THE RESEARCH:

_____ 1. Educators should recognize that identity development has the potential for influencing children's and adolescents' entire lives and their perceptions of cultural backgrounds.

_____ 2. Educators should respond affirmatively to

> children and adolescents develop positive individual and cultural identities.
>
> _____ 3. Educators should provide appropriate multicultural educational experiences for all learners in a deliberate attempt to avoid name-calling, labeling, cultural misperceptions, and stereotyping.

Source: Mendelberg, H. E. (1986). Identity conflict in Mexican-American adolescents. *Adolescence, 21,* 215–224.

MULTICULTURAL EDUCATION: THE SCHOOL'S RESPONSE TO DIVERSITY

Emergence of Multicultural Education

For many years, the American nation has opened its doors to people of diverse cultural, ethnic, and racial origins. Some people entered the country with new hopes of the American dream, and some immigrated as a means of getting away from oppressive conditions. Others were actually brought against their will, and were expected to become culturally similar to the Anglo-American population. Still others, who first inhabited the land on which the American nation now exists, were expected to adopt the "white man's" ways. Through activities commonly associated with daily living and working together, these people were expected to adopt "American" customs and values, and through a "melting pot", actually become mainstream "Americans".

During the first half of the twentieth century, schools sought to assimilate all children into the American culture as quickly as possible. Children were expected to forsake their native languages and learn to speak and write in English, the accepted language of the nation. The United States functioned as huge melting pot in which culturally diverse people were expected to give up cultural differences, and become a people who were very much alike (Tiedt & Tiedt, 1990). For any number of reasons, however, many culturally diverse people rejected the "melting pot ideology" and adopted a "salad bowl" approach that actually resulted in an increasingly pluralistic nation. As schools head into the twenty-first century, the melting pot theory is even more inappropriate, because today, cultural diversity is perceived positively and as a strength, rather than as a weakness in need of eradication (Tiedt & Tiedt, 1990).

Multicultural education emerged as people recognized that the melting pot theory did not work, and that cultural diversity is to be valued and respected. However, it is necessary to point out that several court decisions and laws set the precedent for the present multicultural education movement.

Contemporary court decisions have ruled toward equal opportunity and human rights. Court cases and other events promoted multicultural understandings and recognition of equal rights for all people. The Supreme Court in *Brown vs. Topeka Board of Education* (1954) ruled that segregating black and white children in schools was illegal. State laws which provided separate schools for black and white learners were declared unconstitutional. Three years later, in 1957, the United States Commission on Civil Rights was established to investigate complaints which alleged the denial of civil rights. In 1968, the Bilingual Education Act (BEA) was passed as part of Title VII of the Elementary and Secondary Education Act. The U.S. Commission on Civil Rights issued a report in 1975 called *A Better Chance to Learn: Bilingual-Bicultural Education*, which was designed for educators as a means of providing equal opportunity for language-minority students. Although this brief listing provides only a few representative examples of events that recognized cultural diversity and equal rights, these were the forerunners of the movement to recognize and teach respect for culturally different people. Schools continue to have a major responsibility in breaking down stereotypes, promoting multicultural understandings, and making a difference in the lives of individual learners (Tiedt & Tiedt, 1990).

Definitions and Purposes

Multicultural education has been defined in numerous ways by various groups and individuals. Some definitions address the perspectives of specific disciplines, such as education, anthropology, sociology, and psychology. Other definitions represent the views of accrediting agencies and professional organizations that are concerned with what teachers need to teach and what students need to learn (Hernandez, 1989). Although the varying definitions result in confusion among educators, the differences probably result from goals unique to particular situations, rather than disagreements concerning the need for multicultural education. Even among the array of differing opinions and definitions, sufficient similarities exist for educators to understand that the primary purpose of multicultural education is to provide an environment that recognizes differences among people, perceives cultural differences as strengths rather than weaknesses to be remediated, and emphasizes the importance of all differences and exceptionalities in the education process.

Providing several definitions illustrates the differing perspectives, and at the same time shows the movement's commitment to all people:

Two experts on multicultural education:
Multicultural education is the popular term used increasingly by educators to describe education policies and practices that recognize, accept, and affirm human differences and similarities related to gender, race, handicap, and class (Sleeter & Grant, 1988).

A teacher education accrediting agency:

A multicultural perspective is a recognition of: (1) the social, political, and economic realities that individuals experience in culturally diverse and complex human encounters; and (2) the importance of culture, race, sex, ethnicity, religion, socioeconomic status, and exceptionalities in the education process (National Council for Accreditation of Teacher Education, 1986, p. 47).

A leading authority on multicultural and multiethnic education:

Multicultural education refers to a reform process whose aim is to create an educational environment in which a wide range of cultural groups, such as women, ethnic groups, and various regional groups, will experience educational equity (Banks, 1981, p. 13).

Educational policies and practices derived from such definitions vary widely, yet all tend to include:

knowledge of cultures and subcultures with emphasis on significant minority groups;

awareness of how specific cultures shape student responses to schooling;

minimizing prejudice and maximizing tolerance for different others (Tesconi, 1984, p. 88).

Regardless of the various definitions, purposes, or specific goals, multicultural education strives for a total school program that respects and plans appropriate experiences for students from differing ethnic, cultural, religious, and socioeconomic backgrounds.

A Brief Historical Overview

The fact that, prior to 1978, the *Education Index* did not include *multicultural education* in its listings illustrates that few pedagogical journals addressed the topic. However, during the last two decades, increasing numbers of articles and books that focus on multicultural education have appeared (Tiedt & Tiedt, 1990). Three forces contributed to the emergence of the multicultural education movement: The Civil Rights Movement came of age, school textbooks were critically analyzed, and assumptions underlying the deficiency orientation were considered from a more positive perspective (Gay, 1983). The Civil Rights Movement began as a passive, nonviolent, means of changing laws that oppressed specific racial groups. By the late 1960s, the movement had matured into an energetic coalition joining all Americans of color, directed toward self-determination and power. The United States' school system was severely criticized because of its segregation, and a curricula that focused attention only on the Anglo culture. Similarly, few teachers knew about minority groups, their rich cultural diversity, their individual strengths and weaknesses, and their learning styles. In fact, schools primarily considered cultural and ethnic differences to be weaknesses in need of remediation (Sleeter & Grant, 1988).

CASE STUDY 1-4 looks at the importance of having a multicultural education program that considers diversity in its broadest forms.

CASE STUDY 1-4: Toward an All-Encompassing Definition of Multicultural Education

The administration, faculty, and staff at PS 105 decided on a broad approach to their multicultural education program. Rather than addressing only "cultural backgrounds", this group agreed that their program should direct attention to a broad number of differences: ethnicity, race, gender, social class, and individual. Children and adolescents of respective cultures are vastly different. For example, the many different cultures which comprise the Hispanic-American population, the vast differences among Asian-Americans, and the diversity among African-Americans.

The question to be answered was how to address so many differences. The decision was to examine each difference, its influence on learning and other school-related activities, and then look at the curriculum, instructional approaches, print and non-print media, school policies, extracurricular activities, and the cultural composition of the administration, faculty, and staff.

Although this constituted a task of some magnitude, the group recognized the advantages of having a multicultural education program which genuinely addressed diversity in its broadest definition.

In the 1970s, multicultural education developed as a more comprehensive approach. With cultural diversity and equal opportunity serving as an impetus, multicultural education examined and considered the relationships among culture, ethnicity, language, gender, handicaps, and social class in developing educational programs. *Education That Is Multicultural and Social Reconstructionist* is a more recent and more controversial approach that represents an extension of multicultural education toward more definitive social action. This approach incorporates a curricular emphasis on: (1) active student involvement in social issues such as sexism, racism, and classism; (2) the development of problem-solving ability and political action skills; and (3) curricular adaptations, cooperative learning, and decision-making skills (Hernandez, 1989).

Banks used phases to place multicultural education in its proper historical perspective. During Phase I (monoethnic studies courses), the Black civil rights movement began and African-Americans demanded more African-American teachers; more control of community schools; and the rewriting of textbooks to provide a more accurate portrayal of African-Americans, their culture, and their contributions. Phase II (multiethnic studies courses) provided courses that focused on several minority groups and viewed experiences of ethnic groups from comparative perspectives. During Phase III (multiethnic education), an increasing number of educators recognized that reforming courses was insufficient to result in genuine educational reform. In Phase IV (multicultural education), some educators became interested in an even broader development of pluralistic education that focused on reform of the total school environment. The term, *multicultural education* emerged as the preferred concept because it enabled educators to focus on a wider range of groups rather than a limited focus on racial and ethnic minorities. Phase V is a slowly occurring process that has strategies designed to increase the pace and scope of the institutionalization of multiethnic-multicultural education within schools (Banks, 1988).

Although ethnic studies became more widespread during Phase III (multiethnic education), an increasing number of educators recognized that reforming courses was necessary, but that this approach was not sufficient to result in genuine educational reform. Two factors contributed to this reasoning: The negative attitudes of many teachers rendered their use of the new ethnic materials ineffective, and in some cases harmful; and second, educators realized that such ethnic studies courses could not enable minority groups to meet the achievement levels of most Anglo-American students.

In Phase IV (multicultural education), some educators became interested in an even broader development of pluralistic education that focused on a more broadly conceptualized education reform that included the total school environment. The term *multicultural education* emerged as the preferred concept because it enabled school districts and universities to focus on a wider range of groups, rather than a limited focus on racial and ethnic minorities. Phase V is a slowly-occurring process that has strategies designed to increase the pace and scope of the institutionalization of multiethnic-multicultural education within schools (Banks, 1988).

The two World Wars, mass immigrations to the United States, the intercultural movements, and the racial disturbances all contributed to the emergence and development of multicultural education.

SUMMING UP

Educators who wish to plan an appropriate response to the various cultural groups in the United States, and to provide effective multicultural edcuation programs should:

1. Understand the melting pot ideology and the more humanistic contemporary perspectives toward cultural diversity.

2. Understand that cultural differences should be valued and considered as enriching to the United States society.

3. Understand terms such as culture, ethnicity, race, social class, and gender.

4. Address and stand against racism in all forms, and in all situations.

5. Provide appropriate instruction and a classroom environment and climate that will contribute positively to cultural and individual identities.

6. Understand the rationale for multicultural education, provide a historical overview, and suggest appropriate educational experiences for children and adolescents of all cultures.

7. Form a perspective on culture and cultural diversity that perceives differences as "positives" rather than entities to be eliminated.

SUGGESTED LEARNING ACTIVITIES

1. Survey a number of elementary or secondary schools to determine the cultural composition of the student body. What has been the school's response to meeting the needs of culturally diverse students? What efforts have been made to teach majority cultures about minority cultures?

2. Suggest several methods of helping children and adolescents develop positive individual and cultural identities. What would be your response to an educator who stated, "My job is teaching content and academic matters—improving cultural identities is not my job!"

3. Offer several examples that show that the "melting pot" did not work, and that what we now have is a "salad bowl." Suggest reasons why culturally diverse people might be unwilling or hesitant to forsake cherished cultural values for Anglo values.

4. Give at least four or five examples of racist acts, and offer a solution (indeed, a difficult task) for reducing each type of racist act. To what extent should reducing racism be a role of schools?

5. Name four or five stereotypical images of culturally diverse children and adolescents. Suggest how such images may have started, and how schools can provide an appropriate response.

Expanding Your Horizons: Suggested Journal Readings and Books

HERNANDEZ, H. (1990). *Multicultural education: A teacher's guide to content and practice*. Columbus: Merrill. In her excellent text, Hernandez looks at bilingualism, special/gifted education, the hidden curriculum, and various other topics and issues.

MANNING, M. L. (1989). "Multicultural education." *Middle School Journal, 21(1)*, 14—16. Manning examines multicultural education, its importance to contemporary schools, and other topics such as the goals, fundamentals, unresolved issues, and characteristics of teachers.

PINE, G. J., & HILLIARD, A. G. (1990). "Rx for racism: imperatives for America's schools." *Phi*

Delta Kappan, 71, 593–600. First, Pine and Hilliard maintain that the conscious and unconscious expressions of racism in the United States society should be eliminated; and second, they offer several recommendations on how to accomplish the task.

STOVER, D. (1990). "The new racism." *American School Board Journal, 177(6),* 14–18. Stover examines the new racism plaguing United States schools and offers suggestions for breaking racism's hold and reducing its detrimental effects.

2

Understanding Native-American Children and Adolescents

Understanding the material and activities in this chapter will help the reader to

1. Describe the cultural, socioeconomic, and familial characteristics of Native-American children and adolescents;
2. Explain special problems and challenges that confront Native-American children and adolescents;
3. Describe Native-American learners and their development, achievement levels, language problems, and learning styles;
4. List several educational practices which impede the Native American learners' educational progress;
5. Offer several suggestions and strategies for improving the Native-American learner's self-concept and cultural identities;
6. List several points that educators of Native-Americans should remember when planning teaching and learning experiences;
7. Suggest appropriate children's literature, implement research findings, and provide culturally-appropriate experiences for Native-American learners.

OVERVIEW

Native-American children and adolescents have special needs that warrant educators' understanding: cherished and unique cultural characteristics, language problems, familial traditions, and learning problems that present schools with special challenges. Yet teacher education programs traditionally have not prepared prospective teachers to understand multicultural populations and the special characteristics and learning problems of Native-American learners or, in reality, any other multicultural groups. This chapter examines Native-American learners by providing a cultural portrait that focuses on their culture, language issues, families, achievement levels, learning styles, and overall school programs.

THE NATIVE-AMERICAN PEOPLE

Origins

Banks (1987) contended that scholars do not know exactly when people first came to the Americas. While many archaelogists have concluded that the lack of fossils rules out the possibility of men and women evolving in the Western Hemisphere, some Native-American groups believe that they originated in the Americas. Despite their contentions, archaelogists continue to believe that the ancestors of Native-Americans originally came from Asia (Banks, 1987).

Whatever explanation of origins one accepts, it is a fact that the ancestors of these people, who are today known as Indians, American Indians, or Native-Americans, have continuously occupied North America for 30,000 years or longer (Dorris, 1981). The white man came and began a crusade of taking their land and building homes and communities. A somewhat paradoxical situation exists: Rather that immigrating from other lands and being faced with cultural assimilation into the majority culture, Native-Americans faced the problem of the white man coming to their land and expecting them to relinquish cherished cultural traditions. Although the Native-American origins may continue to be in dispute, it is well-known (Wax, 1971; Banks, 1987) that these people had a distinct and cherished heritage from the beginnings of their existence.

Native-Americans Today

Contemporary Native-Americans are in a unique population, cultural, legal, and historical situation. While their population numbers are growing, they will probably never be a powerful political force. However, they still have treaty rights and a special relationship with the federal government that other cultural groups do not have (Banks, 1987).

Several factors suggest that Native-Americans may have improved lives and more affluence in future years: Some of their land is rich in raw materials, and the current emphasis on cultural diversity gives increasing recognition of Native-American rights in a predominantly Anglo society. Also, the many and varied contributions of Native-Americans are being recognized and accepted. While historical Native-American figures are being recognized by the United States population, other, more contemporary, figures are making their mark on society.

The following exercise provides an opportunity for readers to test their knowledge of Native-Americans, both historical and contemporary. As readers consider their success on the exercise, they should realize that the contributions and accomplishments of Native-Americans have not received widespread attention in social studies texts, or by the contemporary media. A deliberate and planned effort may be necessary for readers to enhance their knowledge of Native Americans and their contributions to American society.

The Culture Quiz: Contemporary Native-Americans

Directions: Match the individuals with their contributions or achievement by placing the appropriate letter before the name.

_____ 1. Vine Deloria, Jr.

a. First Native-American to serve as United States Commissioner of Indian Affairs

_____ 2. Watie Strand

b. A Sioux leader in the fight for Indian rights in the U.S.; wrote *Custer Died For Your Sins*

_____ 3. Jim Thorpe

c. Seminole-Creek and a member of the Oklahoma Senate

_____ 4. Ely Samuel Parker

d. Rural sociologist; a Cherokee-Choctaw; wrote *American Indians: The First of This Land*

_____ 5. Kelly Haney

e. The only Native-American brigadier general in the Confederate Army

_____ 6. C. Matthew Snipp

f. One of the greatest athletes in history; first president of the American Professional Football Association (now National Football League)

_____ 7. Susan LaFlesche

g. Sioux physician and

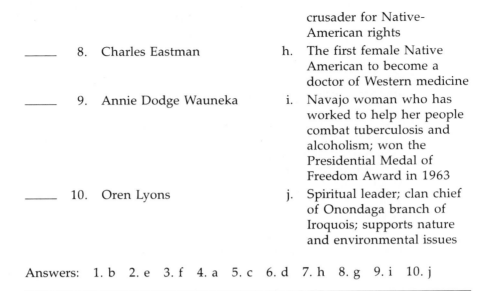

		crusader for Native-American rights
___	8. Charles Eastman	h. The first female Native American to become a doctor of Western medicine
___	9. Annie Dodge Wauneka	i. Navajo woman who has worked to help her people combat tuberculosis and alcoholism; won the Presidential Medal of Freedom Award in 1963
___	10. Oren Lyons	j. Spiritual leader; clan chief of Onondaga branch of Iroquois; supports nature and environmental issues

Answers: 1. b 2. e 3. f 4. a 5. c 6. d 7. h 8. g 9. i 10. j

___

Stereotyping of Native-American Children and Adolescents

Although stereotypical images often accompany the terms "Indian children", and "adolescents", this culture and these developmental periods constitute a highly diverse group. While the Native-American population varies significantly physically and culturally, differences in developing children and adolescents vary even more significantly. Not all Native-Americans are slow learners, shy, and undependable; likewise, not all adolescents are rebellious and experiencing difficult and stressful times. Although some common characteristics emerge when studying Native-American children and adolescents, one must use caution not to oversimplify or ignore individual differences.

CASE STUDY 2-1 shows the importance of forming accurate perceptions of Native Americans.

___

CASE STUDY 2-1: Forming Accurate Perceptions of Native-Americans

Upon completing her teacher education program in the east, Miss Stein joined several friends who went to a western state in hopes of finding teaching positions. Miss Stein accepted a position teaching eighth-grade social studies in a school that was predominantly Native-American. Trying to be objective as possible, Miss Stein questioned her beliefs about Native-American learners. She asked herself and her friends: "Are Native-Americans really different? Are they all poor? What will I do about their lower achievement?" She had heard so many stories. She wondered whether they were true and how she should separate facts from stereotypes.

Miss Stein and her future students are fortunate in at least one aspect—Miss Stein realizes that she does not know what to believe, and she is willing to question stereotypical generalizations. Miss Stein decided on the following strategy:

1. Speak with several professionals in the school—teachers, administrators, and the special services personnel such as the speech therapist and the librarian. Obtain an objective cultural portrait by forming opinions based upon objective information about the Native-Americans' culture, families, religions, socioeconomic status, and language.

2. Look at each student's permanent record in order to learn academic strengths and weaknesses.

3. Learn as much as possible about the learners' families and their role in the education process.

4. Read about the Native-American culture, its contributions, and its proud heritage.

5. Read children's books such as nonfiction and basic informational books which provide insights into the Native-American culture.

6. Talk to Native-American learners and express an interest in their cultural backgrounds.

7. Seek information from organizations promote Native-Americans, their overall welfare, and their determination for equality.

NATIVE-AMERICAN CHILDREN AND ADOLESCENTS

Cultural Characteristics

A product of both culture and parents, Native-American children and adolescents have unique and special cultural and developmental characteristics. The Native-American culture plays a major role in the shaping of children and adolescents as they develop. Educators must make the extra effort to seek accurate information, and to understand American history and the Native-American culture both from the point of view of the Native-American, and from the child and adolescent's perspective (Banks, 1987). Educators should also think through their own cultural beliefs, and realize the dangers in cultural substitution where Native-American learners are expected to change cultural viewpoints to coincide with Anglo middle-class expectations.

USING CHILDREN'S LITERATURE: Informational Books

ALIKI. *Corn Is Maise: The Gift of the Indians.* Crowell, 1976. (Reading Level: 2; Interest Level: 5-9.) Aliki provides an interesting and excellent history of corn, how it grows, and how it was first used.

ASHABRANNER, BRENT. *To Live in Two Worlds: American Indian Youth Today.* Dodd, Mead, 1984. (Reading Level: 7; Interest Level: 11 and above.) Ashabranner provides true accounts as Indians youths tell about their own lives.

ASHABRANNER, BRENT. *Morning Star, Black Sun: The Northern Cheyenne Indians and America's Energy Crisis.* Dodd, Mead, 1982. (Reading Level: 7; Interest Level: 11 and above.) This informative text traces the history of the Northern Cheyennes and discusses their fight to save their lands.

POATGIETER, ALICE HERMINA. *Indian Legacy: Native-American Influences on World Life and Culture.* Messner, 1981. (Reading Level: 5-7; Interest Level: 9 and above.) This text provides readers with an informative account of Native North and South American contributions to democratic attitudes and culture.

Although physical and cultural diversity has long characterized the Native-Americans, certain similarities exist to allow a synopsis of the Native-American learner. Banks (1987) warns, however, that the term "Indian" often connotes stereotypical images in the popular mind when, in fact, Indians' height, hair texture, and facial features vary greatly, and skin colors range from dark brown to very light. This diversity also includes a wide variety of personality traits, cultural practices, and lifestyles (Lum, 1986).

Values and beliefs that Native-Americans hold in esteem also differ from those of Anglo-Americans. Whereas Anglo-Americans believe that individuals have freedoms as long as their actions remain within the law, Native-American children are taught that actions must be in harmony with nature. Other values conveyed to children and adolescents include a degree of self-sufficiency, and being in harmony with knowledge gained from the natural world. Youth are taught to respect and protect the aged, who provide wisdom and acquaint the young with traditions, customs, legends, and myths (Axelson, 1985).

Activity:

Learn more about Native-American students by asking about their values and beliefs. For example, question how they feel about competition, achievement, self-sufficiency, and their opinions of school rules.

Achievement in the Anglo-American culture may not equate with achievement in the Native-American culture, and vice versa, and to place a value judgment on one or the other constitutes a serious mistake. Sanders (1987) hypothesizes that this cultural conflict and incompatibility contributes significantly to the academic failure of many Native-American children. Native-American children function at the average to superior range until the fourth grade. Thereafter, academic achievement typically declines each year so that by the tenth grade, Native-American students are doing below-average work.

USING CHILDREN'S LITERATURE: Biographies

TOBIAS, TOBI. *Maria Tallchief*. Crowell, 1970. (Reading level: 4; Interest Level 8-12.) The biography of Maria Tallchief, a world-renowned ballerina born in Fairfax, Oklahoma.

FALL, THOMAS. *Jim Thorpe*. Crowell, 1970. (Reading Level: 2; Interest Level: 7-10.) A biography for young children, this story focuses on Jim Thorpe, a great athlete and Olympic hero.

GRANT, MATTHEW. *Squanto: The Indian Who Saved the Pilgrims*. Publications Associates, 1974. (Reading level: 3; Interest Level: 6-10.) This is an illustrated biography of the Wampanoag, who played an important role in the lives of early settlers in New England.

BROWN, MARION MARSH. *Homeward, The Arrow's Flight*. Abington, 1980. (Reading Level: 6; Interest Level: 9-11.) The story of the first female Native-American to become a doctor of western medicine.

Native-American tribes, organizations, and communities play vital roles in the improvement of educational opportunities for Native-American children. More than 100 tribes operate the Head Start programs that serve 16,548 Native-American children. Many public schools, the Bureau of Indian Affairs, and tribal schools also strive to provide special education and culture-related learning designed to assist the development and early education of Native-American children (Walker, 1988).

Societal and cultural beliefs and traditions of the Native-American people particularly influence developing adolescents and their evolving identities. Adolescents living in Native-American families and attending Anglo-American schools, whether on or off the reservation, experience degrees of cultural confusion, and often question allegiance to a cultural identification. Such a dilemma can pose a particularly serious problem for adolescents who want to retain their rich cultural heritage while seeking acceptance in the Anglo-American schools and society.

FOR ADDITIONAL INFORMATION

Indian Youth of America, 609 Badgerow Building, P.O. Box 2786, Sioux City, IA 51106. This Native-American organization sponsors cultural enrichment projects, summer camp programs, and a resource center in its attempt to improve the lives of Native-American children.

Council for Indian Education, 517 Rimrock Rd., Billings, MT 59102. The CIE seeks to improve and secure higher standards of education for American Indian children, promotes quality children's literature in the Indian culture, and publishes books about American Indian life, past and present, on reading programs.

Natural Indian Education Association, 1819 H St. NW, Suite 800, Washington, DC 20006. This organization designs programs to improve the social and economic well-being of American Indians and Alaskan natives. The primary emphasis is on an exchange of ideas, techniques, and research methods among participants in American Indian education.

Native-American adolescents must also resolve the cultural differences surrounding the concept of sharing. Sharing represents a genuine and routine way of life in the Native-American culture. Yet this cultural belief which is so deeply ingrained in the Native-American culture does not equate with the Anglo-American custom of accumulating private property or savings. The Anglo-American's "worth" and social status are measured by the accumulation of material possessions, while the Native-American considers the ability and willingness to share to be most worthy (Lewis & Ho, 1989). While younger children may wish to share only with adults, an acceptance and allegiance to the cultural tradition of sharing increases as the child or adolescent develops. Adolescence is a unique time to develop a concept of sharing that is congruent with Native-American cultural expectations.

CASE STUDY 2-2 shows the need for teachers to understand the Native-American concept of sharing.

CASE STUDY 2-2: The Native-American Concept of Sharing

Mrs. Jason was upset with eight-year-old Bill when she learned that he had taken a pencil off another child's desk. Just last week, he had taken a pencil off her desk. What's wrong with Bill, she wondered? She asked a friend, "I told him about taking other people's things—I just cannot understand him—why does he continue to take things that do not belong to him?"

Her friend thought that the problem might be more Mrs. Jason's than Bill's. Although Mrs. Jason needs to discuss with Bill that taking things can be misconstrued by Anglos as stealing, Mrs. Jason also needs to understand Bill's perception of the situation, and his cultural concepts of sharing: Bill had forgotten his pencil, and to his culture, taking another's pencil is not perceived as a problem (she had others didn't she?). He would not have objected if someone had taken his pencil when he had more than one. Upon listening to Bill's perception, Mrs. Jason realized that what she had perceived as stealing was perceived as sharing (and culturally permissible and encouraged) to Bill. She decided that two steps would be appropriate: First, she needed a better understanding of sharing in the Native-American culture; and two, she needed to explain to others in the class that Bill was not stealing their pencils.

Several reasons exist for adolescents becoming increasingly cognizant and accepting of this cultural expectation. Adolescents have more advanced intellectual abilities that enable them to recognize that it is possible for two people to want the same thing at the same time, that shared possessions can be retrieved, and that sharing can be reciprocated. Also, developing intellectual skills allows an adolescent to understand the difference between sharing temporarily and donating permanently. The adolescent can understand, as well as make clear to others, which intent is meant (Kostelnik, Stein, Whiren, & Soderman, 1988).

Activity:

Talk to Native-American children and adolescents concerning their feelings about sharing. Learn specifically how they feel and the reasons. Also, see how they perceive Anglo-American attitudes toward possessions and ownership.

Other notable cultural characteristics of Native-Americans which become an integral part of children's and adolescents' evolving identity are the tendencies toward patience and passive temperaments. Native-American are taught to be patient, to control emotions, and to avoid passionate outbursts over small matters. As the Native-American adolescent develops an identity, cultural characteristics such as poise, self-containment, and aloofness become ingrained. These cultural habits conflict with the Anglo-American custom of impatience and competitiveness, and often result in the Native-American being mistakenly considered lazy, uncaring, and inactive (Lewis & Ho, 1989). This demeanor or personality trait is also demonstrated in the Native-Americans' tendency to lower their voices to communicate anger, unlike Anglo-American adolescents, who learn to raise their voices in order to convey a message (Kostelnik, Stein, Whiren, & Soderman, 1988).

Non-interference with others, and a deep respect for the rights and dignity of individuals, constitute a basic premise of Native-American culture (Banks, 1987). Although such practices may have caused people of other cultures to consider the Native-American as uncaring or unconcerned, the actual case is quite the contrary. Native-Americans are taught early to respect the rights and privileges of other individuals, and the responsibility of working together toward a common goal in harmony with nature.

Socioeconomic Status

Two decades ago, Wax (1971) used "the culture of poverty" to describe the lower socioeconomic status of the Native-American population. In reality, many Native-Americans continue to live in poverty. Dorris (1981) painted a bleak picture for Native-Americans:

Statistically they remain among the poorest economically, the least employed, the unhealthiest, the lowest in education and income level, and the worst-housed ethnic group in America—but there are signs of improvement in each area. (p. 63)

Because of Civil Rights legislation and the strong will and the determination of Native-American population, there is evidence that these people are improving their lot in life. For instance, some of their lands contain rich energy resources. Specifically, the Southern Utes in Colorado, the Uinta-Ouray Utes in Utah, and the Blackfeet in Montana, have gas and oil reserves, as do the Shoshones and Arapaho in Wyoming. Similarly, the Bannocks and Shonsones, whose reservations are in Idaho, own one of the largest phosphate deposits in the West. The Navajo and Hopi reservations in the Southwest contain vast oil and gas fields, as well as uranium reserves (Dorris, 1981).

Attempting to break the bonds of poverty, other Native-Americans today are making notable achievements. Such attitudes as " . . . we never, never give up" (p. 40), some Native-Americans have engaged in business ventures that have yielded considerable successes. The Navajo Nation produces electronic missile assemblies for General Dynamics; the Choctaws of Mississippi build wire harnesses for Ford Motor Co.; the Seminoles in Florida own a 156-room hotel; and the Swinomish Indians of Washington State plan a 60-acre boat basin, an 800-slip marina, and a three-story office and commercial headquarters. *Newsweek* continues to report that such aggressive approaches to business were previously unheard-of on the reservations. High unemployment, high rates of alcoholism, and poverty-level living conditions have characterized the Native-American people for many decades. Critics charge that these successful business ventures have not helped the entire culture: Unemployment affects 35% of some tribes, young people often must leave home to find work, and some critics worry that economic development will threaten the cultural identity of Native Americans (Indian tribes, incorporated, 1988).

Families

Native-American adolescents place a high priority on both the immediate and the extended family. The immediate and extended family, tribe, clan, and heritage all contribute to the child's cultural identity, and play a significant role in overall development.

Grandparents retain an official and symbolic leadership in family communities. Children seek daily contact with grandparents and grandparents monitor the children's behavior and have a voice in childrearing practices (Lum, 1986). Although the adolescent's social consciousness and awareness doubtless cause a transition from a family-centered to a more peer-centered environment, the traditional Native-American respect and commitment to the family continues (Lum, 1986).

Adult perceptions of childhood and childrearing practices also influence the developing person significantly. For example, Richardson (1981) contends that the Indian family considers children to be gifts worthy of sharing with others, while the Anglo perception holds that children constitute private property to be disciplined as deemed necessary. In essence, children in the Indian family have few rules to obey, while the Anglo children have rules with strict consequences.

The Native-American parent provides children with early training in self-sufficiency and also, contrary to the individualism prized in the Anglo-American society, the Native-American family places importance on group welfare (Axelson, 1985). Sanders (1987) provides examples of the Native-American emphasis on group welfare in her reports of high school absenteeism. Any crisis in the home or within the family will precipitate an absence from school until the crisis has been resolved and the family situation returns to normal.

Native-American childrearing practices and differing cultural expectations for behavior can result in confusion and frustration for the children. Native-Americans who confront an incompatibility with their Anglo-American counterparts appear to demonstrate growing feelings of isolation, rejection, and anxiety that can result in alienation, poor self-image, and withdrawal (Sanders, 1987). Such feelings undoubtedly affect the behavior and achievement aspirations of the Native-American children and adolescents.

Activity:

Talk with Native-American learners about their parents and extended families. Try to understand the Native-American concept of family, and the role of extended family members in the lives of children and adolescents.

Young people seek social acceptance and approval from older members of the family as well as the younger family members. Unlike the Anglo-American culture, which emphasizes youth and the self, Native-American adolescents place family before self, and have great respect for elders and their wisdom. The wisdom of life is received from the older people, whose task it is to acquaint the young with the traditions, customs, legends, and myths of the culture. All members of a family care for the old, and consider death as an accepted fact of life (Axelson, 1985).

The early training in self-sufficiency which Native-Americans receive from their families and other significant adults continues to have an impact during the adolescent years. Although the adolescent continues to recognize the loyalty and dependence upon the immediate and surrounding family, adolescents develop independence and confidence in their abilities to deal with the world outside the family. This attitude of self-sufficiency, however, must be considered from the Native-American point of view. For example, not sharing with one's fellows, and the accumulation of great wealth and materialistic possessions, would not be included in self-sufficiency. The cultural expectation must be compatible with the knowledge of the natural world and in harmony with others. Achieving self-sufficiency and self-gain cannot be at the expense of family or tribal members, or at the expense of harming any aspect of the natural world (Axelson, 1985).

Religion

According to Native-American belief, the world is interconnected, and everything, including human beings, lives according to the same process. Each being has its power, function, and place in the universe. Every part of nature has a spirit which many tribes believe possesses intelligence, emotion, and free will. Praying, in fact, is praying to one's own power. Because the Great Spirit is everything, in all of nature, there is no need to question the existence of a god. Since nature is the essence of God, nature would stop if God no longer lived (Axelson, 1985).

God is the great power above everything. It is "the force which is responsible for action, and which can actually have control over man's destiny" (Zychowicz, 1975, p. 15). Man, nature, and the universe were created by God, and instructions were given on how to live in the land. The inner spiritual power, or the word "God," was called "orenda" by the Iroquois, "manitou" by the Algonkian tribes, "ahone" by the Powhatans, and "wakan" or "wakonda" by the Sioux. The Sioux also used the expression "wakan tanka," meaning all of the "wakan" beings. The spiritual god of the Native-Americans is positive, benevolent, and part of daily living. God's knowledge and advice are transmitted through traditional Native-American wisdom. Ideal action toward God is accomplished by helping others understand and get along with people, and by comprehending the natural world, of which everything (living and nonliving) is a part (Bryde, 1971). All of nature's objects are equally respected as both physical and spiritual entities (Axelson, 1985).

As in any other culture, the Native-American culture contains norms and standards for behavior, but Native-Americans are inclined to judge each person as a separate individual, taking into consideration the reasons for actions ahead of the norms of the society. The dominant society judges behavior as right or wrong, good or bad, and considers how things "should" be and not necessarily "how" they are. The practice of judging the behaviors of others is an important value in the mainstream society (Axelson, 1985).

Native-Americans have a close relationship between spiritual realization and unity, and their cultal practices. While Catholic and Protestant clergy have sought to Christianize Native-Americans, there has been a continuation of indigenous religious rituals, and beliefs in the healing power of nature. Natural forces are associated with the life process itself, and pervade everything that the believing Native-American does. Community religious rites are a collective effort that promote this mode of healing, and increase inward insight and experiential connection with nature. Native-American individuals can utilize the positive experiences resulting from ceremonial events, power-revealing events (omens, dreams, visions), and contact with a tribal medicine man in the healing process. Helping to discover and reinforce the therapeutic significance of Native-American religious and cultural events can be a learning task for social workers (Lum, 1986).

Language

Language and communication, whether verbal or nonverbal, may constitute the most important aspects of an individual's culture, and characterize the general culture, its values, and its ways of looking and thinking (Bruner, 1966). Educators should develop a consciousness and appreciation for the many Native-American languages, and also recognize the problems that may result when educators and the children have differing language backgrounds.

The cultural mannerisms and nonverbal communication demonstrated by the Native-American child add other personal entities to both culture and language. During the last decade, anthropologists, counselors, sociologists, and teachers have begun to awaken to the urgent need to understand these "silent languages." Gestures, body movements, practices due to attitudes toward time and space, and general social behavior all provide valuable information about the client (Jensen, 1985). Professionals should recognize communicational differences (both verbal and nonverbal) between Native-American and Anglo-American children, such as the Native-American's inclination to speak softer and at a slower rate, to avoid direct identification between speaker and listener, and to interject less frequently with encouraging communicational signs such as head nods and "uh huh." (Sanders, 1987)

Native-American adolescents, like adolescents of all cultures, need the security and psychological safety that a common language provides, yet they experience significant language problems during this crucial period of development. Of the approximately 400,000 Native-Americans under 21 years of age in 1974, over three-fourths obtained their education on reservations, or in special boarding schools off the reservation. The considerable diversity in their language has resulted in some adolescents speaking their Native-American language, some speaking only English, and others being bilingual. Both the self-concept and the identity are being formed during this transition from the family-centered world of the immediate and extended home. No longer is communication possible only with elders, parents, and siblings. Native-American adolescents' ability to reach out to a wider world will depend greatly on his or her ability to speak and understand the language of the majority and other cultures (Youngman & Sandongei, 1983).

Activity:

Observe Native-American nonverbal communication patterns. How might communication be misunderstood? Discuss with Native-Americans how nonverbal communication is important for all cultures, and the importance of considering nonverbal mannerisms not only from one's own cultural perspective.

Native-American children and adolescents often have to decide which language to speak. This may be an even more difficult task, considering that Native-Americans consider language to be a crucial aspect of the culture, and a cherished gift which should be used whenever possible (Richardson, 1981). Such a belief conflicts with the Anglo-American opinion that English is the Native-American's means to success, and that English should be the predominant language.

The following cultural comparison shows how Native-American and Anglo-American children and adolescents differ.

CULTURAL COMPARISON

Native-American and Anglo-American Children
and Adolescents

Native-American	*Anglo-American*
Elders to be honored	The future lies with youth
Learning through legends	Learning found in books and schools
Sharing—everything belongs to others	Ownership rather than sharing
Immediate and extended family comes first	Think of oneself
Humble/cooperative	Competitive
Carefree—unconcerned with time	Structured—be aware of time
Expects few rules	Expects rules for every contingency
Avoid looking in the eye	Shows listening by looking directly in the eye
Dance is for religious expression	Dance is for expression of pleasure
Family-centered	Peer-centered
Question which culture for identification	No question about cultural identification

Great respect for elders	Elders not in the "real world"; respect for youth
Patience and passive temperaments	Impatience; active
Speak softer to make points	Speak louder to make points

Source: Richardson, E. H. (1981). "Cultural and historical perspectives in counseling American Indians" in D. W. Sue *Counseling the culturally different*. New York: John Wiley 225-227.

NATIVE-AMERICAN LEARNERS IN THE SCHOOL

Educators' Understanding Native-American Learners and Their Culture

An understanding of the Native-American culture is necessary for educators working with these children. The Native-American's reflection and passivity, and short-term orientation (Lum, 1986) deserve understanding in the light of the Native-American culture, rather than through attempts to persuade the Native-American to respond to the Anglo-American culture.

Educational and societal factors, as well as the clash of cultures, during these crucial developmental years have the potential for developing the feelings of frustration and hopelessness that often result in alienation. Such alienation has been attributed to the Native-American's general loss of confidence and decline in motivation. These feelings during adolescence may also result in considerable confusion in the classroom. The Native-American adolescent may demonstrate behavior that teachers perceive as excessive shyness, inactivity, or lack of motivation. Adolescents who have teachers who misunderstand, or culturally misconstrue, these characteristics along with the adolescent's usual steady decline in achievement may develop feelings of hopelessness and alienation. These problems might result from Native-American early childrearing techniques, e.g., the precepts, "do not set yourself apart from others," "material success is not as important as the natural aspects of life," and "the importance of being humble" might continue to influence their behavior (Wax, 1971).

IMPLEMENTING RESEARCH 2-1 shows how Native-American and Anglo-American learners differ, and how educators can use the information to help Native-American learners.

IMPLEMENTING RESEARCH 2-1: Cultural Conflicts

Sanders (1987) examined the cultural characteristics of the Native-American students and showed the differing cultural orientations between these students and their predominantly Anglo-American teachers. Sanders (1987) presents the following comparison:

Native-American	*Anglo-American*
Speak softly, at a slower rate	Speak louder and faster
Avoid speaker or listener	Address listener directly, often by name
Interject less	Interrupt frequently
Use fewer "encouraging signs"	Use verbal encouragement
Auditory messages treated differently—delayed responses	Use immediate response
Nonverbal communication	Verbal skills highly prized
Cooperation	Competition
Group needs considered more	Personal goals considered
Present goals considered important	Plan for future
Encourage sharing	Acquisitiveness
Privacy and non-interference valued	Need to control and affect others
Patience—allowing others to go first	Aggressive and competitive

IMPLEMENTING THE RESEARCH:

_____ 1. Educators should be aware of cultural diversity, and respond by accommodating the goals of education while allowing Native-American students to preserve their values and self-worth.

_____ 2. The interaction styles and communication practices within the educational system must be recognized as incompatible with the American Indian style of interacting and communicating, and this incompatibility must be addressed.

_____ 3. Curricular materials and instructional procedures could be revised to maximize the excitement and potential that cultural diversity can bring to the classroom.

_____ 4. It is easier to be comfortable with, and talk to, those with whom one can identify. Therefore, the presence of American Indian teachers and staff would give American Indian students mentors who share their cultural background.

_____ 5. The inherent abilities of American Indian students to perform and achieve at high standards should be recognized as a function of the self-fulfilling prophecy, because support and encouragement by teachers would establish a student's belief in himself or herself, and promote a good self-image.

Source: Sanders, D. (1987). "Cultural conflicts: An important factor in the academic failures of American Indian students." *Journal of Multicultural Counseling and Development, 15*, 81-90.

Educators can benefit from understanding the Native-Americans' all-too-often predicament in predominantly Anglo schools.

1. In contrast to their Anglo-American counterparts, Native-American children must deal with the centuries of injustice that have resulted in significant feelings of suspicion and distrust of Anglo-American professionals and institutions (Lum, 1986).

2. Communicational problems may result in an inability to understand, trust, and build rapport with peers and professionals of other cultures. Differences in "home language" and "school language" of the Native-American's nonverbal communication might hinder educational efforts. Native-American learners may appear to be unconcerned with educational progress when, in fact, they may be painfully shy and overly-sensitive to strangers due to language problems and mistrust of Anglo-Americans.

3. Native-American adolescents develop in an often unique and difficult situation. Not only must they reconcile allegiance to the values and customs of both the Native-American and the Anglo-American cultures, the usual problems of adolescence, e.g., the possibility of experiencing role confusion or differences associated with building a positive identity, are also encountered.

4. Native-American learners face decisions regarding whether the Native-American or Anglo-American culture (or some "cultural combination") should provide the basis for the identity, whether to attempt proficiency in both the Native-American language *and* English, how to maintain harmony with family and nature while surviving in the Anglo-American world, and how to accept the vast cultural differences in situations where the Anglo-American is unlikely to attempt cross-cultural understandings or acceptance.

Also, perceptive educators understand (and plan educational experiences accordingly) that survival in the predominant and powerful Anglo-American culture often requires Native-Americans to place low priority on several culturally-precious aspects such as language, rituals and customs, and the commitment to the family. During this crucial time for identity formation and the development of positive self-concept and cultural identities, giving up long-respected customs and traditions to survive in a culture that places little value on nature, sharing, being humble, honoring elders, and cherishing one's language, presents Native-Americans with formidable tasks.

In an investigation of study habits and attitudes of Native-American learners, Gade, Hulbert, and Fuqua (1986) studied students in grades seven to twelve, and concluded that poor study habits and attitudes, especially in the junior high school years and among boys, were related to teacher ratings of low achievement, insufficient cooperation, and poor work habits. Gade, Hulbert, and Fuqua (1986) offered several implications for professionals in today's schools. First, they emphasize the importance of understanding that study habits and attitudes involve all school personnel, not just classroom teachers. Second, those students who have poor opinions of teachers and their classroom behaviors and methods indicates the need for more recruitment of Native-American teachers and counselors. Third, Native-American learners need direct instruction on study skills and attitudes toward their education.

CASE STUDY 2-3 shows the efforts of Mr. Thomas who realized that the low-achieving students in his classes needed additional assistance.

CASE STUDY 2-3: Helping the Low Achiever

Mr. Thomas pondered his class—the achievers, the low achievers, and those who seemed to be in a constant struggle just to make passing grades. As Mr. Thomas thought about his students, he also wondered whether his lack of knowledge of how Native-Americans learn actually contributed to their learning difficulties. Mr. Thomas asked himself, "What can I do and what should I know about the way Native-Americans learn to improve their academic achievement?"

Mr. Thomas went to several authorities on Native-American children and adolescents to seek advice on how he could better understand the learner, make his teaching more effective, and maximize teaching/learning efforts. Advice he received included:

1. Understand the short-term time orientations of many Native-Americans.
2. Understand the need to understand families and involve them in school activities and their children's learning.
3. Understand the need to improve the Native-American learners' self-concepts and their belief in their ability to learn.
4. Understand the need for genuinely positive and caring relationships between teachers and students.
5. Understand the need to design curricula which reflects the Native-American's backgrounds and contemporary needs.
6. Understand Native-American learning styles, and how the curricula and teaching methods can be changed to match student's learning styles.

Developmental Theory: Children and Adolescents

Being able to plan and implement effective teaching/learning experiences and appropriate multicultural experiences requires an understanding of the learner's developmental perspectives. Developmentally, children and adolescents are gaining in ability to think at higher levels, are engaging in wider social circles, and are becoming physically taller and heavier. Such changes are accompanied by fluctuating self-concepts and interpretations of their cultural identities.

Although the learner's development should always form the basis for educational experiences, it is important to consider these changes from a cultural perspective. Children who are forming identities while developing into adolescents need successful experiences to ensure healthy opinions of themselves and their Native-American culture. Considering their developmental periods and their culture, what school experiences do Native-Americans need? These youngsters need opportunities to be successful, both in their Native-American culture and in the predominantly Anglo culture. Their steadily increasing ability to think requires that educators provide them with opportunities to think and to reason. Their budding self-concepts and cultural identities also suggest the need for curricular materials that portray Native-Americans in a positive light, and their psychosocial development requires opportunities to form cross-cultural friendships and to widen their circle of peers. In essence, rather than following verbatim a prescribed curriculum designed for middle-class Anglo learners, educators need to address the unique developmental and cultural needs of Native-American learners.

Activity:

Examine several curricular materials to determine their feasibilitiy for Native-American learners. Do the materials recognize Native-Americans and convey a respect for Native-American values such as sharing and noninterference with others?

Achievement Levels

Several studies suggest that tests and teacher reports show that Native-American children function at the average-to-superior range until the fourth grade. After the fourth grade, academic functioning typically declines each year so that by grade ten, Native-American learners' academic achievement falls below their Anglo-American peers. Several complex factors may contribute to this predicament, such as the growing feelings of isolation, rejection, and anxiety that are felt by Native-American learners as they confront the incompatibility of their cultural value system with that of their Anglo-American peers. These feelings contribute to alienation, poor self-image, and withdrawal (Sanders, 1987).

Adherence to Native-Americans' cultural traditions and mannerisms often conflicts with schools that may have differing orientations. How can the clash of values between Native-Americans and Anglo-Americans affect educators? Anglo-American teachers view behaviors exhibited by American Indian students as rude or insulting. For example, if these students avoid the teacher's gaze, do not volunteer answers, or delay response, as their cultural background has taught them to do, the students are seen as lazy or uncomprehending. Anglo-Americans see Native-American students as lacking time-management skills or being self-centered because of their present-time orientation. The American Indian concept of time means that what is happening now is more important than what is not happening now; that what is happening now deserves full attention; and that what one will be doing at this time tomorrow will be more important than what one is doing now, or what one will *not* be doing tomorrow (Sanders, 1987).

Whether or not the educational problems experienced by Native-American adolescents are caused by "cultural teachings" or the "cultural differences" in Anglo-American schools, the result is the same: Native-Americans continue to have one of the highest dropout rates of any ethnic group at the high school level, regardless of region or tribal affiliation (Sanders, 1987). The reasons for dropping out of school include: (1) an uneven application of school rules; (2) factors pertaining to teacher-student relationships, e.g., teachers not caring about students, and not providing sufficient assistance; (3) disagreements with teachers; and (4) the content of schooling, which the students perceive as not important to what they want to do in life (Coladarci, 1983).

Perceptive educators should demonstrate genuine care, understanding, and encouragement with which Native-American learners can identify; ensure that the curriculum addresses Native-American needs and provides culturally-relevant curricular experiences; and understand the home problems of some Native-Americans such as separations and divorces, unemployment, alcoholism, and child abuse.

Language Problems

Native-Americans speak about 2,200 different languages, which further complicates the language problem (Wax, 1971). This broad and diversified language background, albeit personal and sacred to the Native-American, has not provided the rich cultural and language experiences that contribute to the Anglo-American definition of school success. Wide-scale differences exist in the Native-American's ability to speak English. In some cases, as few as 4 percent of Native-Americans speak "excellent" English, with a far greater percentage speaking either "good" or "poor" English. The children, Vontress (1976) contends, who have attended English-speaking schools of course speak better English than their elders. This tremendous diversity of languages has also contributed to difficulties in school, e.g. teachers and students speaking different languages, and curricular materials being written in unfamiliar languages.

Attending a school staffed with Anglo-American teachers, and facing daily the academic and social problems associated with not being understood and not understanding the language of others, significantly affects the adolescent's self-perception. Language may also be a contributing factor in the adolescent's tendency to decline in academic achievement, especially since the lack of cognitive and academic skills does not appear to be a major factor (Sanders, 1987).

CASE STUDY 2-4 looks at how a fifteen-year-old boy experiences difficulty due to his language problems.

CASE STUDY 2-4: The Native-American's Language Problem

Harry, a fifteen-year-old boy, has several problems that result, at least in part, from his lack of proficiency in English. He is faced with functioning in a bilingual world. While his family continues to rely on the language it has spoken for centuries, he must speak English at school. (Some of his friends have been punished for not speaking English.) Meanwhile, his grades are failing, he does not always understand the teacher (and vice versa), and he experiences difficulty as he ventures outside the social confines of his culture.

Harry's teacher, Mrs. Rivers, can take several steps to assist him. She can:

1. Arrange for Harry to visit the language specialist or a bilingual teacher who can determine the extent of his problem and plan an appropriate course of action.
2. Seek the services of the remedial or resource teacher to provide Harry with appropriate remedial assistance.
3. Arrange for Harry to visit the guidance counselor, who may be able to help him widen his circle of friends.
4. Talk with Harry to let him know that she and the other school personnel are interested in him as a person and as a learner.

Learning Styles: Cultural Considerations

Effective education for Native-American learners requires consideration of each individual's learning styles—the learner's strategies used to acquire knowledge, skills, and understanding. Readers are reminded of the necessity for considering the multitude of differences among the Native-American people. To assume that all Native-Americans have similar learning styles shows a disregard for nations, tribes, and individuals, as well as educational and socioeconomic backgrounds. Table 2-1 provides a brief overview of several learning areas and their implications for Native-American learners.

Table 2-1 Native-American Learning Styles

Area	Implications
Many Native-American learners prefer to learn using visual/perceptual/spatial information rather than verbal means.	Present new or different material in a visual/perceptual/spatial mode; also, many students need to improve their skills in the verbal mode.
Many Native-American learners use mental images to remember or understand words and concepts rather than word associations.	Present metaphors, images, or symbols, rather than dictionary-style definitions or synonyms when teaching difficult concepts.
Many Native-American learners process information in a global/analytic manner, e.g., they focus on the whole rather than the part.	Present material in a manner whereby overall purpose and structure are clear, rather than presenting information in small, carefully sequenced bits.

Although Table 2-1 provides representative examples of learning styles and implications, perceptive educators can see the need to consider individual learners, teaching and communication styles, internal cognitive processes, and the external conditions which affect learning outcomes. This can only be accomplished by using appropriate diagnostic instruments and learning style inventories and by getting to know individual learners and their learning styles.

IMPLEMENTING RESEARCH 2-2 examines how educational practice should reflect Native-American learning styles.

IMPLEMENTING RESEARCH 2-2: Styles of Learning

Swisher and Deyhle use specific classroom examples to illustrate the learning styles and interactional styles of various groups of Native-American and Alaskan Native youth. This paper is based on the premise that "people perceive the world in different ways, learn about the world in different ways, and demonstrate what they have learned in different ways" (p.2). Specific differences include learning to learn, visual approaches to learning, the influence of culture, cooperating and competing, and adapting one's teaching styles to Native Americans' learning styles. Contemporary emphases include educational researchers and practitioners continuing to search for instructional methods that address the relationship of how children have "learned to learn" and the ways in which they are expected to demonstrate learning in the classroom.

IMPLEMENTING THE RESEARCH:

_____ 1. Educators should discuss students' learning styles, and assist in understanding the learning process and the learner's role in the process.

_____ 2. Educators should recognize (and respond appropriately to) Native-American cultural characteristics, such as students not liking to be "spotlighted" or having excessive attention; students wanting a degree of distance in closeness; and students being uncomfortable with rigid and inflexible pacing of activities.

_____ 3. Educators should organize the classroom to meet the interactional needs of the students, and provide activities that encourage both independence and cooperation.

Source: Swisher, K., & Deyhle, D. (1989). "The styles of learning are different, but the teaching is just the same: Suggestions for teachers of American Indian youth." _Journal of American Indian Education, Special Issue_ (August), 1-11.

SCHOOL PRACTICES IMPEDING NATIVE-AMERICANS' PROGRESS

Since some techniques taught to educators are incompatible with Native-American cultural traditions, it is imperative that educators use strategies that are appropriate for the culture. What specifically should educators avoid?

1. Methods designed to increase positive self-talk, such as "something I like about myself" or "a sport I can play well," often work well with Anglo or Black children; however, the Native-American child may be reluctant.

2. Attempts to convince Native-Americans to be competitive (such as being the first, best, fastest, or smartest) are incompatible to children and adolescents taught to value cooperation and harmony.

3. Educators often expect eye contact, and perceive the Native-American's tendency to look the other way as signs of withdrawal, embarrassment, or discomfort.

4. Educators and counselors often rely extensively on verbal participation by children in the class. While verbal interaction is valued by Anglo, Black, and Hispanic cultures, such interaction is not valued by Native-Americans.

Promoting Positive Self-Concepts and Cultural Identities

Educators working with Native-American learners readily recognize the many personal and social factors that affect children's and adolescents' self-concepts and cultural identities. Injustice and discrimination, poverty, low educational attainment, and perhaps growing up on reservations, in foster homes, or in a predominantly Anglo society may result in Native-American learners questioning their self-worth and the worth of their culture.

Although self-concept scales reveal little difference in the level of self-concept between preschool Native-American and Anglo-American children (Bruneau, 1985), other evidence suggests that Native-American learners experience conflict upon entering school (Soldier, 1985). One study compared Native-American and Anglo-American children, and concluded that various tribes, e.g., the Cree, Miccosukee, and the Seminole, have scored lower on self-concept scales (Rotenberg & Cranwell, 1989). Such measures and conclusions, however, Rotenberg and Cranwell (1989) warn, may be misleading, because attributes assessed by the self-concept scales may be more culturally revelant for Anglo-Americans than for Native-Americans. Although one cannot and should not automatically assume that Native-Americans have lower self-concepts, educators do have the responsibility of diagnosing the self-concept of Native-American children and adolescents, and of providing appropriate school experiences that contribute to positive perceptions of one's self and one's culture.

IMPLEMENTING RESEARCH 2-3 shows how educators can provide positive and productive educational experiences that can lead to enhanced self-concept of Native-American students.

IMPLEMENTING RESEARCH 2-3: Positive and Productive Educational Experiences

This paper shows how teachers can use self-esteem exercises, reinforcement of clear rules and directives, and parent involvement, to help students have a positive and productive educational experience. Efforts include greeting students at the door to determine their state of mind; self-esteem exercises such as "I am," "I have," "I want," and "I will influence the world by . . . ."; rarely raising one's voice; weekly and monthly reports home; and extensive efforts to involve both parents and grandparents. The premise of the approach is that teachers need to encourage Native-Americans. One of the most effective means of accomplishing this task is to model encouraging and positive behavior.

IMPLEMENTING THE RESEARCH:

1. Educators should understand the importance of modeling respect and acceptance for all students. Educators should plan and implement self-esteem exercises for all culturally different learners that address distinctive cultural characteristics.

2. Educators should plan and implement self-esteem exercises

for all culturally different learners that address distinctive cultural characteristics.

3. Educators should include both immediate and extended family members in school activities in an attempt to build positive individual and cultural identities.

4. During all teaching and learning activities, educators should remember that "the goal is to assist the student in achieving success in the white man's culture while preserving the Indian way of life" (p. 165).

Source: Uthe-Reyno, M.G., & MacKinnon, L.J. (1989). "Teacher's modeling encourages learning in Indian students." *Educational Horizons, 67,* 163-165.

What, then, can educators do to contribute to positive self-concepts and cultural identities among Native-American children and adolescents? Mitchum (1989) provides a group activity for improving self-concepts and cultural identities.

Activity:

Young Native-American children might become involved by being given a drawing or a silhouette of an Indian child. They may be asked to write words or draw symbols to illustrate their favorite food, favorite game, favorite sport, and perhaps something they like to think about.

After making their pictures, non-Indian children would be asked to explain their pictures to the other children in the group. Native-American children, however, may benefit more by simply looking at their pictures, together, as a group. They may look for some similarities in their pictures to identify their group's favorite foods, or some things their group likes to think about. After sharing, the children may combine their pictures into a collage incorporating all of the pictures into a "group personality." The purpose, then, of this type of self-disclosing activity for Indian children is twofold: First, they see a type of collective group personality emerge. Second, they begin to think of themselves as a part of the group. They do not compare themselves individually with other members of the group. Instead, they gain a sense of their contribution to the group and the ways in which they belong and identify, not with individuals in the group, but with the group as a whole.

CULTURAL PORTRAIT: John—A Native-American Learner

Fourteen-year-old John attends a school off the reservation. The student population is a mixed group of Native-Americans, some Hispanic-Americans, a few Black Americans, and some Anglo-Americans.

Although the school is represented by several culturally-diverse groups, most teachers are Anglo-American, and the school environment and educational program indicate an orientation toward traditional Anglo expectations.

John has several academic and social problems: he makes below average grades, feels he does not have many friends, and generally feels uncomfortable while in school. Everything is rushed, cooperation is second to competition, his teachers feel he is not trying, and the overall curricular emphasis makes little sense to him. He has an interest in the ancient traditions of his people, yet his teachers rarely address his cultural needs or, in fact, any of his individual needs. He realizes that his grades need to improve, yet he does not always understand the teacher or the way she teaches. Also, although he has Native-American friends, he has few friends among the students of the other cultures. School days are often frustrating for John as he strives to make another day.

What John's Teacher Can Do

John's teacher can take several specific steps to help him improve his academic and social progress. First, she can spend some time alone with John to determine his strengths, weaknesses, and interests. Second, she can consult the language specialist to determine whether John's academic (or social) problems can be attributed to his using a second language. Third, she can arrange for John to have individual assistance from the remedial specialist. Fourth, she can reassess her teaching techniques to see whether her teaching methods match John's learning styles. Last, she can build upon John's interest in his cultural heritage through appropriate reading and other curricular materials. Reading and studying about his own cultural background might show John that the curriculum values his Native-American culture, and recognizes his individual needs and interests. Just as important, the teacher will provide a curriculum that gives other learners an appropriate multicultural understanding of the Native-American culture. Although almost any number of suggestions could be listed to help John and to improve his feelings about school and himself, John's teacher should recognize the importance of showing interest in John, and in providing first-hand and individual help in improving his academic and social progress.

SUMMING UP

Educators who plan teaching and learning experiences for Native-American children and adolescents should:

1. Remember that Native-American people have a proud history of accomplishments and notable contributions, and that these should be incorporated into school curricula.

2. Avoid providing curricular and instructional practices that indicate only Anglo, middle-class expectations, and that might seem alien to Native-American learners.

3. Remember that achievement levels and school dropout rates need to be addressed by educators who understand Native-Americans and the possible cultural basis for educational problems.

4. Promote the positive self- and cultural images among Native-American learners that might be one of the most effective means of improving academic achievement and school-related problems.

5. Adapt teaching styles and other school practices to meet the Native-American's learning styles, demonstrating that educators are caring and interested in improving school achievement and overall school success.

6. Understand the Native-American culture and the learners' cultural characteristics, religious orientations, and socioeconomic backgrounds.

7. Provide learning experiences so that learners of other cultures may develop a better understanding of their Native-American peers.

8. Understand the learner's development, and provide school experiences based upon developmental and cultural characteristics.

9. Consider Native-Americans as "individuals" who differ in nations, tribes, socioeconomic levels, and educational attainment.

SUGGESTED LEARNING ACTIVITIES

1. Observe a Native-American learner and record the cultural mannerisms that might be contrary to behaviors expected in schools. How might the behavior of Native-Americans be misinterpreted? How might educators better understand Native-American learners and their behavior?

2. List several stereotypical beliefs about Native-Americans. What is the basis of those beliefs? How might those beliefs affect educators' perceptions of these learners? What steps can multicultural educators take to lessen the effect of stereotypical beliefs?

3. Study (observe, examine school records, talk with, test) two Native-American learners, one who has attended reservation schools, and one who has attended Anglo schools. What differences can you list? What has been the effect of acculturation? What differences might be attributed to social class or tribal affiliation? Considering all these differences, how can educators gain an accurate perception of the Native-American learner?

4. Talk with several teachers of Native-American learners to see what first-hand experiences they have to offer. Specifically, learn their

perception of the following characteristics: cultural characteristics, the influence of families, achievement levels, and language problems. What advice could these teachers offer?

5. Sanders (1987) wrote: "American Indians continue to have the highest dropout rate of any ethnic group at the high school level, regardless of region or tribal affiliation" (p.81). In a plan to reduce this dropout rate during the 1990s and beyond, address the following points:

Extent of the problem

Reasons for the problem (be sure to examine cultural factors)

Possible solutions or plans to reduce the dropout rate

Ways to involve parents, administrators, and special school personnel

Expanding Your Horizons: Additional Journal Readings and Books

HARVEY, K. D., Harjo, L. D., & Jackson, J. K. (1990). *Teaching about Native-Americans* (Bulletin No. 84). Washington, DC: National Council for the Social Studies. The authors take a comprehensive look at Native-Americans and focus on issues such as culture and diversity, change and adaptation, conflicts, and current issues. The book contains an excellent chapter on "Resources for Teachers and Students."

LIGHT, H. K., & Martin, R. E. (1986). "American Indian families." *Journal of American Indian Education, 26(1)*, 1-5. Light and Martin provide an overview of American Indian families and focus attention on such aspects as family support and communication.

MITCHUM, N.T. (1989). "Increasing self-esteem in Native-American children." *Elementary School Guidance and Counseling, 23*, 266-271. Mitchum examines the effects of the school experience on Native-American learners, explains how cultural differences affect their self-esteem, and offers several strategies for increasing self-esteem among Native-American learners.

RINDONE, P. (1988). "Achievement motivation and academic achievement of Native-American students." *Journal of American Indian Education, 28(1)*, 1-8. Although Rindone's work focuses on Native-American college students rather than children and adolescents, her work provides important insights into the role and influence of the family on a young person's motivation and achievement.

SANDERS, D. (1987). "Cultural conflicts: An important factor in the academic failures of American Indian students." *Journal of Multicultural Counselling and Development, 15*, 81-90. Sanders presents a detailed study of Native-American cultural expectations and values and their influence on academic achievement.

Expanding Your Students' Horizons: Appropriate Native-American Books for Children and Adolescents

ASHABRANNER, BRENT. *To Live in Two Worlds: American Indian Youth Today.* Dodd, Mead, 1984.

BAKER, BETTY. *Killer-of-Death.* Harper, 1963.

BAKER, BETTY. *Little Runners of the Longhouse.* Harper & Row, 1962.

BATHERMAN, MURIEL. *Before Columbus.* Houghton Mifflin, 1981.

BAYLOR, BYRD. *And It Is Still That Way: Legends Told by Arizona Indian Children.* Scribners, 1976.

BAYLOR, BYRD. *The Desert Is Theirs.* Scribners, 1975.

BELTING, NATALIA. *Whirlwind is a Ghost Dancing.* Dutton, 1974.

BULLA, CLYDE ROBERT. *Squanto, Friend of the White Man*. Crowell,1956.
CROMPTON, ANNE ELIOT. *The Ice Trail*. Harcourt, 1970.
CARLSON, VADA & WITHERSPOON, GARY. *Black Mountain Boy*. Navajo Curriculum Center Press, 1982.
COHEN, CAREN LEE. *The Mud-Pony*. Scholastic, 1988.
DALGLIESH, ALICE. *The Courage of Sarah Noble*. Macmillan, 1987.
de PAOLA, TOMIE. *The Legend of Bluebonnet*. Putnam's, 1983.
DODGE, NANABAL CHEE. *Morning Arrow*. Lothrop, Lee and Shepherd, 1975.
FRITZ, JEAN. *The Double Life of Pocahontas*. Putnam, 1983.
GEORGE, JEAN CRAIGHEAD. *The Talking Earth*. Harper and Row, 1983.
GIRION, BARBARA. *Indian Summer*. Scholastic, 1990.
HASELEY, DENNIS. *The Sacred One*. Warner, 1983.
HIGHWATER, JAMAKIE. *Legend Days*. Harper, 1984.
GOBLE, PAUL. *The Girl Who Loved Horses*. Bradbury, 1978.
MILES, MISKA. *Annie and the Old One*. Little, Brown, 1971.
O'DELL, SCOTT. *Sing Down the Moon*. Houghton Mifflin, 1970.
RICHTER, CONRAD. *The Light in the Forest*. Knopf, 1953.
ROBINSON, MARGARET. *A Woman of Her Tribe*. Scribner, 1990.
ROOP, PETER. *Little Blaze and the Buffalo Jump*. Council for Indian Education, 1984.
SNEVE, HAWK VIRGINA DRIVING. *When Thunder Spoke*. Holiday, 1974.
SPEARE, ELIZABETH GEORGE. *The Sign of the Beaver*. Houghton Mifflin, 1983.
SPEARE, ELIZABETH G. *Calico Captive*. Houghton Mifflin, 1957.
WOLFSON, EVELYN. *Growing Up Indian*. Walker, 1986.

3

Understanding African-American Children and Adolescents

Understanding the material and activities in this chapter will help the reader to:

1. Describe the cultural, socioeconomic, familial, and language characteristics of African-American children and adolescents.

2. List several stereotypes of African-American children and adolescents, and explain how these beliefs affect curriculum and school practices.

3. Describe the educational achievement of African-American children and adolescents, and be able to explain the importance of self-concept on learning achievement.

4. Understand African-American English dialect as a valued cultural trait, and be able to explain its importance to school achievement and self-concept development.

5. Explain the importance of understanding learning styles and how African-American learning styles may differ.

6. List several points that educators should remember when planning educational experiences for African-American children and adolescents.

7. Incorporate practical activities, suggest appropriate children's liter-

ature, implement research findings, and respond appropriately in school situations involving African-American learners.

OVERVIEW

A responsive multicultural curriculum recognizes the cultural diversity of African-American children and adolescents, and provides appropriate educational experiences based upon an understanding of both the individual and the culture. African-American children's and adolescents' culture, socioeconomic class, family, and language play significant roles, and interact in a complex fashion to create unique learners with individual strengths and needs. Providing appropriate teaching and learning experiences for African-American learners requires an understanding of the individual's development, learning styles, achievement levels, and self-concepts. This chapter examines African-American children and adolescents, and explores educational issues germane to these learners.

THE AFRICAN-AMERICAN PEOPLE

Origins

African-American people have lived in America for many centuries. Originating in Africa, and arriving either as explorers or slaves, African-American people have experienced a long history of struggle. The first Africans in America were explorers: Columbus' last voyage to America included an African man, Balboa's crew brought an African man, and an African explored present-day Kansas with Coronado. In addition to exploring this land, Africans were among the first non-Indian settlers, e.g., African people were included in the ill-fated South Carolina colony in 1526, San Miguel de Gauldape; African people also helped to establish Saint Augustine, Florida, in 1665.

Other Africans were brought to America on slave ships and endured degrading and dehumanizing conditions. Upon completing the long and arduous trip, Africans worked as slaves on large plantations that specialized in growing tobacco and cotton (Banks, 1987). One important distinction deserves understanding: Many multicultural groups elected to immigrate to America in hopes of improving their lives, to seek religious freedom, or to get away from oppressive conditions or war-torn areas. Most Africans, on the other hand, were forcibly transported to a foreign land and forced to work and live in cruel and inhumane conditions.

USING CHILDREN'S LITERATURE: Understanding Slavery and Racism

ARMSTRONG, WILLIAM. *Sounder*. Delacorte, 1983. This story describes the racism and prejudice experienced by a black sharecropper and his family. (Reading Level: Grade 6; Interest Level: Ages 10 and above.)

FOX, PAULA. *The Slave Dancer*. Bradbury, 1973. A young boy plays the fife on a slave ship. (Reading Level: Grade 7; Interest Level: 12 and above.)

TAYLOR, MILDRED D. *Roll of Thunder, Hear My Cry*. Dial, 1976. A Black family in Mississippi in 1933 experiences humiliating experiences, yet retains its pride.

African-Americans Today

African-Americans presently comprise the nation's largest ethnic minority group. The latest annual population estimates indicate that African-Americans totaled 29.9 million in 1987, compared with 26.8 million in the 1980 census. In 1985, 16 states had African-American populations in excess of one million. Two of these states, New York (2.7 million) and California (2.1 million), had African-American populations of more than two million. Ten states and the District of Columbia had between 200,000 and 1,000,000 African-Americans in 1985, and eight additional states had between 50,000 and 200,000 African-Americans (U. S. Bureau of the Census, 1989, *Current population reports*, Series P-25, No. 1040).

The Culture Quiz: Contemporary African-Americans

Directions: Match the individuals with their contributions or achievements by placing the appropriate letter before the name.

_____	1. Rosa Parks	a.	First African-American actor to win an Academy Award (for role in *Lilies of the Field*)
_____	2. Thomas Bradley	b.	Confirmed as the first African-American to hold nation's top military post
_____	3. Martin Luther King, Jr.	c.	First African-American mayor of Los Angeles
_____	4. Thurgood Marshall	d.	Congresswoman from Texas, first African-American woman from a southern state to serve in Congress
_____	5. Andrew Young	e.	Author of Pulitzer Prize winner *The Color Purple*
_____	6. Guion S. Bluefield	f.	Syndicated columnist
_____	7. Alice Walker	g.	Former President of Morehouse College; Civil Rights leader, minister and educator

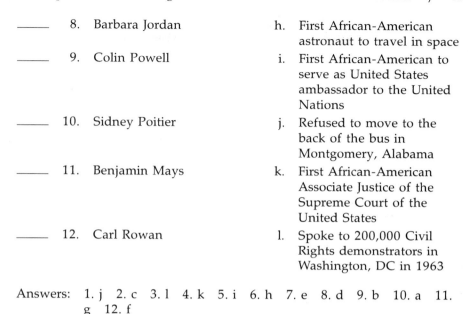

_____   8.   Barbara Jordan

h.   First African-American astronaut to travel in space

_____   9.   Colin Powell

i.   First African-American to serve as United States ambassador to the United Nations

_____   10.   Sidney Poitier

j.   Refused to move to the back of the bus in Montgomery, Alabama

_____   11.   Benjamin Mays

k.   First African-American Associate Justice of the Supreme Court of the United States

_____   12.   Carl Rowan

l.   Spoke to 200,000 Civil Rights demonstrators in Washington, DC in 1963

Answers: 1. j   2. c   3. l   4. k   5. i   6. h   7. e   8. d   9. b   10. a   11. g   12. f

The African-American population has been growing faster than the total population, and its proportion to the total population increased from 11.8% in 1980 to 12.2% in 1987 (_Black population is growing . . ._ , 1988). Several interesting demographic facts have implications for educators teaching in multicultural settings: First, the African-American population increased by 8.2% between 1980 and 1985, and is expected to continue to increase. Second, African American population growth during the next few decades will probably outpace Anglo population growth because of the relatively young age of the African-American population (U. S. Bureau of the Census, 1986, _Current population reports_, Series P-25, No. 985). Table 3-1 shows the estimated population growth of the African-American people:

Table 3-1   Estimated Population Changes of African-Americans

1990—2000 Number (1,000)	
Year	_Estimated Population_
1990	30,934
1995	33,000
2000	34,939

Compiled from: U. S. Bureau of the Census, 1988b; _Statistical Abstracts of the United States: 1988_ (108th Edition).

About one-half of the African-American population lives in the Southern states, with the remainder living in large cities in the East, Midwest, and West. While African-Americans had been moving North from the South in large numbers since World War I, the trend reversed during the last half of the 1970s. In fact, 53% of all African-Americans presently live in the South (Banks, 1987). As Table 3-2 indicates, significant increases in the African-American population can also be detected when considering the age structure of the population:

Table 3-2 Age and African-American Population: 1985, 1990, 2000

Age	1985[1]	1990[2]	2000[2]
		Numbers (1,000)	
5-17	6,898	7,170	7,895

Sources:

1. U.S. Bureau of the Census (1986). *Current Population Reports*, Series P-25, No. 985, "Estimates of the Population of the United States, by Age, Sex, and Race: 1980-1985." U.S. Government Printing Office, Washington, DC.
2. U.S. Bureau of the Census. *Statistical Abstracts of the United States: 1988b*. (108th Edition).

USING CHILDREN'S LITERATURE: Nonfiction Books About the African-American Experience

PATTERSON, LILLIE. *Frederick Douglass: Freedom Fighter*. Garrand, 1965. A story of Douglass' life in slavery, protest against slavery, escape from slave owners and slave hunters, and his championing of rights for all people. (Reading Level: Grade 3; Interest Level: age 8 and above.)

DEKAY, JAMES T. *Meet Martin Luther King*. Random House, 1969. Dekay stresses King's tremendous work and his reasons for fighting against injustice and prejudice. (Reading Level: Grade 4; Interest Level: Ages 7-12.)

Activity:

Make a list of historical and contemporary African-Americans who have contributed to their culture and to the nation. Include such leaders of the past as George Washington Carver and Frederick Douglass, and contemporary African-Americans such as Jesse Jackson and Colin Powell. Show their contributions, and list how their actions have contributed to the betterment of all cultures.

STEREOTYPING OF AFRICAN-AMERICAN CHILDREN AND ADOLESCENTS

Being both a child or adolescent and a African-American in a predominantly Anglo-American society can carry a double stigma. Many stereotypical statements concerning the African-American culture and its young people have resulted in negative images. During this time of identity formation, it is especially important that social, cultural, and age differences be accepted objectively, and that people be given fair opportunities to develop identities that are appropriate for the African-American culture and the child or adolescent. Categorizing African-American young people as language-deficient due to their use of English dialect, and as being lower achievers and having behavioral problems, negates diversity and individual differences. A closer and more objective look at the child and the adolescent in the African-American culture results in a better understanding of the learner and the world in which she or he lives. Similarly, such knowledge and understanding provides educators with an objective and sound foundation for a multicultural curriculum that focuses on the strengths and needs of the African-American culture.

CASE STUDY 3-1 shows the detrimental effects of stereotypical statements.

CASE STUDY 3-1: Dealing With Stereotypical Situations

Mrs. Brown hears at the grocery store, "African-American students have ruined that school—their achievement is low, they speak a language nobody can understand, they are always misbehaving—that school has gone to the dogs. It used to be such a nice school, too."

Direct confrontation in a grocery store with a person making such a remark will probably prove unsuccessful; however, this does not imply that the person should not be politely told of the school's many accomplishments. Perhaps a community-wide campaign is needed to change the school's image: Make public the school's accomplishments; encourage the school's young people to take an active role in the community; and encourage business leaders to take a greater role in schools and to publicize successful efforts. Even though such efforts may improve the school's image, a serious problem still exists with the dangers of stereotypical statements. These problems will require more objectivity toward, and acceptance of, differing cultures, and will require a larger-scale effort and change of attitudes.

AFRICAN-AMERICAN CHILDREN AND ADOLESCENTS

Cultural Characteristics

Considerable diversity characterizes African-American children and adolescents. Differences exist between lower, middle, and higher socioeconomic groups, between younger and older generations, between African-Americans residing in the various geographic locations of the United States, and between urban and rural African-Americans. Understanding this diversity among African-American children and adolescents contributes to the multi-cultural curriculum based on objective and factual information.

Activity:

Make a list of cultural differences between African- and Anglo-Americans. Then, keeping in mind the characteristics you listed, make another list of social class differences. Are the cultures more alike or different? Are the social class differences more alike or different? Are African and Anglo members of the same social class more alike than African members of differing social classes?

USING CHILDREN'S LITERATURE: The African-American Experience in Children's Books

KEATS, EZRA JACK. *The Snowy Day*. Viking, 1962. Keats captures the mood of the African American experience on this book. Illustrated with collage. (Reading Level: Grade 2; Interest Level: Ages 2-7.)

STEPTOE, JOHN. *Stevie*. Harper & Row, 1969. Robert is unhappy when Stevie wants to play with his toys. (Reading Level: Grades 3-7; Interest Level: Ages 2-8.)

HAMILTON, VIRGINIA. *Zeely*. Macmillan, 1967. Geeder is convinced that her neighbor is a Watusi queen. (Reading Level: Grade 4; Interest Level: Ages 7-12.)

African-American children daily face two cultures: The African-American culture of the home/neighborhood, and the Anglo-American culture of the schools and other social institutions. African-American children, and children from other cultures, need opportunities to learn about one another's cultures, and to understand that "different" does not imply "wrong." Curricula which are responsive to the multicultural concerns of children provide experiences which emphasize the positives of the culture: the inventors, doctors, leaders, artists, and other contributors. By recognizing cultures as different and unique, rather than inferior, educators provide learners of all ages and cultures with opportunities to understand and appreciate cultural diversity. Since education has focused for many years solely on historical and contemporary Anglos, educators sometimes justifiably complain that their education did not provide them with examples of the contributions of African-Americans. During the past several decades, attempts to instill pride and a better understanding of the African American culture have resulted in learning materials which show the many positives of the culture.

FOR ADDITIONAL INFORMATION

National Black Child Development Institute, 1463 Rhode Island Ave. NW, Washington, DC 20005. This organization is dedicated to improving the quality of life for African-American children and youth, and focuses on issues such as health, child welfare, education, and child care.

Minority Caucus of Family Services America, 34-1/2 Beacon Street, Boston, MA 02108. This organization participates in policy-making groups, works toward the needs of minority families, and helps combat racism.

National Black Youth Leadership Council, 250 W. 54th Street, Suite 800, New York, NY 10019. This council provides training and motivation workshops, resources, information, skills, and strategies for fostering leadership development.

Although cultural generalizations must be offered cautiously, cultural characteristics include: Larger families, respect for immediate and extended families, and nonverbal communication that differs from the Anglo culture (for example, interrupting the speaker to show support, not feeling that looking the speaker in the eye is necessary). African-American children are generally more expressive emotionally, assertive, and highly verbal in dealings with peers and adults (Rotherman-Borus & Phinney, 1990). Once again, readers are reminded that individuals within a culture differ, and cultural characteristics vary with socioeconomic class and geographic region.

IMPLEMENTING RESEARCH 3-1 explains early adolescents' friendship patterns and provides suggestions for educators.

IMPLEMENTING RESEARCH 3-1: Friendship Patterns in Early Adolescence

DuBois and Hirsch (1990) conducted research to determine friendship patterns of 292 black and white early adolescents who attended an integrated junior high school. Specifically, their investigation explored the nature of black and white children's friendships across school and non-school contexts. Their review of the literature revealed that among children and adolescents own-race friendship choices are more common than other-race choices; racial cleavage in friendship patterns increases between the elementary and secondary school years; and the increased separation of the black and white peer groups, and the conflicts between the groups, help to make interracial friendships more and more rare during adolescence.

DuBois and Hirsch concluded that their research indicated that there may be important differences in the peer friendship networks of black and whites during early adolescence.

_____ 1. More than 80% of both blacks and whites reported having an other-race school friend.

_____ 2. Fewer students, yet still more than half, reported

having an other-race school friend with whom they were close.

_____ 3. A smaller group reported having a close other-race school friend who was frequently seen outside of school.

_____ 4. Blacks are almost twice as likely as whites to report having a close other-race school friend whom they saw frequently outside of school.

IMPLEMENTING THE RESEARCH:

1. Educators should recognize the importance of friendships in social development during the early adolescence years (and, indeed, for all children and adolescents).

2. Educators should encourage cross-cultural friendships and provide opportunities for such friendships to develop such as cooperative learning and cross-age tutoring.

3. Educators should encourage cross-cultural friendships outside of school.

Source: DuBois, D. L., & Hirsch, B. J. (1990). "School and neighborhood friendship patterns of Blacks and Whites in early adolescence." *Child Development, 61,* 524-536.

USING CHILDREN'S LITERATURE: Contributions of African Americans to the Fine Arts

BYRAN, ASHLEY. *I'm Going to Sing: Black-American Spirituals, Volume 2.* Athenum, 1982. This book includes words and music that help African-American children understand their heritage. (Interest Level: All ages.)

HASKINS, JAMES. *Black Theater in America.* Crowell, 1982. This text traces the contributions of African-Americans from minstrel shows through contemporary protest plays. (Reading Level: 7; Interest Level: Age 9 and above.)

Understanding the African-American culture allows educators to understand the cultural predicament of many African-Americans. A difficult situation exists when African-Americans want to retain their cultural heritage, the culture of their ancestors, and the culture with which they can relate and feel comfortable. However, some African-Americans may also feel that some acculturation with the Anglo-American culture is necessary for economic and psychological survival. A middle ground must be achieved where African-American adolescents can retain their African heritage and still feel successful in contemporary society.

Socioeconomic Status

Social class and ethnicity, and their complex interactions on the shaping of human behavior, have received considerable attention. Within a complex society, social classes and ethnicity are two major sociologic structures that produce diversity in human life-style and development (Havighurst, 1976; Hale-Benson, 1986). Six determinants provide indications of socioeconomic status: income, wealth, occupation, education, prestige, and power (Gollnick & Chinn, 1990). The racism, injustice, and discrimination experienced by African-American people have resulted in a lack of educational and employment opportunities, and have prohibited significant social mobility. Long deprived of equal opportunities and the chance to improve themselves educationally and economically, African-American people find themselves represented disportionately in the lower socioeconomic classes.

Many African-American children today live in a desolate world where struggles for physical survival reign, where fear and hopelessness are everyday occurrences, and where the future seems to hold little hope. African-American children in the future need to be at the forefront of attention, where adequate nutrition, health care, and education receive priorities (Edelman, 1989).

The socioeconomic plight of the African-American child has been described as:

- Nearly one of every two African-American children lives in poverty
- Almost two-thirds of young African-American children live in homes relying on public assistance
- African-American children generally receive poorer health care than Anglo children (Clark-Johnson, 1988).

The future, however, looks brighter for African-American children. Surviving years of segregation and discrimination in employment and education, contemporary African-Americans have more equality, and better access to education and more equitable salaries. Through Civil Rights legislation, Affirmative Action programs, and equal opportunity employment, African-Americans are able to obtain an education and seek employment. Such gains will result in improved conditions for children. The problem of poverty, however, continues for many people, and requires the attention of government, school, and other organizations concerned with the children's welfare.

Activity:

_____ 1. Understand the effects of being a member of a lower socioeconomic group.

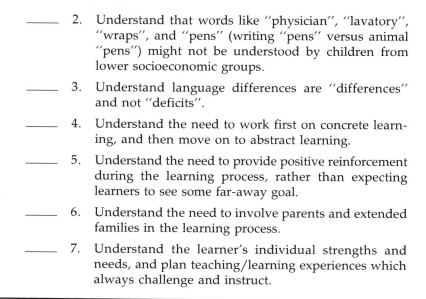

    _____ 2. Understand that words like "physician", "lavatory", "wraps", and "pens" (writing "pens" versus animal "pens") might not be understood by children from lower socioeconomic groups.

    _____ 3. Understand language differences are "differences" and not "deficits".

    _____ 4. Understand the need to work first on concrete learning, and then move on to abstract learning.

    _____ 5. Understand the need to provide positive reinforcement during the learning process, rather than expecting learners to see some far-away goal.

    _____ 6. Understand the need to involve parents and extended families in the learning process.

    _____ 7. Understand the learner's individual strengths and needs, and plan teaching/learning experiences which always challenge and instruct.

Families

Educators who work with African-American learners need a historical understanding and perspective of the African-American family. Such a task might prove difficult, since African-American families have been mistreated, ignored, and distorted in American scholarship (Billingsley, 1968). Often, the majority-culture educator's misconceptions may cause him or her to question African-American cultural traditions. Throughout centuries of cultural oppression and repression, for example, the African-American family has developed, perhaps through necessity rather than choice, a network of "significant others" who have close ties and are willing to assist. Understanding and accepting this African-American family tradition continues to be a prerequisite to effective educational decisions (Conger, 1977).

    African-American children grow up in homes that are very different from the homes Anglo-American children and adolescents experience. Minority extended families and kinships function on the principles of interdependence and an extensive reliance on family kinship networks, which include blood relatives and close friends called kinsmen. For example, young African-American children are often taken into the household of elderly grandparents (Lum, 1986). These arrangements sometimes result in a sense of corporate responsibility, where children belong to an extended family clan, not merely to the parents. Consequently, uncles, aunts, cousins, and grandparents have considerable power in the family, and are responsible for the care and rearing of children, and for teaching appropriate skills and values (Lum, 1986).

USING CHILDREN'S LITERATURE: Families in African-American Children's Books

MATHIAS, SHARON BELL. *The Hundred Penny Box*. Viking, 1975. This story focuses on the life and love of Great-great Aunt Dew, an aged African-American woman, and Michael, a young boy. (Reading Level: Grade 3; Interest Level: Ages 6-10.)

FLOURNOY, VALERIE. *The Patchwork Quilt*. Dial, 1985. This is the story of a grandmother's and a granddaughter's developing relationship while constructing a quilt. (Reading Level: Grade 4; Interest Level: Ages 5-10.)

GREENFIELD, ELOISE. *She Come Bringing Me That Little Baby Girl*. Lippincott, 1974. Kevin dislikes all the attention his new baby sister receives; shows changing emotions in a warm, loving story. (Reading Level: Grade 3; Interest Level: Ages 6-9.)

YARBROUGH, CAMILLE. *Cornrows*. Putnam, 1979. An African-American great-grandmother braids a young girl's hair and relates the history of her people. (Reading Level: Grade 3; Interest Level: Ages 6-10.)

These strong kinship bonds probably originated from the two guiding principles of the African ethos, the survival of the tribe, and the oneness of being. Children see early that their families develop a kinship in the African-American community, and that African-Americans refer to each other as "sister", "brother", "cousin", "blood brother", or "homeboy" to imply a family closeness even where actual kinship does not exist (Hale-Benson, 1986, p. 49).

IMPLEMENTING RESEARCH 3-2 examines how professionals can respond to children of mixed parentage.

IMPLEMENTING RESEARCH 3-2: Children of Mixed Parentage

Wardle (1989) maintains that there are 632,000 interracial marriages in the United States, of which 125,000 are African/Anglo marriages. Children of these mixed racial and ethnic marriages have unique needs that professionals may not be prepared to address. Historically, children of mixed marriages were identified with the parent of color, i.e., if one parent was African-American, the child was also considered African-American. Contemporary positions on interracial children take three directions: (1) Some insist that the child is "human above all else" (p. 11); (2) some choose to raise their children with the identity of the parent of color; and (3) some (and a growing group) parents are insisting that the child have the racial and cultural heritage of both parents.

IMPLEMENTING THE RESEARCH:

Wardle's suggestions for professionals working with interracial children and families include:

_____ 1. Encouraging parents and children to discuss openly all aspects of a mixed heritage such as skin and eye color, national origin, and language difficulties.

_____ 2. Providing parents and children with the right words and responses to defend themselves from those who do not appreciate the differences resulting from mixed families.

_____ 3. Being aware of the vast individual differences within racial and ethnic groups, including socioeconomic class, culture, religion, and education.

_____ 4. Encouraging interracial families, and programs serving these families, to provide a variety of books, music, dolls, and art materials that reflect the rich variety of the family backgrounds (Wardle, 1989).

Source: Wardle, F. (1989). "Children of mixed parentage: How can professionals respond?" *Children Today, 8(4)*, 10-13.

Another difference in African-American family life is the large number of people living in the same household. A counselor visited the home of an honor student and remarked, "There just seem to be too many people in that house . . . there was the grandmother; then a couple of cousins stopped by. It was ridiculous . . . " (Smith, 1981, p. 170.)

Activity:

Interview several African-American families (maybe you can include extended family members, too) to determine their expectations of the schools. What do they want for their children? What questions do they have? What do they feel good about? What are their frustrations? Based upon this information, how can the schools become more responsive to the educational needs and expectations of African-American families?

Religion

Religion, another powerful aspect of the African-American family orientation, has almost never been documented empirically. Rather than studying the church and religion in relation to children, writers usually focus attention on the role of religion in the Civil Rights Movement, economic leadership, and the quest for equal opportunities. However, children undoubtedly perceive the role of the African-American church as a socializing institution, a hub of social life, the provider of a peer group, and a means of leadership in the community. Rather than church membership being limited to Sunday morning services, children see the church as a integral aspect of African-American family life (Hale-Benson, 1986).

Language

Educators will benefit from objective and reliable information about African-American language. Although the child may not experience difficulty at home or in the neighborhood, language differences may result in problems when significant variations exist between home/neighborhood and school languages. African-American children are faced with a problem: Their language is "worthy" at home, yet may be "different" and unworthy in school. Hall (1981) summarizes the situation with:

> [African-American children] come to school equipped with rich and different dialect ideally suited to the multiple needs of the Black culture, only to be told that what they spoke was a degraded, substandard form of English. (p. 32)

Considerable diversity exists in the degree to which children speak an English dialect, and varies according to socioeconomic class, geographic location, and the acculturation of both the child and the parents. Children of educated and socially-mobile urban African-American parents may not speak the dialect of rural and less fortunate parents. African-American English is used in varying degrees depending on the individual person and the situation. However, one estimate suggests that 80-90% of all African-Americans use this dialect at least some of the time (Smitherman, 1972).

Activity:

Do a case study of several African-American families to determine cultural, intracultural, and social class differences. How do they differ in dress, food, customs, and family behaviors? Is it just as difficult to say that all African-American families are alike as it is to say that all Anglo families are alike? How can the school provide a curriculum which responds to the African-American family?

African-Americans, as do members of other cultures, have developed effective nonverbal communication that may be questioned by other cultures. For example, African-American children may learn early that active listening does not require always looking the speaker in the eye. Neither is it necessary to nod one's head, or make little noises to show that one is listening (LaFrance & Mayo, 1978).

The language of African-American children, albeit an excellent means of communication in the African-American culture, may result in communication difficulties and other problems generally associated with not being understood outside ones' social community. Further, children who hear negative statements about their language, and who are urged to change to a more "standard" form of English, undoubtedly have a lower self-concept and opinion of cultural backgrounds.

CULTURAL COMPARISON

African-American and Anglo-American
Children and Adolescents

African-American	*Anglo-American*
Language "worthy" at home; "unworthy" at school	Language "worthy" both at home and at school
Not always necessary to look speaker in the eye	Look speaker in the eye
Seek support from larger families/ "kinship networks"	Seek support from smaller, more immediate family
Childrearing—result of extended family	Childrearing—result of immediate family
Cultural pride	Individual pride
Usually (but not always) lower educational attainment	Usually (but not always) higher educational attainment
Faces overt and implied racism	Does not face racism
May interrupt speaker with encouraging remarks	Uses nods and few words to encourage speakers

Sources: Axelson (1985); Pinkney (1975); Boykin (1982); Hall (1981)

AFRICAN-AMERICAN LEARNERS IN THE SCHOOL

Educating African-American learners requires several considerations: Building upon their cultural backgrounds, utilizing the family as a resource, understanding their language, understanding their achievement levels, addressing their learning styles, and promoting their self-concept and personal identities. This section explores the African-American learner in the school and provides understanding and direction for educators.

Educators' Understanding of African-American Learners and Their Culture

African-American children growing up in a predominantly Anglo society may face several problems that handicap their overall development into adults. African-American children often face language differences, lower academic achievement, and lower self-concepts due to cultural differences, daily inequities, racism and injustices. Although this constitutes a realistic picture for some African-American children, it is imperative that educators remember and consider intracultural, geographic, socioeconomic, and individual differences, rather than perpetuating stereotypical images of African-American learners.

Developmental Theory: Children and Adolescents

It is crucial that educators planning multicultural teaching and learning experiences understand the childhood and adolescence years: Slow maturers, fast maturers, developing self-concepts and positive cultural identities, moving from dependence to independence, and equating family and peer expectations. The many positives of the African-American culture deserve objective understanding during these developmental periods. Valuing one's cultural background and heritage, and taking pride in personal and cultural accomplishments, contribute to learners' psychosocial development. Increasing intellectual skills and thinking abilities also allow a better understanding of one's (and others') cultures. Educators can contribute by providing positive and realistic opportunities to successfully meet the various tasks and crises for developmental stages.

IMPLEMENTING RESEARCH 3-3 examines beliefs and achievement in Black, Anglo, and Hispanic children.

IMPLEMENTING RESEARCH 3-3: Beliefs and Achievement in Black, White and Hispanic Children

Stevenson, Chen, and Uttal (1990) investigated school achievement among African-, Anglo-, and Hispanic-American elementary school children, and the children's and mothers' beliefs about academic achievement. Their study included interviews with approximately 1000 mothers and their children, and also the administration of achievement tests in reading and mathematics to approximately 3000 first, third, and fifth graders. Interviews with mothers and children revealed several interesting findings: (1) Minority mothers and children showed a greater emphasis on, and concern about, education than did majority families; (2) minority mothers and children evaluated the children and their academic abilities highly; they were positive about education, and held high expectations for the children's future prospects for education; and (3) mothers of minority children and teachers in minority schools believed more strongly than Anglo mothers and teachers in the value of homework, competency testing, and a longer school day as a means of improving children's education.

IMPLEMENTING THE RESEARCH:

_____ 1. Educators should question the often-quoted stereotype and myth that culturally diverse mothers do not care about their children's education.

_____ 2. Educators should recognize the culturally diverse mother's concern for her children's education, and build upon her efforts whenever possible.

_____ 3. Educators should seek the culturally diverse mother's involvement and participation in school activities whenever possible.

Source: Stevenson, H. W., Chen, C., & Uttal, D. H. (1990). "Beliefs and achievement: A study of Black, White and Hispanic children." *Child Development*, *61*, 508-523.

Achievement Levels

The African-American child's achievement (which is closely related to self-concept) must be considered objectively, rather than by relying on traditional stereotypes of achievement expectations. Nationally, the school dropout rate for African-American youth is almost 28%, and approaches 50% in some areas (Clark-Johnson, 1988). Other reports contend that nationally, African-American pupils lag behind Anglo-American pupils on standardized tests, and the debate rages over where the responsibility for low academic performance lies. School officials too often blame the child's "disadvantaged" or "culturally deprived" home, while many African-American educators maintain that generations of Anglo-American and Oriental immigrants have performed successfully in schools and have achieved social mobility. These African-American educators call for effective schools where teachers have an objective understanding of African-American children, and have similar expectations for both African-American and Anglo-American children (Pinkney, 1975). Boykin (1982) agrees that studies have typically found that African-American children's performance on cognitive tasks and their achievement on academic areas are lower than Anglo-American children. Such findings usually result in "blaming the victims" rather than in examining the underlying causes of the problem.

USING CHILDREN'S LITERATURE: African-American Learners in the Schools

MURRAY, MICHELE. *Nellie Cameron*. Seabury, 1971. Nine-year-old Nellie has difficulty learning to read. While she felt "dumb," Nellie thought reading was a mountain she could never cross. (Reading Level: Grade 3; Interest Level: Ages 8-12.)

Many African-American parents have stressed to their children the importance of exceeding Anglo children's achievement and behavior, because falling short reflects unfavorably upon the group. In fact, evidence indicates that achievement orientation is a strength of African-American families: Most African-American college youths came from families whose members were not college-educated. One poll indicated that over 75% of African-American children said that their mother wanted them to be one of the best students in the class; similarly, lower-income maternal warmth (i.e., use of reinforcement, consultation with the child, and sensitivity to the child's feelings) appear to be conducive to intellectual achievement (Hale-Benson, 1986).

Although indications reveal lower academic achievement, the situation must be understood in its historical perspective. For years, many African-Americans attended segregated schools where instruction and materials were often substandard. While substantial progress has been made toward the provision of educational resources to African-Americans, educational opportunities are not generally equal. Standards of academic performance in schools that serve predominantly African-American learners are not equivalent to those that serve predominantly Anglo learners. Likewise, the amount of encouragement and support provided for educational achievement and attainment are not equal (Jaynes & Williams, 1989).

African-American learners face a brighter and more optimistic future. First, African-Americans now attend the same schools as their Anglo counterparts, and are receiving more equitable educational opportunities. Second, their parents have more opportunities in employment, education, and housing, and this will allow an improved standard of living. Third, educators are better trained in diagnostic and remediation approaches and individualized education. Fourth, the research on effective teaching, which has grown considerably during the past twenty years, is being translated into practical application.

CASE STUDY 3-2 looks at a teacher who feels overwhelmed, and several suggestions for her as she works with African-American learners.

CASE STUDY 3-2: Improving Academic Achievement Among African-American Learners

Miss Carter, a new teacher in your school, commented: "I just graduated from the teacher ed program and they didn't teach me about all this! I taught students in a nearly all-white school in the suburbs. Now, I have all these African-American students. I looked at their achievement test scores and I am floored. What can I do?"

There are several suggestions for Miss Carter:

1. First, and foremost, Miss Carter should understand the dangers of believing and making blanket statements that downplay the academic performance of an entire cultural group in the school.
2. She needs to understand African-American students, their culture, and the dangers of labeling all the students as being academically slow.
3. She needs to consider individual students to determine those who are behind academically, and she should make a list of individual strengths and weaknesses.

4. She needs to plan diagnostic-remediation efforts for individuals who have documented learning problems.

5. She needs to plan developmentally- and academically-appropriate instruction for average and above-average learners, and to seek assistance from administrators, remedial and resource personnel, and special district personnel as she plans instruction for students who are behind academically.

Activity:

1. Get to know individual children, and their strengths and weaknesses.

2. Give interest inventories to determine needs and areas where instruction might be most effective.

3. Administer culturally appropriate diagnostic tests to determine which areas require remediation.

4. Work to improve self-concept and convince learners that they can learn and achieve.

5. Work to improve the learner's attitude about the African-American culture.

6. Teach, evaluate, and re-teach basic skills.

Language Problems

The language of African-American children is a function of their culture, and plays a significant role in their self-concept, their school achievement, and their social and psychological development. Although the child may not experience communication difficulties at home or in the neighborhood, language differences may result in problems when significant variations exist between home/neighborhood and school languages. Children's language skills are crucial in their education, and much of what is being measured as "intelligence" and "achievement" are actually language and communication skills (Hale-Benson, 1986).

The grammatical structure of African-American speech patterns frequently leads listeners to conclude that a genuine structural pattern does not exist. Linguists acquainted with the various vernaculars of African-American English realize the fallacy of such thinking. Dillard (1972) contends that the African-American speaker who says "Mary hat" and "he book" does indeed have as much knowledge of possessives in grammar as the speaker who says "Mary's hat" and "his book".

IMPLEMENTING RESEARCH 3-4 looks at an article that proposes that Black English might inhibit the learning of mathematics and science.

IMPLEMENTING RESEARCH 3-4: Is African-American English dialect hindering learning?

Eleanor Wilson Orr, co-founder of a private high school in Washington, DC, published *Twice as Less*, which asks the question: Does Black English dialect stand between African-American students and success in mathematics and science? Orr's conclusions proved to be controversial:

- African-American students are being classified as "learning disabled" in disproportionately high numbers.
- Studies have shown that English dialect is continuing to evolve away from standard English, despite earlier predictions that television, radio, and movies would serve as a homogenizing influence on language.
- The lack of prepositions, conjunctions, and relative pronouns does not allow speakers to communicate effectively in mathematics and science.

IMPLEMENTING THE RESEARCH:

_____ 1. Educators should de-emphasize the importance of test scores that promote reliance on memorizable patterns.

_____ 2. Educators should challenge students to think through word problems.

_____ 3. Educators should consider the differences between African-American English dialects and standard English that might cause misunderstandings.

Source: Heys, S. (1988, February 14). "Is Black English standing in the way of learning?" *The State Newspaper* (Columbia, SC). *1B, 6.*

CASE STUDY 3-3 illustrates how Mrs. Johnson becomes annoyed with dialectical differences, and how she should consider such differences.

CASE STUDY 3-3: Dialectal Differences and Standard English

"I ain't got no pencil!" "That Paul pencil . . . ; I seen him with it!" Mrs. Johnson, a teacher for many years, gets irritated when learners do not speak the standard English that she and the textbooks try to present. Although Mrs. Johnson is annoyed by these language dialects, she really does not know what to do. She has tried to "change" the students' language to a more acceptable dialect, but nothing seems to work.

First, Mrs. Johnson should avoid a perspective that promotes a "blame the victim" attitude. Second, her attempts to "change" the students' language (which has only resulted in frustration for her and her students) shows a lack of understanding of the students and their cultural heritages.

Rather than trying to change language habits, or considering "differences" as "deficits", Mrs. Johnson needs to understand that these students' language dialects and communication patterns work perfectly well in their homes and neighborhoods. It is only in schools and outside the African-American community that "others" have difficulty understanding.

Learning Styles: Cultural Considerations

Educators have long recognized that learners respond differently to instruction. While some students learn most efficiently reading alone in a quiet atmosphere, others learn best in a group or cooperative learning project that discusses issues. The "means or conditions" under which one learns most effectively and efficiently can be termed the students' "learning style." In essence, learning styles include a complex relationship of personal, social, cultural, and behavioral elements that vary among individuals and cultures.

Although the relationship between culture and learning styles is not fully understood, it is an important one: "Culture shapes the way we think (cognition), the way we interact (behavior), and the way we transmit knowledge to the next generation (education)" (Collier & Hoover, 1987, p.7). Hernandez (1989) explains that cultural and cognitive development are closely intertwined, and that social and environmental factors influence cognitive and affective preferences. These, in turn, reflect themselves in incentives, motivation, interpersonal relationships, and patterns of intellectual abilities (Ramierez & Castaneda, 1974; Hernandez, 1989).

Hale-Benson (1986) lists several factors to consider when determining how African-American students learn most effectively. Factors with the most relevance for multicultural teaching and learning situations include:

1. African-American people tend to respond to things in terms of the whole picture, rather than its parts.
2. African-American people tend to prefer inferential reasoning to deductive or inductive reasoning.
3. African-American people tend to approximate space, numbers, and time, rather than stick to accuracy.
4. African-American people tend to prefer focusing on people and their activities, rather than on things.
5. African-American people tend in general not to be "word" dependent, and tend to be proficient in nonverbal communication.

Knowing African-American learners' cultural characteristics and their learning styles represents an essential first step when planning and implementing a multicultural curriculum that meets the needs of African-American learners.

School Practices Impeding African-Americans' Progress

Educators sometimes develop and implement curricula that either overlook or ignore cultural diversity. African-American learners may find themselves in a world of Anglo rules, expectations, and orientations. Rather than recognizing cultural diversity and teaching learners as individuals, learners are treated as groups with homogeneous characteristics. School practices that may impede learning achievement and appropriate behavior include:

1. Failing to understand African-American learners and expecting all learners to conform to Anglo standards and expectations;
2. grouping by homogeneous ability may result in learners being segregated by culture and by social class;
3. providing insufficient or inappropriate positive reinforcement;
4. downgrading or even punishing learners for using English dialects;
5. providing for African-American learners too many worksheets and drill times without a meaningful purpose;
6. using Anglo-oriented textbooks and curricular materials;
7. basing academic and behavior standards and expectations on stereotypical expectations.

IMPLEMENTING RESEARCH 3-5 looks at a proposal which suggests that African-American males should teach in the primary school grades.

IMPLEMENTING RESEARCh 3-5: Educating Young African-American Males

The inability of urban public schools to effectively address the problems of African-American male children is all too obvious. The most common reasons cited for social and academic failings include: Boys coming from poor, single-parent, female-headed households that lack positive role models. Whether or not these accurately reflect the reasons, the widespread "blame-the-victim" syndrome does little to ease the males' problem. Evidence of the schools' failure includes large numbers of young African-American males who end up in prison, and homicide rates of young African-American males that remain high. Inner-city African-American males without positive, literate, male role models in schools contributes to their social and academic problems. Holland (1987) suggests creating all-male classes in kindergarten through the third grade, and that these classes be taught by African-American male teachers.

_____ 1. Educators should examine Holland's suggestion to determine its feasibility.

_____ 2. Educators should provide positive primary school experiences for all children, yet pay particular attention to those children who may be at risk for any reason.

_____ 3. Educators should insist on positive role models, both at school and in the community.

Source: Holland, S. H. (1987). "Positive primary education for young Black males." *The Education Digest, 53(3)*, 56-58.

School practices related to the assessment of African-American children and adolescents is another area which can impede the learners' progress. The use of assessment devices designed primarily for middle-class Anglo learners does not always provide an accurate assessment of African-American learners. Table 3-3 provides examples of four tests which have been recommended for African-American learners.

Table 3-3   Assessing African-American Children

The Black Intelligence Test of Cultural Homogeneity (BITCH), a test whose major objectives are to identify early indicators of intelligence in Black children. Test items include Black American folklore, history, life experiences, and dialect that the author feels is more relevant and fairer to the Black culture.

Themes of Black Awareness (TOBA), a 40-item sentence-completion instrument that elicits thematic material relating to an individual's level of Black awareness.

Themes Concerning Black (TCB), another measure of Black personality that examines various aspects of the Black person's underlying personality or psychopathology.

Multicultural Pluralistic Assessment (SOMPA), a test to be used with five- to eleven-year-old, culturally-diverse children, based upon the fundamental assumption that the American society is pluralistic, both culturally and structurally. This battery includes an interview with parents, a medical examination and a Wechsler IQ test.

Adapted from: Isen, H. G. (1983). "Assessing the Black child: A strategy." *Journal of Non-White Concerns, 11*, 47-58.

CASE STUDY 3-4 shows educators should listen to and offer a response to parents' concerns.

CASE STUDY 3-4: Responding to Parents' Demands

Feeling that the education African-American children are receiving does not meet their needs, a vocal and militant group of parents presents a list of demands for improving the school system. Among these demands are

Holland's suggestion to create all-male classes, and to have African-American males teachers for kindergarten through grade three. It is clear that some action is necessary to improve these parents' attitudes toward their schools, and to have a school which better meets the needs of African-American learners.

Failing to listen to the parents' concerns, and failing to respond appropriately whenever possible, can only result in frustration for both parents and school officials, and for the children attending the school. The school's response should include:

1. Whether or not the school is meeting African-American students' needs, the parents perceive their needs are not being met. Therefore, their demands should be heard in an atmosphere without hostility or defensiveness.
2. Complete a multicultural assessment of the overall school curriculum and environment to determine the extent to which the needs of African-American learners are being addressed.
3. Form an advisory committee consisting of parents, an administrator, teachers from the school, and several people in the community to provide an open forum to discuss issues of concern to the African-American parents.
4. Explain the inconclusive evidence of having Black males in Kindergarten through third grade, and the shortage of Black male teachers willing to teach the lower grades.

Promoting Positive Self-Concepts and Cultural Identities

Several studies have sought to ascertain the effects of minority group status on personality development during identity formation. These studies provided concrete evidence for long-held opinions that the society and the culture in which African-Americans live adversely affects their personality development, self-concepts, and educational achievements. African-Americans often face either overt, or sometimes blatant, racism that has been handed down for generations (Smith, 1981). Lee and Lindsey (1985) maintained that racism and oppression hinders the positive development of the African-American child's self-concept.

Self-concept may be the most influential factor in the learners' development. The African-American child or adolescent's self-perception influences not only academic achievement, but also many other social and psychological aspects of development. Distinctive aspects affecting the self-concept include children's perception of themselves, what others perceive children to be, and the views of others that children adopt. For example, the African-American child may tend to accept others' views, either negative or positive, that may characterize the African-American culture (Axelson, 1985).

Research through the 1960s concluded that "self-hatred" existed in much of the African-American community. However, the African-American power movement and the pride in African-American identity resulted in considerable gains in African-American self-concept (Axelson, 1985). Other gains in self-concept can be attributed to African-American parents fostering positive self-concept development in their children. Bolstering egos with "You're just as good as anybody else" (p. 64) may sooth anxieties that may arise when their children engage in a social comparison with Anglo children (Hale-Benson, 1986).

Activity:

Using the case study method, compare and contrast two learners, one with a positive self-concept, and one with a negative self-concept. What are the differences in areas such as: Attitudes toward self, school, and the teacher; academic achievement; and overall mental health and psychosocial development. What might you do to help learners with low self-concepts? What might you suggest to parents and extended family members?

Considerable concern has been generated for the African-American adolescent's identity formation, especially in poverty-ridden households and in father-absent homes. Evidence, however, indicates that this concern may be ill-founded, because the African-American adolescent might not be as detrimentally-affected as once believed. Specifically, individuals from female-headed homes do not usually perceive their families as "broken", since fathers and the extended family and kinship network continue to play a role in their lives (Bell-Scott & McKenry, 1986). The physical presence or absence of adult males in the home says little about the availability of other male models. Adolescent males living in single-parent households often identify male role models in their neighborhood, in classrooms, and even in instruction from their mothers (Rubin, 1977).

Activity:

_____ 1. Be open and honest in relationships with African-American children.

_____ 2. Learn as much as possible about one's own culture.

_____ 3. Seek to respect and appreciate culturally-different attitudes and behaviors.

_____ 4. Take advantage of all available opportunities to

participate in activities in the African-American community.

_____ 5. Keep in mind that African-American children are members of their unique cultural group, and are unique individuals as well.

_____ 6. Eliminate all behaviors that suggest prejudice or racism.

_____ 7. Implement practices that acknowledge the African-American culture.

_____ 8. Hold high expectations of African-American children, and encourage all who work with African-American children to do likewise.

_____ 9. Ask questions about the African-American culture.

_____ 10. Develop culturally specific strategies, mechanisms, techniques, and programs to foster the psychological development of African American children (Locke, 1989).

CULTURAL PORTRAIT: Paul—An African-American Learner

Paul J., a ten-year-old African-American learner, attends a large urban elementary school which is approximately half African- and half Anglo-American. Paul is a lower achiever, speaks an English dialect, and has a low self-concept. When speaking of Paul's lower academic achievement, Mrs. Smith, Paul's teacher, feels he does not listen. "He looks away when I talk to him. I have tried to get him to look at me," Mrs. Smith stated. Paul claims he is listening, even though he does not look directly at Mrs. Smith as she speaks. Regarding his language, Paul knows Mrs. Smith does not approve of his English dialect, but his language works fine at home and on the playground, so he doesn't see any need to change. Paul feels he is in a bind: He tries to make higher grades, but he just cannot seem to do so. He sees himself in the "middle". Some African-American students make better grades that he does, and others make worse. Paul feels the frustration of coping in a school that appears to cater to Anglo students, and appears to expect African-Americans to conform to Anglo expectations.

How Paul's Teacher Can Respond
Mrs. Smith's response can take several directions:

1. First and foremost, she needs to understand that the people of the African-American culture do not feel that looking someone in the eye is necessary for listening to occur.

2. Mrs. Smith also needs to recognize that Paul's English dialect works well for him at home, on the playground, and in the neighborhood.

3. As for Paul seeing himself in the "middle", Mrs. Smith's response should be to administer the proper diagnostic tests to determine Paul's achievement, and to identify any special strengths and weaknesses.

4. The fourth response extends further into the school itself as it focuses attention primarily toward an Anglo orientation. Rather than the school being genuinely multicultural in nature (and celebrating cultural diversity), it might be continuing an orientation toward Anglo perspectives, and dealing with Paul (and other African-American learners) as problems or liabilities to be expected in urban schools.

SUMMING UP

Educators planning a culturally responsive curriculum and school environment for African-American learners should:

1. Understand both historical and contemporary perspectives of the African-American culture and its people.

2. Understand the close correlation between socioeconomic class and academic achievement among African-American learners (and learners of other cultures).

3. Address the dilemma surrounding African-American English, which needs understanding and appropriate action: African-Americans understand one another in home and community situations, and yet they sometimes experience difficulty in school and teaching/learning situations. Remember that "different" does not equate with "wrong" or "inferior."

4. Promote the positive self-concepts and cultural identities that are crucial to African-American learners' academic achievement, psychosocial development, and general outlook on life.

5. Consider and address African-American students' learning styles when planning teaching/learning experiences.

6. Consider intracultural, geographic, socioeconomic, urban and rural, and other differences that result in "individuality", rather than categorizing all African-American learners as a homogeneous group.

7. Understand several factors (appropriate diagnostic/remediation procedures; improving self-concepts; basic skills instruction) that

have the potential for improving African-American academic achievement.

8. Adhere to the commitment that African-American learners should not be stereotyped or labeled as slow learners, and should not be grouped in organization patterns that result in segregation by either culture of social class.

SUGGESTED LEARNING ACTIVITIES

1. Complete a case study of two African-American learners, each from a different social class, e.g., one from a lower class, and one from a higher social class. Compare and contrast differences in culture, language, familial traditions, food, and life expectations.

2. Conduct an in-depth study of English dialects. Why is it valued in the African-American culture? How can children and adolescents communicate in home and community situations, yet experience difficulties in school? Survey textbooks to determine usage and other problems African-Americans might encounter.

3. Using an actual student achievement permanent record (with academic grades, standardized test scores, and anecdotal comments), outline what appear to be the learner's strengths and weaknesses. Administer two *different* diagnostic instruments designed to determine strengths and weaknesses. With this information, outline a teaching/learning plan designed to improve academic achievement and self-concept.

4. The family, both immediate and extended, is a valued aspect of the African-American culture. How can educators utilize this resource? What can educators do to involve African-American families? What special concerns should be remembered during parent conferences?

Expanding Your Horizons: Additional Journal Readings and Books

CLARK-JOHNSTON, G. (1988). "Black children." *Teaching Exceptional Children, 20*(4), 46-47. This article examines African-American children in the United States today. After quoting some disturbing statistics from the National Black Child Development Institute and the Children's Defense Fund, the author discusses assessment bias, and parent and community involvement.

EDELMAN, M. W. (1989). "Black children in America." In J. Dewart (Ed.), *The State of Black America* (pp. 63-76). New York: The National Urban League. Edelman examines the condition of African-American children in America: poverty, health and nutrition, and education.

HALE-BENSON, J. E. (1986). *Black children: Their roots, culture, and learning styles* (rev. ed.). Baltimore, MD: Johns Hopkins. This excellent resource on African-American children explores such issues as African backgrounds, culture and childrearing, and how culture shapes cognition.

JAYNES, G. D., & WILLIAMS, R. M. (1989). *A common destiny: Blacks and American society.* Washington, DC: National Academic Press. This text from the National Research Council contains the summary and conclusions of a report from the Committee on the Status of Black Americans. Issues such as African-American participation, racial attitudes and behaviors, children and families, economics, and schooling are examined.

LOCKE, D. C. (1989). "Fostering the self-esteem of the African-American child." *Elementary School Guidance and Counseling, 23,* 254-259. Locke offers suggestions for improving the self-concept of African-American children, and provides specific activities for each grade, levels kindergarten through six.

Expanding Your Students' Horizons: Appropriate African-American Books for Children and Adolescents

BLUME, JUDY. *Iggie's House.* Bradbury, 1970.
BOGART, JO ELLEN. *Daniel's Dog.* Scholastic, 1990.
BYARD, CAROLE. *The Black Snowman.* Scholastic, 1989.
CLIFTON, LUCILLE. *Everett Anderson's Goodbye.* Holt, Rinehart and Winston, 1983.
CUMMINGS, PAT. *Clean Your Room, Harvey Moon.* Bradbury, 1991.
DESBARATS, PETER. *Gabrielle and Selena.* Harcourt Brace Jovanovich, 1968.
FLOUROY, VALERIE. *The Patchwork Quilt.* Dial, 1985.
FOX, PAULA. *How Many Miles to Babylon.* D. White, 1967.
FUFUKA, KARAMA. *My Daddy Is a Cool Dude.* Dial, 1975.
GREEN, BETTY. *Philip Hall Like Me, I Reckon Maybe.* Dial, 1974.
GREENFIELD, ELOISE. *Sister.* Crowell, 1974.
HAMILTON, VIRGINIA. *The House of Dies Drear.* Macmillan, 1968.
HAMILTON, VIRGINIA. *M.C. Higgins the Great.* Macmillan, 1974.
IRWIN, HADLEY. *I Be Somebody.* Macmillan, 1984.
HOWARD, ELIZABETH FITZGERALD. *Aunt Flossie's Hats (and Crab Cakes Later).* Clarion, 1991.
KATZ, WILLIAM LOREN. *Breaking the Chain: African-American Slave Resistance.* Atheneum, 1990.
KEATS, EZRA JACK. *Hi Cat.* Macmillan, 1970.
KEATS, EZRA JACK. *John Henry: An American Legend.* Pantheon, 1965.
McKISSICK, PATRICIA. *Jesse Jackson: A Biography.* Scholastic, 1989.
MATHIAS, SHARON BELL. *The Hundred Penny Box.* Viking, 1975.
MURRAY, MICHELE. *Nellie Cameron.* Seabury, 1971.
MYERS, WALTER DEAN. *Fallen Angels.* Scholastic, 1989.
PINKWATER, JILL. *Tails of the Bronx.* Macmillan, 1991.
RINALDI, ANN. *Wolf by the Ears.* Scholastic, 1991.
STEPTOE, JOHN. *Daddy Is a Monster . . . Sometimes.* Lippincott, 1980.
TAYLOR, MILDRED D. *Song of the Trees.* Dial, 1973.
TAYLOR, MILDRED D. *Roll of Thunder, Hear My Cry.* Dial, 1976.
WASHINGTON, VIVIAN E. *I Am Somebody, I Am Me: A Black Child's Credo.* C. H. Fairfax, 1983.

4

Asian-American Children and Adolescents

Understanding the material and activities in this chapter will help the reader to:

1. Describe the cultural, socioeconomic, familial, and language characteristics of Asian-American children and adolescents.
2. Explain the "model minority" stereotype and its effects on Asian-American children and adolescents.
3. Describe Asian-American learners and their development, achievement levels, language problems, and learning styles.
4. List several practices which impede the Asian-American learners' educational progress.
5. Offer several concrete suggestions for improving the Asian-American learner's self-concept and cultural identities.
6. List several points that educators of Asian-Americans should remember.
7. Suggest appropriate children's literature, implement research findings, and provide culturally-appropriate experiences for Asian-American learners.

OVERVIEW

Planning teaching and learning experiences for Asian-American learners requires an understanding of their developmental characteristics, achievement levels, language problems, learning styles, and cultural characteristics. The diversity among Asian-American learners also requires a consideration of their geographic, generational, and socioeconomic differences, as well as intracultural and individual characteristics. Although learners from all cultures have been plagued with stereotypical beliefs, the notable successes of the Asian-American people have resulted in a "model minority" stereotype that sometimes leads educators to expect exemplary achievement and behavior. This chapter examines the cultural characteristics of Asian-American children and adolescents, and then focuses attention on these learners in teaching and learning situations.

THE ASIAN-AMERICAN PEOPLE

Origins

Many Asians arrived in the United States during the late eighteen- and early nineteen hundreds as farm and construction laborers and were subjected to cruel treatment. Many young men headed for the promised land of America risking violation of sacred family traditions and actually breaking a law against immigration from the homeland. Their journey was rough and hazardous, and their arrival was met with suspicion (Banks, 1987). Asian-Americans met many hardships and often were forced to accept the lowest paid, most menial jobs. They were often denied the right of citizenship and the right to own land. At one time or another, this ethnic group has been the victim of appalling forms of discrimination (Sue, 1981). Chinese immigrants' strange clothing, language, the queue hairstyles, and skin color made them victims of curiosity and racism. Often denied the opportunity of living and working outside the cultural community, Asian-Americans formed their own cultural enclaves, e.g., Chinatown. In such isolation, Asian-Americans often continued to speak their native language, maintained their close-knit families, and continued old-world traditions (Banks, 1987).

Table 4-1 shows the various countries of origin of the Asian-American people:

Asian-Americans Today

More recent influxes of Southeast Asians include people from Vietnam, Cambodia, Thailand, and Laos. The already considerable diversity among these people becomes even greater as one considers geographic, socioeconomic, generational, and educational differences. Asian-Americans have increased in numbers from 1.4 million in 1970 to 3.5 million in 1980, an increase of 141 percent (Banks, 1987). Of the cities with populations of 250,000 or more, those with the greatest concentrations of Asian-Americans

Table 4-1   Asian Immigrants by Country of Birth 1961-1986 (Ten with Highest Number of Immigrants) Numbers (000)

Country of Birth	Number of Immigrants
Philippines	735.5
China	518.6
Korea	509.6
Vietnam	448.8
India	353.9
Iran	135.6
Laos	127.8
Japan	110.4
Hong Kong	103.8
Thailand	81.6

Compiled from: U.S. Bureau of the Census. (1988). *Statistical Abstracts of the United States: 1988* (108th Edition).

include Buffalo, Chicago, Honolulu County, Los Angeles, New York, and San Francisco (U. S. Bureau of the Census, 1980).

FOR ADDITIONAL INFORMATION

Chinese Cultural Center, 159 Lexington Ave., New York, NY 10016. The Cultural Center provides classes, and library and information services to promote better understanding of the Chinese culture.

Chinese Cultural Association, P. O. Box 1272, Palo Alto, CA 94302. This worldwide organization promotes communication and better understanding between the Chinese and people of other cultures.

Southeast Asian Center, 1124-1128 W. Ainslie, Chicago, IL 60640. The Southeast Asian Center promotes the independence and well-being of Lao, Hmong, Cambodian, Vietnamese, and Chinese peoples.

The total enrollment of Asians and Pacific Islanders in the San Diego school district doubled between 1982 and 1986 (Divoky, 1988). Several characteristics can be identified with the cultures of Southeast Asian countries, differences that could be misunderstood by professionals working with children. Many people refer to any Southeast Asian child as "Vietnamese" without realizing that serious insults may result due to different cultural heritages. Such labeling fails to realize the bitter feelings among various nationalities and ethnic groups:

> Children may not know one another's language. They may not be of the same religion; their parents may have been opposing enemies; or they may harbor feelings of superiority, inferiority, or resentment toward one another. (West, 1983, p. 85-86)

Activity:

Visit an elementary or secondary school that has a significant number of Asian-American student subgroups. What are the educators in the school doing to address the diversity among the Asian groups? What else might they do?

The Culture Quiz: Contemporary Asian-Americans

Directions: Match the individuals with their contributions or achievement by placing the appropriate letter before the name.

_____	1.	Akio Morita	a. Probably the best known superconductivity scientist in the world; director of Texas Center for superconductivity
_____	2.	Paul Chu	b. Chairman of the SONY Corporation
_____	3.	Laurence Yep	c. Chinese-American CBS News correspondent
_____	4.	I. M. Pei	d. Vietnamese actress starring in *Casualities of War*
_____	5.	Connie Chung	e. Chinese-American architect; known for creative urban designs, e.g, the J.F.K. Library in Boston
_____	6.	Thuy Thu Lee	f. Chinese-American writer of children's books about Asian-Americans, e.g, *The Rainbow People* (1989)
_____	7.	An Wang	g. Shot in the foot at seven in Laos; he is now a leading apprentice jockey in the United States
_____	8.	Chin Yang	h. Engineer from Shanghai who built a $600.00 investment into a multibillion dollar company

Answers: 1. b 2. a 3. f 4. e 5. c 6. d 7. h 8. g

Children of all cultures can read developmentally appropriate books about the Asian-American culture for more enhanced knowledge and better understanding.

USING CHILDREN'S LITERATURE: The Asian-American Experience

YEP, LAURENCE. *The Rainbow People.* Harper & Row, 1989. A book of folktales, this book shows a lively and enjoyable picture of Chinese culture.
ASIAN CENTRE FOR UNESCO. *Folktales from Asia for Children Everywhere.* Weatherhill, 1977. These three volumes contain folktales from many Asian countries.
CLARK, ANN NOLAND. *To Stand Against the Wind.* Viking, 1978. An eleven-year-old Vietnamese boy's memories return to the beautiful land before it was destroyed by war.
YAGAWA, SUMIKO. *The Crane Wife.* Morrow, 1981. In this Japanese traditional tale, greed and its consequences become clear.

STEREOTYPING OF ASIAN-AMERICAN CHILDREN AND ADOLESCENTS

Because of their notable educational, occupational, and economic successes, Asian-Americans are often called the "model minority" (Banks, 1987). Yao (1988), reflecting upon the model minority stereotype, describes Asian-American children as:

> Not all of them are superior students who have no problems in school. Some have learning problems; some lack motivation, proficiency in English, or financial resources; and some have parents who do not understand the American school system, because of cultural differences, language barriers, or their own single-minded quest for survival. (p. 223)

The media like to portray the contemporary image of Asian-Americans as a highly successful minority that has achieved success in the Anglo-American society. For example, some reports that applaud the educational achievements of Asian-American students have resulted in the model minority stereotype. Young Asian-Americans, largely those with Chinese, Korean, and Indochinese backgrounds, have outpaced their Anglo-American counterparts in several academic areas. These young people are reported to spend more time on homework, take more advanced high school courses, and graduate with more credits. In addition, a higher percentage of these young people complete high school and college than do Anglo-American students (*The new whiz kids . . .* , 1987).

CASE STUDY 4-1 shows how Mrs. Black addressed the stereotypical statement that all Asian-Americans are alike.

CASE STUDY 4-1: "They're all alike!"

Mrs. Black, an experienced tenth grade teacher, overhears several students saying, "Those Asian-American students—they are all alike: Smart, polite, putting their family first, and they look and act alike!" Mrs. Black calmly continued walking down the hall, but she began considering how best to address such attitudes. She knew that all Asian students were not alike, that they came from different geographical areas, and had many intracultural differences. However, an even greater problem was surfacing: The myth that all Asians students are alike—void of diversity.

Mrs. Black decided on a deliberate plan of action to help the students understand that Asian-Americans are a highly diverse group, and that all students do not fit stereotypical images.

1. She planned a unit on cultural diversity to show that, first, not all Asian cultures are alike, and second, that students have many intracultural, as well as individual, differences.
2. She planned cooperative learning teams (four or five members per group) which crossed cultural, socioeconomic, and ability groups.
3. She planned discussion groups (led by teachers, counselors, and other school professionals) designed to help students to understand individual differences, strengths, and weaknesses.

Still concerned, Mrs. Black decided to propose a school-wide approach to promote cultural diversity and understandings.

Other stereotypes include viewing the Asian-American as a clumsy, inarticulate learner who is good with numbers, but poor with words. Such stereotypes might accentuate discrepancies by setting up rigid educational expectations. In essence, although many Asian-Americans have proven themselves quite successful educationally, educators should remember to view each child as an individual with unique strengths and weaknesses (Sue, 1981).

While some Asian-Americans have demonstrated remarkable succcess, IMPLEMENTING RESEARCH 4-1 shows the importance of considering individuals.

IMPLEMENTING RESEARCH 4-1: The "Model Minority"

Hartman and Askounis (1989) questioned the popular and professional literature description of Asian-American students as "a model minority," "whiz kids", and "problem-free". Are these accurate descriptions? Do these perceptions mask individuality and problems? The researchers reminded readers of the tremendous cultural and individual diversity among Asian-Americans, e.g., the 29 distinct subgroups that differ in language, religion, and customs. In addition, diversity exists within cultural groups. Rather than categorizing all Asian-Americans as being a model-minority, professionals should get to know individuals and determine each one's strengths and weaknesses.

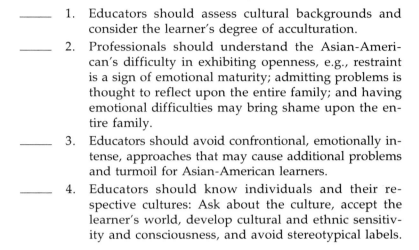

IMPLEMENTING THE RESEARCH:

_____ 1. Educators should assess cultural backgrounds and consider the learner's degree of acculturation.

_____ 2. Professionals should understand the Asian-American's difficulty in exhibiting openness, e.g., restraint is a sign of emotional maturity; admitting problems is thought to reflect upon the entire family; and having emotional difficulties may bring shame upon the entire family.

_____ 3. Educators should avoid confrontional, emotionally intense, approaches that may cause additional problems and turmoil for Asian-American learners.

_____ 4. Educators should know individuals and their respective cultures: Ask about the culture, accept the learner's world, develop cultural and ethnic sensitivity and consciousness, and avoid stereotypical labels.

Source: Hartman, J.S., & Askounis, A.C. (1989). "Asian-American students: Are they really a 'model-minority'?" *The School Counselor, 37,* 109-112.

The enviable academic successes of some Asian-Americans has led to a perception that all Asian-Americans are exceptional in all pursuits. To assume, however, such scholarly expertise on the basis of culture alone does not have any greater validity than does saying all Black-Americans are incapable of high academic achievement, or that all Native-Americans live on reservations. Cultural misconceptions of oneself can have a detrimental effect on the forming identities, and can result in undue and unrealistic pressures and demands.

CASE STUDY 4-2 shows steps that can be taken to learn about Asian-Americans as individuals, rather than assuming the model minority stereotype.

CASE STUDY 4-2: The Model Minority Stereotype

Miss Carter, an Anglo-American and a first-year teacher, has a large percentage of Asian-American learners in the class. She has heard about the excellent reputation of some Asian-American learners, and wants to challenge them to excel in as many areas as possible. However, she is also realistic, in the sense that she knows all Asian-Americans are not "model students", "problem free", and "whiz kids". She wonders how she can have high expectations for learners capable of excelling, yet not be too demanding of students unable to excel.

Although recognizing possible discrepancies between stereotypes and realities is to be commended, Miss Carter now has to determine a means of discovering which students can excel, and which need assistance. What can she do?

1. Check permanent records to determine previous achievement, and areas of strength and weaknesses.
2. Request a diagnostic or achievement test (as free from cultural bias as possible) from the district assessment personnel.
3. Meet with each student to discuss achievements and areas in which assistance is needed.
4. Request that the school language specialist meet with each student for an individual language assessment.
5. Seek any assistance the guidance counselor can offer in terms of tests, inventories, and scales to determine capabilities.

ASIAN-AMERICAN CHILDREN AND ADOLESCENTS

Cultural Characteristics

The many diverse nationalities that compromise the Asian-American culture make overall descriptions difficult. These people constitute a highly diversified ethnic group, and vary greatly in physical characteristics, attitudes, values, and ethnic institutions (Banks, 1987). Teachers often think of Asian-American children as studious, high-achieving, and well-behaved students (Yee, 1988; Huang, 1976) who are expected to excel in the American culture, and yet retain the Asian-American cultures, values, and traditions. Conforming to both the Asian-American and the Anglo-American cultures results in high expectations and considerable problems for developing personalities and identities.

Emphasizing the need to recognize and understand cultural differences, Divoky (1988) writes:

> But too often we forget that those whose roots are in Asia are not necessarily alike; a recently arrived Hmong refugee has virtually nothing in common with an affluent Japanese-American student whose parents were born and raised in the Midwest. (p. 220)

Differences between the Asian-American culture and the Anglo-American culture, and the many long-accepted traditions, customs, and values of Asian-American families (both immediate and extended), also contribute to the developing child's sense of confusion regarding role expectations. Chil-

dren growing up in such a multicultural setting may develop an ethnic identity problem as they are confronted with two major role expectations. Developing children can, indeed, become confused as their identities are formed.

Educators who work with Asian-Americans should remember the personality differences between these children and Anglo-American children.
These differences deserve to be recognize as cultural variations, and should
be placed in proper perspective. For example, Japanese-Americans have
been described as quiet, reticent, or aloof in interethnic situations (Padilla,
1981), and as more dependent, conforming, and obedient to authority, and
more willing to place family welfare over individual wishes (Sue, 1981).

Distinct differences also exist in the respect for education and for teachers. West (1983) tells the story of a teacher who felt that she was not "reaching" a Vietnamese student. Although he was not disruptive, he was not
participating fully in class. When she requested a parent-teacher conference,
the father came to school feeling disgraced and sure his son had done something terrible. The teacher repeatedly explained that she liked the student,
and that she was only trying to improve communication. The father ordered
the boy to apologize, which he did. However, the father struck the child, and
ordered him to kneel during the apology. The boy immediately obeyed, only
to be joined by the teacher, who informed him and his parents that no one in
America had to kneel to anyone.

Activity:

Meet with a group of Asian-American parents and extended family members
to discuss their perceptions and expectations of educators and schools. Allow
sufficient time for questions and discussions. Do not be dismayed if parents
do not express themselves, because they sometimes perceive teachers as
authority figures, or place teachers on a pedestal.

Other cultural differences which warrant educators' attention include:
1) Physical contact between members of the same sex is permissible, but not
acceptable between members of the opposite sex; 2) Vietnamese rarely touch
their heads (either a religious belief or the possibility of damaging one's
head) (West, 1983).

Recently-arrived Asian children and adolescents may experience particularly acute conflicts. They are caught between their parents' culture and
the school, and have little power to influence either. These young people
often serve as translators, and may be called upon to complete forms, appli-
cations, and licenses (Chen, 1987; Kitano, 1989).

Socioeconomic Status

The accumulation of wealth allows people more options, opportunities, and
increased amounts of leisure time. Changing one's economic circumstances

also influences a person's social expression, values, and patterns of thinking and behaving (Axelson, 1985). A learner's socioeconomic status is undoubtedly one of the most significant factors affecting learning and achievement. Educators can readily understand the educational and social implications of a learner's socioeconomic status, and of basing curricular and instructional decisions on stereotypical beliefs and assumptions.

Trying to determine the socioeconomic level of Asian-Americans proves difficult at best, due to the diversity among the Asian cultures and the lack of current information on their earning power and social class. Educators must be careful not to rely on the model-minority stereotype by assuming that all Asian-Americans are experiencing social and economic success—at least not according to the common American perception of success as the accumulation of money or other materialistic wealth. In all likelihood, some Asian-Americans (like members of other cultures) have achieved socioeconomic successes, while others have been less fortunate.

What can one say about the socioeconomic status of Asian-Americans? Both Japanese-Americans and Chinese-Americans have moved toward educational, occupational, and social assimilation in the American society; however, the higher proportion of Chinese-Americans who work in service occupations may result from their tendency (either due to choice or discrimination) to remain in traditional settings such as the "Chinatowns". Median family incomes provide a clear comparison: Total United States $19,917; Japanese-Americans $27,354; Chinese-Americans $22,559 (*Asian and Pacific Islander data*, 1988).

Although these higher-than-average family incomes are undoubtedly impressive, several factors should be kept in perspective: First, the tremendous range of incomes among Asian-Americans becomes clear when one considers that the Laotians earned only $5,159, and the Hmongs earned $5,000; similarly, the Cambodians earned $8,712. Educators simply cannot look at the impressive economic successes of the Japanese people, and many of the Chinese people, and generalize or assume that all Asian cultures have experienced comparable success. Second, some Asian-American families have more wage earners, which raises their median family incomes (*Asian and Pacific Islander data*, 1988).

Families

The childrearing techniques of Asian-American families have their foundation in cultural expectations, and emphasize loyalty to the family. There is a powerful message of not bringing embarrassment or shame to the family. The inculcation of guilt and shame are the principal techniques used to control the behavior of family members. Parents emphasize their children's obligation to the family, and their responsibility for abiding by family expectations. Children who act contrary to the family's wishes are considered selfish, inconsiderate, and ungrateful. The behavior of individual members is expected to be a reflection upon the entire family. For example, aberrant behavior is considered to be of great shame, and is usually hidden from the public and handled within the family, and outstanding achievement in some aspect of life is a source of great pride for both the child and the entire family. Such a standard of morality sometimes causes confusion for children who are attempting to satisfy the expectations of two cultures, and yet it emphasizes the importance of unity and honor in the Asian-American family (Sue & Sue, 1983).

In summary, the family as central to the Asian culture contributes to many individual conflicts that may arise, because parents and family reflect traditional ways, while the children are exposed to another way of life (Kitano, 1989).

CASE STUDY 4-3 looks at the powerful influence of the Asian-American family, and shows what educators can do to learn about families.

CASE STUDY 4-3: Understanding the Family

Mr. Jones looked at the research on Asian-American families. Without a doubt, the family plays a major role in determining learner's attitudes, behavior, and academic achievement. He read the following:

> The family is the primary socializing influence in the Asian culture; parents are responsible for interpreting appropriate and inappropriate behaviors (Hartman & Askounis, 1989, p.110).

He wondered how we, as educators, can better understand the Asian family and its influence on children and adolescents. He jotted down a list to consider:

1. Meeting families firsthand (in their homes, if possible) is the best means of learning family values, customs, and traditions.

2. Arrange small group sessions with families (both immediate and extended), perhaps at PTA meetings or other school functions, to learn expectations of schools and children, and to explain school expectations to parents.

3. Learn about families from different Asian cultures for a better understanding of intracultural and individual differences.

4. Learn about generational differences among families, e.g., variations in first-, second-, and third-generation families.

5. Learn about families from differing socioeconomic groups to gain an understanding of values, traditions, and beliefs.

Family problems are approached subtly and indirectly, rather than openly, with much care and effort expended to avoid offending other family members. Members are expected to restrain feelings that might disrupt the harmony of the family. This restraint of possibly disruptive emotions receives an emphasis that has led many Anglo-Americans to consider Asian-Americans as "inscrutable" (Sue, 1981).

Family allegiance, and respect for parents and family play a significant role in the value system, achievements, and behavior of the developing Asian-American child. In the traditional family, age, sex, and generational status are the primary determinants of the child's role behavior. Ancestors and elders are viewed with great reverence and respect, and are actively involved with childrearing. Families are patriarchical; children are taught that the father is traditionally the head of the family, and his authority is unquestioned. The primary duty of the son is to be a good son, and his obligations as a good husband or father come second to his duty as a son. The role of the female in the family is that of subservience to the males, the performance of domestic chores, and the bearing of children (Sue, 1981). Needless to say, such generalizations may vary according to socioeconomic class and generational status.

The Asian-American family is and has been conservative and slow to change. Rigidly-defined family expectations are arranged so that roles do not interfere, and actually work to eliminate or minimize familial conflicts. The welfare and integrity of the family is of great importance, and family members suppress their individual behaviors for the welfare of the family and its reputation (Sue & Sue, 1972).

Religion

The recent influx of Indochinese, Chinese, Koreans, and other groups has increased the religious pluralism in the United States. The Laotians and Cambodians are primarily Buddhists, as are the Vietnamese. Some of the Vietnamese, however, are Taoists or Roman Catholic. Some embrace the philosophy of Confucianism. The majority of Korean immigrants adhere to the teachings of Confucianism, which is more a philosophy than a religion. Most Koreans are likely to be Buddhists. However, a minority are Protestant, and a smaller, but still significant, group are Roman Catholic. The majority of Hong Kong immigrants are Buddhists; some are Taoists. Many of these immigrants are also likely to adhere to the teachings of Confucius (Gollnick & Chinn, 1990).

Asian-Americans tend to practice values such as respect for one's ancestors, filial piety, and avoidance of shame. These moral principles assist many Asian-Americans in family and social functioning by defining their obligation, duty, and loyalty to others. Good performance and achievement bring honor to the family. Shame and dishonor are powerful motivators to minimize unacceptable behavior. This standard of morality may seem harsh and rigid to the outsider, but to many Asian-Americans it maintains honor and harmony in the family (Lum, 1986).

Language

Unquestioningly, the considerable emphasis placed on education, the promise that education holds for successful students, and the parents' insistence that children abide by family wishes, have contributed to the success of many Asian-American children. Language, however, appears to be an area of difficulty for Asian-American children. In one school district in California, the number of Asian-American children with limited English skills grew from 8% to 42% in just seven years (Divoky, 1988). Two of every five Asians and Pacific Islanders aged five and over spoke a language other than English at home, e.g., the proportion was highest for Laotians, Cambodians, and Hmongs (at about 95%), and lowest for Japanese (at about 44%). For Pacific Islanders, the range was 88% for Tongans, and 10% for Hawaiians (*Asian and Pacific Islander data: '80 census goldmine . . .*, 1988).

For a better understanding of Asian-American learners, educators should recognize the problems Asian-Americans have with English. Without doubt, the language barriers and problems confronting Asian-American learners make achievements and educational attainments even more significant. Although many Asian-American parents encourage the use of English, many adolescents still live in homes where the native language continues to be the primary language. This results in learners who speak and understand two languages.

Understanding the spoken word, and being understood while speaking English, often poses a problematic situation, especially in the Anglo-American school system (Sue, 1981). These children have, however, overcome many language problems, and have demonstrated enviable educational successes. Reconciling the loyalties demanded by two different cultural traditions presents the Asian-American child with a second challenge. Our pluralistic society requires that learners maintain their ethnic identities, while meeting the differing cultural expectations of home and school (Sue, 1981).

Activity:

Discuss with a group of Asian-American learners how language affects their lives and progress in school. What language problems exist? What are their opinions about forsaking their native languages and adopting English? How can educators and language specialists assist these learners?

Not only must educators in multicultural settings understand (and be understood in) verbal interactions with Asian-Americans, but it is also necessary to make an equal effort to understand nonverbal communication. Several examples of nonverbal behavior learned by adolescents show the distinctive differences among cultures. First, the forward and backward leaning of the body indicates feelings: A backward lean indicates a withdrawal from a conversation or topic, while a forward lean lets the speaker know that the listener is polite, concerned, and flexible. Other notable differences include Japanese-American females expressing anxiety through increased speaking, and the Japanese-American males expressing anxiety though silence (Bond & Shiraishi, 1974). Third, Japanese-Americans often communicate nonverbally through gestures, many of which are unknown to Anglo-Americans (Ishii, 1973). For educational efforts to be most effective, educators and Asian-American learners should work actively to understand each others' verbal and nonverbal behaviors.

CULTURAL COMPARISON

Asian-American and Anglo-American Children
and Adolescents

Asian-American	*Anglo-American*
Conform to both Asian and Anglo cultures	Conform to Anglo-American culture
Quiet, reticent, aloof	More talkative and outgoing
Dependent, conforming, obedient	Independent, "do my own thing"
Place family welfare over individual desires	Individual desires more than family welfare
Bilingual background	Monolingual background—not as many problems
Respect and reverence for elders	Youth is most valuable
Sons of more value than daughters	Sons and daughters of equal value
Childrearers—parents and extended family	Childrearers—immediate family
Strong family structure exerts control over conduct	Free to do his/her own thing
Child aberrant behavior—great shame must be hidden or shame upon entire family	Child aberrant behavior—behavior sign of independence and freedom
Family priority over peers	Peers priority over family

Sources: Lum (1986), Sue & Sue (1983), Axelson (1985)

ASIAN-AMERICAN LEARNERS IN THE SCHOOL

Educators' Understanding Asian-American Learners and Their Culture

When they first enter the United States, children often experience a clash between their cultures and the expectations of their new homes and schools. Several distinct differences exist between Asian and Anglo expectations and attitudes toward schools and teachers: 1) Teachers in Asia are accorded a higher status than teachers in the United States. The informality between

American teachers and students may seem confusing to Southeast Asian children, and appalling to their families. 2) The cultural backgrounds and values cause children to expect considerable structure and organization.

Obvious differences in values may include: 1) Self-effacement and saving face are highly valued; students wait to be answered or to participate, unless otherwise requested by the teacher. Having attention drawn to oneself, e.g., the teacher putting a child's name on the board for misbehaving, can bring considerable distress. 2) Children have been socialized to listen more than to speak, and to speak in a soft, well-modulated voice. This characteristic is often perceived as shyness. Children have also been taught to be modest in dress, manner, and behavior.

The Anglo-American emphasis on individualism may present challenges for the Asian-American learners who seek to satisfy the demands of contemporary society while feeling loyalty to Asian-American family traditions. Educators need to understand the Asian-American's strong emphasis on the father as head of the family, the additional value placed on sons rather than daughters, and the respect for the older family members. Maintaining loyalty to family tradition while building an identity and life in an Anglo-American society that emphasizes individuality may prove troublesome for children and adolescents.

IMPLEMENTING RESEARCH 4-2 summarizes a study that focused on the reasons Asian-Americans succeed, and provides several suggestions for educators.

IMPLEMENTING RESEARCH 4-2: Why Asian-American High School Students Succeed

Reglin and Adams (1990) reported "an inordinate number of success stories coming from Asian-American students, especially in the areas of math and science" (p. 143). In an attempt to reduce stereotypical generalizations about Asian-American students, Reglin and Adams completed a descriptive study (a 15-item questionnaire) designed to determine whether cultural differences between families of Asian-American high school students and non-Asian-American high school students contribute to the Asian-American's greater success in high school. Although Reglin and Adams provided detailed findings to each item included on the questionnaire, several implications can be gleaned from their overall findings:

IMPLEMENTING THE RESEARCH:

_____ 1. Educators should take advantage of the fact that Asian-American students are more influenced by their parents' desire for them to do well than are their non-Asian counterparts.

_____ 2. Educators should provide a sufficient number of

developmentally-appropriate learning experiences, since Asian-American students (at least in this study) do not start dating until their late teens, have little interest in rock music, television, or athletics.

_____ 3. Educators should recognize that Asian-American students value their leisure time and spend considerable time doing their homework.

Source: Reglin, G.L., & Adams, D.R. (1990). "Why Asian-American high school students have higher grade point averages and SAT scores than other high school students." *The High School Journal, 73*, 143-149.

It is important that educators understand Asian-American parents' perceptions of school behavior and achievement. Asian-Americans come from cultures that often view children's behavior as the result of a lack of will, or supernatural causes. Cases of school failure have resulted in parents' complaining that children are lazy and lack character. Rather than looking for educational reasons, parents often believe that the solution lies in increasing parental restrictions, more homework, and other negative sanctions designed to promote character development. Hard work, effort, and developing character are considered to be the best avenue to improving behavior or school work. As educators quickly realize, such beliefs can be particularly acute for Asian-Americans with limited intellectual (or other) abilities (Kitano, 1989).

Even greater challenges may confront the female Asian-American adolescent. Experiencing the cultural conflict between traditional Asian values and contemporary Anglo-American values can cause females to question their role in life, and the cultural value placed upon their sex. Will they continue to be relegated to second-class status in the Asian-American family, or should they seek the more equitable standing of the Anglo-American family? Since some acculturation will probably occur, the female may be faced at some point with the task of reaching cultural comparisons.

IMPLEMENTING RESEARCH 4-3 emphasizes that teachers should recognize Asian-American learners' strengths, but also that learners should be treated as individuals.

IMPLEMENTING RESEARCH 4-3: The Model Minority Goes to School

Without doubt, the significant increase of Asian-American children challenges educators to deal with language problems, cultural differences, and stereotypes. Studies have shown that Asian-American students earn higher grades as high school juniors and seniors, and virtually out-perform all groups, including Anglo learners. Their academic achievement and their success in earning scholarships from prestigious universities and music conservatories have earned them the reputation of being a model minority.

IMPLEMENTING THE RESEARCH:

_____ 1. Educators should encourage excellence and high academic achievement, but should base expectations on individuals and their ability, rather than stereotypical beliefs.

_____ 2. Educators should not overlook Asian-Americans' problems, and should not expect total self-sufficiency.

_____ 3. Educators should not expect docility and passivity, and should not treat Asian-Americans more harshly when they do misbehave.

_____ 4. Educators should assist other children in understanding the Asian culture, and should try to reduce other childrens' hostility toward Asian-Americans.

Source: Divoky, D. (1988). "The model minority goes to school." *Phi Delta Kappan, 70,* 219-222.

Developmental Theory: Children and Adolescents

The importance of identity formation and personality development during the adolescent years deserves developmental and cultural consideration. These developments are influenced by the childrens' experience and their families' perceptions of historical events, as well as by contemporary perceptions and treatment. Studies of personality development contend that Asian-Americans adopt a more practical and applied approach to life and its problems than do Anglo-Americans, e.g., ideas are evaluated more on the basis of their immediate practical application. Another personality trait is the tendency to prefer concrete, well-structured, and predictable situations over ambiguous situations (Sue & Kirk, 1973). Cultural emphasis is also placed on the restraint of strong feelings, unquestioning obedience to family authority, submergence of the individual to the welfare of the family, and a tendency to avoid outspokenness for fear of retaliation by the larger society (Watanabe, 1973).

Achievement Levels

Although it is imperative that the "model minority" stereotype be avoided at all costs, it appears on the surface that many Asian-American students are highly successful students. However, educators cannot allow the successful experiences of many Asian-American students to be generalized to all Asian learners. The excellence demonstrated by many students might, in fact, impose considerable tolls and hardships on others, especially when the language handicaps that hamper the progress of many Asian-American learners are considered.

However, one can state with a degree of certainty that Asian-Americans undoubtedly have attained enviable accomplishments in United States schools.

It is unrealistic and stereotypical to expect all Asian-Americans to attain such achievement levels. Not all Asian immigrant children are superior students who have no problems at school. Some have learning problems; some lack motivation, proficiency in English, or financial resources; and some have parents who do not understand the American school system because of cultural or language barriers (Yao, 1988).

Contending that Asian-Americans have achieved remarkable educational achievements, Lee and Rong (1988) sought to determine whether the reasons for Asian-American successes included superior intelligence, or concentration, or hard work. They concluded that Asian-American children have an ability to hold a particular problem in mind until they reach a solution. In fact, it is believed that Asian-American children are not far above their peers in native abilities, but that concentration and hard work make up for any deficiencies (Garfinkel, 1983; Lee & Rong, 1988).

Trying to meet the high expectations of parents and educators can result in considerable frustration. While successful Asian-American students credit their families for making sacrifices for their futures, others feel resentment: "My parents will not let me stay after school to play soccer," a tenth grade Cambodian immigrant stated. "They say I have to study. I study and I study and I study . . . If I don't have homework, still I study. They make me do it over and over again. They really want me to do well, but they don't understand about schools here" (Divoky, 1988, p. 221).

Language Problems

Language poses a major barrier to children in a land where few people can speak or write a language other than they own. As one Vietnamese girl observed, to be successful in the U. S., "you have to know English" (First, 1988, p. 206).

Educators who work with Asian-American learners readily recognize the language and communication problems. One of the authors recently taught a Japanese-American learner who excelled over all others in the class. However, her language problems required that she study far longer and more diligently than her classmates. During tests and other written work, she relied extensively on her Japanese-American dictionary, and requested extra time. Despite all her language difficulties, her persistence and determination overcame her deficiencies in English.

CASE STUDY 4-4 tells of Keigo, her language problem, and what her teacher might do to help her.

CASE STUDY 4-4: The Language Problem

Keigo, an Asian-American fourth grader, has a language problem which interferes with several aspects of her life. She often cannot understand her teachers, and she experiences difficulty making friends. Her language at home and in her community does not pose a problem. Her parents and neighbors either speak their native language, or a form of English not much better than Keigo's. Yet, at school, Keigo's language results in her having to study harder and having few friends.

Keigo's teacher can take several approaches to helping her improve her language, make better use of her study time, and improve her friendships. It is important at the outset to avoid a "blame the victim" perspective, in which Keigo would be blamed for her lack of fluency in English. The teacher—and the school as a whole—should understand Keigo's situation and try to help her overcome the language barriers. First, arrangements should be made with the school's language specialist to meet with Keigo, and determine the extent of her problem and the possible remediation efforts. Second, Keigo's teacher might consider placing her in a cooperative learning team in which other students can help her understand. Third, Keigo and other children with language difficulties may be placed in a group that receives extra attention. Regardless of what means is used to help Keigo, it is important that Keigo and her problem are understood, rather than hoping the problem will simply disappear.

Japanese-Americans and Chinese-Americans of both sexes scored lower than Anglo-Americans on the verbal sections of an achievement test. The reasons for language difficulties may include the fact that Asian-Americans often come from bilingual backgrounds; and second, that cultural traditions and customs often restrict or impede verbal communication. For example, many Asian-American families encourage one-way communication, e.g., parents speak to children. Multicultural educators working with such children can avoid several of the pitfalls that may lead to stereotypical thinking. First, educators must remember that Asian-American students may be communicating in a second language. Although English may be the predominant language, these children may continue to hear their parents' native language (Sue, 1981).

Over 50% of Asian-Americans failed an English examination, and this resulted in additional coursework to remediate deficiencies. Specifically, some Asian-Americans have such significant difficulty in understanding English, and, in being understood, that considerable motivation and language study are required for them to be even minimally competent. The direct teaching of English language skills to correct deficiencies indicates a failure to understand the Asian-American's difficulty with English, and has resulted in remedial programs being generally ineffective (Sue, 1981).

Learning Styles: Cultural Considerations

The adjustment of the Asian-American learner's cognitive learning styles to the United States school system deserves attention. Asian children tend to need reinforcement from teachers, and they work efficiently in a well-structured, quiet, learning environment in which definite goals have been established. Asian learners seldom reveal their opinions or their abilities voluntarily, or dare to challenge their teachers. Even when they know an answer to a teacher's question, they may choose to sit quietly—as though they do not know. Older children may perform well in rote memorization and mathematics operations, but may do poorly on creative writing or analytical commentary. Asian children tend to seek teachers' approval and to make their decisions based on what teachers think is best, thus becoming more dependent on teachers for help with school work, and guidance in classroom behavior (Yao, 1985).

Activity:

Observe a group of Asian-American learners doing school work to determine their learning habits, such as time on a given task, individual versus cooperative work, and reliance on bilingual dictionaries. How do they differ from Anglo learners? What could you, as an educator in a multicultural setting, do to help these learners?

Some factors are clear concerning Japanese learners: Their mothers are intensely involved in the children's learning, families celebrate the starting of school, children are introduced to mathematics concepts earlier in life, children must learn a great deal of material quickly, learners must pass strict examinations, teachers teach moral values and character, schools set curfews and dress codes, and children spend more time in school. Although these do not represent learning styles per se, they do show an attitude toward school, and show that learners work conscientiously and diligently to achieve (Papalia & Olds, 1989).

School Practices Impeding Asian-American's Progress

Educators who fail to understand Asian-Americans' cultural backgrounds and their school-related problems may actually contribute to their difficulties in United States schools. Looking at Asian-Americans from an Anglo perspective may promote learning experiences and expectations that are not compatible with Asian-American expectations. Generalizing across Asian customs, and assuming too much homogeneity among learners, negates or overlooks the tremendous cultural diversity between groups, and ignores generational and socioeconomic differences.

What school practices might interfere with the Asian-American academic achievement or psychosocial development?

1. Providing predominantly verbal teaching/learning experiences that place Asian-American learners at a disadvantage.

2. Failing to make school expectations clear to learners and their parents.

3. Expecting Asian-American learners to participate in discussion and sharing times, which may jeopardize their (as in their *family's*) name or reputation.

4. Basing academic and behavioral expectations on stereotypical images of Asian-American learners as "model" learners.

Understanding Asian-American learners, and their cultural backgrounds and diversity, places these practices in proper perspective. Although their accomplishments should be recognized and appreciated, Asian-Americans deserve individual consideration of their differences, abilities, motivation, and attitudes.

CASE STUDY 4-5 shows how Mrs. Bush does not understand her Asian-American students, and what she might to do improve her cultural understandings.

CASE STUDY 4-5: "She will not volunteer!"

Mrs. Bush complains, "I do not know what to do. Those Asian-Americans just will not volunteer, or show any interest at all. I asked for volunteers to participate in a group discussion and not a hand was raised. Are they totally uninterested? I am at my wit's end—I just don't know how to motivate these students."

This perception of Asian-Americans may be all too common in American schools. However, this problem results more from the teacher's lack of understanding than from Asian-Americans being noncommittal toward their education. Still, the teacher's cultural misunderstandings deserve to be addressed. The teacher needs to understand that Asian-Americans, because of their cultural backgrounds, are reluctant to bring attention to themselves, or to stand out among peers. Although the teacher might want to talk with the Asian-American students (alone, rather than in front of the class, which might seem like a reprimand) about class participation, the teacher should not force or coerce these students into participating in an activity that may be culturally or personally threatening.

Suggestions for Understanding and Teaching Asian-American Learners

1. Avoid reprimanding or disciplining the Asian-American learner in front of peers. Having one's name written on the black board or on other public displays may be far more damaging to the Asian child than to the Anglo child (West, 1983).

2. Avoid thinking that all Asian-Americans are high achievers who

reach excellence in all academic areas, and who model impeccable behavior.

3. Help the Asian-American family to understand the United States school system, and its expectations of learners and their families. Also, try to understand how the Asian family perceives teachers, e.g., the higher respect accorded to teachers by Asians. As the family's respect is gained, its assistance and support can also be earned.

4. Understand that behavior (at least to Anglo teachers) which may seem to indicate indifference or disinterestedness (e. g., looking the other way, or not volunteering to answer), is deemed appropriate for Asian learners. For example, learners have been taught to listen more than to speak, and to speak in a well-modulated voice.

5. Other culturally specific traits which should be understood include: Asian-American learners may be modest in dress; girls might be quieter than boys; girls might not want to reveal their legs during physical education activities; and problems might result when assigning girls and boys as cooperative learning partners (West, 1983).

Promoting Positive Self-Concepts and Cultural Identities

Asian-American children have special needs that responsive educators should address. In a school system that might seem different, and perhaps even oblivious to their needs, these learners need teaching and learning experiences that reflect their cultural and social needs. Learners in these formative developmental stages may begin to question their self- as well as their cultural worth. Responsive multicultural educators need to focus their efforts on several directions that will improve the self-concept of Asian-American learners.

First, the actual effects of the school experience on the Asian-American learner deserve consideration. Attending a school that appears to direct attention toward the majority culture can contribute to Asian-Americans questioning their place in the school. Educators can focus attention in several directions: Recognizing Asian-Americans as integral and worthy learners in the school system, recognizing the Asian culture as worthy, and addressing directly the concerns of Asian-Americans, e.g., teachers who often have high expectations based on the model minority stereotype.

Second, educators can respond by understanding the cultural differences that affect Asian-Americans and their academic and social progress in the United States schools. For example, Asian-Americans strive toward the accomplishment that brings pride to the family, in contrast to Anglos, who expect individual acclaim. The custom of many Anglos is to question the teacher, volunteer for an academic activity, or assertively raise one's hand to answer a teacher's question; such traits are in opposition to Asian beliefs. Teachers first need to understand these cultural differences, and then to respond with appropriate teaching behaviors, rather than to expect learners of all cultures to respond in a similar fashion.

Third, responsive multicultural educators need to engage in direct activities to improve the self-concepts of Asian-American learners; by specifically addressing their needs; by asking about their families (using extreme caution not to make the learner feel uncomfortable, or think that the teacher is prying); by genuinely and truthfully conveying to the learner that other students would benefit from knowing more about the Asian culture; and by making these learners feel that their culture and presence are understood, accepted, and appreciated by both school personnel and other children and adolescents.

Activity:

_____ 1. Educators can read aloud culturally appropriate children's books on Asian-Americans.

_____ 2. A sense of welcome or belongingness needs to be communicated that makes children feel welcome, a part of the class, and that their presence is wanted in the classroom.

_____ 3. Making a "Me" collage that demonstrates both the individual and the Asian culture.

_____ 4. Encouraging learners to engage in "Open-Ended Writing" where they can probe their feelings and express them without fear of sharing.

_____ 5. Writing about "What I Like About My Life" (and perhaps culture) or "Ten Things About Me", in which learners can feel free to express opinions and emotions (Tiedt & Tiedt, 1990).

Educators should remember the importance of the family in efforts to improve self-concepts. Asians generally have close-knit families, and one's feelings about oneself usually include a consideration of one's feelings about the family (and vice versa).

CULTURAL PORTRAIT: Mina—An Asian-American Learner

Mina, a 10-year-old Asian-American girl, attends a large urban elementary school whose population is approximately half Anglo, one-fourth Black, and one-fourth Asian and Hispanic. Mina makes above-average grades, but does not make the high grades that her family and teachers expect. Her problem with the English language is probably the major factor for her grades not being among the highest, but other factors also contribute, such as: Her family and teachers have expectations which are unrealistically high; she does not to want to volunteer for special assignments; she does not want to raise her hand to answer; and she does not always understand the Anglo learner's attitude toward school, teachers, and people.

Mina feels a little "lost". Her teachers are either Anglo or Black; they are friendly and appear to want to help her, but they do not seem to understand her and the way she feels children should act around adults, especially teachers. She perceives the school as being oriented toward Anglo expectations, and perhaps a little toward the Black perspective, yet very little toward the Asian or the Hispanic expectations. While she feels somewhat frustrated with this arrangement, she also realizes that she has to do her best school work and that her behavior must be exemplary. Otherwise, her family might feel shame or disappointment.

How Mina's Teacher Can Respond

Responding to Mina's psychosocial and intellectual needs first requires understanding her as an individual learner, and then as a member of the Asian-American culture. After a determination of her strengths and weaknesses, her teacher should focus attention in several directions:

1. Help Mina to understand both the Asian culture and the American culture.

2. Maintain high (but not unrealistic) expectations for Mina, and avoid relying on cultural stereotypes.

3. Understand that Mina's reluctance to volunteer or raise her hand during class is a reflection of her cultural background, and that it does not indicate indifference.

4. Provide appropriate multicultural experiences that teach learners of all cultures about the Asian culture, its diverse characteristics, and its many contributions.

5. Assign a professional in the school to be the advisor or mentor who will help Mina deal with daily school routines.

6. Meet with Mina's family to explain the philosophy and expectations of American school systems, and work to gain the understanding, respect, and support of Mina's family.

7. Decide how special service personnel, i.e., guidance counselors, speech and language specialists, and other school support personnel, can assist Mina.

SUMMING UP

Educators planning educational experiences for Asian-American learners should:

1. Reflect upon both historical and contemporary Asian cultural experiences, and plan teaching/learning experiences accordingly.
2. Undertake objective assessments, rather than believing all learners are members of a "model minority".
3. Understand that language warrants understanding because of its cultural basis (and the cultural value placed upon it), and because of the problems many Asian-Americans have with the English language.
4. Understand (and plan appropriate activities) that positive self-concepts and cultural identities are crucial to Asian learners' psychosocial development and general outlook on life.
5. Recognize that students have their distinct culture with its unique cultural characteristics, rather than grouping all Asian-American learners into one "Asian" culture.
6. Consider the tremendous diversity among learners: individual, generational, socioeconomic, and urban and rural dwellers, rather than categorizing all Asian-American learners into one homogeneous group.
7. Exercise extreme caution not to expect all Asian-American learners to be high achievers.
8. Recognize the family and its powerful influence (i.e., the encouragement not to bring shame and embarrassment on the family) on children and adolescents.

SUGGESTED LEARNING ACTIVITIES

1. Select an Asian-American learner and evaluate his or her language problem. Specifically, diagnose the exact problem, list several educational areas which might be affected, and devise a plan to remediate the language problem.
2. Select three Asian-Americans: a Japanese-American, a Chinese-American, and a Pilipino-American. After getting to know these three learners and their families, show similarities and differences among the three cultures. Specifically consider cultures, families, academic achievement, socioeconomic accomplishments, and any other area where similarities and differences are evident.
3. Choose two to three learners of similar cultural backgrounds but of differing generational and/or socioeconomic status. Compare the

similarities and differences that reflect the effects of socioeconomic class or generational differences.

4. Complete a case study of a high-achieving Asian-American. Specifically, (1) show his or her outstanding accomplishments; (2) show how the family has contributed to his or her successes; (3) show any problems or frustrations the student may experience; (4) explain how one can account for outstanding achievements, even though language problems exist; and (5) ask how can the schools address the student's problems. Show how it is imperative that educators not base teaching/learning experiences on the "model-minority" stereotype.

5. Survey several educators who have taught Asian-American students. Develop a survey designed to determine the strengths and weaknesses of Asian-American learners, the educators' opinions of Asian-Americans attitudes and achievements, and how schools can respond to meet the individual needs of Asian-American learners. What attempts can be made to educate parents and gain their support? Generally speaking, what can you suggest to educators who work with Asian-American learners of varying cultural backgrounds and individual differences?

Expanding Your Horizons: Additional Journal Readings and Books

DIVOKY, D. (1988). "The model minority goes to school." *Phi Delta Kappan, 70,* 219-222. Divoky maintains that Asian-Americans' success has created a model minority stereotype. She urges that Asian-Americans be perceived as individuals with strengths and weaknesses.

HARTMAN, J.S., & Askounis, A.C. (1989). "Asian-American students: Are they really a 'model-minority'?" *The School Counselor, 37,* 109-112. Hartman and Askounis emphasize the need to recognize individual differences: language, religion, customs, and family. Also, concrete suggestions for working with Asian-Americans are discussed.

"The new whiz kids: Why Asian-Americans are doing so well, and what it cost them." (1987, August 31). *Time,* pp.42-51. *Time* examines the extraordinary accomplishments of many Asian-Americans and looks at their problems.

YAO, E. L. (1988). "Working effectively with Asian immigrant parents." *Phi Delta Kappan, 70,* 223-225. Yao believes that the importance of working with parents has been well documented; however, schools must use strategies that reflect the unique cultural characteristics of Asian parents and families.

YAO, E. L. (1985). "Adjustment needs of Asian immigrant children." *Elementary School Guidance and Counseling, 19,* 222-227. Yao examines adjustment needs, such as changes in life-styles and family structure, the parent-child relationship, and the importance of the teachers and other school personnel.

YEE, L. Y. (1988). "Asian children." *Teaching Exceptional Children, 20(4),* 49-50. Yee looks at many teachers' perceptions of Asian-Americans, and focuses attention on what teachers can do to assist these learners.

WEST, B. E. (1983). "The new arrivals from Southeast Asia." *Childhood Education, 60,* 84-89. In this article, destined to become a classic, West provides concrete and specific information about Asian-American learners, and addresses such issues as their origins, differences in schooling and values, and how the teacher can make a difference.

Expanding Your Students' Horizons: Appropriate Asian-American Books for Children and Adolescents

ASHABRANNER, BRENT & ASHABRANNER, MELISSA. *Into a Strange Land*. Dodd, Mead, 1987.

CLARK, ANN. *To Stand Against The Wind*. Viking, 1978.

DAVIS, DANIEL. *Behind Barbed Wire: The Imprisonment of Japanese-Americans During World War II*. Dutton, 1982.

DUNN, MARY LOIS & ARDATH, MAYHAR. *The Absolutely Perfect Horse*. Harper & Row, 1983.

FRIEDMAN, INA. *How My Parents Learned To Eat*. Houghton Mifflin, *1984*.

HAUGAARD, ERIK CHRISTIAN. *The Boy and the Samurai*, Houghton-Mifflin, 1991.

LEVINE, ELLEN. *I Hate English!*. Scholastic, 1989.

LORD, BETTY BOA. *In the Year of the Boar and Jackie Robinson*. Harper & Row, 1984.

MAHY, MARGARET. *The Seven Chinese Brothers*. Scholastic, 1990.

MOSEL, ARLENE. *The Funny Little Woman*. Dutton, 1972.

NHUONG, HUYNH GUANG. *The Land I Lost: Adventures of a Boy in Vietnam*. Harper & Row, 1982.

RAU, MARGARET. *Holding Up The Sky*. Lodesta Books, 1983.

SURAT, MICHELE. *Angel Child, Dragon Child*. Raintree, 1983.

UCHIDA, YOSHIKO. *Journey to Topaz*. Scribner, 1971.

WALLACE, IAN. *Chin Chiang and the Dragon's Dance*. Athenaeum, 1984.

WATERS, KATE, & SLOEVENZ-LOW, MADELINE. *Lion Dancer: Ernie Wan's Chinese New Year*. Scholastic, 1990.

YAGAWA, SAMIKO. *The Crane Wife*. Morrow, 1981.

YASHIMA, TARO. *The Umbrella*. Viking, 1958.

YEP, LAURENCE. *Child of the Owl*. Harper & Row, 1977.

YEP, LAURENCE. *Dragonwings*. Harper & Row, 1975.

YEP, LAURENCE. *Sea Glass*. Harper & Row, 1979.

YEP, LAURENCE. *The Serpent's Children*. Harper & Row, 1984.

YEP, LAURENCE. *The Rainbow People*. Harper & Row, 1989.

5

Understanding Hispanic-American Children and Adolescents

Understanding the material and activities in this chapter will help the reader to:

1. Describe the cultural, socioeconomic, familial, and language characteristics of Hispanic-American children and adolescents.

2. Understand the dangers of stereotyping Hispanic-American learners and know how to respond appropriately in teaching/learning situations.

3. List and describe the educational characteristics and problems of Hispanic-American learners.

4. Name several practices that impede the educational process of Hispanic-American children and adolescents.

5. List several points that educators of Hispanic-American children and adolescents should remember.

6. Incorporate practical activities, suggest appropriate children's literature, implement research findings, and respond appropriately to school situations involving Hispanic-American learners.

OVERVIEW

Understanding Hispanic-American children and adolescents requires knowledge of their families, their religion, their language, their culture's contributions, and their school-related problems. "Knowing, understanding, and appreciating" Spanish-speaking learners are prerequisites, yet not enough: Educators must also understand the interrelatedness of the cultural characteristics of Hispanic learners, their differences as learners, and their school-related problems. The educators' emphasis should focus on understanding cultural diversity, and genuinely demonstrate appreciation and respect for Hispanic cultures. Educators should focus on teaching learners of all multicultural populations to appreciate the cultural differences of other learners as well as their own cultural differences. This chapter explores various cultural aspects of Hispanic-American children and adolescents, and then examines these learners in school-related contexts.

THE HISPANIC-AMERICAN CULTURE

Origins

The Hispanic-Americans may be identified as Mexican-Americans, Chicanos, Spanish-Americans, Latin-Americans, Mexicans, Puerto Ricans, Cubans, Guatemalans, and Salvadorans. All these multinational Americans are recognized as Hispanics and share many values and goals (Gonzalez, 1989). In some aspects, Hispanics constitute members of a single cultural group with a fairly common history, and the sharing of language, values, and customs, while other aspects point to a significant heterogeneous population that should be conceptualized as an aggregate of distinct subcultures (Ruiz, 1981). Tremendous cultural diversity exists among Hispanic-Americans, such as the differences among Mexican-Americans and Cuban-Americans, between generations, and between people living in different geographic locations in the United States. Although this section only examines several Hispanic cultural characteristics, educators are encouraged to learn about individual learners and their respective cultural characteristics.

Activities:

Learners often want to know more about their place of origin. Using a map, globe, or current reference book, teachers can focus efforts in several directions: Showing learners their place of origin, and teaching about the area—its terrain, its climate, its people and their contributions, and its history and place in Spanish history. What is the place like? What are the people like? Upon answering these questions, Hispanic learners can write reports, stories or poems in which they provide factual knowledge and share personal feelings.

Hispanic Americans Today

The Hispanic population increased by 34%, or about 5 million persons, from 1980 to 1987. In 1980, one out of every sixteen people in the United States was of Hispanic origin. (*The Hispanic population of the United States: March 1988*, 1988). How will the steadily-increasing Hispanic-American population affect schools? Table 5-1 shows the estimated population increases for Hispanic-American children and adolescents:

Table 5-1   Estimated Population Changes
Hispanic Children and Adolescents Numbers (000)

Age	1990	1995	2000
5-17	4,825	5,555	6,207

Based on information from U.S. Bureau of the Census. *Statistical Abstracts of the United States: 1988* (108th edition).

In 1988, 55% of all Hispanic-Americans resided in two states, Texas and California (*The Hispanic population in the United States: March 1988*, 1988). Table 5-2 shows the states with the largest populations of Hispanics in 1988:

Table 5-2   Geographic Distribution of the Hispanic Population: March 1988

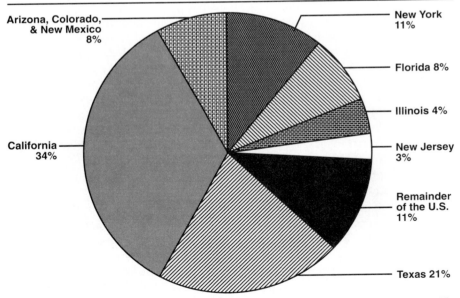

Source: U.S. Bureau of the Census, Current Population Reports, Series P-20, No. 431, *The Hispanic Population in the United States: March 1988 (Advance Report)*, U.S. Government Printing Office, Washington, DC, 1988.

Olsen (1988) describes the effects of today's unprecedented racial and ethnic diversity in California classrooms. Although referring to both Southeast Asian and Hispanic learners, Olsen reports issues affecting learners as being demographic changes, changes resulting from war, "undocumented children," the cultural changes, language and academic needs, and the problems created by coping with a strange educational system.

The Culture Quiz: Contemporary Hispanic-Americans

Directions: Match the individuals with their contributions or achievement by placing the appropriate letter before the name.

_____ 1. Eliana Schippel	a.	First person of Mexican descent to win election as mayor of a major United States city
_____ 2. Pauline Gomez	b.	Prepared report on "The Children of Mariel," which examined programs designed to cope with 15,000 non-English-speaking students
_____ 3. Isabel Schon	c.	Leading spokesman for Mexican-American farmers in the 1960s—led strike against grape growers
_____ 4. Jose Pedro Greer	d.	An illustrator with a law degree, a sense of history, and a talent for making children laugh
_____ 5. Caesar Chavez	e.	Former alcoholic who runs alcohol treatment program—La Posada—in Dallas
_____ 6. Henry G. Cisneros	f.	Born blind; founded the Nation Federation of the Blind in New Mexico
_____ 7. Juan Ramon Jimenez	g.	Reviewed recently published children's books and concluded stereotypes and misconceptions continue
_____ 8. Jose Aruego	h.	Operates free clinic in

			Miami—Camillus Health Concerns; 200 volunteers and 12 staff members
_____	9.	Lupe Anguiano	i. Responsible for creating several Hispanic women's groups
_____	10.	Helga Silva	j. Winner of 1956 Nobel Prize for Literature

Answers: 1. e 2. f 3. g 4. h 5. c 6. a 7. j 8. d 9. i 10. b

As children learn about the Hispanic culture and people, teachers can suggest developmentally appropriate children's informational books.

USING CHILDREN'S LITERATURE: Informational Books

STEIN, R. CONRAD. *Enchantment of the World: Mexico.* Children's Press, 1984. Text and a variety of colored photographs describe the geography, history, culture, and people. (Reading level: Grade 5; Interest level: Age 9 and above.)

BEHRENS, JUNE. *Fiesta.* Children's Press, 1978. This informational book describes the modern-day celebration of the Cinco de Mayo fiesta. (Reading level: Grade 4; Interest level: Ages 5-8.)

MELTZER, MILTON. *The Hispanic Americans.* Crowell Publishing, 1982. Another informational book that explores Spanish influences and the history and contributions of the Hispanic people. (Reading level: Grade 6; Interest level: Ages 9-12.)

STEREOTYPING OF HISPANIC-AMERICAN CHILDREN AND ADOLESCENTS

As with other culturally diverse learners, Hispanic-American children and adolescents may experience "double jeopardy" if educators label learners, and base teaching and learning decisions on cultural stereotypes. In essence, children and adolescents may be perceived erroneously as exhibiting undesirable behavior, while the Hispanic culture may be viewed as having tendencies toward emotional and violent behavior. Educators inflict an injustice upon learners when educational decisions are based on such stereotypes as Hispanic-American learners are not as "well-behaved" as the Asian-American learner, are not as "intelligent" as the Anglo-American, and are not as "docile or peaceful" as Native-American learner. In fact, a self-fulfilling prophecy may occur where Hispanic learners achieve and behave in accordance with the educator's stereotypes and academic/behavior expectations. What action should educators take? All school personnel should examine the validity of their cultural "baggage" seriously, and work toward an objective understanding of Hispanic-American children and adolescents. Educators have several avenues which will lead to a more enlightened picture of Hispanic-American learners: Meeting Hispanic-Americans first-hand, learning their proud and diverse history, becoming acquainted with their parents and extended families, understanding the culture's contributions, understanding their allegiance to the Spanish language, understanding what being an Hispanic-American child or adolescent is really like, and realizing the potentially disastrous consequences of basing educational programs on cultural misperceptions.

As CASE STUDY 5-1 indicates, teachers also must accept the often difficult responsibility for changing the cultural attitudes of children.

CASE STUDY 5-1: Name-calling

Nine-year-old Juan wonders what his second day at his new school will be like. He quickly recognizes that most children are either Anglo or Black. During the first classes of the day, Juan notices that no one seems to want to be his friend, but he thinks things will improve during recess. However, at recess, the other children still do not pick him when choosing teams for kickball. Finally, he hears three children laughing, and although he could not hear exactly what was said, he did hear "wetback". Juan is angered and hurt; he feels like crying, but wonders whether he should fight. The teacher sees and hears the entire episode.

Juan's teacher recognizes that such a situation has the potential for damaging Juan's self-concept and Mexican-American identity. Although she does not want to call a great deal of attention to the situation, she does want to respond appropriately. She feels that several steps are in order:

1. She will have a class discussion on name-calling, e.g., show how name-calling labels or stereotypes children, and how one can be hurt by being called derogatory names.
2. She will plan activities to involve Juan so that students can know him as an individual and learn about the contributions he can offer the class.
3. She will integrate multiculturalism into her curriculum so that all students can understand and value each others' cultural heritages.

HISPANIC-AMERICAN CHILDREN AND ADOLESCENTS

Educators who plan and implement a multicultural curriculum can benefit from knowledge, understanding, and appreciation of Hispanic learners and their culture. Steinberg, Blinde and Chan (1984) concluded that studies of Hispanic youngsters do not sufficiently differentiate among the different

Spanish-speaking ethnic groups. Differing cultures, generational and socio-economic differences, and acculturation factors exist which should be considered when understanding Hispanic-American learners. Whenever possible, specific Hispanic cultures should be addressed to avoid stereotyping and cultural misrepresentations. This section examines Spanish-speaking children and adolescents, and the cultural, socioeconomic, familial, religious, and language aspects of their lives.

Cultural Characteristics

A cultural description of Spanish-speaking peoples should include an understanding of certain values and traits (Gonzalez, 1989; Christensen, 1989).

Activities:

It is important that educators of Hispanic children and adolescents understand and appreciate important concepts of the Hispanic culture. Upon understanding these cultural characteristics, try to identify related behaviors in Hispanic learners.

"corazon"	heart
"sensibilidad"	sensitivity
"afecto"	warmth and demonstrativeness
"dignidad"	dignity
"respecto"	respect
"machismo"	biological superiority of the male

The Hispanic experience may best be seen in appropriately-written children's literature.

USING CHILDREN'S LITERATURE: Understanding the Hispanic Experience

POLITI, LEO. *The Nicest Gift*. Scribner's, 1973. Carbitos lives in the barrio of East Los Angeles with his family and his dog. (Reading Level: Grade 6; Interest level: Ages 5-8.)

BELPRE, PURA. *Santiago*. Warner Publishing, 1969. The story of a young Puerto Rican boy in New York as he shares pictures of his favorite pet. Santiago's mother and teacher help his friends appreciate the Puerto Rican experience. (Reading level: Grade 5; Interest level: Ages 5-8.)

MOHR, NICHOLASA. *Felita*. Dial Publishing, 1979. Eight-year-old Felita has lived in her Puerto Rican neighborhood in New York City for as long as she can remember. She experiences problems when she must leave her close friends and her grandmother. (Reading level: Grade 2; Interest level: Ages 9-12.)

Educators can gain considerable insight into the culture by understanding several unique characteristics. First, Hall (1981) points out that the Hispanic-American who is not a member of an elite group tends to avoid any competition or activity that will set him apart from his own group. To stand out among one's peers is to place oneself in great jeopardy, and is to be avoided at all costs.

Second, "machismo" plays a significant role in the Puerto Rican culture and significantly influences the behavior and attitudes of adolescent males during this time of identity formation. It suggests a clear-cut distinction among the sexes whereby the male can enjoy rights and privileges denied women. Used as a flattering term among Hispanic-Americans, both Hispanic-American boys and girls learn that "machismo" refers to the male's manhood, to the courage to fight, to the manly traits of honor and dignity, to keeping one's word, and to protecting one's name. On a more subtle level of analysis, "machismo" also includes dignity in personal conduct, respect for others, love for the family, and affection for children (Ruiz, 1981; Fitzpatrick, 1987). Third, many children are taught early that Anglo-Americans cannot be trusted. Mexican-Americans, for example, often teach their children to look toward Anglo-Americans with fear and hostility. Children who are taught such attitudes have difficulty believing that Anglo-American professionals have their best interests at heart (Vontress, 1976). Fourth, although acculturation is undoubtedly affecting Hispanic learners, many would not agree that the Anglo-American ideas of equality within the family, and self-advancement, are necessary to sustain the ideals of freedom, democracy, and progress (Mirandé, 1986).

In general, Mexican-American children who are group-oriented, and who change their own behavior to adapt to an interpersonal challenge rather than trying to change situations, are less assertive in expressing themselves to peers and adults, and rely on authority figures to resolve interpersonal problems (Rotheram-Borus & Phinney, 1990).

Activities:

Educators have realized for many years the advantages of knowing as much as possible about learners. However, when teaching multicultural students, it is also important that learners' cultural backgrounds be understood so as to maximize learners' opportunities to improve learning experiences and self-concepts. What can educators do to learn about Hispanic learners' cultural backgrounds?

_____ 1. Read objective literature about the Hispanic culture to learn about its historical background and its place in Spanish history.

_____ 2. Understand the Hispanic peoples' contributions,

cherished cultural traits, and how they are different and similar to the majority culture and other minority populations.

_____   3.   Learn about Hispanic families—both immediate and extended—and understand the value placed on the family.

_____   4.   Understand individual Hispanic learners, rather than reaching broad generalizations based on isolated incidents or only on having read about cultures.

_____   5.   Visit Hispanic learners in their homes to learn first-hand about students' home lives.

Readers who want a better understanding of Hispanic children and adolescents and the contributions of the Hispanic cultures may want to write the listed organizations.

FOR ADDITIONAL INFORMATION

Association of Hispanic Arts (AHA), 200 E. 87th Street, New York, NY 10028. Founded in 1975, AHA promotes the general concept of Hispanic arts, specifically dance, music, art, and theatrical performances.

Hispanic Institute for the Performing Arts (HIFPA), P. O. Box 32249, Calvert Station, Washington, DC 20007. HIFPA began in 1981, and seeks to promote a better understanding of Hispanics by conducting educational and cultural activities.

Socioeconomic Status

The increasing odds that the Hispanic-American young people will live in poverty conditions deserves recognition by educators. In fact, the overwhelming majority of all Hispanic students come from working class and lower-income homes (Valdivieso, 1986). Some reports contend that 38.7% of all Hispanic children live at the poverty level, with 71% living in homes in which the head of the household is female (Colburn and Melillo, 1987; Valero-Figueira, 1988).

Fitzpatrick (1987), referring to Puerto Rican-Americans, contends that a puzzling concern has been the continuing level of poverty. Although the second generation has improved in socioeconomic terms, poverty and its effects continue to be widespread. Two interrelated factors contribute to this cycle of poverty among Hispanic-Americans: The unemployment rate of Puerto Rican males is twice as high as the Anglo-American rate, while the number of female-headed households continues to increase.

Table 5-3 Proportion of Families with Income Below the Poverty Level: 1981 to 1987

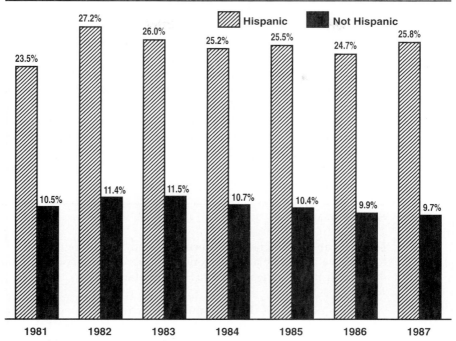

Source: U.S. Bureau of the Census, Current Population Reports, Series P-20, No. 431, *The Hispanic Population in the United States: March 1988 (Advance Report)*, U.S. Government Printing Office, Washington, DC, 1988.

Are there indications that the socioeconomic status of Hispanic-American children and adolescents will improve? One could provide an affirmative answer to this question if Hispanics improve their educational levels and improve the English skills which will allow them to venture from Spanish-speaking communities into mainstream United States society. Although educators should recognize (and respond appropriately to) the effects poverty often has on academic achievement, it would also be a serious mistake to categorize all lower socioeconomic Hispanics into an unmotivated or unachieving academic groups.

FOR ADDITIONAL INFORMATION

The Hispanic Policy Development Project, Suite 310, 1001 Connecticut Avenue NW, Washington, DC 20036. This organization examines the problems of Hispanic youth living in the United States today and suggests public and private strategies for helping these youth.

Families

Family lifestyles and activities in the Hispanic-American culture contribute greatly to the developing child and adolescent, and also act as socializing agents to inculcate the child into the culture. A basic feature of the Hispanic-American family is the "extended family", which plays a major role in each family member's life. These are families in which there are strong bonds and frequent interaction among a wide range of kin. Grandparents, parents, and children may live in the same household, or nearby in separate households, and will visit frequently. A second feature is the emphasis on cooperativeness, and on placing the needs of the family ahead of individual concerns. This has led to the erroneous conclusion that the family impedes individual achievement and advancement. Observers of the Hispanic-American culture are responsible for distinguishing between being cooperative and respectful, and being docile and dependent (Mirandé, 1986).

Activities:

Learning about the Hispanic learner's family might be one of the best ways to improve academic achievement and improve self-concept. Educators can do several things to learn about Hispanic families:

_____ 1. Invite families to school on special occasions just to visit. While the family learns about the school and its policies and expectations, teachers can become acquainted with these families.

_____ 2. Request that students write a story or essay on their families. Be sure to emphasize including parents, grandparents, brothers and sisters, cousins, and other relatives living in the home. Keep an open mind, and remember the importance of the extended family. Tell students prior to writing the story whether or not their stories or essays will be shared with the class.

_____ 3. Educators who teach in heavily-populated Hispanic areas may want to schedule a day for just Hispanic families to visit. Have individual meetings to determine how the family influences school achievement and attitudes toward school. (If possible, speak Spanish to families with limited English-speaking skills.)

_____ 4. Schedule individual meetings with Hispanic students to discuss their families, but be careful that students understand the purpose of these discussions. Allow and respect learner's privacy.

Latino-American children learn early the importance of (1) a deep sense of family responsibility; (2) sex roles being rigidly defined; (3) the elderly being treated with respect and reverence; and (4) the male's position of respect and authority in the family. Although some of the male's authority appears to be relaxing as the woman's role is redefined, women in the Hispanic-American culture continue to occupy a subordinate position. Fathers have prestige and authority, while sons have more and earlier independence than daughters (Lum, 1986).

FOR ADDITIONAL INFORMATION

Puerto Rican Family Institute (PRFI), 116 W. 14th Street, New York, NY 10011. This organization was established in 1960 for the preservation of the health, well-being, and integrity of Puerto Ricans and other Hispanic families in the United States.

Chicano Family Center (CFC), 7145 Avenue H, Houston, TX 77011. CFC, founded in 1971, seeks to enhance understanding and appreciation of the Chicano culture.

The Latino and Chicano families also value the extended family structure and interaction in their daily life. The value placed on adults other than the immediate parents is evidenced by parents often arranging for godparents or "companion parents" for the child. These "parents" also have a right to give advice and correction, and are expected to be responsive to the child's needs (Fitzpatrick, 1987). IMPLEMENTING RESEARCH 5-1 examines the importance of taking advantage of the close Hispanic family relationships by involving parents in their children's learning.

IMPLEMENTING RESEARCH 5-1: Hispanic Parents' Role in Word Recognition Skills

Goldenberg investigated the role Hispanic parents played in nine first-grade children's acquisition of word-recognition skills. This report is part of a larger ethnographic study of home and school influences on the reading achievement of at-risk, low income, Hispanic first graders. Goldenberg's (1987) research suggests that Hispanic parents' involvement in their children's education may be helpful in ameliorating the chronic school failure among large segments of the United States Hispanic population. (p. 149)

IMPLEMENTING THE RESEARCH:

_____ 1. Rather than educators presupposing that lower-class parents neglect their children's education, attempts should include enlisting the aid of parents.

_____ 2. Educators should encourage parents to read to children, with the child seated alongside, following as the parent reads.

_____ 3. Educators should explore other ways of involving minority parents in children's school achievement.

Source: Goldenberg, C.N. (1987). "Low-income Hispanic parents' contributions to their first-grade children's word-recognition skills." *Anthropology & Education Quarterly, 18,* 149-179.

Religion

Even after considering the diversity of the Spanish-speaking people, one can safely conclude that religion plays a central role in their lives. Although the section explores the role of religion in the Puerto Rican-American culture, many generalizations can be reached that cross other Hispanic boundaries.

The Spanish colonial experience brought about a distinct culture penetrated by the Catholic faith. Catholicism was originally Spanish in the United States. The first Mass on what is now American soil was celebrated at Saint Augustine, Florida, in 1565. Spanish missionaries were active in the Southwest as early as 1539, and California missions were being founded between 1770 and 1782 (Fitzpatrick, 1987).

Fitzpatrick (1987) also believes that Hispanics make up 40% of the present Catholic membership. Numbers from *The Gallup Report* substantiate the belief that Hispanics predominantly adhere to the Catholic faith: Protestant (18%); Catholic (70%); others and those not claiming a religious preference (12%) (*Religion in America*, 1985). Fitzpatrick (1987) writes " . . . within the parishes of Puerto Ricans in New York City there is a spirit, a vitality, a sense that brings a new life to the church" (p. 138).

Language

There are many varieties of Spanish spoken among the Hispanic people in the United States. These varieties depend on where the speakers live, how long they have lived in this country, and where they came from originally. Spanish in the Southwest is different from Spanish in the Midwest, the Northeast, and Florida. Even in New York City, there are important cultural and linguistic differences between speakers from Puerto Rico, Cuba, the Dominican Republic, Colombia, Ecuador, Peru, Mexico, Venezuela, Bolivia, and other South American areas (Tiedt & Tiedt, 1986).

Children who feel pressure to speak Spanish at home and English at school may develop problems in both languages, and may become bilingual, or avoid English-speaking situations. Such a situation can result in dual cultural identification, additional language conflicts, and chronic anxiety (Padilla, 1981). Successes, failures, and problems encountered while developing language proficiency significantly influence the child's self-concept and developing identity.

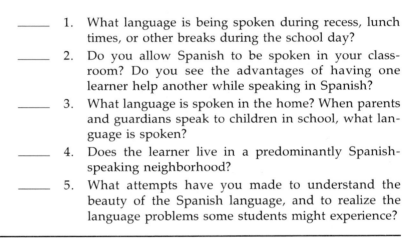

Activities:

Educators often assume that everyone speaks English at school and at home. With the increasing Spanish-speaking populations, it is becoming easier for Hispanic people to live in sections in which Spanish continues to be the mother tongue. Educators who teach children and adolescents from Hispanic backgrounds can take several steps to understand the extent to which learners continue to speak Spanish:

_____ 1. What language is being spoken during recess, lunch times, or other breaks during the school day?

_____ 2. Do you allow Spanish to be spoken in your classroom? Do you see the advantages of having one learner help another while speaking in Spanish?

_____ 3. What language is spoken in the home? When parents and guardians speak to children in school, what language is spoken?

_____ 4. Does the learner live in a predominantly Spanish-speaking neighborhood?

_____ 5. What attempts have you made to understand the beauty of the Spanish language, and to realize the language problems some students might experience?

Some Hispanic-American learners' language poses a problem outside the immediate neighborhood, because they tend to retain the native tongue rather than making a cultural transition to English. Instead of making an attempt to learn English, many do not perceive a need to develop proficiency in English, and continue to risk survival in a bilingual world. Language difficulties experienced by learners may have a major impact on self-concept and the developing identity.

USING CHILDREN'S LITERATURE: Learners With Language Problems

LEWITON, MINA. *Candita's Choice*. Harper & Row, 1959. Candita, a Puerto Rican girl, refuses to speak at all until she can speak well enough to make her teacher proud.
BOUCHARD, LOIS. *The Boy Who Wouldn't Talk*. Doubleday, 1969. Carlos' family moves from Puerto Rico to New York City, and he experiences so many language problems that he decides not to speak English or Spanish.

Nonverbal language, as in other cultures, also plays a major factor in the Hispanic-American culture, and must be recognized and understood by professionals of other cultures. Although a complete list of nonverbal behaviors is impossible, and would deny individual and intracultural differences, several examples will serve to indicate their significance. Many Hispanic-Americans stand closer together while communicating, touch to communicate, and often avoid eye contact. Other examples may include behaviors unique to boys and girls, e.g., boys' assertion of "potential manhood" and the girls' tendency toward a retiring and reserved attitude (Padilla, 1981).

CULTURAL COMPARISON

Hispanic-American and Anglo-American
Children and Adolescents

Hispanic-American	*Anglo-American*
Does not want to be set apart from group as being different or excelling	Competitive—wants recognition for skills and abilities
Distrust toward Anglo-American professionals	Trust toward Anglo-American professionals
Bilingual—Strong commitment to Spanish as native language	Monolingual—English to be language of "worth"
Stand closer, touch, avoid eye contact	Respect distance, avoid touch, look in the eye
Respects extended family/"kinship networks" and companions' parents	Loyalty to immediate family
"Personalismo"—preference for contact and individualized attention	Favor a more organizational approach following impersonal approach
Male biologically superior; clear-cut distinction among sexes	Equality among males and females
Tendency toward lower academic achievement	Tendency toward higher academic achievement
Strong commitment to dignidad, machismo, and respeto	Do not share these cultural characteristics

Sources: Mirandé 1986; Fitzpatrick, 1987; Christensen, 1989

HISPANIC-AMERICAN LEARNERS IN THE SCHOOL

Upon reaching an understanding of the social and cultural characteristics of Hispanic-American children and adolescents, educators can proceed with understanding the "learner" in the Hispanic culture. Santiestevan (1986) maintained that "Nationwide, United States Hispanics agree that the single most crucial problem they face today is education" (p. 396). This section considers Hispanic-American learners, and looks for answers to several questions related to their educational progress: What special school-related problems do Hispanic learners experience? Are Hispanic learners penalized by Anglo expectations and stereotypes? Are Hispanic learners labeled? How do learning styles of Hispanics differ? What school practices might impede Hispanics' progress? As these and other questions are explored, readers are reminded that intracultural, generational, and socioeconomic differences require that individual learners be considered when reaching educational decisions.

Educators' Understanding Hispanic-American Learners and Their Culture

Prior to educators' planning appropriate educational experiences for Hispanic learners, there must be an understanding of Hispanic learners, their unique cultural characteristics, and their school-related problems. First, the aforementioned aspects such as culture, socioeconomic status, language, and religion must be respected, and their influence on school achievement understood. However, there exists yet another dimension which has only recently been recognized. In her essay on Hispanic children, Valero-Figueira (1988) wrote:

> . . . there is among Hispanic and other linguistically and culturally different groups a new and not-so-young population that must be considered. They are the immigrant children from countries of war, who come to the United States and are expected to attend school and learn the language and subject matter just as any other child would. Many of these children are not performing well in school . . . where a different language is spoken and things are done in a way that is foreign to them. (p. 48)

Prior to getting to know the strengths and weaknesses of learners, teachers and other school personnel need to know the individual.

Activities:

_____ 1. Meet the learner's family—both immediate and extended, if possible.

_____ 2. Give an "interest inventory" to determine the areas where learners might be the most motivated.

_____ 3. Administer appropriate diagnostic instruments to determine the learner's strengths and weaknesses. Be sure instruments are designed to take into account Hispanic learning styles.

_____ 4. Talk with the child or adolescent to learn more about the Hispanic culture, the family, areas of interest or confusion, fears, expectations, and any other factors that would help in planning culturally and developmentally appropriate instruction.

_____ 5. Seek the advice and input of other professionals in the school (speech correctionists, guidance counselors, and remedial, resource, and gifted teachers) who have knowledge of the Hispanic learner.

Developmental Theory: Children and Adolescents

It is imperative that children and adolescents be understood as developing individuals with unique interests and characteristics. Rather than being a developmentally homogeneous group, children and adolescents develop at differing rates that vary according to heredity and environmental/cultural factors. However, Erikson and Havighurst have identifed several psychosocial crises and developmental tasks that all children and adolescents must successfully meet. For example, Erikson (1963) suggested that children demonstrate eagerness and diligence to achieve a sense of industriousness; learn significantly from older children; and may experience feelings of despair and inadequacy if they can not identify with peers. Havighurst (1972) suggested that learners must complete developmental tasks such as learning physical skills necessary for ordinary games, learning appropriate sex roles, and achieving personal independence. It is also important to understand that development in all cultures might not correspond to these developmental theories. As has been stated repeatedly, both the culture and learners in the culture deserve consideration when planning educational programs.

IMPLEMENTING RESEARCH 5-2 examines the social expectations of African- and Mexican-American children, and shows how educators might respond appropriately.

IMPLEMENTING RESEARCH 5-2: Social Expectations of African- and Mexican-American Children

Rotheram-Borus and Phinney (1990) asked 213 African- and Mexican-American third and sixth graders to respond to 8 videotaped scenes of everyday social encounters with same-ethnic, unfamiliar peers at school. The goal of the study was to examine the effects of enculturation and acculturation on the social expectations of African- and Mexican-American children, and to examine the self-esteem of the two groups. Their findings demonstrated clear ethnic differences in the social expectations between African- and Mexican-American school children. Specific results included:

_____ 1. Mexican-American school children were more group-oriented and more reliant on authority figures for solving problems.

_____ 2. African-American school children were more action-
oriented and expressive;

_____ 3. African-American children responded with more
emotional expressiveness and had more active coping
strategies than their Mexican-American counterparts.

_____ 4. Both African- and Mexican-American children de-
ferred to authority.

While African-American children were reported as apologizing more frequently than Mexican-American children, Mexican-American children were
more likely to feel bad, a different way of responding to authority.

IMPLEMENTING THE RESEARCH:

_____ 1. Educators should recognize that learners' cultural
differences affect how they will respond in social
situations.

_____ 2. Educators should provide social experiences, i.e.,
cooperative learning or cross-age tutoring that recognizes and reflects learner's cultural backgrounds.

_____ 3. Educators should recognize that, due to acculturation,
one cannot assume that all learners of a particular
culture react in a similar manner.

Source: Rotheram-Borus, M. J., & Phinney, J. S. (1990). "Patterns of social expectations
among Black and Mexican-American children." *Child Development, 61,* 542-556.

Achievement Levels

The news media raised several issues concerning the level of educational
achievement of Hispanic-American students, e.g., the relatively low number
of Hispanic-American students eligible for college—in some cases, at least
45% between the 10th and 12th grades, with as many as 40% leaving school
before the 10th grade. By the senior year, only 31% of Hispanic-American
high school students are enrolled in college preparatory courses. Of the Hispanic students graduating from high school, only about 10-15% are academically qualified to enter state universities in California (*Closing the educational
gap for Hispanics:* . . . 1987). Hispanic-Americans' academic achievement
has been described as:

> Hispanic students score lower than do their white, middle-class counterparts
> on tests of academic achievement. They are more likely to fail one or more
> grades in school, be placed in special education, and drop out altogether. Atti-
> tudes toward school are negative, with Hispanic students reporting a higher
> degree of alienation and disenchantment with school and school personnel
> (Goldenberg, 1987, p. 149).

Teachers should not let stereotypes and erroneous conclusions interfere with their academic and behavior expectations of Hispanic learners.

CASE STUDY 5-2 underscores the necessity of perceiving Hispanic-American learners objectively, and as individuals.

CASE STUDY 5-2: Basing School Expecations on Long-Held Beliefs

"Hispanic students always experience learning problems in American schools," Mrs. Miller was saying in the teachers' workroom. "They have so many problems—language, poverty, and those big families! What more can you expect? It has always been that way."

One of the professionals in the workroom should explain to Mrs. Miller the danger and futility of such statements. Expecting poor academic achievement as a result of language problems and poverty situations may set the stage for students' failure. Without doubt, Mrs. Miller needs a better understanding of Hispanic cultural heritages, more recognition of the differences within the Hispanic culture, and more objectivity with regard to Hispanic students. Mrs. Miller should also understand intracultural differences among the many Hispanic cultures, and individual differences resulting from generational factors, geographic origins, and socioeconomic factors.

In general, Mrs. Miller continues to perpetuate an Anglo-oriented school in an increasing multicultural society. Though unfortunate, far more serious consequences exist for culturally different learners, in this case, the Hispanic-American learners in the school.

Activities:

It is time for school systems to do their part to enhance the Hispanic learner's academic record by:

_____ 1. Considering the Hispanic learner objectively, and by avoiding labels;

_____ 2. developing a more individualized instructional program that recognizes Hispanic learning styles;

_____ 3. implementing a curriculum that recognizes, respects, and builds upon Hispanic learners' cultural diversity;

_____ 4. involving parents by explaining the role and purposes of schooling, and by showing what they can do to help the child in school.

Language Problems

Undoubtedly, many of the problems Hispanic-American learners experience stem from their difficulties with the English language. Hearing the Spanish language at home, yet being required to communicate in English at school, often results in academic and behavioral problems, lower self-concepts and cultural identities, and a general pessimism toward teachers and schools, and also affects their ability to perform in American schools.

Activities:

Names and their meanings are special to learners of all cultures and ages. Teachers, other school personnel, and students should understand the special meaning and value the Hispanic cultures place on names.

Soledad	(solitude)	Dolores	(sorrows)
Concepcion	(conception)	Mercedes	(mercies)
Salvador	(savior)	Jesus	(Jesus)

Source: Tiedt, P.L., & Tiedt, I.M. (1990). *Multicultural teaching: A handbook of activities, information, and resources.* Boston, MA: Allyn and Bacon.

Olsen (1988) reports that 9% of the children in California with limited English proficiency are not receiving native-language support, nor are they involved in any English language program. Olsen (1988) continues with the story of Socorro:

> I just sat in my classes and didn't understand anything . . . Sometimes I would try to look like I knew what was going on; sometimes I would just try to think about a happy time when I didn't feel stupid. My teachers never called on me or talked to me. I think they either forgot I was there or else wished I wasn't. I waited and waited, thinking someday I will know English. (p. 216)

CASE STUDY 5-3 shows the importance of being understood and what Mr. Donaldson did to help Maria.

CASE STUDY 5-3: The Importance of Understanding and Being Understood

Mr. Donaldson, an elementary school teacher, had a fourth grade child whose lack of proficiency in English left her virtually unable to learn. Rather than being a meaningful learning experience, the school day became a time of boredom and frustration. Devastating consequences awaited Maria (and other, similar, culturally diverse learners) who felt "stupid", or who felt that teachers forgot she were there or else wished she were not. Even though language proficiency takes time and effort, Maria needed to feel that teachers and other school personnel cared and wanted to help her. Mr. Donaldson decided to take several steps to help Maria have meaningful school experiences:

1. Request that the bilingual (or other) language specialist meet with Maria to determine an immediate plan of action.

2. Arrange for a professional, perhaps an aide, to work closely with Maria to show a sense of caring and concern.
3. Call on or talk to Maria about anything: School, the Hispanic culture, or activities on the playground.
4. Administer an "interest inventory" to learn about Maria's interests, likes, and dislikes, then plan instruction and communication accordingly.

Activities:

Educators can help second-language learners through bilingual programs, ESL programs, English remediation classes, and instruction in Spanish for at least part of the day. Other suggestions include:

_____ 1. Read aloud to students
_____ 2. Respect students' efforts
_____ 3. Provide opportunities for oral communication
_____ 4. Provide opportunities for students to speak and write
_____ 5. Use a variety of methods and materials—small-group speaking situations, tapes, choral speaking, and records
_____ 6. Respect the student's native language

See also: IMPLEMENTING RESEARCH 5-3 on the Integral Education Model.

In the Southwestern United States, many Hispanic-American people live in Spanish-speaking communities isolated from the English-speaking community. In fact, children often enter the English-speaking world for the first time when they begin their public school education. Then, to make matters worse, these children are often threatened in school environments with punishment for speaking Spanish (Vontress, 1976).

IMPLEMENTING RESEARCH 5-3 provides a brief discussion of a language model for Hispanic learners.

IMPLEMENTING RESEARCH 5-3: A Language Program for Teaching Hispanics

Hall and Reck (1987) examine the language program for the Hispanic child in the Catholic school. The authors focus attention on the achievement record of Hispanic students, the Bilingual Education Act of 1965, the purposes of bilingual education, and the Integral Education Model. The model implements an academic program that includes the culture and values of the

Hispanic people, and is closely related to the expression of the Catholic faith. The model assumes that Spanish-speaking students need help with beginning formal education in an English-speaking country, and recognizes that, although the primary focus should be in English, Spanish should also be allowed in social school situations, and encouraged at home.

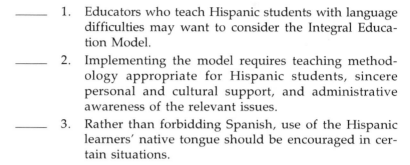

IMPLEMENTING THE RESEARCH:

_____ 1. Educators who teach Hispanic students with language difficulties may want to consider the Integral Education Model.

_____ 2. Implementing the model requires teaching methodology appropriate for Hispanic students, sincere personal and cultural support, and administrative awareness of the relevant issues.

_____ 3. Rather than forbidding Spanish, use of the Hispanic learners' native tongue should be encouraged in certain situations.

Hall, S., & Reck, C. (1987). "What about the language program in teaching Hispanics?" *Momentum, 18,* 52-55.

Learning Styles: Cultural Considerations

As mentioned in the previous chapters on culturally diverse children and adolescents, educators can determine learning styles by observing the learner's overt behavior (Keefe, 1987). What cultural or sociological elements should educators consider in the Hispanic-American learner? Learners can provide clues while demonstrating any number of behaviors. Some learners work and achieve when left alone; distractions such as others' presence, movements or sounds create disturbances. Other children learn best when among peers working on case studies, small-group activities, or team learnings (Dunn & Dunn, 1979).

Activity:

Hispanic students' better understanding of their learning style can be an excellent means of improving their learning performance. As learners better understand how they learn, perceptive educators can also gain insight into how learning experieces should be planned and implemented. Learners can ask themselves several questions:

_____ 1. Do you prefer to (a) think through a learning experience to reach a conclusion, or (b) be told the conclusion and then think out how the conclusion was reached?

_____ 2. Do you think your most effective learning experiences are in the morning, the afternoon, or at night?

_____ 3. Do you prefer a quiet learning environment, or can you learn better when there is background noise?

_____ 4. Do you prefer teaching/learning experiences that require you to see, listen, or feel?

_____ 5. Do you prefer to study and learn alone, or with a friend?

These represent only a few determinants of learning styles. FOR ADDITIONAL INFORMATION provides readers with sources for learning more about learning styles.

FOR ADDITIONAL INFORMATION

Learning styles, especially with multicultural learners, have considerable potential for teachers and learners. The following resources are recommended for teachers who wish to match teaching and learning activities with the students' learning styles:

DUNN, R., BEAUDRY, J.S., & KLAVAS, A. (1989). "Survey of research on learning styles." _Educational Leadership, 46(6)_, 50-58. In this theme issue dealing with diversity, Dunn, Beaudry, and Klavas comprehensively survey the research on learning styles.
KEEFE, J.W. (1987). _Learning Style: Theory and Practice_. Reston, VA: National Association of Secondary School Principals. This succinct 48-page monograph provides an overview of learning styles, and focuses on assessment and application.
Theory Into Practice, 23, (Winter, 1984). This entire issue deals with learning styles, and provides 12 excellent readings which range from the theoretical to practical application.

Determining the most appropriate learning styles for Hispanic-Americans requires that educators, whether regular classroom teachers or remedial/resource teachers, observe both individual and cultural differences that may affect learning styles. Although the previously-mentioned aspects focus on the "individual", effective multicultural educators should look at specific Hispanic cultural characteristics to determine their potential effects on learning. CASE STUDY 5-4 looks at several cultural characteristics that may affect learning styles. As with other chapters on cultural diversity among learners, educators are urged to use caution in considering both the culture and also the "individual within the culture".

CASE STUDY 5-4: Cultural Characteristics and Learning

Mr. Smith, an Anglo teacher in his fourth year of teaching, received his class roll for the upcoming school year, and learned that nearly half his class was Hispanic. Although he had some background in providing educational experiences in multicultural situations, he was unsure how to relate Hispanic cultural characteristics to learners' teaching/learning experiences. Mr. Smith met with colleagues to discuss the challenge and received the following suggestions:

Cultural Characteristic	*Implications For Learning*
Does not want to be set apart as excelling	Provide opportunities for group work so group will excel, not individual
"Personalism"—wanting personal contact	Learner needs opportunities to have first-hand contact with teacher and others in school
"Machismo"—biological superiority of the male	Sexes may feel uncomfortable working with each other; may feel that the male must lead and reach decisions

While these characteristics and implications are only representative, Mr. Smith saw that learning could and should be based on the cultural characteristics of learners.

School Practices Impeding Hispanic-Americans' Progress

Is it possible that well-meaning teachers, either Anglo or of another culture, actually encourage school practices that may prove detrimental to Hispanic students? A look at many American schools causes one to answer in the affirmative.

The already somewhat-overwhelmed Hispanic child or adolescent may be even more startled at the verbal emphasis in America's schools. Elkind (1972) wrote:

> What impresses me about American education, at all levels, is its extreme verbalism. (p. 10-11)

Although Elkind was speaking of English-speaking students, even more profound consequences await learners with limited English-language skills.

A second, related, practice occurs when well-meaning teachers forbid and actually punish Hispanic students for speaking Spanish. Understanding such a situation proves difficult for learners who are proficient in Spanish, but who are experiencing considerable difficulty with their second language.

A third practice involves an entanglement of values and cultural orientations. Believing in the American cultural tradition of excelling among one's peers, teachers often motivate learners by encouraging Hispanic learners to excel above others in the class. Causing oneself to stand out among one's peers goes against Hispanic cultural traditions and expectations.

Activities:

_____ 1. Is there genuine respect for the Hispanic learners and their culture?

_____ 2. Are there efforts to understand the cultural assets and contributions of Hispanic learners?

_____ 3. Are Hispanic people being employed by the school, and in what positions? Are Hispanics serving on committees and in decision-making capacities?

_____ 4. Are there efforts to teach cultural understanding and acceptance?

_____ 5. Are learners provided with chances to feel that their culture and individuality are appreciated?

_____ 6. Are there policies (either overt or covert) that limit opportunities to participate, e.g., extra-curricular activities?

_____ 7. Are there efforts to diagnose and remediate specific learning problems of Hispanic learners?

Another problem results when teachers from Anglo and other cultural groups have stereotypical beliefs of Hispanic learners. How many educators believe that Hispanic learners are slow, violent, prone to emotional, erratic behavior, and generally speaking, unable to perform academically in American schools? So (1987) believed that Anglo-American teachers harbored biases against Hispanic-American students. In his research, So concluded that Anglo-American teachers assigned a "good" or "bad" label to students, and then gave different treatment to some students. The students began to accept the teacher's label, and responded appropriately. Such practices can also affect students' motivation and academic achievement.

Labeling, repeatedly mentioned in this text as being a dangerous educational practice, is examined in IMPLEMENTING RESEARCH 5-4.

IMPLEMENTING RESEARCH 5-4: Are Hispanic Students Labeled?

So (1987) designed a study to determine if Hispanic students were being labeled and, if so, the consequences. Questions studied included:

_____ 1. Do Hispanic-American teachers make better teachers for Hispanic-American students?

_____ 2. What is the impact of labeling on those students who have received "good" labels?

_____ 3. Would Hispanic- and Anglo-American teachers treat "good" Hispanic-American students the same way as they treat "good" Anglo-American students?

So concluded that:

_____ 1. Anglo-American teachers gave more positive treatment to Anglo-Americans than to Hispanic-American learners;

_____ 2. Hispanic-American students received more positive treatment from Hispanic-American teachers than they received from Anglo-American teachers;

_____ 3. Once the label of "going to college" was assigned to a Hispanic-American student, then Anglo-American teachers treated this student the same way as they treated other college-bound Anglo-American students.

IMPLEMENTING THE RESEARCH:

_____ 1. Educators must treat all learners equally, and base academic and behavioral expectations on objective and unbiased opinions free from prejudice and stereotypes.

_____ 2. Schools need to recruit more Hispanic teachers who understand both the Hispanic- and Anglo-American cultures.

_____ 3. Anglo teachers need to recognize and understand the harmful consequences of labeling.

So, A. Y. (1987). "Hispanic teachers and the labeling of Hispanic students." _The High School Journal, 71,_ 5-8.

Promoting Positive Self-Concepts and Cultural Identities

The educator's role in promoting positive self-concepts and cultural identities among learners will always be of paramount importance. Purkey and Novak (1984) have clearly demonstrated the relationship between self-concept and school achievement. Emphatically stated, a student who feels "worthless", "not-so-good", and "inferior" will experience academic difficulties in spite of the teacher's most conscientious efforts. Drill, memorization, and worksheets cannot overcome learners' feeling that they (or their culture) are inferior. Although the problems associated with speaking one's mother tongue in a predominantly English-speaking environment deserves consideration, allowing (or even encouraging) Hispanic children to read appropriate children's literature written in Spanish might enhance their self-concepts and cultural identities.

USING CHILDREN'S LITERATURE: Books Written in Spanish

De la VARA, ARMINDA. *El Tornviaje*. (The Return Trip). Organizacion Editorial Novaro, 1982.
Eleven-year-old Andresito manages to join his uncle on an expedition to the Philippines.
NERSEYS, FELIPE. *Cuentos de Guane*. (Stories from Guane). Casa de la Americans, 1976. In smalltown life in the Cuban countryside, the 90-year-old grandfather, the grandmother with long white braids, the 14 aunts and uncles, and their family episodes bring smiles and laughter.
Al Onto Lado de la Peurta. (On the Other Side of the Door). Organizacion Editorial Novaro, 1982. A wealthy 18th-century girl discovers that life in the streets and the mines of the poor lacks the comfort and security of her home.
ROXLO, CONRADO NALÉ. *La Esculela de las Hadas*. (A School for Fairies). Editorial Universitaria, 1963. This wonderful fantasy is about a young school girl who is admitted to a very special school for fairies.
WALSH, MARIÁ ELENA. *Dailan Kifki*. (Dailan Kifki). Sudamericana, 1977. Walsh takes her readers on an uninterrupted series of adventures with an abandoned elephant named Dailan Kifki.

Source: Ada, A. F. (1987). "Hispanic American classic and best loved books for children." *Journal of Reading, 30,* 195-202.

Specifically, what can educators do to promote positive feelings of self-worth and cultural identity? First, all efforts should be genuinely and honestly undertaken; learners will detect hypocrisy if teachers say one thing yet demonstrate contrary actions. Second, programs can be planned that teach about the Hispanic culture, and the proud history and accomplishments of the Spanish-speaking people. Third, rather than having "Spanish Art, Music, and Foods Week", a curriculum must be developed that shows an appreciation for cultural diversity, and which fully incorporates the Hispanic culture into all areas of the school curriculum. Last, educators can use bibliotherapy and any other method or activity that improves learner self-concept, enhances cultural identities, and increases the appreciation of cultural differences.

Activities:

One way to improve Hispanic-American learners' self-concept might be to take advantage of their strong sense of family. Learning of one's family can reveal proud contributions and accomplishments. Activities may include:

My Name—   Discuss names, how names were chosen, what names mean, and how one feels about the name.

Choosing Names—Ask children how they got their names—after a relative or more than one relative?

Surnames—	What are they? Where do they come from? Discuss the origins of Castaneda, Chavez, Feliciano, and Vasquez.
Family Roots—	Students can ask their families about family history and write information on a chart

	Name	*Birthplace*	*Date*
Mother			
Father			
Brothers			
Sisters			

Family Tree—	Children can construct a family tree using the information collected under "Family Roots".

Learning more about one's self and family has the potential for allowing learners to see the "uniqueness" or "special qualities" of all people and families.

Source: Tiedt, P.L., & Tiedt, I.M. (1990). *Multicultural Teaching* (3rd ed.). Boston, MA: Allyn and Bacon.

CULTURAL PORTRAIT: Carlos—An Hispanic-American Learner

Carlos S., a twelve-year-old boy of Spanish origin, is one grade level behind in his public elementary school, which is composed predominantly of Black- and Hispanic-American children. A small percentage of Anglo students attend Carlos' school; while the majority of the teachers are Anglo, a few are Black, and one is Hispanic. Carlos lives in a lower-socioeconomic, Spanish-speaking neighborhood near the school. Carlos has several problems: His family speaks Spanish at home, but he is forbidden to speak Spanish at school; his difficulty with the English language has resulted in lower reading grades and achievement test scores (thus, the grade level behind); and he sees older boys dropping out of school and wonders when he can end his frustrations with school. Carlos admits his frustrations to his best friend, another Hispanic-American boy: Why does the teacher keep asking him to excel? Why does she say ignore Blacks and Anglos when they pick on Hispanic children? Why doesn't she allow him to speak Spanish when his family (including his grandparents, aunts and uncles, and cousins) continues to speak Spanish? Carlos knows he has problems, and he thinks his teachers have almost given up on him.

What Carlos' Teacher Can Do

Carlos' situation calls for immediate attention. First, whenever possible, Carlos needs to be allowed to speak Spanish. This is the language in which he is most proficient, and he cannot understand the reason for not being allowed to speak a language that both his family and his friends speak. Second, Carlos needs English-language instruction from qualified professionals who understand second-language instruction, and who understand the problems Hispanic learners face. Third, Carlos needs appropriate diagnostic testing to determine his strengths and weaknesses, and carefully-planned remediation to address his weaknesses.

Equally important is that the teachers in Carlos' school understand the Hispanic culture and situations of students like Carlos. Additionally, since the cultural diversity of the school population is not reflected in the teaching staff, the curriculum and learning environment probably reflects an Anglo perspective. More effort should be directed toward making Carlos' school more multicultural in nature, and in this case, more understanding and accepting of Hispanic-American learners.

SUMMING UP

Educators who plan teaching/learning experiences for Hispanic-American children and adolescents should:

1. Provide an educational environment in which Hispanic-American children and adolescents feel that educators, and other significant adults and peers, respect their Spanish culture and background.

2. Allow Spanish to be spoken in schools, since it is the language spoken at home and in the neighborhoods, although learners should be taught to speak English.

3. Understand that language problems and differences should be considered as partly responsible for most academic problems.

4. Consider differences in learning styles when planning and implementing education programs.

5. Promote positive feelings toward learners' self and their culture since learners' self-concepts and cultural identities influence school achievement and social development.

6. Understand and appreciate cultural diversity to the degree that Hispanic learners do not feel their culture, socioeconomic class, families, religion, and language are wrong or inferior.

7. Use utmost caution not to label Hispanic learners on a basis of myth, stereotypes, prejudices, racism, or any other form of discrimination.

8. Use test data carefully, and remember that achievement tests, in-

telligence tests, and other measurement instruments might be culturally biased toward Anglo standards and cultural expectations.

SUGGESTED LEARNING ACTIVITIES

1. Survey a group of Puerto Rican-American and Mexican-American children to compare cultural, language, religious, and familial differences. What similarities and dissimilarities exist? Suggest ways educators can address intracultural differences within varying Spanish-speaking cultures.

2. Choose a typical Spanish-speaking student (any of the Spanish-speaking cultures) and write a case study that explores individual and cultural characteristics. Consult with the school guidance counselor to better understand the child and his or her culture. After listing specific individual and cultural characteristics, plan an educational program that will meet the needs of this individual child.

3. Observe the overt learning behaviors of an Hispanic child to determine his or her learning style. Consult with a remedial or resource teacher for help in interpreting the behaviors. After specifically determining the child's learning styles, tell how educators can plan appropriate learning opportunities based on these styles.

4. Choose a lower-achieving Hispanic-American student and assess his or her language proficiency. To what extent is the student's lower academic achievement a product of poor English skills? Interview the student to determine whether his or her immediate and extended families speak Spanish or English. In what ways can the school's speech correctionist (working with language development specialists) assist with this child? Last, plan an instructional program which addresses the student's problems with language and academic achievement.

Expanding Your Horizons: Additional Journal Readings and Books

FITZPATRICK, J. P. (1987). *Puerto-Rican Americans* (2nd ed.). Englewood Cliffs, NJ: Prentice-Hall. Fitzpatrick examines the Puerto Rican-American's community, family, schools, and such problems as poverty, welfare, and drug abuse.

MOLL, L. C. (1988). "Some key issues in teaching Latino students." *Language Arts, 65,* 465-472. Moll documents the persistent, high rate of educational failure among Latino students, and then discusses two fifth grade teachers and their attempts to organize instruction for these students.

VALDIVIESO, R. (1986). "Hispanics and schools: A new perspective." *Educational Horizons, 64,* 190-197. Valdivieso, offering a new perspective, contends the Hispanic-American's problems with academic achievement are complex in nature, and do not result solely from bilingual programs.

VALERO-FIGUEIRA, E. (1988). "Hispanic children." *Teaching Exceptional Children, 20(4),* 47-49.

This excellent article examines the growing Hispanic population, the problem with poverty, and several educational outreach techniques to identify and assist Hispanic learners.

WALSH, C. (1987). "Language, meaning, and voice: Puerto Rican students' struggle for a speaking consciousness." *Language Arts, 64,* 196-206. Walsh examines the competing tensions of school and community languages for Puerto Rican learners and the meanings behind their use of words. The author also examines communicative strategies students develop to deal with this situation.

Expanding Your Students' Horizons: Appropriate Hispanic Children's Books

BELPRE, PURA. *Once in Puerto Rico.* Warner, 1973.
BELPRE, PURA. *Santiago.* Warner, 1978.
BOUCHARD, LOIS. *The Boy Who Wouldn't Talk.* Doubleday, 1967.
BROWN, TRICIA. *Hello, Amigos.* Holt, Rinehart, & Winston, 1986.
de PAOLA, TOMIE. *The Lady of Guadalupe.* Holiday, 1980.
DELACRE, LULU. *Arroz Con Leche.* Scholastic, 1990.
DELACRE, LULU. *Las Navidades.* Scholastic, 1990.
ETS, MARIE HALL. *Gilberto and the Wind.* Harper & Row, 1984.
FIFE, DALE H. *Rosa's Special Garden.* Whitman, 1985.
HALL, LYNN. *Danza.* Scribner, 1981.
KRUMGOLD, JOSEPH. *And Now Miguel.* Harper & Row, 1984.
KURTYCZ, MARCOS, & KOBETH, ANA GARCIA. *Tigers and Opossums.* Little, Brown and Company, 1984.
LAMPMAN, *Go Up the Road.* Atheneum, 1973.
LEXAU, JOAN. *The Christmas Secret.* Dial, 1963.
MANN, PEGGY. *How Juan Got Home.* Coward-McCann, 1972.
MARKUN, PATRICIA. *Central America and Panama.* Watts, 1983.
MOHR, NICHOLASA. *Felita.* Dial, 1979.
O'DELL, SCOTT. *Carlota.* Dial, 1979.
POLITI, LEO. *Song of the Swallows.* Scribner's, 1949.
ROE, EILEEN. *Con Mi Hermano/With My Brother.* Bradbury, 1991.
SCHWEITZER, BYRD BAYLOR. *Amigo.* Macmillan, 1973.
SINGER, JULIA. *We All Come From Puerto Rico.* Athenum, 1977.
SONNEBORN, RUTH A. *Friday Night is Papa Night,* 1987.
TAHA, KAREN T. *A Gift for Tia Rosa.* Dillion Press, 1986.

6

Multicultural Education

Understanding the material and activities in this chapter will help the reader to:

1. Define multicultural education and explain its fundamental purposes.
2. List several goals, assumptions, concepts, and principles of multicultural education.
3. Explain briefly the historical milestones and precedents of multicultural education.
4. List several characteristics of responsive multicultural education programs.
5. List the challenges facing multicultural education and suggest possible solutions for each.
6. List several current controversies in multicultural education.
7. Recognize several areas of controversy surrounding multicultural education and suggest possible resolutions for each.

OVERVIEW

The tremendous diversity of cultural, ethnic, religious, and socioeconomic groups in schools today calls for multicultural education programs which reflect understanding and respect for children's and adolescents' differences. The multicultural education movement has particular relevance for the 1990s and beyond because of the continuing influx of culturally diverse people into the United States, and because of the more humane recognition that cultural diversity enriches, rather than weakens, a nation. This chapter examines the fundamentals and principles of multicultural education and considers the various aspects which make programs successful.

The Culture Quiz: Multicultural Education

Directions: Mark the following as True or False.

_____ 1. Multicultural education should be an integral part of the elementary, but not the secondary, curriculum and should focus on academic matters.

_____ 2. Multicultural education programs are only needed in schools that have considerable cultural diversity among learners.

_____ 3. Multicultural education programs should emphasize to all learners the importance of assimilating toward majority culture expectations.

_____ 4. Multicultural education programs should use a unit or thematic teaching approach, rather than being incorporated into all areas of the curriculum.

_____ 5. Multicultural education programs should address as many culturally diverse groups as possible.

_____ 6. Multicultural education programs are a political tool used to force cultural diversity on Anglo-Americans.

_____ 7. Multicultural education programs do not interfere with the academic areas of learning.

_____ 8. Multicultural education is a popular trend in education, and will likely lose its impetus as its popularity wanes.

_____ 9. Multicultural education should focus on cultural and ethnic diversity, as well as racism, sexism, classism, and the acceptance of handicapped conditions.

_____ 10. Multicultural education can have a significant and positive impact on the education reform currently occurring in the United States.

Answers: 1. F   2. F   3. F   4. F   5. T   6. F   7. T   8. F   9. T   10. T

MULTICULTURAL EDUCATION IN PLURALISTIC SCHOOLS

The Need for Understanding and Appreciating Cultural Diversity

The rich cultural diversity of the United States population, and the increased recognition and awareness of cultural differences, adequately demonstrate the need for appropriate multicultural education experiences that are designed to help learners understand and appreciate others' cultural diversity as well as their own cultures. Although cultural diversity becomes increasingly evident as one continues to learn about the four cultural groups just discussed, still other differences deserve recognition and understanding: gender, age, language, backgrounds, religious beliefs, politics, the work world, physical and mental abilities, and experiences (Tiedt & Tiedt, 1990).

⚹ The need to understand differences among people, and groups of people, will continue to be acute as more immigrants and refugees enter the United States, and as cultural and other forms of diversity are understood. In many situations even during the 1990s, however, respect for diversity among people may be the exception rather than the rule, as can be seen in continuing forms of racism and racist acts (*Lessons from bigotry 101 . . . ,* 1989). Multicultural education programs that try to instill appropriate attitudes and perceptions toward others, and try to teach the dangers of racism, sexism, and ageism, should begin with children and adolescents who are forming lifelong beliefs and attitudes.

⚹ Some educators believe that if racial problems are not visible, then multicultural education programs are not needed. CASE STUDY 6-1 examines a just such a situation.

CASE STUDY 6-1: "We don't need a multicultural education program."

After the faculty meeting in which the principal has just formed a committee to plan a multicultural education program, you hear Mr. Brown say, "But we don't need a multicultural program in our school. We do not have any racial problems."

School professionals and parents sometimes feel that multicultural education is not needed unless racial problems exist. However, Mr. Brown is missing an important goal of multicultural education. First, students in his school need a better understanding of each others' cultural backgrounds. Second, forming a multicultural education program after racial disturbances emerge may be too late, and may be hurriedly implemented without sufficient thought.

Responsive Multicultural Education Programs

As there are varying definitions of multicultural education, goals and objectives also vary in emphasis and focus. For example, while some multicultural education programs may direct attention toward specific, culturally diverse groups, others may include handicapped conditions, gender issues, or other differences. However, the underlying premises continue to place emphasis on the recognition and respect for all people, regardless of the degree and type of differences. This section looks at basic concepts, and several goals, assumptions, and principles which form the basis for responsive multicultural education programs.

Concepts

Payne (1984) suggested that it is important that educators understand three concepts of multicultural education, especially since one's concept of the term determines a program's direction and issues to be addressed.

First, multicultural education is viewed as a product, whereby emphasis is given to the study of ethnicity, e.g., the contributions or characteristics of an ethnic group. Since this view addresses teaching about different ethnic and cultural groups, this concept may be best described as ethnic studies.

Second, multicultural education emphasizes the role of oppression, and the atonement or compensation for past injustices. Dealing primarily with targeted oppressed groups (and possible solutions to their problems), this view considers multicultural education to be a concern only of minorities.

The third perception views multicultural education as a teaching process, and includes aspects such as product *and* entitlement. It extends even further than these two aspects, because teachers focus on the concept of culture as a separate entity from ethnicity. It emphasizes the intrinsic aspects of culture, and its influence on teaching/learning processes. Such a concept of multicultural education recognizes the entitlement aspect by believing that to obtain what one is entitled to includes both a fair system, and an equal chance to acquire social and academic skills. It incorporates the product view in that (1) certain historical facts and events must be taught, and (2) an adequate understanding of present conditions, as well as general human behavior, is aided by a knowledge of historical facts. This idea of multicultural education as a process includes all educational variables, such as methodology, curriculum, and instructional techniques (Payne, 1984).

Goals of Responsive Programs

An integral aspect of all multicultural education focuses on the development of skills and attitudes necessary to function in a culturally diverse society. Educators should not only learn about other cultures, but also should develop the attitudes and skills to function in multicultural situations. These attitudes and skills include an awareness, understanding, and acceptance of cultural differences. Additionally, empathy with members of other cultures, and modifications of one's own cultural values, may also need to be developed (Cordova & Love, 1987). One goal of multicultural education is to change the total educational environment so that it promotes a respect for a wide range of cultural groups, and enables all cultural groups to experience equal educational opportunities (Banks, 1987, p. 29). Developing cross-cultural competency is another goal, and includes the skills, attitudes, and knowledge needed to live within the individual's own ethnic culture and the universal American culture, as well as within and across ethnic cultures (Banks, 1987, p. 35-36).

Goals of Multicultural Education

Educators should be enlightened on the social, political, and economic realities encountered in a culturally diverse and complex society.

Specifically, goals should lead people to:

Recognize, understand, and respect the nature of differences and similarities between cultures;

know that differences exist within family groups of different and like cultures;

develop a better understanding of the nature and impact of racism, and the implications for positive or negative influence;

develop a positive attitude toward one's own ethnicity, accepting and using that cultural background as motivation for becoming a significant contributor to society;

provide developmentally appropriate experiences that will better equip children with skills, knowledge, and attitudes necessary to live in a multicultural/multiethnic society; and

recognize similarities in cultures such as:

all children play games;

all cultures celebrate holidays;

all cultures have some family structure; and

all cultures provide for the same basic needs—food, clothing, and shelter.

Source: *Multicultural Education: A Position Statement.* (1988). Little Rock, AR: Southern Association for Children Under Six.

Ramsey (1987) offered several goals that differ slightly from those of Banks and the professional organization. First, in her goals for teaching from multicultural perspectives, Ramsey felt that it was necessary "to help children develop positive gender, racial, cultural, class, and individual identities, and to recognize and accept their membership in many different groups" (p. 3). Another goal was to encourage social relationships in which there was "an openness and interest with others, a willingness to include others, and a desire to cooperate" (p. 4). A third, different, goal was to "empower children to become autonomous and critical analysts and activists in their social environment" (p. 4). Another difference, which is a major focus of this text, is the inclusion of immediate and extended families. Ramsey wrote: "To promote effective and reciprocal relationships between schools and families" (p. 5).

Assumptions

Several assumptions underlie multicultural education, and are, in fact, the philosophy on which *Multicultural Education of Children and Adolescents* is based.

Assumption 1: *Cultural diversity is a positive, enriching element in a society because it provides individuals with increased opportunities to experience other cultures and thus to become more fulfilled as human beings* (Banks, 1988). Rather than being perceived as a weakness to be remediated, cultural diversity should be viewed as a strength with the potential for helping people better understand their own culture. Similarly, as people reach higher levels of understanding and acceptance of other cultures, it is hoped that people will achieve similar heights of understanding and sensitivity in areas such as racism, sexism, and classism.

Assumption 2: *Multicultural education is for all students* (Hernandez, 1989). Some people believe that multicultural education is only for minority children and adolescents. For example, some states require multicultural education only in districts having at least one school with 25% minority student population (Hernandez, 1989; Baker, 1979). This and other, similar, policies are based upon the assumption that only minority youngsters need multicultural education. This assumption completely fails to recognize that majority cultures can benefit from a better understanding of cultural differences, and eventually of their own cultural backgrounds.

Assumption 3: *Teaching is a cross-cultural encounter* (Hernandez, 1989). All teachers and students have their own cultural baggage—their backgrounds, values, customs, perceptions, and, perhaps, prejudices. These cultural aspects play a significant role in teaching/learning situations, and can have a substantial effect on behavior and learning. Socioeconomic status, ethnicity, gender, and language have a powerful and dynamic effect upon one's outlook and attitude toward school, and upon one's actual school achievement (Hernandez, 1989).

Assumption 4: *Multicultural education should permeate the total school curriculum rather than taking a "one-course" approach or a teaching unit approach.* Responsive multicultural education programs cannot accomplish lasting and worthwhile goals though "one-shot" approaches. The school must be genuinely multicultural: The curriculum, as defined in the broadest sense (every aspect of the school with which learners come in contact); the composition of the administration, faculty, and staff; expectations that reflect an understanding of culturally different groups, their attitudes toward school success, and their learning styles; and the recognition of all other aspects which may affect both minority- and majority-culture learners. Culturally different learners will feel like "intruders" or "outsiders" in a school which appears to address only Anglo needs and expectations.

Assumption 5: *The education system has not served all students equally well* (Hernandez, 1989). Generally speaking, members of minority groups, students from lower socioeconomic groups, and students who are culturally different, or speak a language other than English, have not fared well in United States school systems. Any number of reasons may exist for the lack of achievement among such students: differing achievement orientations, problems resulting from language backgrounds, differing learning styles, curricula, and school policies that are unresponsive to minority student needs, testing and assessment procedures that may be designed for middle-class (or higher) Anglo students, and a lack of understanding or acceptance of cultural differences. In any event, the high dropout rate among Native-Americans (Sanders, 1987), African-Americans (Wilson, 1989), and Hispanic-Americans (*Closing the gap for Hispanics*, 1988) substantiates the position that culturally different learners often do not experience success in United States schools.

Assumption 6: *Schools will continue to experience and reflect increasing cultural diversity due to influxes of immigrants and refugess and due to the high birthrates of some culturally-diverse groups.* It is an understatement to say that American society continues to grow more diverse. Increasing numbers of culturally different people, increasing recognition of gender issues, the many religious groups, differing socioeconomic groups, varying sexual orientations, and geographical differences, are a few representative examples. Multicultural education programs have the responsibility for reflecting the rich diversity that characterizes the United States society.

Assumption 7: *It is the responsibility of elementary and secondary schools to implement appropriate multicultural education programs that contribute to better understandings of cultural differences, show the dangers of stereotyping, and reduce racism, sexism, and classism.* Families are undoubtedly children's first teachers as values, opinions, and attitudes are instilled during the early years. Ideally, families teach acceptance and respect for all people and their differences. Realistically speaking, however, children may learn that their culture, race, or ethnic backgrounds are "right", while others are "wrong" or "inferior". Since the United States educational system is characterized by considerable cultural diversity, elementary and secondary schools are the most feasible transmitters of understanding and respect for cultural diversity. However, rather than having a multicultural education program "in name only", responsive programs need to teach genuine respect, and need to work toward reducing racism, sexism, and classism. Admittedly, this is an undertaking of considerable magnitude; however, teaching and modeling respect for all people may have the most dramatic impact during these formative years.

Principles

Providing appropriate multicultural education requires more than just teaching cultural information about ethnic groups. Several "fundamentals" are needed to promote effective multicultural education that allows learners and teachers of various cultures to maintain integrity and dignity. First, appropriate curricular materials are needed for culturally different students. These materials should enhance self-concept, maintain interest in classroom learning, and provide examples, vocabulary, and models with which culturally different students can relate (Grant & Sleeter, 1985). Second, major curricular focuses should include skills in analysis and critical thinking (Grant & Sleeter, 1985). Third, materials, activities, and experiences should be designed to help students understand ethnic differences and cultural diversity by being authentic and multidimensional, and include both cognitive and affective skills (Gay, 1975).

Interdisciplinary Approaches

Multicultural education should be an interdisciplinary approach integrated into the total program (Grant & Sleeter, 1985). First, multicultural education should be an integral aspect of all curricular areas, rather than just the social studies course. Likewise, the "once-a-year" Multicultural Week or unit focusing on African-American history, tacos, and Oriental dresses and customs will not suffice. Such approaches have not worked, and will not work, because being aware of diversity does not necessarily result in acceptance and respect of individuals within the cultural group. The curriculum, learning environments, and the mindset of learners and faculty and staff should become genuinely multicultural in nature, and should reflect the cultural diversity of the school. Second, well-meaning multicultural education programs may serve only cosmetic purposes if students and school personnel harbor long-held cultural biases and stereotypes. In essence, to be effective, responsive multicultural education programs recognize the need to both inform and to change negative attitudes and long-held prejudices.

CASE STUDY 6-2 shows the advantages of an interdisciplinary approach to multicultural education.

CASE STUDY 6-2: Interdisciplinary Approaches

The administrators, faculty, and staff at Browning High School worked conscientiously toward developing their multicultural education program. The committee had decided to offer their total commitment to an interdisciplinary program. Decisions had been reached concerning the goals, curriculum content, instructional practices, and school policies, and how best to evaluate both print and non-print media. Although the committee recognized the legitimacy of unit approaches, and that multicultural education was one subject, it also recognized that an interdisciplinary approach would be most effective for several reasons.

Specifically, the interdisciplinary approach could:

1. Provide a means of including multicultural education experiences in *all* subject areas, e.g., showing the contributions of culturally-diverse people in the various disciplines.
2. Ensure broad involvement of all educators responsible for the various discipline areas.
3. Show culturally diverse students and majority-culture learners that the school is committed to serious multicultural education efforts.
4. Provide a wide variety of instructional approaches and learning experiences.
5. Make all school personnel feel that they are a part of the multicultural education program and responsible for the success of the effort.

The educators at Browning felt good about their multicultural education efforts: Everybody was involved, curricular and instructional practices were being examined, school policies were being reconsidered, and efforts crossed discipline lines.

Developing Multicultural Attitudes

Teaching and interacting with culturally diverse learners requires an awareness of the learners' cultural backgrounds, knowledge of how culture affects motivation and learning, and the skills necessary to work in close interpersonal situations with learners of cultures different from one's own.

Probably related too closely to be perceived separately, awareness, knowledge, and skills function in a complementary fashion, and contribute to the overall attitudes necessary for multicultural education programs. The educator with awareness, but without the necessary knowledge and skills, will in all likelihood be ineffective in providing appropriate multicultural experiences. Although this section addresses each area, readers are reminded of the complex interrelationships between the three.

Awareness

Responsive educators working in multicultural situations have the dual responsibility of developing their own awareness of cultural diversity, and also of instilling cultural awareness in the children and adolescents under their tutelage.

First, educators should develop an awareness of learners' cultural backgrounds, their attitudes toward school and orientations toward achievement, and their learning styles. Being aware or recognizing that all learners are not Anglo and middle class (DeCosta, 1984) represents a significant step toward providing appropriate education experiences.

Second, since children (and often adults) may feel that "different" is wrong or something to be feared, it is the educator's responsibility to instill an awareness of cultural diversity in children. Many factors contribute to children's multicultural awareness: culture, various kinds of media (TV programming, advertising, and children's books, for example), other children, and adults. Parents and teachers play a major role in enhancing multicultural awareness in children. Teachers can support parents in expanding their appreciation of diverse cultures. Parents can become involved in the classroom to promote cultural awareness in children (SACUS, 1988).

ENHANCING MULTICULTURAL AWARENESS: TEACHERS' ROLES

Develop positive attitudes and values that are conveyed to children directly or indirectly;

create learning environments for young children that facilitate their multicultural awareness and are developmentally appropriate, providing for active, concrete learning with other children and adults;

use appropriate teaching, curricular, and interaction strategies to accommodate different learning styles;

foster the development of self-esteem in young children, thereby increasing their ability to learn; and

model for children respect and concern for all people (SACUS, 1988).

Knowledge

During the past several decades, the professional literature has increased (and undoubtedly will continue to increase) educators' knowledge of cultural diversity. More than ever before, educators have access to valuable objective information describing Native-, African-, Asian- and Hispanic-Americans. No longer should decisions concerning a learner's education be based on inaccurate generalizations and stereotypical generalizations. Through first-hand contact, journals, books, and other sources of information, professional decisions regarding a learners' family, language, and unique problems can be reached with a degree of accuracy and objectivity. The Native-American's concept of sharing, the African-American's unique language and extended family, the Asian-American's concept of generational and family relationships, and the Hispanic-American's belief in machismo and commitment to the Spanish language can be understood and can form an accurate basis for teaching and learning. Equally important is the knowledge and understanding that these cultural characteristics may or may not hold true with each culturally diverse learner, and may vary according to generation, socioeconomic status, and geographic location.

Knowledge of the rich cultural diversity among learners, the impact of centuries of oppression on culturally diverse people, and how culturally different learners function in predominantly Anglo school systems are crucial as educators plan and implement multicultural education programs. First, educators should understand individual learners, their histories, their cultural backgrounds, their families, and their language. Second, knowledge of the effects of racism, sexism, and classism are necessary as educators strive to understand learners in schools. Third, it is important that educators understand how Anglo students perceive and feel about minority youngsters, and vice versa. Promoting, maintaining, and modeling positive interpersonal relationships between minority- and majority-culture learners is also crucial.

Skills
Although having awareness and knowledge of culturally-different learners is of paramount importance, educators should also have the skills and ability to teach and relate to learners: They should be able to recognize and respond appropriately to learners' strengths and weaknesses; address areas in need of remediation; respond to the relationship between learning styles and culture, and provide school experiences based upon learners' orientations toward school and academic success; select standardized tests and evaluation instruments with the least cultural bias; and utilize teaching methods that have proven especially appropriate for minority children and adolescents. Other skills include understanding and helping others to understand nonverbal communication, understanding and responding appropriately to the concerns of culturally different learners, and arranging for appropriate school and community resources for learners with additional or specialized assistance.

CHALLENGES FACING MULTICULTURAL EDUCATORS

Historical perspectives reveal that the culturally different have been the recipients of cruel and inhumane treatment. Just a few examples include the injustices imposed upon Native-Americans and their land; the racism and discrimination in education, employment, and housing that have affected the progress of African- and Hispanic-Americans for centuries; and the Asian-Americans' cruel treatment upon arrival in the United States. During the 1990s and the twenty-first century, educators will be challenged to mold a more humane and equitable society by providing multicultural education programs that teach respect for cultural differences, address the need for positive cultural identities, and respond with decisive action to the often disastrous effects of racism and stereotyping.

Changing Attitudes in the United States

Although considerable racism and discrimination continue to exist and to restrain minority entrance into mainstream America, the 1990s can be a time for recognition and acceptance of cultural diversity. Factors and events that may contribute to such recognition include: The increasing numbers of culturally diverse people; the efforts being directed at children and adolescents (e.g., multicultural education courses) in elementary and secondary schools; the multicultural emphasis of the National Council for Accreditation of Teacher Education; the increasing recognition that the nation actually benefits from cultural diversity; and increasing numbers of organizations working to instill cultural pride.

Ethnocentrism

Ethnocentrism is the belief that one's cultural ways are not only valid and superior to those of others, but also universally applicable in evaluating and judging human behavior (Hernandez, 1989, p. 25). Persons with strong ethnocentric attitudes and beliefs, especially when these are unconscious, may have difficulty appreciating and accepting the range of cultural differences which exist in societies (Hernandez, 1989). Because culture influences the way we think, feel, and act, it becomes the "lens through which we judge the world" (Gollnick & Chinn, 1986, p. 13). Culture becomes the only natural way to function in the world, i.e., common sense in one's own culture becomes the norm or the expected for common sense in other cultures of the world. The result is that other cultures are evaluated by one's cultural standards and beliefs, thus making it virtually impossible to view another culture as separate from our own (Gollnick & Chinn, 1986). In essence, ethnocentrism is an universal characteristic in which one's own cultural traits are viewed as natural, correct, and superior, while others' culture may be perceived as odd or inferior (Yetman & Steele, 1975).

CASE STUDY 6-3 examines the problem of ethnocentrism and offers several suggestions for addressing the problem.

CASE STUDY 6-3: Reducing Ethnocentrism

People all too often believe that their culture and cultural traditions are "correct", while all others are "wrong". Dr. Farnsworth was one of these people. For example, he either misunderstood, or was unwilling to accept, that culturally diverse people have different opinions of what is important, different perceptions of immediate and extended families, and different degrees of allegiance to the elderly. Such opinions and perceptions may have become ingrained early in Dr. Farnsworth's life, and he never considered this ethnocentrism objectively.

Educators with these views, or who teach children and adolescents with ethnocentric views, should take action: First, educators must address their (and their colleagues') ethnocentrism; and second, they must seek ways to reduce ethnocentrism in their colleagues and students. Although reducing ethnocentrism represents a task of some magnitude, educators can use several approaches to further this goal with children and adolescents:

1. Instill in children and adolescents the idea that cultural differences should not be considered as right or wrong, superior or inferior.

2. Arrange teaching/learning situations (e.g., cooperative learning and cross-age tutoring) whereby learners of varying cultures can have firsthand experiences with each other.

3. Model acceptance and respect for all people.

4. Respond appropriately to statements indicating a lack of understanding or acceptance of cultural differences.

5. Encourage respect for *all* differences—cultural and ethnic, socioeconomic, handicapped conditions, gender, and other characteristics which contribute to diversity among individuals.

The challenge for educators in multicultural situations is to understand ethnocentrism, to recognize its dangers, and to respond appropriately. For example, ethnocentrism can be perpetuated in textbooks and other instructional materials in subtle ways that educators may find difficult to recognize. Since a perspective consistent with one's own vantage point, attitudes, and values is likely to be accepted without question, it might not even occur to educators that another cultural perspective exists (Gollnick & Chinn, 1986).

Responding appropriately to ethnocentrism is a significant challenge, since one of the primary goals of any multicultural program is to encourage and instill an acceptance for others' culture and cultural backgrounds. First, it is crucial for educators to recognize their own ethnocentrism and its potential for clouding their objective judgments. A second challenge is to attempt to convince children and adolescents to realize that, while their cultural beliefs are "right" in their perceptions, other cultures also consider their beliefs to be "right". Convincing learners of the dangers of ethnocentrism, and teaching them to perceive others' cultural differences and beliefs in a more positive light, may be a major undertaking, especially since the educator may be challenging long-held beliefs that may have been taught or encouraged by the learner's family.

Developing Positive Cultural Identities.

Identity has been defined as answers to questions such as: "Who am I?" and "Who am I to be?" Identity is a person's sense of place within the world, or the meaning that one attaches to oneself in the broader context of life (Vander Zanden, 1989). It is important that educators show children and adolescents that people may have several identities at once, i.e., one might be Hispanic-American, a member of any of the Spanish-speaking cultures, one's brother, a Catholic, an inhabitant of a specific geographic region in the U.S., or any number of identities.

Activity:

Encourage all children and adolescents to understand that they have various identities. For example, an adolescent may have a number of different and changing identities:

I am a:
- . . . Hispanic-American, Cuban-American, and a resident of Florida
- . . . a person of Spanish descent
- . . . a member of a minority group
- . . . an adolescent boy or girl
- . . . a member of a particular school and grade
- . . . a son, a grandson, and a nephew or niece
- . . . somebody's best friend

The educator's first challenge is to view students as different and unique individuals, rather than as a homogeneous group. As DeCosta (1984) suggested, educators often assume too much similarity among learners:

> They (teachers) have come to see the classroom as a homogeneous group—assuming a sameness or similarity in all children's social, economic and ethnic backgrounds. (p. 155)

Educators who treat students in such a manner contribute to children and adolescents feeling they must conform to Anglo (or some other) standards.

The second challenge for multicultural educators becomes clear as one considers learners from culturally diverse backgrounds. Culturally-diverse individuals need to be able to clarify personal attitudes toward their cultural and ethnic backgrounds. The educator's goal is to teach individuals to learn self-acceptance, thus developing the characteristics needed to accept and respond more positively to other ethnic groups. Similarly, educators should strive to instill in learners an acceptance and understanding of both the positive and negative attributes of their cultural or ethnic groups, and to teach learners the importance of acquiring genuine ethnic pride, rather than hate or fear (Banks, 1988).

Individuals who have positive ethnic, national, and global identifications value their ethnic, national, and global communities highly, and are proud of these identifications. They both desire and have the competencies to take actions that will support and reinforce the values and norms of their ethnic, national, and global communities (Banks, 1988).

Racism

Often defined as the domination of one social or ethnic group by another, racist individuals have used an ideological system to justify the discrimination of some racial groups against others. The evidence of racism toward minority groups in the United States is all too evident: African-Americans have faced discrimination in housing, employment, schooling, and in various other areas, despite civil rights legislation. Latino-Americans have been exploited as migrant farmworkers, Asian-Americans were excluded as immigrants into the United States during the early 1900s, and Native-Americans had their land taken and were placed on reservations (Lum, 1986).

Although the authors continue to hope that the twenty-first century will bring greater acceptance and recognition of cultural diversity, they must report that discrimination, racism, and bigotry continue in the United States, i.e., racial incidents have occurred at 250 colleges since the fall of 1986 (*Lessons from bigotry 101 . . .* , 1989). Whether by overt racism, such as the Ku Klux Klan's acts of violence and hatred, or the more covert forms of racism and discrimination often found in employment and housing, African-Americans and other minorities continue to experience inequities and inequalities. Although the overt acts and John Crow attitudes are not as visible as they were several decades ago, racial injustices continue to affect minorities' progress and well-being. Educators of all cultures may have to deal with problems resulting from these realities in the United States, and may have to sort though their own personal biases and long-held cultural beliefs.

How can multicultural education programs respond to the racism that has affected people for centuries? Although the events of the past, such as racism, are important and deserve to be addressed, multicultural education should not focus just on past events. It must provide an impetus for changing the future. Educators are challenged to implement effective multicultural education programs that reduce the ignorance that breeds racism, and to develop the understanding and actions people need to become antiracist (Bennett, 1986). Racism has permeated the entire United States school system for many years through teacher preparation, textbooks, and other curricular materials. Therefore, for multicultural education to counteract racism, it will have to be equally broad in scope, and inclusive in application (Payne, 1984).

IMPLEMENTING RESEARCH 6-1 looks at reducing the impact of racism on students.

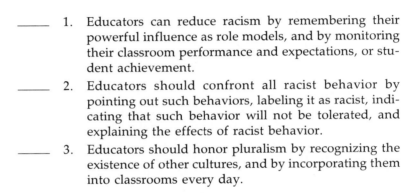

IMPLEMENTING RESEARCH 6-1: Reducing Racism

Racism continues to be a major force that affects the attitudes and behavior of children today. Racism is such a strongly negative emotional experience that minority students' attention may be diverted from academic pursuits and toward responding to racism in unconstructive ways. Educators sometimes do not respond because they feel unable to change students' experiences, or because such actions take away from academic subject areas. Educators who fail to respond to racism send signals to students that racism is either acceptable, or a trivial issue. Since failure to counteract racism has two damaging consequences, educators have a responsibility to respond appropriately.

IMPLEMENTING THE RESEARCH:

_____ 1. Educators can reduce racism by remembering their powerful influence as role models, and by monitoring their classroom performance and expectations, or student achievement.

_____ 2. Educators should confront all racist behavior by pointing out such behaviors, labeling it as racist, indicating that such behavior will not be tolerated, and explaining the effects of racist behavior.

_____ 3. Educators should honor pluralism by recognizing the existence of other cultures, and by incorporating them into classrooms every day.

Source: Pollard, D. S. (1989). "Reducing the impact of racism on students." *Educational Leadership, 47(2),* 73-75.

REDUCING RACISM: ASSUMPTIONS

1. It is worthwhile for educators to focus on the reduction of racial/ethnic prejudice and discrimination, even though powerful sectors of the society and the world do not presently value this goal.

2. It is appropriate for schools to teach certain humanistic values, such as the negative effects of racial and ethnic prejudice and discrimination.

3. A reduction of racial/ethnic prejudice and discrimination is possible through appropriate educational experiences (Bennett, 1986, p. 211–212.)

Stereotypes, Prejudices, and Generalizations

Lum (1986) defines stereotyping as "the prejudicial attitude of a person or group that superimposes on a total race, sex, or religion a generalization about behavioral characteristics" (p. 135). Stereotypes produce a generalized mental picture that usually results in a judgment (negative or positive) of a person or an entire culture. Although stereotypes might be partially valid, it is imperative that educators approach all stereotypes with skepticism, and acknowledge that most are accompanied by prejudice, like or dislike, or approval or disapproval of the culture group (Axelson, 1985). Recognizing that stereotypes all too often contribute to people being beneficiaries or victims of racism and ageism, effective multicultural educators seek to understand and respond appropriately to others' and to their own cultural and age-level beliefs about people.

Counteracting Biases and Stereotypes

How can educators counter biases and stereotypes? How can multicultural education programs be designed to encourage understanding and reduce stereotypical beliefs?

1. Educators should be aware of their own biases and stereotypes.
2. Educators should expect as much from culturally diverse learners as from Anglo students.
3. Educators should examine and confront biases and stereotypes held by other students.
4. Educators should ensure that library materials and other instructional materials portray characters in a realistic, non-sexist, non-racist, non-stereotypical manner.
5. Educators should provide heterogeneous classes that allow students an opportunity to build interethnic and interracial relationships with other students over a sustained period of time.
6. Educators should provide role-playing situations and simulation activities that allow students a better understanding of stereotyped groups (Garcia, 1984).

Stereotypes and generalizations that surround cultures have the potential for severely damaging interpersonal counseling and the outcome of educational efforts. Whether one believes that all culturally diverse learners are underachievers or that all adolescents are involved in drugs and sex, stereotypes and generalizations can be detrimental to learners, educators, and teaching/learning relationships. For example, one who bases educational decisions on the images presented by the mass media might conclude that all African-Americans are dealing in drugs, or that they survive only as welfare recipients. Consider the following young African-American woman's predicament (Raybon, 1989):

> This is who I am not. I am not a crack addict. I am not a welfare mother. I am not illiterate. I am not a prostitute. I have never been in jail. My children are not in gangs. My husband doesn't beat me. My home is not a tenement. None

of these things defines who I am, nor do they describe the other Black people I've known and worked with and loved and befriended over these 40 years of my life.

Nor does it describe most of Black America, period. (p. 11).

Raybon (1989) sums up only too well the situation facing minorities. Too often, cultural stereotypes and generalizations are considered "truisms and facts", and become the basis for professional decisions affecting personal lives.

Myths and Realities

Myths and misconceptions that influence attitudes and actions toward those who are culturally different must be eliminated. Examples of myths and misconceptions currently existing are:

All children of the same ethnic background have the same needs and intellectual abilities.

All children who speak broken English and/or a dialect are intellectually deficient.

All minorities are disadvantaged, lazy, and on welfare.

All Oriental children are academically gifted.

All minorities are inferior—i.e., Blacks, Hispanics, Puerto Ricans, American Indians, Cubans, Jamaicans, and Haitians.

Other myths and misconceptions exist about people from different cultural and socioeconomic backgrounds. Clearly, cultural stereotyping tends to develop negative attitudes about one's self and others, lessens cultural value perceptions and cultural appreciations, and destroys the democratic fiber of our society (SACUS, 1988).

Understanding Cultures and the Learner's Individual Culture

Recognizing the diversity in cultural backgrounds challenges all educators, especially those with a powerful sense of ethnocentrism and a steadfast belief that their culture is superior to others. These educators may assume that culturally diverse learners should change cultural values and beliefs to meet the expectations of predominantly Anglo school systems. Such assumptions challenge the educators who may not understand cultural diversity and its effect on teaching and learning situations.

A basic rationale of this text is that educators must understand individual learners and their cultural diversity. Professionals who have a genuine caring attitude are to be commended, yet educators must also understand culturally diverse learners' families, language, religion, and other significant aspects of their lives. Educators are challenged continually to learn what it is like to be a child or adolescent in a specific culture, how it feels to attend a school that often appears to have strange rules and expectations, and how it feels to experience communication problems.

Better Understanding the Culturally Diverse Learner

1. Read textbooks, journal articles, and other written material on cultural diversity and teaching/learning in multicultural settings.
2. Request information from organizations that disseminate objective information and promote the various cultures.
3. Meet on a first-hand basis culturally diverse learners and their families (perhaps in their homes) to gain a better understanding of what it means to be a culturally different learner.
4. Attend conferences that focus on cultural diversity and working with children and adolescents from the various cultures.
5. Read about cultural diversity in books and magazines that are written primarily for children and adolescents.

CONTROVERSIAL ISSUES IN MULTICULTURAL EDUCATION

Although the last several decades have seen multicultural education emerging as a means of promoting understanding, acceptance, and good will among people, it is somewhat ironic that these programs have not been wholeheartedly accepted in some circles. In some cases, multicultural education has resulted in criticism and controversy. It is important for multicultural educators to recognize several controversial areas and the claims of the critics.

First, Bennett (1986) summarized an anthropological study by Gibson (1984) in which Gibson analyzed approaches to multicultural education and concluded that serious limitations plagued the various approaches. Education for the culturally different is basically a condescending approach that assumes that a student's failure in school results from cultural differences. Education about cultural differences is designed to teach the value of cultural differences, the understanding of the concept of culture, and the acceptance of others' differences. It also leads to stereotyping by ignoring similarities among all groups, and by neglecting differences within any one group. Gibson also maintained that multicultural education overlooked the impact of racism, because one could not assume that developing ethnic literacy and cultural appreciation would end racism, prejudice, and discrimination (Bennett, 1986).

Second, Glazner (1981) argued that most immigrant groups who came to the United States chose to become Americanized as soon as possible, rather than to maintain their foreign language and culture. In fact, Glazner believed this argument to be valid for all cultural groups (e.g., Cuban-Americans), not just the people classified as immigrants.

A third criticism of multicultural education is based upon the belief that "the American society does not promote sufficient love and interpersonal caring for a fulfilling existence" (Sleeter & Grant, 1988, p. 165). This criticism holds that multicultural education becomes misdirected by emphasizing cognitive knowledge about cultural groups over the exploration of interpersonal feelings. Although students might be provided a broad knowledge base, it is necessary to stress and experience interpersonal relationships for attitudes and prejudices to change (Sleeter & Grant, 1988).

A fourth criticism results from the fact that the words *culture*, *race*, and *class* have multiple interpretations. Some people perceive these words as connoting accusations of prejudice, fears of job or housing discrimination, or isolation and alienation from the larger society. Ramsey (1987) wrote:

> One Head Start teacher talked about the resistance of her low-income white parents whenever she said the word *multicultural*. It appeared from the parents' comments that the term meant glorifying "those people who get all the jobs and services." Because the teacher knew the community and was aware of the controversies and cutbacks related to jobs and welfare, she understood that, before the parents could hear anything positive about other groups of people, they had to explore and share their own feelings of economic and social threat. After some of their anger was dissipated, she tried to help them feel more personally powerful and optimistic, through activities designed to foster their feelings of self-appreciation and confidence. After several sessions, the parents were more receptive to the idea of multicultural education. (p. 176)

Ramsey (1987) pointed out that some parents who identify with the mainstream of society feel threatened by the arrival of culturally different people, and may resent schools' efforts to have their children think positively about these groups. Responsive educators recognize that these problematic situations have the potential for limiting the success of multicultural programs, and also realize the crucial need for planning appropriate responses for changing parental and community attitudes.

SUMMING UP

Educators planning multicultural education programs should remember to:

1. Plan and implement multicultural education programs that address the wrongs of the past such as racism, prejudice, and discrimination. However, the primary focus should be on understanding, respecting, and accepting culturally different people.
2. Consider multicultural education as an emerging concept that will continue to evolve as necessary to meet the needs of an increasingly culturally diverse society.

3. Plan and implement a multicultural education program that transmits facts and knowledge, includes teaching an awareness of cultural diversity, helps learners to develop the skills necessary to interrelate, and deals positively with people of culturally diverse backgrounds.

4. Consider multicultural education as a total school curricular approach that integrates cultural diversity into all teaching/learning situations.

5. Recognize multicultural education as an endeavor that has received considerable recognition and respect. However, several areas of controversy and criticism continue to exist, and deserve to be addressed.

6. Design a multicultural education that directs attention to issues such as sexism and classism, creates more positive attitudes toward the handicapped, and eliminates the racism, prejudice, and discrimination that plagues the United States society.

7. Since people draw conclusions based on their cultural expectations and beliefs, plan multicultural education experiences that address the ethnocentrism of both learners and educators.

8. Insist on multicultural education programs in all schools, rather than just schools with considerable cultural diversity in the student population.

SUGGESTED LEARNING ACTIVITIES

1. Select a school that is known for its culturally diverse student population. Assess the extent to which the school has responded to cultural diversity. Formulate an instrument (survey or checklist) to assess the school's efforts in areas such as multicultural education programs; cultural/racial/ethnic composition of faculty, staff, and other professional personnel; whether organization and grouping methods segregate learners by race; and whether the curriculum and instruction materials reflect the cultural diversity of the school.

2. Outline a multicultural education program for a school which has a population of 50% Anglo-American, 25% African-American, 20% Hispanic-American, and approximately 5% other culturally diverse groups. Respond specifically to decision areas such as: The extent to which each culture should be addressed; a determination of the content of the program, and attitudes to be examined; appropriate in-service sessions for the administration, faculty, and staff; appropriate curriculum and instruction methods and materials; and methods of assessing the program.

3. Respond to the following statement: "There are more differences in

social class than there are differences in culture. For example, middle- or upper-class people of various cultures may be more alike (e.g., food, clothing, customs, traditions, and religious customs) than people of a given culture or race. In essence, social class may be the distinguishing factor among people." Agree or disagree? To what degree do social class differences characterize people? Interview several people from differing social classes and several people from differing cultural backgrounds to determine differences and similarities.

4. Examine and compare the multicultural education programs of several schools. How do schools differ in philosophy, commitment, approaches (unit or total curriculum integration), goals and objectives, treatment of holidays, and overall attempts to have a truly "multicultural" school.

Expanding Your Horizons: Additional Journal Readings and Books

BANKS, J. A. (1988). *Multiethnic education* (2 ed.). Boston: Allyn and Bacon. Banks, a noted authority on multiethnic education, examines the history, goals, and practices of multiethnic education and looks at conceptual and philosophical issues.

GOLLNICK, D. M., & CHINN, P. C. (1990). *Multicultural education in a pluralistic society.* Columbus: Merrill. Gollnick and Chinn examine the tenets of multicultural education, and then focus attention on class, ethnicity, gender, exceptionality, religion, language, and age.

HERNANDEZ, H. (1989). *Multicultural education: A teacher's guide to content and process.* Columbus: Merrill. In this excellent text, Hernandez approaches multicultural education as both content and a process.

MANNING, M. L. (1991). "More than lip service to multicultural education." *The Clearing House, 64,* 218. The 1990s will be a time for comprehensive school approaches which make the curriculum, instructional practices, and school environment more multicultural in nature.

(Theme Issue), *Theory Into Practice, 22* (Spring 1984). This issue focuses on multicultural education, and has twelve articles which direct attention toward several aspects of multiculturalism. Both theoretical and practical aspects are examined.

7

Curricular Efforts

Understanding the material and activities in this chapter will help the reader to:

1. Distinguish between the purported changes and the actual progress achieved by culturally diverse people in the United States society.
2. Prepare a multicultural teaching unit that addresses the needs of culturally diverse learners, and teaches Anglo learners about diversity.
3. State several reasons needing a multicultural education program that emphasizes "across-the-curriculum" and the total school environment.
4. List and describe several methods of extending the multicultural education curriculum to the community, and to extracurricular activities.
5. Understand the importance of having school administrators, faculty, and staff reflect the cultural diversity of the student body.

OVERVIEW

The tremendous cultural diversity that characterizes United States school systems provides a strong message to educators and curriculum developers in both elementary and secondary levels: A curriculum should be developed that addresses the needs of culturally different learners, and creates a school environment that reflects cultural diversity. Efforts should encompass a wide array of perspectives, such as an across-the-curriculum approach, careful selection of bias-free materials, selection of evaluation instruments that take into account cultural differences, appropriate community involvement, and extracurricular activities that involve all learners. These tangible aspects, however, are not any more important than the more-difficult-to-pinpoint aspects such as the "hidden curriculum", or the acts of unconscious (or perhaps even conscious) racism, discrimination, or prejudice that continue to plague our schools. This chapter suggests that children and adolescents of all cultures need a multicultural education program that emphasizes across-the-curriculum approaches, and school environments that offer a positive response to the increasing cultural diversity.

The Culture Quiz: Multicultural Education Curriculum Efforts

Directions: Mark the following as True or False.

_____ 1. Multicultural efforts should be a total curricular and instructional approach, because less ambitious approaches might not be construed by learners as a serious effort.

_____ 2. An example of the "hidden curriculum" is when culturally diverse learners perceive that school decisions and instructional practices indicate that middle-class Anglo learners are being favored.

_____ 3. Current levels of racism, discrimination, and injustice indicate that relations between cultures in the United States are positive, and may be at an all-time high.

_____ 4. Even if relations between children and adolescents are positive and without serious incident, multicultural education is still needed so that knowledge of, and respect for, cultural diversity can be emphasized.

_____ 5. Homogeneous ability grouping may result in an insidious form of segregation whereby children and adolescents are separated by race or socioeconomic class.

_____ 6. Textbooks and other written material which portray middle-class Anglo characters and values rarely affect culturally diverse children and adolescents, because learners expect instructional materials to reflect the majority culture.

_____ 7. Enthnocentrism is the belief that one's culture is in some way better than another person's cultural background and heritage.

_____ 8. Multicultural education efforts should avoid adopting an interdisciplinary focus (which includes all subject areas) because individual teachers have their own strengths, weaknesses, and interests.

_____ 9. Multicultural education efforts should focus on extracurricular activities so as to provide equal access and opportunities to all learners, regardless of cultural backgrounds.

_____ 10. The curriculum should endorse bilingual education and a multilingual society.

Answers: 1. T 2. T 3. F 4. T 5. T 6. F 7. T 8. F 9. T 10. T

TOWARD A SCHOOL CURRICULUM THAT RESPECTS AND PROMOTES CULTURAL DIVERSITY

Overall school curriculum and teaching/learning situations should reflect the cultural diversity of our nation. Although the Brown desegregation case and the Civil Rights legislation of a number of years ago contributed to better treatment and acceptance of culturally diverse groups, educators should place change and progress in proper perspective.

The Illusion of Change and Progress

Acquiring an objective understanding of culturally diverse people requires a careful analysis of progress, and of hurdles yet to be surmounted. Without doubt, progress toward better relations between culturally diverse groups has been commendable. The accomplishments of culturally diverse people and of women are recognized; many educators welcome handicapped youngsters into their classrooms; most teachers work to reduce racist and sexist behavior in their classrooms; and many work to develop or obtain curricular materials free from bias and prejudice (Sleeter & Grant, 1988).

However, to avoid the illusion of change, one has to consider the continuing vestiges of racism, sexism, and bias toward culturally different and handicapped people. Two areas surface as being particularly in need of change: Society in general, and the teaching and learning practices that are often found in United States schools. First, racism and nonacceptance continue to plague society: there is increasing evidence of racism and bigotry (Pine & Hilliard, 1990), and a growing popularity of "skinheads" or neo-Nazi groups. Second, school practices often document either a lack of understanding of culturally diverse learners, or a lack of acceptance and respect for their cultural differences. As the following excerpts indicate, careful attention should be devoted to school practices (Sleeter & Grant, 1988) that may hamper or actually impede culturally diverse learners' progress.

The Continuing Need for Change in Educational Practices

African-American students suffer academically because their learning styles tend to be oriented toward cooperation; content about people; discussion and hands-on work; and whole-to-part learning (Shade, 1982).

Young Navajo learners sometimes interpret tests as games (in contrast to Anglo students who take a more serious attitude). This was a result of home socialization (Deyhle, 1985).

Bilingual education teachers often find themselves in conflict with regular classroom teachers over the specific needs of limited English proficiency students (Sleeter & Grant, 1988).

Educators interact with, call on, and praise students who are Anglo, male, and middle class more than other students in the same classroom (Jackson & Cosca, 1974; Sadker & Sadker, 1982).

Although curricular materials and textbooks more accurately reflect cultural diversity, Native-, Asian-, and Hispanic-Americans are still barely visible in the curriculum (Sleeter & Grant, 1988).

Students are often grouped homogeneously. This has the tendency to segregate culturally diverse learners and children from lower socioeconomic groups (Manning & Lucking, 1990).

The social conditions in the United States, and the examples just provided, lend credence to the hypothesis that much of the purported progress toward equality is little more than an illusion. There continues to be much room for genuine change in teaching and learning situations, compatible treatment of handicapped and culturally diverse people, improvement of the cultural and ethnic compositions of school faculty and staff, and equitable representation of culturally diverse people in textbooks and other curricular materials. This discussion and the accompanying recommendations do not downplay the significant progress that has already been made in our society and schools. It is necessary, however, to perceive society and schools objectively, and to plan an appropriate agenda for positively reconstructing society and schools during the 20th century.

From Illusion to Reality: Responding to Racism, Discrimination, Ethnocentrism and Stereotypy

Garcia (1984) contended that schools should accept responsibility for translating illusion into realities, and that they can serve as a significant force in countering discrimination and the various "isms" which affect culturally diverse people, women, and the handicapped.

Racism has many damaging and long-lasting effects on the lives of children and adolescents, the character of society, the quality of our civilization, and peoples' prospects for the future. Before an illusion of racial harmony and justice for all can become a reality, it will be necessary for schools to take a powerful and pivotal role in teaching about racism, and in working toward acceptance and respect for all people, regardless of racial and cultural backgrounds. Schools can play a powerful role in combating racism and educational inequities by confronting and challenging racism, increasing the pool of culturally diverse teachers, developing and implementing a genuine multicultural curriculum, improving pedagogical practices that address the needs of all learners, and teaching character development and improvement of self-esteem (Pine & Hilliard, 1990).

IMPLEMENTING RESEARCH 7-1 looks at students' efforts to combat racism in their schools.

IMPLEMENTING RESEARCH 7-1: Combating Racism

Polakow-Suransky and Ulaby (1990) contended that, although the explosive conditions which once sparked race riots in high schools have faded somewhat, an environment continues to exist that perpetuates "a tense undercurrent of mutual misperception, fear, and resentment" (p. 601). A student-designed survey was administered to determine racial problems in the city schools, to learn the extent of racial tension, and to raise the consciousness of students. Upon completion of the survey, the students presented to the school board an in-depth report that offered several recommendations: (1) Arranging immediate follow-up activities to the survey, i.e., workshops, class discussions, and assemblies in all high schools; (2) re-evaluation of the district's policies on tracking, with the goal of discontinuing the practice; (3) requiring students to take a course that would enlighten them concerning racial oppression in the United States; and (4) establishing a task force to evaluate the entire high school curriculum from a multicultural perspective.

IMPLEMENTING THE RESEARCH:

_____ 1. Like these students, educators need to recognize that racism in some form and degree most likely exists in their schools.

_____ 2. An attempt (such as the survey, or perhaps small group discussions in heterogeneous settings) should be made to determine the racial unrest in the school.

_____ 3. Either through a curriculum revamping, or a course or unit if total revamping is impossible, the racial consciousness of all students should be raised to a point where there is better understanding and acceptance of racial differences.

_____ 4. As with these high school students, all efforts should be wide-scale, and should include students, staff, and all tiers of the administration.

Source: Polakow-Suransky, S., & Ulaby, N. (1990). "Students take action to combat racism." *Phi Delta Kappan, 71,* 601–606.

Garcia referred to ethnocentrism as the notion that one's group is better than other groups. Degrees of ethnocentrism can be placed on a scale extending from mild group pride at one end to extreme group pride and arrogance at the other end. The complexity of responding to ethnocentrism can be understood as one realizes that, while some ethnocentrism is good, too much group pride can result in a negative force, for example, the claims that the Aryan race is superior to all others. A society and its schools must seek to understand the many forms of ethnocentrism, and work toward better control of ethnocentrism among individuals and students (Garcia, 1984).

Schools' responsibilities in our multicultural society extend to countering the dangers of stereotyping to all cultural groups, but most especially when learners have educators who base educational decisions on stereotypical beliefs. What steps can educators take to transform illusions of equality and justice into reality?

First, teachers should be aware of their own biases and stereotypes. Through self-examination or through cultural awareness workshops, educators can gain a better understanding of their attitudes toward culturally diverse people, women, and the handicapped. Second, as cultural understandings clarify stereotypical beliefs, educators will see the need for expecting as much from culturally diverse learners as they do from any other student. Too often, teachers tend to "make it easy for the downtrodden" (Garcia, 1984, p. 107). Although the plight of minorities should be recognized, these learners should be encouraged to excel in all areas of academic pursuits. Third, curricular materials should be examined for stereotypical images and connotations. Specifically, does the material present females and minorities in a realistic, nonstereotypical, manner? Does the material accurately reflect a holistic view of the past in terms of the contributions of females and culturally diverse people in American history (Garcia, 1984)? Fourth, classes grouped homogeneously by ability levels have the potential for segregating students by race or socioeconomic group, and should be replaced with heterogeneous classes or cooperative learning activities (Garcia, 1984; Manning & Lucking, 1990).

In summary, the United States society should be commended for its considerable progress toward a just society for all people. Through landmark court decisions and Civil Rights legislation, and through overall improved race relations, the United States society is not as divided racially and culturally as it was several decades ago. Still, we must not allow reality to be overshadowed by illusions of grandeur. Racism, discrimination, and stereotypes continue to exist, and take a heavy toll on culturally diverse people, women, and the handicapped. Rather than accepting the status quo as the most equitable we can achieve, school curricula should deliberately instill in children and adolescents a sense of respect and acceptance for all people, regardless of their cultural and individual differences.

PLANNING AND IMPLEMENTING A MULTICULTURAL EDUCATION CURRICULUM

Emphasis on Across-the-Curriculum and the Total School Environment

The major focus of this text is that a genuine multicultural curriculum and environment should be an integral part of the school. Educators who plan an occasional multicultural education class or unit probably have honorable intentions; however, in all honesty, a far more comprehensive program is needed. Multiculturalism should extend to, and permeate throughout, all aspects of the school. In fact, multiculturalism should be such a basic part of the school that it becomes a natural and accepted aspect of the daily routine.

One way that multiculturalism can permeate the curriculum is through a literature approach that incorporates culturally-appropriate children's and adolescents' literature in teaching the various areas of the curriculum. Norton (1990) recommends a multicultural reading and literature program that crosses curriculum areas. Multicultural literature is essential to all areas of the curriculum, because these materials meet the needs of students and help them grow in understanding of themselves and others. Through carefully selected and shared multicultural reading materials, students learn to identify with the people who created the stories, whether of the past or present. They can discover folktales, myths, and legends that clarify the values and beliefs of people. Upon discovering the great stories on which cultures have been founded, they can discover the threads that weave the past with the present, and the themes and values that interconnect the people of all cultures.

Activity:

Divide the class into small groups and have each select a different cultural group to research. The following questions may serve as guidelines:

_____ 1. Where did the racial, religious, or ethnic group you're studying originate?

_____ 2. Why did they leave their homeland?

_____ 3. Where in the United States did they originally settle?

_____ 4. What kind of work did they do when they first came here?

_____ 5. What was their native language?

_____ 6. What was their dominant religion?
_____ 7. What is a popular myth or legend from their culture?
_____ 8. What are three notable themes from their literature?
_____ 9. Who are three notable authors from this group?

Source: Minderman, L. (1990). "Literature and multicultural education." *Instructor, 99(7)*, 22–23.

IMPLEMENTING RESEARCH 7-2 looks at the diverse gifts brought to school by young children, and suggests that appropriate multicultural education experiences should begin at the kindergarten level.

IMPLEMENTING RESEARCH 7-2: Multicultural Education in Kindergarten

Williams maintained that early childhood teachers can and should make valuable use of the social and cultural gifts that children bring to school. Previously, the emphasis had been on individual children and their physical, psychological, and cognitive development. While these are important aspects for teachers to consider, children's cultural backgrounds also deserve consideration. Kindergarten teachers often reject the notion that young children cannot understand the concept of culture; however, " 'culture' consists of all the people, objects, and events that impart meaning to our lives" (p. 3). Culture, therefore, serves as a thread that allows young children to share in the connection between groups of people.

IMPLEMENTING THE RESEARCH

_____ 1. Kindergarten teachers should recognize that culture can be understood by young children, and that age-appropriate cultural experiences should be provided.

_____ 2. Educators can allow children to explore their family's cultural traditions by examining family names, customs, traditions, and photographs.

_____ 3. Educators can request that culturally different grandparents, or other community people, visit the classroom to show how all people have cultural similarities and dissimilarities.

_____ 4. Kindergarten educators should provide developmentally-appropriate reading materials that incorporate multiculturalism throughout all curricular areas.

Source: Williams, L. R. (1989). "Diverse gifts: Multicultural education in the kindergarten." *Childhood Education, 66(1),* 2–3.

Reform Efforts

The traditional curriculum in United States schools has taken an one-sided approach that predominantly addressed subjects, events, and people from Anglo, middle-class, perspectives. Whether this approach was conscious or unconscious, the result was the same: Many culturally diverse learners perceived that their culture had contributed little or nothing positive or of worth to the history of the world.

As stated earlier, approaches using teaching units are appropriate, and often serve as a viable means of reaching specific objectives. However, serious reform efforts toward a more realistic portrayal of culturally diverse people will require a major overhaul of elementary and secondary school curricula (Manning, 1991). Specifically, what steps can educators take to ensure that elementary and secondary school curricula reflect the cultural diversity of the United States society? The following suggestions represent guidelines for a curriculum that recognizes, reflects, and respects cultural diversity (Sleeter & Grant, 1988). As previously mentioned, a curriculum must have more than multicultural components. Multicultural aspects must genuinely permeate the entire curriculum and the total school environment.

GUIDELINES FOR DEVELOPING MULTICULTURAL CURRICULA

1. The curriculum should be reformed in such a way that it regularly presents diverse perspectives, experiences, and contributions. Similarly, concepts should be presented and taught that represent diverse cultural groups and both sexes.
2. The curriculum should include materials and visual displays that are free of race, gender, and handicap stereotypes, and which include members of all cultural groups in a positive mannner.
3. The curriculum should include concepts related to diverse groups, rather than teaching fragments of information.
4. The curriculum should provide as much emphasis on contemporary culture as on historical culture, and groups should be represented as active and dynamic, e.g., while the women's suffrage movement should be addressed, more contemporary problems confronting women also should be addressed.
5. The curriculum should be viewed as a "total effort", with multicultural aspects permeating all subject areas and all phases of the school day.
6. The curriculum should ensure the use of non-sexist language.
7. The curriculum should endorse bilingual education and the vision of a multilingual society.
8. The curriculum and the teaching/learning methods should draw

on children's experiential background, and the community and curricular concepts should be based on children's daily life and experiences.

9. The curriculum should allow equal access for all students, i.e., all students should be allowed to enroll in college preparatory courses or other special curricular areas.

Adapted from: Sleeter, C. E., & Grant, C. A. (1988). *Making choices for multicultural education: Five approaches to race, class, and gender.* Columbus: Merrill, pages 153–155.

Although the Sleeter and Grant (1988) list goes far toward developing a multicultural curriculum, Bennett (1986) provides still other perspectives and suggestions for making the curriculum more relevant and responsive to multicultural populations, and for showing the contributions of the various cultures. First, Bennett maintained that the traditional curriculum was filled with inaccuracies and omissions concerning the contributions and life conditions of major ethnic groups within United States society. Curricular reformers should address this omission, for the benefit of both culturally diverse learners and majority-culture learners.

IMPLEMENTING RESEARCH 7-3 shows how multicultural education experiences can be incorporated in the educational experiences of even the youngest children.

IMPLEMENTING RESEARCH 7-3: Multicultural Education in Infant and Toddler Settings

Whaley and Swadener (1990) provide considerable, convincing, information to document that multicultural education should begin with children at a very young age. Their evidence pertains to children's discrimination skills (i.e., distinguishing friendly and unfriendly voices), children's early development of preferences for people, and the way children's behavior is affected by the emotional reactions of parents. Infant and toddler multicultural education should develop and nurture self-esteem, and should include goals such as creating a familiar, home-like atmosphere, providing exposure to diverse cultures, and fostering a child's own cultural identity.

IMPLEMENTING THE RESEARCH:

_____ 1. Educators who work with very young children should learn the backgrounds and cultures of each family, build self-esteem by allowing children to feel competent, encourage creativity, and portray both genders in nurturing roles.

_____ 2. Educators can avoid gender-stereotyped toys, use various types of music, talk about feelings and emotions, and encourage and expect empathy and altruistic behavior from children.

_____ 3. Educators can put up pictures of different cultural experiences, recognize language differences, and be sure materials represent various cultures and lifestyles.

Source: Whaley, K., & Swadener, E. B. (1990). "Multicultural education in infant and toddler settings." *Childhood Education, 66(4)*, 238–240.

The Hidden Curriculum

While some aspects of the curriculum are readily discernible to children and adolescents attending a school, other aspects are more subtle, and may be equally influential. For example, one does not have difficulty in determining whether culturally diverse people are addressed honestly and adequately in textbooks and other curricular materials. One can also ascertain with relative ease whether tracking and ability grouping have resulted in all culturally diverse people or lower-class students being segregated, or relegated to second-class status. There is, however, another equally important curriculum, one which has a powerful influence on children and adolescents. This "other" curriculum is the "hidden curriculum", a very subtle curriculum which affects learners of all races and cultures.

Referring to the "hidden curriculum", Jarolimek and Foster (1989) wrote:

> The hidden curriculum is pervasive in a classroom and school and reflects the attitudes of the teacher, the administration, and the children. Without saying so directly, the teacher, through a combination of circumstances, conveys to the children much about the expectations and values that are prized. Through the hidden curriculum, children learn the extent to which life at school suits them and their needs. Lessons learned through informal interaction with other children may condition a child's social skills and human relationships for a lifetime. Children learn, often without being told, which models of behavior are highlighted for emulation. They learn which behavior is likely to gain favor and which is not. They know a great deal about how the teacher feels toward social issues, groups, and individuals, and, again, without ever having been told explicitly (Jarolimek & Foster, 1989, p 65).

Mrs. Brunson in CASE STUDY 7-1 takes a stand against the "hidden curriculum" in her school.

CASE STUDY 7-1: The "Hidden Curriculum"

Mrs. Brunson at Calhoun Middle School knew she would have to take a stand at the faculty meeting. No longer could she let injustice prevail—her only decision was how to make her point in such a way that positive action would result.

"We have a hidden curriculum," she said calmly and matter-of-factly. She continued to say that, while their school's philosophy offered a belief in equality and equitable treatment for all, this was not the case.

Early adolescents were learning from a hidden curriculum that taught as much or more than the planned curriculum. She had numerous examples to substantiate her point: School policies which only recognized middle-class Anglo expectations; the media center, which was predominantly Anglo-oriented; instructional practices and academic expectations that addressed Anglo learning styles; and mostly Anglo students participating in extracurricular activities. What were they conveying to culturally diverse learners? While one curriculum sought to show acceptance and respect for diversity, the hidden curriculum conveyed an almost totally opposite picture. Culturally diverse learners often felt unaccepted, and perceived that they must adjust to middle-class Anglo values and customs.

Although there was some skepticism, it was apparent that the faculty had not considered the impact of the hidden curriculum. In fact, the school was not as "multicultural" as some believed. Ms. Brunson felt better; genuine change would be slow, and efforts would be challenged by supporters of the status quo, but at least the problem had been recognized. This was a first and significant step.

What specific aspects might this "hidden curriculum" include? This "hidden curriculum" may be comprised of any number of events, behavior expectations, and attitudes that might appear relatively unobtrusive to Anglo, middle-class learners, yet might appear out of character or context to culturally diverse learners. Although trying to list all possible aspects of a "hidden curriculum" is an impossible task, representative examples might include: Teacher behaviors and expectations conveyed both verbally and nonverbally; textbooks and other curricular materials that portray Anglo, middle-class values and orientations; segregation due to tracking or ability grouping policies; educators' and other students' acceptance and attitudes toward culturally different learners; and acceptance or lack of acceptance of language differences. In other words, middle- or upper-class Anglo students might not be surprised when their teacher encourages them to compete and excel above others in the class, but this exact same teacher expectation might be anathema to Native-American learners. Educators must make a deliberate effort to examine all their behaviors (both conscious and unconscious) to determine hidden messages they are conveying and, also, to carefully assess every aspect of the curriculum and the total school environment to determine whether culturally diverse learners are being given a different message from that sent to Anglo students.

The Multicultural Curriculum Respecting Cultural Diversity

Guidelines

As with all curricular efforts, a multicultural curriculum should be matched carefully with goals and objectives, and use established guidelines. Although each program should reflect the needs and goals of the respective school, the following guidelines serve as a basis for multicultural curricular development (Hernandez, 1989; Banks, 1981; Calfornia State Department of Education, 1979):

> Emphasize multiple groups (i.e., ethnic, religious, regional, socioeconomic, language), rather than treating individual groups separately or in isolation. Such multiple-group emphasis diminishes the likelihood of stereotyping, and facilitates integration of multicultural content into the overall curriculum.

> Provide an interdisciplinary focus for the integration of multicultural perspectives, as appropriate, in all content areas. Although most frequently associated with the social sciences, language, literature, art, and music, multicultural perspectives are valid and applicable in areas such as mathematics, science, home economics, and physical education.

> Use a variety of instructional approaches and materials appropriate to the maturity level of students. In particular, teaching strategies should aim to accommodate differences in learning styles and to maximize academic achievement.

> Focus on the development of both cognitive and affective skills. Learning outcomes should be assessed in terms of knowledge, attitudes, and skills.

> Emphasize school and area populations, locally-oriented activities, and community resources (Hernandez, 1989, p. 176–177).

In a basic premise of this text, Banks (1988) contended that ethnic pluralism should permeate the total school curriculum and environment. Similarly, school policies and procedures should foster positive cross-cultural interactions and understandings among students, teachers, and staff members. The entire curriculum and school environment should reflect the learning styles of all learners, and should provide students with continuous opportunities to develop a more positive self-concept and cultural identity. Other guidelines suggested by Banks (1988) include:

1. The multicultural curriculum should help students understand the totality of the experiences of ethnic groups.
2. The multicultural curriculum should help students understand that there is always a conflict between ideals and realities in human societies.
3. The multicultural curriculum should explore and clarify ethnic alternatives and options within society.
4. The multicultural curriculum should promore values, attitudes, and behaviors that support ethnic pluralism.

5. The multicultural curriculum should help students develop the skills necessary for effective interpersonal and interethnic group interactions.

6. The multicultural curriculum should be comprehensive in scope and sequence, should present holistic views of ethnic groups, and should be an integral part of the total school curriculum.

7. The multicultural curriculum should include interdisciplinary and multidisciplinary approaches.

8. The multicultural curriculum should use comparative approaches in the study of ethnic groups and ethnicity.

9. The multicultural curriculum should maximize use of local community resources.

10. The multicultural curriculum should include assessment procedures which reflect individual ethnic cultures (Banks, 1988).

Assessing the Need for Curricular Change

Prior to planning the multicultural curriculum, a needs assessment should be made to determine the direction and extent of the change. Also, curricular assessment should be viewed as an ongoing and integral part of curriculum development (Ramsey, 1987). Representative examples of criteria to be considered in a needs assessment are listed below.

1. Do multicultural perspectives permeate the entire school curriculum and environment?

2. Do the attitudes of teachers, administrators, and staff members indicate a willingness to accept and respect cultural diversity?

3. Do textbooks and other curricular materials recognize the value of cultural diversity, and gender and social class differences?

4. Do curricular activities and methods provide learners with opportunities to work together in a cooperative fashion?

5. Do extracurricular activities reflect cultural diversity?

6. Do curricular planning efforts reflect the views and opinions of parents and other community people?

7. Do curricular efforts include bilingual perspectives, or provide assistance for students with limited English-speaking skills?

CASE STUDY 7-2 shows how the educators at Lockhaven Elementary decided to assess the need for change in their school.

CASE STUDY 7-2: Assessing the Need for Change

The educators at Lockhaven Elementary knew that their school was experiencing demographic changes. Many of the Anglo families had moved to the suburbs; the African-American population had grown to some extent; and there had been an influx of Asian- and Hispanic-American students. Even with these changes, the curriculum and educational practices had stayed basically the same. The counselor was the first to mention a need for change. However, others had begun to recognize that the school was no longer designed to meet the needs of the current student population.

That the school should assess the need for change became clear, but the questions remained of where to begin and what to assess. Suggestions poured in as the counselor took notes:

1. The actual cultural composition of the school and the community.
2. The cultural composition of the administration, faculty, and staff.
3. The curriculum and the extent to which it addresses cultural diversity.
4. The instructional practices and the extent to which they meet the learning styles of culturally diverse learners.
5. The school policies and expectations of students.
6. The extracurricular program and its accessibility to all learners.
7. The attitudes (recognition, respect, acceptance) of the educators.
8. The media center and the extent to which its holdings demonstrated a respect for diversity of all types.

The list could go on and on, the counselor thought, but the initial effort had been made. The need for change had been recognized, and a needs assessment was underway.

Toward Bias-Free Curricular and Teaching-Learning Materials

This section on textbooks and other curricular materials shows the significance and influence of textbooks. It provides examples of omission, stereotypical images, and the outright racism and sexism often found in teaching/learning materials, and suggests guidelines for the selection of objective materials. Although this effort and goal are worthy of all elementary and secondary curricula, it might be of greater importance in a curriculum specifically designed to teach the values of cultural diversity.

Textbooks, workbooks, worksheets, and virtually all materials used for teaching have a powerful impact on learners' cognitive and affective domains. Not only is factual information taught, but these materials also affect students' attitudes and beliefs toward themselves, other people and cultures, and world views. In essence, teaching materials have the potential for transmitting an "approved culture", which in most cases has been the Anglo, middle-class perspective. As the Association of American Publishers (1984, n.p.) pointed out: "The words and pictures children see in school influence the development of the attitudes they carry into adult life. These words and pictures not only express ideas—they are part of the educational experience which shapes ideas." With such a powerful influence as this, one can readily comprehend the damage inflicted upon culturally diverse children through-out the decades as they came into contact with images and perceptions that either ignored their culture, or dealt with their culture only in erroneous or stereotypical terms.

The influence of characterizations on children and adolescents can be affected by several factors. First, the extent to which attitudes and stereo-types are internalized and retained seems to be determined, at least in part, by the amount of time spent interacting with the materials. For example, the longer children are exposed to stereotypical images or omissions, the greater the effect of the materials. Second, children vary in their emotional involve-ment and identification with the individuals and situations portrayed. In reading, mathematics, and social studies, for example, student performance is enhanced when content is perceived to be relevant and interesting. On the positive side, culturally relevant materials can facilitate the process of learn-ing to read, making it both easier and faster. On the negative side, the absence of characters and situations with which children are able to identify may contribute to, and reinforce feelings of, security, inferiority, or superior-ity, depending upon an individual's group identity. These non-academic aspects of textbook content affect variables associated with academic achievement, e.g., perserverance, motivation, retention, and skills develop-ment (Hernandez, 1989).

Klein (1985) contended that stereotyping occurs when all individuals in a particular culture are depicted as having the same attributes, e.g., all Asian-American students are whizzes in mathematics and science, and in fact, excel in all areas. Other stereotypes found in textbooks include Native-Americans as warlike, Hispanics as poor and violent, and African-Americans being depicted only in entertainment or sports roles (Gollnick & Chinn, 1990; U. S. Commission on Civil Rights, 1980).

Activity:

How might the following be stereotyped?

Hispanic-American adolescents are ————————————————— .

The elderly are ————————————————————— .

The lower classes are ———————————————————— .

Adolescent girls are ————————————————————— .

Considering your own culture, ethnic background, gender, and social class, and considering a person with similar characteristics, what conclusions can you reach concerning?

. . . the vast differences among people.

. . . the vast differences among cultural groups.

. . . the vast differences among social classes.

One can easily conclude that even people with similar backgounds and personal characteristics differ greatly, and that describing people according to specific characteristics risks the dangers of stereotyping.

Other equally important concerns related to bias in textbooks are omissions and distortions. Simply put, omission refers to information left out of an account presented in a textbook, while a distortion is a lack of balance or systematic omissions. Because of omissions, members of some cultural and ethnic groups are virtually "invisible" in textbooks. Although some progress undoubtedly has been made, Hispanic-Americans, Asian-Americans, Native-Americans, and women continue to be under-represented in educational materials (Hernandez, 1989). This invisibility implies that these groups have less value or significance in United States society, and occurs most often with women, culturally-diverse people, handicapped individuals, and the elderly (Gollnick & Chinn, 1990; Sadker & Sadker, 1978).

Distortions result from inaccurate or unbalanced impressions. History and reading materials too often ignore the presence and realities of certain groups in contemporary society, confine treatment to negative experiences, and provide a single point of view on events that may be technically correct, but are nevertheless misleading (Hernandez, 1989).

Sexism or sexist language is another factor to consider when selecting textbooks and other teaching materials. Gollnick, Sadker, & Sadker, (1982) and Pyle (1976) have called attention to the sexism often found in children's and adolescents' textbooks. Especially at the elementary school level, children asked to draw an early caveman drew only pictures of cave-*men*. In contrast, when instructed to draw "cave people," the children generate drawings of men, women, and children. In classrooms, teachers can point out to students words that appear to exclude women as full participants in society, or that limit their occupational options, e.g., mail carrier and police officer as alternatives to mailman and policeman (Gollnick et al., 1982).

The challenge facing multicultural educators is to select textbooks and other materials that objectively represent the various groups and people who have been traditionally either ignored or misrepresented. Table 7-1 provides educators with a means of evaluating written material to determine its feasibility in our increasingly multicultural schools.

Table 7-1   Ways to Analyze Books for Racism and Sexism

The guidelines below are a starting point, and are designed to detect racist and sexist bias in story books—children's picture books, primers, fiction, etc.

1. Check the illustrations.

    Look for stereotypes. A stereotype is an oversimplified generalization about a particular group, race, or sex, and generally carries derogatory implications. Look for variations which in any way demean or ridicule characters because of their race or sex.

    Look for tokenism. If there are culturally diverse characters, are they just like Anglo-Americans, but tinted or colored? Do all culturally diverse faces look stereotypically alike, or are they depicted as genuine individuals?

    Look at the lifestyles. Are culturally diverse characters and their settings depicted in such a way that they contrast unfavorably with an unstated norm of Anglo-American middle-class suburbia? For example, culturally diverse people are often associated with the ghetto, migrant labor, or "primitive" living. If the story does attempt to depict another culture, does it go beyond oversimplifications of reality and offer genuine insights into another lifestyle?

2. Check the story line. Civil Rights legislation has led publishers to weed out many insulting passages and illustrations, particularly in stories with Black themes, but the attitudes still find expression in less obvious ways. The following checklist suggests some of the various subtle forms of bias to watch for:

    Relationships: Do Anglo-Americans in the story have the power and make the decisions? Do culturally diverse people function in essentially subservient roles?

    Standard for success: What does it take for a character to succeed? To gain acceptance, do culturally diverse characters have to exhibit superior qualities—excel in sports, get A's, etc.?

    Viewpoint: How are "problems" presented, conceived, and resolved in the story? Are culturally diverse people themselves considered to be "the problem"? Do solutions ultimately depend on the benevolence of an Anglo-American?

    Sexism: Are the achievements of girls and women based on their own initiative and intelligence, or is their success due to their good looks or to their relationships with boys? Are sex roles incidental or paramount to characterization and plot? Could the same story be told if the sex roles were reversed?

3. Consider the effects of the book on the child's self-image and self-esteem. Are norms established that limit the child's aspirations and self-concepts? What does it do to African-American children to be continuously bombarded with images of white as beautiful, clean, virtuous, etc., and black as evil, dirty, menacing, etc.? What happens to a girl's aspirations when she reads that boys perform all the brave and important deeds? What about a girl's self-esteem if she is not fair of skin and slim of body?

4. Consider the author's or illustrator's qualifications. Read the biographical material on the jacket flap or on the back of the book. If a story deals with a culturally diverse theme, what qualifies the author or illustrator to deal with this topic? If they are not members of the culturally diverse group being written about, is there anything in the author's or illustrator's background that would specifically recommend them for this book?

Similarly, a book that has to do with the feelings and insights of women should be more carefully examined if it is written by a man . . . unless the book's avowed purpose is to present a male viewpoint.

The above observations do not deny the ability of writers to empathize with experiences other than those of their own sex or race, but the chances of their writing as honestly and as authentically about other experiences are not as good.

5. Look at the copyright date. Books on culturally diverse themes—usually hastily conceived—suddenly began appearing in the mid-1960s. There followed a growing number of "culturally diverse experience" books to meet the new market demand, but these were still written by Anglo-American authors, and reflected an Anglo point of view. Only in the late 1960s and early 1970s did the children's book world begin to even remotely reflect the realities of a multiracial society, and it has only just begun to reflect feminists' concerns.

Adapted from: "Ten quick ways to analyze children's books for racism and sexism." (November 3, 1974). *Interracial Books for Children, 5(3)*, 6–7.

Evaluation: Curricular Efforts

Evaluating the multicultural curriculum to determine overall program strengths and weaknesses, and to assess how well it meets individual learner needs, is as important as the actual content and teaching methods being used. One basic criterion is to determine whether teaching and learning situations reflect multiculturalism. For example, if children are taught a history, content and instruction should include accomplishments of all people, and should not focus solely on wealthy Anglo males (Sleeter & Grant, 1988).

Other recommended measures of program effectiveness include oral and written tests (teacher-made and standardized), sociograms, questionnaires, surveys, student projects, interviews, anecdotal information, and discussion groups. Indicators such as attendance records, class participation, and incidence of disruptive behavior also provide clues about student acceptance of, and interest in, the program. Many of these procedures are conducive to staff, parent, and student involvement. Whatever evaluation is used, the information collected should be well-documented, relevant, and useful. The validity of evaluation depends upon the questions asked, behaviors observed, and efforts made to sample randomly and to apply common standards (California State Department of Education, 1979).

A Multicultural Education Unit

While the basic premise of *Multicultural Education for Children and Adolescents* is that multicultural education should be a total school curriculum and environment approach, rather than an occasional unit, the authors do recognize that the situation should not be considered an "either/or" situation, and should not become a multicultural education curriculum versus the unit approach. The authors firmly believe, however, that a once-a-year semester (or even a semester) effort in the form of a multicultural week, or perhaps a two- or three-week unit, will not be sufficient to teach a knowledge of, and a respect for, cultural diversity. Therefore, readers are reminded to consider units as a part of a total curriculum effort, perhaps as a means of addressing one or more specific objectives.

Considerations. Before examining an unit designed to convey knowledge and understanding of cultural diversity, it is important to define the unit approach, and to look briefly at what units usually include. First, units (sometimes called modules) are designed to teach a specific body of information over a time lasting more than a class meeting or two. For example, the unit might last one, two, three days? weeks? years? other? (or longer in some instances). Second, units contain goals, objectives, content, activities, materials, enrichment resources, and evaluational instruments. Although educators may differ on what the unit should include, generally speaking, it is a comprehensive guide which differs from the one-day lesson plan.

Example. The next several pages provide an example of an instructional unit. It is important to remember that this unit serves only as an illustration. Educators should assess their students' own developmental needs, levels of knowledge, and attitudes, and then plan instruction based on individual needs.

A MULTICULTURAL EDUCATION UNIT

I.   Rationale
     In most classes, oppression is dealt with only from the standpoint of how people are oppressed and not why people feel the need to be oppressors. It is important to understand the reasons people want to oppress others rather than solely studying the effects of oppression. If these reasons are not understood, they are most likely to continue to result in new forms of oppressions.
     Students must understand that prejudice and stereotypic attitudes lead to oppressive interactions between people. They should be aware that they may be oppressors of other students and teachers as well as being oppressed by others in the classroom setting.

II. Statement of Specific Objectives
     A.   To introduce the meaning of culture, ethnic groups, prejudice, and oppression through the use of definition and examples.
     B.   To develop an awareness of oppression through small group studies pertaining to oppression of different ethnic groups.
     C.   To reinforce group participation through the technique of group studies.
     D.   To study and discuss why people feel the need to oppress others.
     E.   To study and discuss means by which people oppress others, i.e., slavery, holocaust, and internment.
     F.   Through viewing a film, to gain an awareness of the meaning of stereotype and its effect upon people.
     G.   To gain an awareness of the relationship between stereotypic beliefs and the willingness to oppress others.

  H. To gain an awareness of the presence of oppression in the classroom through actual classroom experiments.

  I. To experience and discuss the feeling of oppression.

III. Procedure

  A. Day One

    1. The experience of oppression

      a. Discussion of definition of terms

        (1) prejudice

        (2) culture

        (3) ethnic group

        (4) oppression

      b. Handout on the comparison between factual information and prejudice

      c. Discussion on feelings experienced during the classroom experiment on oppression

  B. Day Two

    1. Introduction to group activities

      a. divide students into groups

      b. independent group study work

  C. Day Three

    1. continuation of Day 2

  D. Day Four

    1. Presentation of group studies

      a. discussion of questions and answers pertaining to group studies on oppression

      b. discussion of extraneous ideas or comments as a result of class participation

    2. Summation of group presentations

  E. Day Five

    1. Introduction to prejudice and stereotypes

      a. role playing exemplifying cultural differences

      b. discussion of role playing

    2. Presentation of film, "Bill Cosby on Prejudice"

    3. Discussion of film and summation of unit

IV. Materials

  A. A list of questions assigned for group studies:

    1. The Japanese Group (see Daniels, 1972: Yin, 1973)

      a. List some of the lessons the Japanese have taught us. (Include other lessons that could be learned, but have not.)

      b. Before the evacuation of the Japanese from the West Coast, there were many stereotypes concerning the Japanese. Write a paragraph, summarizing each of the following stereotypes:

        (1) the Chinese legacy

        (2) the "Yellow Peril"

        (3) Hollywood and the Oriental

      c. Describe General DeWitt's feelings and position concerning the evacuation of the Japanese

      d. Describe in detail the evacuation (include living conditions in the concentration camps, jobs, and income)

      e. In December of 1944, the army changed its control over the Japanese from "mass exclusion" to "individual exclusion." Describe individual exclusion and detention.

(Include in your description explanations of expatriation and renunciation.)

2. The Mexican American Group
    a. In the book, *Aztecas Del Norte* (DeForbes, 1973), the author speaks in the chapter, "Life in the U.S.: The experience of a Mexican – 1929," as one of the immigrants. Read the chapter and include in your summary the following:
        (1) jobs, wages, and availability
        (2) education
        (3) the Mexican contribution to agricultural and industrial expansion
    b. In the book *Ando Sangrando (I am Bleeding)* (Morales, 1972), Chapter Four states many stereotypes given to Mexican Americans by different groups. Read the chapter and list several stereotypes. Be sure to include some of the developmental history of the stereotypes.
    c. In the book, *Viva La Raza* (Nava, 1973), the last chapter describes and conveys a feeling of triumph for the Mexican American. Read the chapter and describe the Mexican American's triumph and feelings.
    d. In the book, *Ando Sangrando* (Morales, 1972), "The Problem of Passivity" is discussed in the first chapter. Read the chapter and write a description stating the thesis of the "passive" nature of the Mexican American. Also list other stereotypes. Be critical!

3. The Black Group
    a. In the book, *The Nature of Prejudice* (Allport, 1954), the author states several stereotypes given to blacks. List 10 stereotypes and also compare the difference between children's stereotypes of blacks to that of adult stereotypes.
    b. In the book, *Race, Creed, Color, or National Origin* (Yin, 1973), read "The Treatment of Negro Families in American Scholarship." Write a summary of the article, including the following:
        (1) a critical description of the Moynihan Report
        (2) a brief outline on the different phases of studies done on Negro families
    c. In the book, *Race, Creed, Color, or National Origin*, read the article, "Can a Black Man Get a Fair Trial?" Write a brief summary.
    d. In the book, *White Racism and Black Americans* (Bromley & Longino, 1972), the authors attempt to define *white racism*. They divide the term into three subgroups: individual racism, institutional racism, and cultural racism. Read and briefly discuss each subgroup.
    e. In the book, *The Challenge of Blackness* (Bennett, 1972), read the chapter "Reading, 'Riting, and Racism," and write a brief summary. Include the following:
        (1) education and its relationship to racial oppressions
        (2) the injustices forced upon the blacks by the educational system
        (3) strategy of reform in education to aid the blacks

4. The Jewish Group
   a. In the book, *The Nature of Prejudice* (Allport, 1954), the author states several stereotypes and an example of contradictory stereotypes.
   b. There are four main phases in the history of the Jewish ghettos. Briefly describe each phase and its intended outcome.
   c. Describe the Jewish labor camps; include in your description the following:
      (1) who was given the opportunity to work?
      (2) what type of work was provided?
      (3) how was the Jewish worker treated?
   d. In the book, *Anthology of Holocaust Literature* (Glatstein, Knox, & Margoshets, 1973), read "The Death Train" and write a summary of the true story.
   e. What did Hitler mean by "the Jewish problem" and what did he feel would be the outcome for the Jews if Germany was the victor of a second world war?
5. The Indian Group (see Wissler, 1966)
   a. Describe life on the Indian reservation. Include in your description the following:
      (1) the high death rate and its cause.
      (2) the power of the "agent" on the reservation
      (3) how the Indians rebelled on the reservations
   b. List some achievements made by the Indians.
   c. The white man gave the Indian three "gifts": the gun, the horse, and liquor. Describe the effects of each gift and what that gift meant to the Indian.
   d. Describe how you think the Indian must have felt. (There are many stereotypes placed on the Indians due to their actions.) Read and find the *real* reasons behind their actions.
   e. Stories give the impression that the Indian lived a simple life, enjoyed ideal freedom, and was always happy, and therefore lived the most desirable life. Find some contradictions to this.

B. Conclusion

The following was included in all five group studies as the final question:

Why were and are the _____ oppressed?
(Payne & Davis, 1978)

Source: Payne, C. (1984). "Multicultural education and racism in American schools." *Theory into Practice, 23,* 129–131.

EXTENDING THE MULTICULTURAL EDUCATION CURRICULUM

Parental and Community Involvement

It is important that efforts to provide multicultural education curricula and accompanying school environments include active approaches that extend the program beyond the confines of the school. Two basic reasons support this supposition: First, children and adolescents need to perceive evidence of recognition and respect for cultural diversity in the home *and* in the community. The home and the community can serve as powerful and positive forces to help reinforce the efforts of the school. Second, both as valuable resources and as promoters of the school's efforts to promote respect for cultural diversity, parents and other community members (and organizations) should be aware of school efforts, and should feel that their advice and opinions are sought and respected. These two entities can also provide considerable financial and volunteer support for the multicultural education program.

There are, however, still other positive aspects to be gained as schools implement efforts to obtain support and involvement. As parents become involved in their children's education and learn more about the school's goals (especially in relation to the goals and materials used in the multicultural education curricula), there is likely to be more overall support for school programs. Parents will in all likelihood become more interested in their children's school success, and be better able to assist the school in its efforts.

Activity:

Name several ways to involve culturally diverse parents and extended family members in the curricular efforts of the school. Perhaps it would be best to divide the list into two groups, one for classes, and one for the overall school programs. Also include ways that special school personnel (i.e., the counselor and the communications specialists) can most effectively involve parents and extended family members.

Questions also should be asked as to whether the community supports the school and its academic and social tasks. Is the leadership of the community concerned about school effectiveness? Does the community support efforts toward school improvement? Are the achievements of all students and teachers celebrated in the community at public occasions? Are the role models in the community educated persons? If the community is not strongly positive, the matter should be brought to the attention of progressive community leaders with the suggestion that they sponsor a determined effort to improve the community environment (Tyler, 1989).

As can be seen in CASE STUDY 7-3, involving the community can be a task of some magnitude, but one that offers many rewards.

CASE STUDY 7-3: Community Involvement

The school personnel at HS 170, a secondary school in an urban area, had reached basic agreement on their multicultural education program. Specific objectives had been established for the program, one of which was to involve the community. First, extending the program outside the school showed genuine commitment. Second, parents, families, and other community members had a chance to provide input and to offer their involvement.

The group decided on several approaches: Notices sent home with the students explained the basic premises of the program, and how parents, families, and the community could respond; radio and television stations were asked to donate brief air time to inform the community of the effort; posters designed by the students were placed in businesses and other public places.

Several meeting times and locations were listed which recognized the varying work schedules of community members. The purposes of the meetings were outlined as follows:

1. Explain the program's purposes, and how it fits in with the existing academic program.
2. Explain the phases of implementation, and the rationale and objectives for each phase.
3. Explain that all aspects of the program will be evaluated and reviewed for changes and revisions.
4. Form a committee to review library and media acquisitions.
5. Explain that the program will be interdisciplinary, and will permeate all areas of the school: curriculum, instruction, materials, teaching/learning environment, and teacher attitudes and behaviors.

Perhaps of greatest importance during the meetings, the group will demonstrate the objectives of the program itself: recognition, acceptance, appreciation, and respect for all people, regardless of differences.

Extracurricular Activities

Perceptive educators readily recognize the need for an equitable representation of all races and ethnic groups in extracurricular activities.

1. Baker (1983) suggested that athletic programs include minority students and women, and that cheerleading teams include both sexes and culturally diverse students.
2. Baker (1983), and Gollnick and Chinn (1990) recommend that clubs and organizations not perpetuate racial or gender segregation, and that positions of student leadership not be dominated by one group.

3. Baker (1983) also recommended that females should be encouraged to participate in all sports, and that special arrangements be made for students who were unable to participate for financial or other reasons.

Extracurricular Activity Checklist

1. Do extracurricular activities accurately reflect the racial and ethnic groups in the school?
2. Are financial resources equitably distributed among extracurricular activities?
3. Are extracurricular activities segregated along racial lines?
4. Do sponsors or advisors of extracurricular activities encourage culturally diverse learners to participate in the activities they sponsor?
5. Are arrangements available to support students who might lack the financial (or other, e.g., travel) resources to participate in extracurricular activities?
6. Are there conscious efforts to include students of differing socio-economic groups, and to involve both boys and girls in the school's extracurricular program?
7. Do the efforts to involve all children and adolescents in extracurricular activities receive the wholehearted support (not just token support) of all administrators, teachers, special service personnel, and staff members?

THE LANGUAGE OF THE CURRICULUM

Although language and language policies are addressed as issues in Chapter 12, it is necessary to mention language in this chapter, which places a major focus on school curriculum and environment, and to show how educators' actions and attitudes toward languages spoken in the schools transmits a message of acceptance or rejection. In most United States schools, the lack of proficiency in the English language places the learner at a grave disadvantage (Banks, 1988).

Activity:

Visit a school to determine its efforts to help limited English-speaking children and adolescents. What special considerations are made for these learners? What language programs are in place? What professional staff is available to offer help? What remedial programs are available? Are learners allowed to speak their native languages in school?

It is important to note that the number of students with limited English proficiency (those whose first language is not English) has increased during the past decade, and will continue to increase during the 1990s and beyond. Educators in areas such as California, Texas, New Mexico, Arizona, and Hawaii will be particularly challenged to provide a curriculum and environment in which these children and adolescents are able to succeed (Hernandez, 1989).

What are the educational implications for educators who strive to provide a curriculum and overall school environment that reflects the cultural diversity of United States society? First, educators should recognize that language is an integral aspect of our social system; Their ability to respond appropriately will to some extent determine the effectiveness of the education system. Second, since all children bring to school the language systems of their culture, it is the obligation of educators to ensure the right of each child to learn in the language of the home until the child is able to function well in English. Such a provision might include the use of English as a Second Language (ESL), or bilingual programs for students who are limited in English proficiency. Third, the environment should be such that educators understand cultural and linguistic differences, and recognize the value of these differences while they work to enhance the learner's skills in the dominant language (Gollnick & Chinn, 1990).

Although these three implications are self-explanatory, the important issue at stake in this chapter is that educators must understand how learners perceive both the language of the curriculum, and the overall acceptance of children's native languages. School situations in which educators value children's native language capabilities, and who try to build upon existing language strengths, convey positive feelings of acceptance and support for language diversity. Some instruction and curricular materials are in the students' native language; similarly, students are allowed to converse in their native language with peers and teachers who share the language. The opposite situation also holds true. Educators who punish children for speaking their native language convey a lack of acceptance of language diversity and, subsequently, of learners themselves.

This section does not downplay the importance and reality of English as a vehicle to economic and social mobility in the United States. Its purpose is to show that the manner in which language diversity is treated in the curriculum and overall school environment conveys a message of the degree to which cultural diversity is accepted.

SUMMING UP

Multicultural educators planning and implementing culturally-responsive curricula should remember that the curriculum and school environment should:

1. Reflect and recognize that the United States has experienced considerable progress toward acceptance of cultural diversity; that racism, discrimination, and prejudice continue to exist in the United States; and that curricular efforts and overall school environment should demonstrate an emphatic respect for cultural diversity.

2. Place reform efforts on an across-the-curriculum approach and the overall school environment, rather than on a once-a-year or unit approach.

3. Have a sound multicultural basis: A careful assessment of overall needs; established guidelines; the selection of bias-free curricular materials; and the provision of evaluative procedures for both learners and curricular efforts.

4. Include extensive involvement of community resources, and should permeate extracurricular activities as well as the academic curricular aspects.

5. Respect and build upon as much as possible learners' native language.

SUGGESTED LEARNING ACTIVITIES

1. Visit a school with considerable cultural diversity to evaluate the cultural diversity reflected in the textbooks and workbooks. Answer the following questions to determine whether appropriate cultural perspectives are included (feel free to include your own questions):
   a. Are culturally diverse students portrayed in meaningful, non-stereotypical manner?
   b. Are various social classes portrayed?
   c. Are women and handicapped people portrayed in meaningful roles?
   d. Are Native-, Asian-, and Hispanic-Americans portrayed as well as African-Americans?
   e. Are provisions made for learners with limited English-speaking skills?

2. Interview a curriculum coordinator of a large school (or school district) with a large percentage of culturally diverse students. What approach is being taken to implement a multicultural education program? What mechanism is in place to ensure that all levels of educators are involved in the multicultural education program? After the interview, carefully consider your findings, and write a brief paper which summarizes your findings (and offer what you think would be appropriate suggestions).

3. Prepare a multicultural unit (designed for perhaps two or three

weeks) that could be integrated into an overall multicultural education program. In this unit, be sure to include goals, objectives, activities, curricular materials, provisions for evaluation (both student and the unit itself), and provisions for children and adolescents with limited English-speaking abilities.

4. Prepare a list of curricular materials that reflects cultural diversity. Specifically, look at textbooks, workbooks, worksheets, audiovisuals, and any other curricular materials commonly used in elementary or secondary schools. Are culturally diverse children and adolescents portrayed with stereotypes and myths? Of the materials on your list, consider the actual numbers of culturally diverse learners, the accuracy and objectivity of their portrayal, and whether differences among people within cultural groups are addressed (e.g., are all Asian-Americans considered to be alike? Are all Spanish-speaking people considered alike?).

Expanding Your Horizons: Additional Journal Readings and Books

BERNSON, M. H., & LINDQUIST, T. L. (1989). "What's in a name? Galloping toward cultural insights—appreciating cultural diversity in the upper grades." *Social Studies and the Young Learner, 1(4)*, 13–16. These two authors provide activities for students in grades 4–7 in which students learn about names. Specific attention is focused upon Chinese naming patterns and developing a Stamp Worksheet.

MANNING, M. L. (1991). "More than lip service to multicultural education." *The Clearing House, 64*, 218. Manning, in urging educators to take multiculturalism seriously, called for the inclusion of multiculturalism into the curriculum, school environment, and the mindset of both learners and faculty.

MINDERMAN, L. (1990). "Literature and multicultural education." *Instructor, 99(7)*, 22–23. Minderman provided practical suggestions on integrating literature and multicultural education. The reading includes cross-curricular projects and excellent suggested readings for Native-, African-, Chinese-, Japanese-, Hispanic-, and Jewish-Americans.

NORTON, D. E. (1990). "Teaching multicultural literature in the reading curriculum." *The Reading Teacher, 44(1)*, 28–40. Norton suggests that learners be provided opportunities to study multicultural literature in the reading curriculum. Likewise, she provides a sequence chart and extensive list of books for Native-, African, and Hispanic-American learners.

OVANDO, C. J. (1990). "Intermediate and secondary curricula: A multicultural and multilingual framework." *The Clearing House, 63*, 294–297. Ovando examines a number of issues that affect the intermediate and secondary curricula: sociocultural and cognitive factors, indigenous and immigrant experiences, students' behavior in school, and structural and developmental issues.

TURKOVICH, M., & MUELLER, P. (1989). "The multicultural factor: A curriculum multiplier." *Social Studies and the Young Learner, 1(4)*, 9–12. Believing the early years to be critical in establishing a foundation for acceptance of multicultural perspectives and realties, Turkovich and Mueller provide concrete curriculum suggestions and activities for expanding the multicultural curriculum of young learners.

WHALEY, K., & SWADENER, E. B. (1990). "Multicultural education in infant and toddler settings." *Childhood Education, 66(4)*, 238–240. Whaley and Swadener provide convincing information that multicultural education should extend to infant and toddler settings.

WILLIAMS, L. R. (1989). "Diverse gifts: Multicultural education gifts in kindergarten." *Childhood Education, 66(1)*, 2–3. Williams maintained that with the advent of more full-day kindergartens, there will be more time including multicultural perspectives in kindergarten classes.

8

Instructional Practices

Understanding the material and activities in this chapter will help the reader to:

1. State the importance of individual and cultural differences among learners, and explain how these differences affect the teaching-learning process.
2. Explain the classroom teacher's role in providing teaching/learning situations that are beneficial to culturally diverse learners.
3. State how socioeconomic conditions, social class, and parents and families affect culturally diverse learners.
4. List the factors to be considered in the evaluation process of culturally diverse learners.
5. List the items to be considered during self-evaluation to determine teaching effectiveness in multicultural situations.
6. Explain special considerations to be addressed when planning teaching/learning experiences with Native-, African-, Hispanic-, and Asian-American children and adolescents.
7. List the characteristics of teachers who are effective in multicultural situations.
8. Explain the importance and necessity of ensuring that multicultural

education permeates the *total school environment,* providing educational experiences that demonstrate acceptance of culturally diverse learners, and promote positive self-concepts and cultural identities.

OVERVIEW

Learners at both the elementary and secondary levels deserve the most effective educational experiences possible. These educational experiences, however, all too often have emphasized predominantly Anglo-American perspectives, while minority viewpoints and issues have been neglected or portrayed as unimportant. Cultural diversity has been considered an obstacle for learners to "overcome", or for teachers to "remediate". Either consciously or unconsciously using this philosophy, educators planned and implemented experiences for Anglo-American learners. Educators expected all students to learn by using similar cognitive processes, to feel or perceive events similarly, to demonstrate similar patterns of behavior, and to demonstrate achievement through the use of evaluation instruments designed predominantly from a middle-class Anglo-American perspective. In essence, culturally diverse learners were expected to shape themselves to fit the Anglo-American mode. Based upon the philosophy that such educational experiences are both unethical and futile, this chapter will explore several teaching/learning contexts: Learners' individual and cultural differences, characteristics of educators, organization and instruction, the teaching/learning environment, and several cultural perspectives that influence the teaching/learning process in multicultural settings.

The Culture Quiz: Teaching and Learning

Directions: Mark the following as True or False.

_____ 1. The multicultural education program should include efforts that permeate the total school environment—the curriculum, instructional practices, and the promotion of positive self-concepts and cultural identities.

_____ 2. Four decades after *Brown vs. Board of Education of Topeka,* many students continue to be segregated by race.

_____ 3. Teachers, often unknowingly, bring to classrooms biases and prejudices toward people different from themselves.

_____ 4. Teacher self-evaluation lacks objectivity and, for all practical purposes, should be avoided.

_____ 5. Research has indicated that ability grouping does not improve academic achievement; however, the research has not indicated that intercultural relationships are hampered.

_____ 6. Ability-grouping patterns appear to be positively correlated to ethnicity and socioeconomic levels, rather than to academic abilities and achievement levels.

_____ 7. Cooperative learning proposes that when students learn cooperatively, it results in increased academic achievement for cooperative-learning classmates.

_____ 8. A major Native-American scholar and author, Lee Little Soldier, wrote that cooperative learning improves academic achievement, and matches Native-American values and behaviors.

_____ 9. Research has indicated that if the classroom teacher demonstrates appropriate multicultural attitudes, it is less important for the overall faculty/staff composition to represent the cultural diversity of the school.

_____ 10. Governmental efforts such as Headstart, Job Corps, Chapter or Title 1 programs, and often educational programs, generally speaking, did not help children and adolescents from culturally diverse families.

Answers: 1. T   2. T   3. T   4. F   5. F   6. T   7. T   8. T   9. F   10. F

TEACHING AND LEARNING CONTEXTS: LEARNERS' INDIVIDUAL AND CULTURAL DIFFERENCES

Valuing Objective Perceptions of All Learners

It is important that elementary and secondary learners be perceived objectively, regardless of cultural, ethnic, racial, social class, or religious differences. Learners need the psychological security of feeling valued and accepted; therefore, all educational decisions should be based on objective evidence and should be reached with the individual's welfare in mind. The tremendous diversity (whether cultural, racial, ethnic, social class, handicapped, or some combination) among contemporary learners means that educators cannot consider an entire class as a homogeneous group of learners who need the same educational experiences. Just as Anglo-American students differ significantly according to social class, geographic location, and family background, learners of other cultures also differ according to these characteristics, and also with values, traditions, and customs. It is the school's responsibility to develop an understanding of each learner, and to base teaching/learning experiences on reliable and objective information.

Recognizing and Accepting Diversity: Culture, Ethnicity, Race, Social Class, and Religion

It is an understatement to suggest that teaching/learning situations must demonstrate an emphatic acceptance of learners and their cultural, ethnic, social class, and religious differences. An environment that promotes this acceptance of diversity does more than pay lip service or have rhetorical goal statements. For culturally diverse learners to feel genuine acceptance, the teaching/learning process must provide concrete evidence of addressing and respecting cultural and ethnic differences (are all cultures and ethnic groups represented in the curriculum?); it must recognize social class (Do children come in contact with children from other socioeconomic levels? Do textbooks portray the various social classes of United States society?); and it must accept all religious groups (Do children feel their religious views are accepted?). The racism and classism that continue to burden the United States society make genuine acceptance difficult. Four decades after the *Brown vs. Board of Education of Topeka* decision, there continue to be inequities in education and outright segregation in some areas. The goal of school environments that demonstrate genuine acceptance will not be achieved outright; in fact, it might be a goal for which people will strive for years to come.

TEACHING AND LEARNING CONTEXTS: CHARACTERISTICS OF MULTIETHNIC/MULTICULTURAL EDUCATORS

Educators who seek a comprehensive understanding of cultural diversity and a working expertise in multicultural education should direct attention to both cognitive and affective factors. It will not suffice for educators to have knowledge of culturally diverse learners, and yet be unable to recognize learners' individual and cultural needs, and the complex relationship between culture and learning. Educators also need to develop appropriate attitudes which show genuine concern and caring. They also need to develop the skills to plan and implement instruction which addresses the culturally diverse students' developmental needs and learning styles.

To help accomplish this task, the National Council for Accreditation of Teacher Education now requires that all prospective teachers have experience with culturally diverse and exceptional populations so that they may gain an understanding of the unique contributions, needs, similarities, differences, and interdependencies of students from varying racial, cultural, religious, and socioeconomic backgrounds (NCATE, 1986).

While this section looks briefly at the knowledge, attitudes, and skills needed by teachers in multicultural settings, it is important to emphasize that these three attributes do not work in isolation. Teachers who work in multicultural situations are responsible for developing expertise in all three areas so they can provide learners with the most effective learning environment.

Knowledge

Teachers may lack factual information about ethnic, racial, and cultural differences, because teacher education programs traditionally did not provide appropriate experiences (both classroom and first-hand) to prepare teachers to teach in an increasingly multicultural world. While knowledge may appear to be somewhat basic, it is a prerequisite to developing appropriate attitudes and skills. A teacher's knowledge base should include culture, race, ethnicity, and social class, and the teacher should comprehend their implications for the teaching/learning process. Similarly, teachers should know and understand the ramifications of racism, discrimination, prejudice, and injustice, and what it means to be culturally different learner in a predominantly Anglo-American school and world. Although it would not be feasible to list all the competencies that teachers need for effective multicultural teaching, suffice it to say that teachers need sufficient knowledge to be able to understand culturally different learners, and to be able to plan both developmentally and culturally appropriate instruction.

Several educators in CASE STUDY 8-1 discuss whether knowledge, attitudes, or skills are most important for educators in multicultural settings, and reach the conclusion that professionals need all three characteristics.

CASE STUDY 8-1: Knowledge, Attitudes, and Skills

The discussion continued in the teachers' lounge at Ocean View Middle School. When working in multicultural situations, what characteristics does a teacher need the most: knowledge, attitudes, or skills? While the discussion was professional in nature, it was growing increasingly intense.

"Knowledge is what it takes," one person said. "If we know about diversity and the cultural characteristics of learners, we can plan appropriate teaching/learning actvities. Plus, we will better understand how others' characteristics differ from our own."

"True," another group responded, "but knowledge is not enough. You need proper attitudes; you need to examine your attitudes toward diversity, and you need to respond to culturally diverse students and their needs. History is full of times when people knew about cultures yet failed to respond when injustices occurred."

"Your arguments are missing a vital point," a person from another group stated. "Even with knowledge and attitudes, you will still fail to provide the most effective educational experiences for culturally diverse learners. You also need skills."

They thought about the issue. Perhaps, it did take all three—knowledge, attitudes, and skills. Some recognized the shortcomings of their positions. While some had tried to improve their knowledge, others had worked to develop more humane attitudes. One had even taken a "skills course" to improve his ability to work with students of varying cultures.

> However, the effective teacher in multicultural education settings needed all three—knowledge, attitudes, and skills. As the educators filed back to their classes, some one said, "Quite a challenge—but just think of the benefits for culturally diverse learners; in fact, for all learners."

Attitudes

Teachers often bring to classroom settings biases and prejudices toward people different from themselves. These attitudes influence the communication of accurate and objective information about ethnic groups in educational settings. Banks (1981) recommended that both pre-service and in-service teachers acquire the following characteristics: (1) more democratic values and attitudes; (2) a multicultural philosophy; (3) the ability to view events and situations from diverse ethnic perspectives and points of view; (4) an understanding of the complex and multidimensional nature of ethnicity in American society; (5) knowledge of the stages of ethnicity, and their curricular and teaching implications; and (6) the ability to function at increasingly higher stages of ethnicity (p. 193).

Teachers, perhaps unknowingly, have long transmitted biased messages to students. Whether lining up students for lunch by sex, or allowing ability grouping to result in racial segregation, teachers often send messages to students that one sex or race is entitled to preferential treatment. Most educators do not consciously or intentionally stereotype students, or discriminate against them; they usually try to treat all students fairly and equitably. Still, teachers, like others in United States society, have learned attitudes and behaviors that are ageist, handicapped, racist, sexist, and enthnocentric. Some biases have been so internalized that they are not realized or recognized. Only when teachers can (and are willing to) recognize the subtle and unintentional biases of their behavior can positive changes be made in the classroom (Sadker & Sadker, 1982; Gollnick & Chinn, 1990).

Changing attitudes is a difficult task, at best. What can teachers do to change their attitudes toward other cultures, races, and ethnic groups? Banks (1988) reported that racial attitudes may be changed positively through direct contact and involvement with people who differ culturally, ethnically, or racially. A five-week intergroup education workshop, consisting of lectures on racial problems, research projects, and visits to community agencies, has had significantly positive effects on racial attitudes. Efforts directed toward change should include diverse experiences such as seminars, visitations, community involvement, committee work, guest speakers, films, multimedia materials, and workshops (Banks, 1988).

Skills

Teaching culturally diverse children and adolescents requires the skill to understand and relate to learners (and their parents and families) of other cultures, ethnic groups, races, and social classes. Although understanding and relating are without doubt important and are not being downplayed, it is equally important to be able to plan and implement culturally appropriate instruction. Teachers are faced daily with understanding many complicated areas: Learning styles, the dangers of ability grouping, the benefits of cooperative learning, culturally different perceptions of motivation and competition, learners who may not want to excel at the expense of their peers, and stereotypical beliefs about a culture's ability to learn or not to learn. A comprehensive list would include aspects too numerous to list here; however, generally speaking, teachers need the skills to teach culturally different children and adolescents, and the ability to convey that teachers genuinely want what is best for learners, both as students and as people.

Teachers, working in a position to speak for change, have a responsibility to do whatever is possible to reduce racism, prejudice, and injustice among children and adolescents, and to instill attitudes of equality and democratic values which may continue for life. Teachers, indeed, should be significant influences on the values, hopes, and dreams of their students. Classrooms should be an open forum of inquiry, where diverse points of view and perspectives are shared and analyzed effectively. In a democratic classroom, both teachers and students who are committed to human freedom should have the freedom to express their views, values, and beliefs with regard to democratic ideals such as human dignity, justice, and equality (Banks, 1988).

Teacher Self-Evaluation

Educators of all grade levels and all cultures probably agree that some type of evaluation is needed periodically to determine whether goals and objectives have been met. Whether of an informal or formal nature, the evaluation instrument should focus on teachers' ability to plan and implement appropriate teaching/learning activities for children and adolescents. Teachers should also use a self-evaluation instrument designed to measure their ability to provide the environment and learning activities that are responsive to culturally diverse learners. Such a self-evaluation should include several questions designed to provide insight into the teacher's knowledge, attitudes, and skills:

1. Have there been efforts to understand and respect cultural diversity among learners, not as a problem to be reckoned with, but as a challenging opportunity and a rich gift?

2. Have there been efforts to provide a classroom in which learners feel free to speak and express diverse opinions? Are students free to express opinions contrary to middle-class Anglo-American beliefs? Did the teacher repress them or allow other students to stifle diverse opinion?

3. Have there been efforts to have the classroom reflect cultural diversity? Do the walls, bulletin boards, and artwork of the classroom demonstrate respect for cultural diversity, or do the contents of the classroom indicate an appreciation or valuing of only one culture?

4. Have there been efforts to provide organizational patterns that do not result in segregation of some learners according to race, culture, ethnicity, or social class?

5. Have there been efforts to understand language differences and differing learning styles? Have organizational patterns and instructional methodologies been developed which might be helpful to culturally diverse learners?

6. Have there been efforts to understand culturally different learners' perspectives toward motivation, excelling among one's peers, competition, group welfare, and sharing?

7. Have there been efforts to understand culturally diverse parents and extended families, and efforts to ensure their participation in learners' academic and social life at school?

8. Have there been efforts to treat each learner with respect, to consider each learner as equal to other students, and treat each learner as a valued and worthwhile member of the class? Are all learners accorded similar academic assistance? Do all learners receive help from the school's special service personnel?

9. Have there been efforts to allow (and indeed encourage) all students to work in cross-cultural groups, to carry on conversation and meaningful dialogue, and to feel a valued member of the group?

10. Have there been efforts to instill multiculturalism as a genuine part of the teaching/learning process and overall school environment?

CASE STUDY 8-2 suggests that teacher self-evaluation can be one of the most effective means of evaluating one's performance.

CASE STUDY 8-2: Teacher Self-Evaluations

Like nearly all teachers, the faculty at PS High School 93 was accustomed to evaluation by their principal, a central office evaluational specialist, and occasionally a peer teacher. However, the teachers were beginning to realize that, while evaluation was necessary and served useful purposes, something was missing. Evaluation forms indicated the degree of success, yet a teacher basically knew, better than the instrument could suggest, whether he or she had met the school's expectations, and whether he or she was working up to maximum potential. There was yet another issue: While the existing instruments evaluated overall performance, they did little to determine the educator's efforts to address the needs of culturally diverse learners.

In keeping with the research on evaluation, the counselor suggested a self-evaluation form for educators. Interested faculty members decided to work as a committee to develop a self-evaluation scale—a measure that might or might not be shared with peers or the administrators. This was a decision to be reached at a later date. While the evaluation committee would study the various possibilities and make final recommendations, broad categories for evaluation might include (with the "specifics" to be added later):

    I.   The Teacher's Knowledge, Attitudes, and Skills
    II. The Teacher's Classroom Environment
    III. The Teacher's Instructional Process
    IV. The Teacher's Curricular Materials
    V. The Teacher's Management System
    VI. The Teacher's Evaluation Process

The specifics to be added later would provide a base for individual educators to evaluate their efforts and commitment to the multicultural education program.

TEACHING AND LEARNING CONTEXTS: ORGANIZATION AND INSTRUCTION—CULTURAL CONSIDERATIONS

Practices Contributing to Exclusivity

Students are often organized for instructional purposes on the basis of test scores, previous grades, teacher recommendations, and other supposedly objective information. The basic rationale for grouping students is to narrow the abilities range, and thus provide teachers with a homogeneous group that is supposedly easier to teach. Two dangers inherent to any grouping process are: placing students in the wrong group; and having an organization pattern that segregates students by race. Although the dangers of grouping students by ability and achievement have been adequately documented (Manning & Lucking, 1990), the issue to be considered in this section is the danger of practicing exclusivity. Emphatically stated, whether considering race, social class, or gender, organizational patterns should not result in segregation, or in some students being educated by inferior teachers or in inferior schools, while other students receive preferential treatment. Organizational patterns should result in a student population which is as representative as possible of the entire school population, and, if possible, the composition of the community at large.

IMPLEMENTING RESEARCH 8-1 looks at how children from minority homes should be educated:

IMPLEMENTING RESEARCH 8-1: Educating Children From Minority Families

Tyler looked at his 68 years of teaching experience for insight into how best to educate children from minority groups. Moving from theory into practice, Tyler recommended that the first step was to identify children in need. The second step was to examine the school environment to determine whether it inhibited or supported learners. The third step, examining the community environment, included such questions as: Was the leadership of the community concerned with the effectiveness of the school? Were there appropriate role models for children? Did the community support school efforts? Tyler also focused on the home and the family, and maintained that these factors were crucial to successful school achievement.

IMPLEMENTING THE RESEARCH

_____ 1. Educators need to focus attention on the school and the learning environment, the community, the students, and the home, rather than looking only to one factor which either inhibits or supports school achievement.

_____ 2. Educators should get to know the individual child, rather than classifying him or her into a stereotypical catergory.

_____ 3. Educators should strive for a supportive school learning environment in which the morale of both student and teacher is high.

_____ 4. Educators should provide a professional and caring response as they work toward resolving personal learning problems of individual students.

Source: Tyler, R.W. (1989). "Educating children from minority families." _Educational Horizons, 67(4)_, 114–118.

Ability Grouping

The possibility that ability grouping may result in a form of segregation should warrant educators' attention and concern. Ability-grouping patterns often parallel students' non-academic characteristics, such as race or ethnic background, socioeconomic class, or personal appearance. Lower socioeconomic status and minority learners often find themselves placed in lower-ability groups. Such practices may be discriminatory, since students are segregated along ethnic and social class lines (Dawson, 1987). Minority students and learners from lower socioeconomic groups are disproportionately represented in lower-ability groups, while students from the higher socioeconomic strata often place in the higher-ability groups. These patterns of grouping appear to be related to ethnicity and socioeconomic standing, rather than purely academic abilities and achievement levels (Riccio, 1985).

CASE STUDY 8-3 shows how ability grouping can result in a form of segregation by placing culturally diverse learners in one group.

CASE STUDY 8-3: Culturally Diverse Groups and Ability Grouping

In a meeting with all the fifth grade teachers, Dr. Mallory, the principal at Southside Elementary School, voiced a concern that some classes consisted almost entirely of culturally diverse students. "How did this happen?" she questioned. While two classes were almost all minority, the other two classes were almost all Anglo.

One teacher explained that the students had been grouped by ability, based on their achievement test scores, reading grades, and the recommendations of their previous teachers. "The groups just worked out that way," he explained.

The principal explained that a form of segregation was occurring, and that students did not have adequate opportunities for social interaction. She further explained that they, as professional educators, had a responsibility to address the situation. Dr. Mallory explained that evidence shows clearly that ability grouping does not improve student achievement in the elementary school; self-concepts of low-ability learners may be seriously impaired by ability grouping; teachers interact differently with students from various ability groups; and ability groups too often parallel students' non-academic characteristics, such as race, ethnicity, and social class. Since the present segregation had to be changed, Dr. Mallory asked for specific suggestions to remediate the situation itself, rather than the causes that had produced the situation.

The fifth grade teachers brainstormed for possibilities: Heterogeneous grouping, individualized instruction, mastery learning, and cooperative learning. The teachers decided that since the principal had mandated change (and that she was correct about students being segregated), they would group heterogeneously, and then try other means of providing appropriate instruction.

Cooperative Learning

People who help one another by joining forces to achieve a common goal generally feel more positively about each other, and are willing to interact more positively when performing collective tasks. Rather than treating academic learning and social or intergroup relations as two distinct entities, cooperative learning has contributed positively to overall intergroup relations, and particularly to improving relations with multicultural/multiethnic students (Sharan, 1985). Cooperative learning procedures can reinforce the efforts of culturally diverse children to continue their schoolwork successfully. Children who work cooperatively in groups, rather than in isolation, are usually motivated to help others carry out the assigned or chosen project (Tyler, 1989). Other research that focused on cooperative learning and intergroup relationships concluded that students' learning cooperatively resulted in greater liking for cooperative-learning classmates. Specifically, cooperative learning increases contact between students, provides a feeling of group membership, engages learners in pleasant activities, and requires that team members work toward a common goal (Slavin, 1983).

Several research studies have indicated that students' working cooperatively can contribute positively to specific multiethnic populations. Aronson et al. (1978) concluded that both Black and Anglo students working in cooperative learning situations liked school better than the same ethnic groups working in competitive classrooms. Other research suggests that working cooperatively seems to have particularly strong effects for Hispanic and Black students, regardless of achievement levels (Slavin, 1987). One study indicated that Anglo- and Asian-Americans, in a learning situation similar to the Jigsaw method, had more positive attitudes towards Mexican-Americans than learners in competitive classes. A study of Jigsaw II-related classes that included recent European and West Indian immigrants, and Anglo-Canadians, documented substantially more cross-ethnic friendships than in the control groups (Slavin, 1983). Concerning specific cooperative learning methods, positive effects have been documented with STAD, TGT, TAI, and Jigsaw II (Slavin, 1987). Studies of Group Investigation also found that improved student attitudes and behaviors toward classmates of different ethnic backgrounds were extended to classmates of different groups (Sharan, et al., 1984). In conclusion, Slavin (1987) summarized by saying that cooperative learning strategies apparently contribute to students' seeing each other in a positive light and forming friendships based on human qualities. IMPLEMENTING RESEARCH 8-2 shows why cooperative learning is appropriate for Native-Americans.

IMPLEMENTING RESEARCH 8-2: Cooperative Learning and the Native-American Student

Little Soldier (1989) feels that cooperative learning improves academic achievement, and matches Native-American values and behaviors such as respect for the individual, development of an internal locus of control, cooperation, sharing, and harmony. Although the cultural relevance of the curriculum is clearly important, *how* (Little Soldier's emphasis, p. 162) to teach Native-Americans is an equally important topic. Little Soldier's work focuses on the serious problems that persist, the cultural characteristics of Native-Americans, their low self-concept and cultural pride, and how cooperative learning techniques work.

IMPLEMENTING THE RESEARCH:

_____ 1. Understand (and plan appropriate instruction to demonstrate) that, despite significant advances in the education of Native-Americans, serious problems continue to exist:

> The dropout rate remains alarmingly high, enrollment in higher education is low, and teen pregnancy, suicide, and substance abuse continue at disportionately high rates. (p. 161)

_____ 2. Work toward improving learners' self-concepts, and overall perceptions of themselves and their Native-American culture, by providing educational experiences designed to teach the accomplishments and contributions of Native-Americans.

_____ 3. Implement cooperative learning strategies that take advantage of Native-American cultural traits such as cooperation, sharing, group welfare, and harmony. Cooperative learning can improve learner attitudes (both toward themselves and others), as well as increase cross-racial sharing, understanding, and acceptance.

Source: Little Soldier, L. (1989). "Cooperative learning and the Native-American student." *Phi Delta Kappan, 71,* 161–163.

Table 8-1 provides a brief summary of several cooperative learning methods and the sources for readers wanting additional information.

Table 8-1 Overview of Selected Cooperative Learning Methods

Method/Proponent	*Brief Description/Comments*
Learning Together (Johnson and Johnson) 1987, 1989/90	Emphasizing cooperative effort, *Learning Together* has five basic elements: positive interdependence (students believe they are responsible for both their learning and the team's); face-to-face interaction (students explain their learning and help others with assignments); individual accountability (students demonstrate mastery of material); social skills (students com-

municate effectively, build and maintain trust, and resolve conflicts); group processing (groups periodically assess their progress and how to improve effectiveness). Uses four- or five-member heterogeneous teams.

Student Teams–Achievement Divisions (STAD) (Slavin 1978)	Four student learning teams (mixed in performance levels, sex, and ethnicity); teacher presents lesson, students work in teams and help others master material. Students then take quizzes; cooperative efforts are not allowed on quizzes; team rewards are earned. Applicable to most grades/subjects.
Teams-Games-Tournament (TGT) (DeVries and Slavin 1978)	Using the same teacher presentation and teamwork as STAD, TGT replaces the quizzes with weekly tournaments in which students compete with members of other teams to contribute points to team scores. Competition occurs at "tournament tables" against others with similar academic records. The winner of each tournament brings six points to her or his team. Low achievers compete with low achievers (a similar arrangement exists for high achievers), which provides all students with equal opportunity for success. As with STAD, team rewards are earned. Applicable to most grades and subjects.
Jigsaw (Aronson, Blaney, Stephan, Sikes, and Snapp 1978)	Students are assigned to six-member teams to work on academic material that has been divided into sections. Each member reads a section; then, members of different teams meet to become experts. Students return to groups and teach other members about their sections. Students must listen to their teammates to learn other sections.
Jigsaw II (Slavin 1987)	Students work in four- or five-member teams as in TGT or STAD. Rather than being assigned specific parts, students read a common narrative (e.g., a chapter). Students also receive a topic on which to become an expert. Learners with the same topics meet together as in Jigsaw, and then they teach the material to their original group. Students take individual quizzes.
Team Assisted Individualization (TAI) (Slavin, Leavey, and Madden 1986)	Uses four-member mixed-ability groups (as with STAD and TGT); differs from STAD and TGT in that it combines cooperative learning and individualized instruction and is applicable only to mathematics in grades three through six. Learners take a placement test, then proceed at their own pace. Team members check one another's work and help with problems. Without help, students take unit tests that are scored by student monitors. Each week, the teacher evaluates and gives team rewards.
Cooperative Integrated Reading and Composition (CIRC) (Madden, Slavin, and Stevens	Designed to teach reading and writing in upper elementary grades, CIRC assigns students to different reading teams. Teacher works with one team, while other teams engage in cognitive activities: reading, predicting story endings, summarizing stories, writing responses, practicing decoding, and

1986)	learning vocabulary. Teams follow sequence of teacher instruction, team practice, team preassessments, and quizzes. Quizzes may not be taken until the team feels each student is ready. Team rewards are given.
Group Investigation (Sharon and Sharan 1989/1990)	Groups are formed according to common interest in a topic. Students plan research, divide learning assignments among members, synthesize/summarize findings, and present the findings to the entire class.

Source: Manning, M. L., & Lucking, R. (1991). The what, why, and how of cooperative learning. *The Clearing House, 64*, page 153.

Language Differences

The number of languages and dialects spoken by children and their families is staggering, and sometimes creates classroom situations in which communication is virtually impossible. These many languages and, in many cases, the school's inability to provide appropriate learning experiences for these children, results in language-minority children not learning the essential lessons of school, and not fully participating in the economic, social, and political life of this country (Bowman, 1989). As decisions are reached concerning organizing students for instruction, culturally sensitive educators recognize the dilemma often faced by learners with limited English-speaking skills.

Maintaining that language differences pose a major stumbling block for Native-American students, Little Soldier (1989) offered several precepts when planning teaching and learning experiences:

1. Cooperative learning techniques should be implemented. Native-Americans, reared to value cooperation and sharing, are not accustomed, culturally, to work alone or to compete for grades and teacher approval. Cooperative learning situations in which warm personal relationships are developed have contributed to language development of pupils.

2. Large-group, formal lessons in the lecture-recitation mode should be avoided. Native-American students tend to withdraw during formal patterns. In less formal situations, these learners feel greater opportunities for student-to-student dialogues and group problem-solving efforts.

3. Encouragement and positive reinforcement should be given liberally. Teaching and learning activities should include language lifting techniques, and modeling of correct language patterns. The correcting of pupils' oral language errors should be avoided, except during formal language lessons (Little Soldier, 1989).

Bowman (1989) offered several suggestions for educators working with language-minority learners:

1. The use of formal language, teacher leadership and control of verbal exchanges, question and answer formats, and references to increasingly abstract ideas often characterize a classroom environment with which many children are unfamiliar. Whenever possible, these new rules for communication are made easier if they overlap with those the learners already know.

2. Language-minority learners should experience familiar communication styles so a basis for communication can be established. This basis may include speaking in the child's primary language, using culturally appropriate styles of address, and relying on management patterns that are familiar to, and comfortable for, children.

3. The meanings of words, of gestures, and of actions may be quite different to children of differing cultural, ethnic, and racial backgrounds. Care should be taken to develop communication and interactive styles that avoid confusion and avoid learners' perceiving their language as inferior or wrong (Bowman, 1989).

It is clear that teachers who plan teaching and learning experiences must consider the language differences among their learners. As can be easily recognized, the complexity of the issue extends beyond verbal communication between teacher and learner to other aspects, such as nonverbal communication and word meanings. As Little Soldier (1989) suggests, educators should carefully consider language differences and developmental levels on all decisions concerning organizing for instruction, e.g., the effect of language differences on working alone or working cooperatively toward educational goals.

Activities. Check district and school policies, procedures, practices, curriculum guides, lesson plans, instructional materials, etc., to be sure they are free of bias toward race, sex, religion, culture and disabilities.

Activities:

Make newcomers feel welcome through a formal program.

Be sure that assignments are not offensive or frustrating to students of cultural minorities. For example, asking students to discuss or write about their Christmas experiences is inappropriate for non-Christian students. Let students discuss their similar holidays.

Form a school-wide planning committee to address the implementation of multicultural education.

Contact your district curriculum coordinators for ideas and assistance.

Let faculty knowledgeable about multicultural topics in-service others or teach their classes.

Take a cultural census of the class or school to find out what cultures are represented; let students be the ethnographers.

Form a multicultural club.

Select a theme to tie various multicultural activities together; hold school programs with art, music, and dramatic presentations; hold a multicultural fair or festival featuring music, art, dance, dress, etc.; adopt a multicultural theme for existing activities.

Hold a school cross-cultural food festival.

Have multicultural celebrations and teach-ins with school-wide activities in all classes.

Decorate classrooms, hallways, and the library media center with murals, bulletin boards, posters, artifacts, and other materials representative of the students in the class or school, or other cultures being studied. Posters and other information are available from foreign government travel bureaus and education agencies, private travel agencies, consulates, the United Nations, ethnic and cultural organizations, etc.

Designate a permanent bulletin board for multicultural news and displays.

Help students develop the skills needed to locate and organize information about cultures from the library media center, the mass media, people, and personal observations.

Have students write to foreign consulates, tourist bureaus, minority organizations, etc., for information and decorative materials.

Supplement textbooks with authentic material from different cultures taken from newspapers, magazines, and other media of the culture. Such materials are available from the DOE Foreign Language Documentation Center.

Use community resources: Representatives of various cultures talking to classes; actors portraying characters or events; musicians and dance groups, such as salsa bands or bagpipe units performing.

Work with the library media center for special bibliographies, collections, displays, and audio-visuals.

Hold a mock legislature to debate current or historical issues affecting minorities and cultural groups.

Hold oratorical, debate, essay, poster, art, brain brawl, or other competitions with a multicultural focus.

Feature stories in the school newspaper on multicultural topics; publish a multicultural newspaper or newsletter.

Make reminders during daily announcements about multicultural activities.

Use your Newspapers-in-Education program.

Develop a radio or television program on multicultural themes for the educational or local community access channel.

Study works in science, art, music, and literature of various cultures, focusing on the contributions of minority individuals.

Have students write short stories or essays on multicultural topics.

Have student debates, speeches, skits, etc., on multicultural topics, and present them to classes, PTO's, nursing homes, and other community groups.

Study the provisions and freedoms of the Constitution as they relate to minorities.

Compare and contrast other cultures with that of mainstream America.

Discuss the issues and personalities involved in various cultures from a historical, political, and literary standpoint.

Use skills and information from various disciplines (math, social studies, geography, language arts, etc.) to compare population, economy, politics, lifestyle, culture, and other data about different culture groups in the United States during different historical periods, and as they are today. Discuss the meaning of the differences.

Discuss the relevance of the Constitution and government in dealing with today's problems that relate to minorities and cultural diversity.

Hold mock campaigns and elections based on multicultural issues.

Hold a video film festival dealing with various cultures and multicultural issues.

Have children of other cultures, or their parents, share native songs with classmates; have students share instruments or recordings of their native cultures.

Take field trips to local multicultural sites, such as a neighborhood, ethnic recreation/social center, workplace, historical site, museum, restaurant, grocery.

Focus on geography skills and knowledge in geography courses as part of related courses.

Establish pen-pal or video exchange programs with students from other cultures.

Discuss the importance of international trade, and the skills needed to be employed in that area.

Focus on the everyday artifacts of cultures that differentiate the way people behave in different cultures, such as greetings, friendly exchanges, farewells, expressing respect, verbal taboos, ways of using numbers, body language and gestures, gender roles, folklore, childhood literature, discipline, festivals, holidays, religious practices, games, music, pets, personal possessions, keeping warm and cool, cosmetics, fashions, health and hygiene practices, competitions, dating and courtship, transportation and traffic, sports, radio and television programs, hobbies, foods, family mealtimes, snacking, cafés and restaurants, yards and sidewalks, parks and playgrounds, flowers and gardens, movies and theaters, circuses, museums, vacations and resort areas, careers.

Discuss what it means to be a member of a minority or different cultural group.

Discuss what it means to be a responsible American citizen.

Source: *Multicultural teaching strategies.* (1990). (Technical Assistance Paper No 9). Tallahassee: State Department of Education.

TEACHING AND LEARNING CONTEXTS: THE SCHOOL ENVIRONMENT

Multicultural Education of Children and Adolescents is based upon the belief that "the school environment" includes all experiences with which learners come in contact: Content, the instructional methods, the actual teaching/ learning process and environment, the professional staff and other staff members, as well as the actions and attitudes of other students. Although this definition of environment is synonymous with curriculum itself, the authors feel that at least a brief discussion of the school environment is warranted to emphasize that multiculturalism must receive more than a token effort. Even the school with the loftiest goals and principles will accomplish little when students feel racism exists, see acts of prejudice and discrimination, see only the majority culture participating in extracurricular activities, see a predominantly Anglo staff in a school comprised mostly of people of color, or experience all learning from middle-class Anglo perspectives.

Working Toward a Multicultural School Environment

It is important that the multicultural environment demonstrate a genuine respect and concern for all learners, regardless of their racial, cultural, or ethnic backgrounds. With a supportive school environment, culturally different children, along with other learners, can learn to take an active role in a democratic society, guided by relevant understanding, and develop skills in communication and computation, social attitudes and interests, and human appreciation. The school environment should support school learning and socialization for all students. A supportive school environment is one in which the morale of both teachers and students is high. The teachers believe in their mission to help guide and stimulate the learning activities of their students, and are pleased with the responsive behavior of their students (Tyler, 1989).

Activity:

Ask your students to help make the classroom better reflect the cultural diversity of the students. Consider things like artwork, displays showing contributions of the various cultures, and holiday displays, just to name a few. Ask the students how school rules, policies, and expectations could better reflect the needs of culturally diverse learners.

Although it is impossible to describe in detail all the factors that make a school environment responsive to cultural diversity, briefly discussing several areas illustrates the "environment" in its broadest sense: the unconditional acceptance of diversity; the promotion of positive self-concepts and cultural identities; and a faculty/staff composition that represents the cultural diversity of the school population. The school environment is by no means limited to these three aspects; however, these three provide examples that have a powerful influence on how learners perceive others' opinions of cultural diversity.

Recommendations for creating a teaching/learning environment that reflects the cultural diversity of the school include:

- A variety of multiethnic/multicultural and self-awareness materials, updated consistently and provided as a part of the daily learning environment;
- planned and vicarious learning experiences that are flexible, unbiased, and inclusive of contributions from diverse cultures;
- human resources that serve as role models, and material resources that focus on problems in a pluralistic society;
- instructional strategies relevant to the physical, emotional, social, and intellectual development of children of multiethnic heritage;
- instructional material that shows individuals from diverse cultural groups working in different occupational and social roles, material that is free from bias, omissions, and stereotypes;
- flexible scheduling that provides ample time and space for children to share their uniqueness through role play, art, conversation, and games; and
- continuous use of ideas and materials that represent cultures throughout the year, not just during a special holiday such as Black History Week, Christmas, Thanksgiving, Hanukkah, and the Chinese New Year (SACUS, 1988).

Believing that an educational setting should provide feelings of acceptance, encouragement, and respect, Banks (1988) offers several insights into creating appropriate school environments in our culturally pluralistic society:

1. The total school environment should be reformed, not just the courses and programs. The school's informal, "hidden curriculum" is as important, or perhaps more important, than the formal course of study.

2. Ethnic content should be incorporated into all subject areas, preschool through grade twelve, and beyond.

3. Learning centers, libraries, and resource centers should include resources on history, literature, music, folklore, views of life, and the arts of the various groups of people.

4. Ethnic diversity should be reflected in assembly programs, classroom, hallway and entrance decorations, cafeteria menus, counseling interactions, and, as previously discussed, extracurricular activities.

5. School-sponsored dances and other such activities should reflect a respect for a culturally pluralistic society.

Promoting Positive Self-Concept and Cultural Identities

It is imperative that educators understand the school environment's influence (perhaps an unconscious or unrecognized influence), on children's self-concept and cultural identities. Without doubt, the school environment affects both the manner in which children perceive themselves, and their cultural images. Although suggestions for improving learners' self-concepts were offered in Part II, this section takes a brief look at how the school environment affects the self-concept and cultural identities of children and adolescents.

Self-concept, sometimes referred to as self-image, is a complex set of beliefs that an individual holds about him- or herself. A person may have more than one self-image, actually holding positive feelings in some areas, and negative images in others. For example, a person might have a positive self-image in intellectual pursuits, while harboring negative feelings toward his or her athletic abilities. Learners' self-concepts are influenced significantly by the actions of others, or the way in which they think others perceive and treat them. A person's self-concept affects behavior, school achievement, and social development, just to name a few aspects (Bennett, 1986).

Activity:

Have students clip magazines and prepare a collage that reveals things about their lives. Talk about the things they might include:

Birthplace—picture, part of the map

Baby pictures

Things they like—food, sports

Their family—people, pets

Where they have lived or traveled

Have the students write a brief biographical description that can be attached to the collage or read to the class.

Source: Tiedt, P. L., & Tiedt, I. M. (1990). *Multicultural teaching: A handbook of activities, information, and resources* (3rd. ed.). Boston: Allyn and Bacon, pages 45–46.

It is important that educators understand the role of the curricular experiences and school environment in shaping a youngster's self-concept and cultural identity. The environment should allow culturally diverse people to feel a sense of being able to cope, or the feeling that they can control their lives at least to some extent. Although few schools may allow students to feel a sense of control over their lives, a conscientious effort should be maintained to make people of color feel that their views are recognized and considered. Youngsters who feel torn between two cultures (i.e., their culture and the predominantly middle-class Anglo culture of their school) may have a low self-image because they assume they cannot be successful in either society (Ramsey, 1987). Luftig (1983) reported a study of Native-American adolescents who felt the need to choose between being part of the Anglo-American culture and being part of their tribal culture. This situation resulted in these adolescents having lower self-esteem than their peers.

Viewed from multicultural perspectives, self-concepts of learners relate not only to their race, culture, and social class, but also to their feelings of power in the school environment. The task facing educators is to help students build positive perceptions about their reference groups, and to develop confidence in actively participating in social discussion and change (Ramsey, 1987).

The educators' goal should be provide a school environment that will either raise, or contribute positively to, the self-concepts and the racial and cultural pride of people of color. Rather than students' feeling like intruders in a school that emphasizes middle-class Anglo values, expectations and perspectives, educators should have as a goal an environment that allows people of color to feel their perspectives are considered, and that they have at least some degree of control over their lives and school environment.

Making Faculty/Staff Diverse: Culture, Ethnic, and Racial Backgrounds

Members of different ethnic groups must be an integral part of the school's instructional, administrative, and supportive staffs. School personnel—

teachers, principals, cooks, custodians, secretaries, students, and counselors—make as important contributions to multicultural environments as do courses of study and instructional materials. Students learn important lessons about culture and cultural diversity by observing interactions among different racial, ethnic, and cultural groups in their school, observing and experiencing the verbal behavior of the professional and support staffs, and observing the extent to which the staff is culturally representative of the student population. It is imperative that school policies should be established and implemented to recruit and maintain a multicultural total school staff (Banks, 1988).

TEACHING AND LEARNING CONTEXTS: CULTURAL PERSPECTIVES

Socioeconomic and Class Differences

The student's socioeconomic level and social class deserve consideration as elementary and secondary educators plan teaching and learning experiences. Jarolimek and Foster (1989) aptly illustrated how social stratification in America places some groups at a disadvantage:

> If a group of individuals has particular characteristics that are valued by a society, the group so identified will enjoy high status. The reverse is also true. Thus, when speaking of upper and lower classes, we are referring to groups of individuals who either have or do not have qualities in common that are prized by the larger society. In America, upper classes are those groups that have wealth, advanced education, professional occupations, and relative freedom concerning material needs. Conversely, lower classes are those groups that live in or on the edge of poverty, have poor education, are irregularly employed or employed in jobs requiring little or no training, often require assistance from government welfare agencies, and are constantly concerned with meeting their basic needs of life (p. 11).

At least two perspectives stand out as being important for educators to consider: First, some social classes may be able to provide their children with additional experiences that may be conducive to education and academic achievement; second, the American belief that determination, hard work, and middle-class values pay rich dividends. The problem with the former is that many students do not bring to school experiential backgrounds that contribute to their education. The latter often results in poorer people being perceived as failures, or lacking the ambition or determination to pursue longterm goals. Realistically speaking, culturally diverse students often come from poorer financial backgrounds, and homes where language differences impede communication and upward social mobility. Such obstacles, however, do not mean that education and school achievement are any less valued by these social classes. It is educators' responsibility to provide teaching/learning experiences which build upon the strengths and backgrounds of all children and adolescents.

As IMPLEMENTING RESEARCH 8-3 suggests, a relationship exists between social class, race, and school achievement:

IMPLEMENTING RESEARCH 8-3: Social Class, Race, and School Achievement

Orstein and Levine (1989) provide insightful information regarding the relationship between the socioeconomics of students' lives and their ability to perform effectively in schools. The research focuses on areas such as studies on social class and school success, and race/ethnicity and school success. Reasons for low achievement include:

1. Differences in teacher/student backgrounds;
2. teacher perceptions of student inadequacy;
3. low standards of performance;
4. ineffective instructional grouping;
5. difficulty of teaching conditions;
6. differences between parental and school norms;
7. lack of previous success;
8. negative peer pressure;
9. inappropriate curriculum and instruction; and
10. delivery-of-service problems.

After explicating these reasons, Ornstein and Levine provide several implications.

IMPLEMENTING THE RESEARCH:

_____ 1. Educational institutions should strive to increase the number of minority teachers.

_____ 2. Educators should build in knowledge components that focus on effective instruction for low achievers.

_____ 3. Classroom management strategies for all teachers should be improved.

Source: Ornstein, A. C., & Levine, D. U. (1989). "Social class, race, and school achievement: Problems and prospects." *Journal of Teacher Education, 40(5),* 17–23.

As suggested in the four chapters in Part I of *Multicultural Education of Children and Adolescents,* substantial numbers of Native-, African-, Asian- and Hispanic-American children and adolescents experience economic deprivation. Although government efforts such as Headstart, Job Corps, Title I (Compensatory Education), Neighborhood Youth Corps, and other educational programs (Gollnick & Chinn, 1990) have improved the lot of many disadvantaged youth, considerable improvement continues to be needed:

> Native-Americans have been described as the poorest economically, the least employed, the unhealthiest, and lowest in income (Dorris, 1981).

> Nearly one of every two African-American children lives in poverty; almost two-thirds of young African-American children live in homes relying on public assistance (Clark-Johnson, 1988).

> Asian-Americans probably have the highest earning power of the culturally diverse populations; however, a tremendous range in income continues to plague this groups. Similarly, some Asian-American families have more wage earners, which raises their income levels (Asian and Pacific Islander data, 1988).

> Among Hispanic-American children, 38.7% of all Hispanic children live at the poverty level, and 71% live in homes in which the head of household is female (Colburn & Melillo, 1987; Valero-Figueira, 1988).

Although these conditions are disturbing, it is important to emphasize the economic advances and achievements of culturally diverse learners and their families during the past decade or two. Educators should objectively consider each learner to determine individual strengths and weaknesses. To equate poverty conditions with a particular culture, race, or ethnic group would be a serious mistake, and would jeopardize a learner's educational future.

What are the implications for educators working with children and adolescents from lower socioeconomic and social classes?

1. Teachers, counselors, and administrators should recognize the dangers of associating negative and harmful expectations with culturally diverse groups and lower classes. In fact, educators should review periodically their beliefs about children and adolescents as well as their behavioral and academic expectations (Gollnick & Chinn, 1990).

2. Educators should examine curricular and instructional efforts to determine whether they reflect only middle-class, Anglo perspectives. Culturally diverse learners and students from lower socioeconomic classes need to see a reflection of their values and lifestyles in the content taught, and the instructional methods employed (Gollnick & Chinn, 1990).

3. Educators should be on a constant lookout for grouping patterns that segregate students along cultural, racial, or ethnic lines. Stu-

dents from lower socioeconomic classes, or culturally diverse students, are often placed in lower ability groups. Such practices may be discriminatory, because students are segregated along ethnic and social class lines (Dawson, 1987; Manning & Lucking, 1990).

Linton and Foster (1990) suggested "powerful environments" (Linton and Foster's term) for students they termed as underclass youth. Referring specifically to African-Americans, Linton and Foster questioned why so many of the poorer classes seem unable to move upward from the horrendous conditions of underclass life. Reasons may include continuing patterns of racism, not enough government assistance, too much government assistance, the large scale loss of jobs from the urban centers, and the abandonment of the ghettos by upwardly mobile African-Americans. To help these underclass youth, Linton and Foster (1990) recommend that inner-city schools have powerful environments where students are "expected to strive and achieve in all dimensions of school life, including curriculum studies and social relationships" (p. 28). The staff would be expected to project a success-oriented, winning attitude for students to internalize. Instead of students being told to meet high expectations, they should be told how to meet teachers' expectations. Included in this "powerful environment" would be academic subject matter, personal and interpersonal skills (how to talk, dress and handle anger) and how to deal with authority figures.

The Role of Parents and Families

While Chapter 10 examines in considerable detail the roles of parents and families in the education process, their role in the teaching/learning process is sufficiently significant to warrant the inclusion of parent involvement in this section. In fact, the importance of involving parents of culturally diverse learners in their child's education cannot be overemphasized.

The importance of parent involvement, and the school's efforts to have cooperative relationships between parents and schools, has been supported by research (Simich-Dudgeon, 1987). First, parental interest and participation in schools and classrooms has a positive influence on academic achievement. Second, parents involved in academic activities with their children gain knowledge that helps them to assess their children's education, and to help with areas of education in which their children need assistance. Third, the results of parent involvement in tutoring limited English-proficient students are consistent with those for native English-speaking students and their families. To be effective as home tutors, all parents need school support and direct teacher involvement (Simich-Dudgeon, 1987).

Yao (1988) contended that the educators must employ special strategies to accommodate the unique cultural characteristics of Asian immigrant parents. Their agenda should include (1) educators asking themselves some difficult questions about their prejudices and stereotypical beliefs about Asian-Americans, (2) understanding Asian beliefs about education, and

(3) providing opportunities for Asian-Americans to participate in school activities, to communicate through newsletters, and to serve on advisory committees (Yao, 1988).

Several points emerge as educators consider the involvement of culturally diverse parents and families in the teaching/learning process. First, the importance that culturally diverse people place in the family warrants including *both* the immediate and extended families. Educators working with Anglo-Americans usually work only with the mother and the father; however, culturally diverse children and adolescents often perceive the roles of grandparents, aunts, and uncles as similar to the mother and the father. For this reason, educators should welcome extended families who are interested in the learner's educational progress. Second, culturally diverse parents and families may not understand the United States school system and its emphasis on competition, and individual welfare and achievement over group accomplishments. Third, suggestions and directions can be offered to parents and families who are able to assist their children and adolescents. The fourth point, which actually benefits the teacher, and subsequently the student, is that culturally diverse families and their values, customs, traditions, and expectations can be better understood. All too often, the benefits of parent involvement are viewed narrowly, rather than considering children, parents, and teachers as beneficiaries.

Learner Evaluation

The evaluation of learners should include a consideration of individual and cultural differences, variations in learning and testing styles, and differences in motivation. Rather than evaluating only what can be measured by paper and pencil, evaluation efforts should also focus on student behaviors, attitudes, and everyday actions. For example, a student might be able to list examples of racist behavior, and offer several valid reasons on paper why racism should be reduced. However, the evaluation process should also include a consideration of actions: Do students make racist remarks? Do students demonstrate racial harmony? Do students engage in segregationist activities? Generally speaking, have students developed respect and acceptance for, as well as knowledge of, our increasing culturally diverse world?

Evaluating Learners' Progress

Sleeter and Grant (1988) offered several recommendations for educators planning and implementing programs which evaluate learners.

1. Evaluation procedures should not include standardized achievement tests that are monocultural in nature, and that sort students into different groups for different and unequal opportunities.

2. Evaluation procedures should not penalize students by requiring

skills that are extraneous to what is being evaluated. For example, a science teacher assessing science concepts should not require students to read and write above their skill level.

3. Evaluation procedures designed to assess students' English language proficiency levels should take into account the different contexts in which school communication takes place, and the different factors involved.

4. Evaluation procedures should be free of sexist or racist stereotypes.

As can be seen, decisions concerning evaluation include both what should be evaluated, and also an actual determination of the evaluation methods. As with all curricular efforts, evaluation should be matched closely with goals and objectives, should measure what was taught, and should measure attitudes and behaviors as well as cognitive knowledge.

SUMMING UP

Educators who plan teaching, learning, and classroom environments in multicultural settings should remember to:

1. Recognize and respect learner diversity: Culture, race, ethnicity, individual, gender, social class, and religion.

2. Develop the knowledge, attitudes, and skills required to teach and relate to culturally diverse children and adolescents.

3. Recognize that some organizational practices contribute to exclusivity and segregation, and that therefore educators should provide instructional methods with which culturally diverse children and adolescents can most effectively relate.

4. Plan a school curriculum and environment that reflects respect for all cultural, ethnic, social class, and religious differences among people, and promotes learners' self-concept and cultural identities.

5. Recognize (and to respond appropriately to) several cultural perspectives that influence the academic achievement and overall school progress of culturally diverse learners, e.g., socioeconomic class and social class, parents and families, and learner evaluation.

6. Implement a teaching/learning environment that affects positively how children and adolescents feel about school, about being culturally different in a predominantly Anglo-American school, and about genuine feelings of acceptance and caring.

7. Provide culturally diverse learners with an administration, faculty, and staff that reflects the cultural diversity of the overall school population.

SUGGESTED LEARNING ACTIVITIES

1. Survey several elementary and secondary teachers to determine their efforts to include multicultural perspectives in their teaching/learning activities. Look specifically at items such as content, teacher expectations for achievement and behavior, grouping strategies, testing and evaluation, and involvement of parents and extended family members. How might you improve on the teachers' efforts?

2. Design a plan for involving culturally diverse parents and immediate families in the teaching/learning process. Explain specifically how you would address the following points: Language barriers between culturally diverse parents and you; explaining school expectations to parents and families who might not understand how United States schools function; and actual ways you might involve parents and families.

3. Use a case study approach to study a culturally diverse learner and to pinpoint cultural differences in how the student learns, perceives events, and behaves. In a paper summarizing your observations and reflections, state how the student's behavior and attitudes might affect school achievement, and how the school might provide more appropriate teaching/learning experiences for this learner.

4. Observe a teaching demonstration to determine a teacher's "unintended bias". Did the teacher call on more girls than boys, more Anglo-Americans than Hispanic-Americans, expect Asian-Americans to answer more difficult questions, or tend to ignore students from lower socioeconomic groups? How might you help this teacher recognize bias? What items would you include on a teacher self-evaluation scale designed to help teachers recognize "unintended bias"?

5. Devise a checklist to evaluate the degree to which the overall school environment reflects multicultural perspectives. Although you should include perspectives which you feel are important, the basic underlying question should be: Does the overall school environment portray multicultural perspectives? Other examples might include: Is there evidence that cultural, ethnic, social class, and religious diversity is accepted? Are there deliberate attempts to promote positive self-concepts and cultural identities? Is cultural diversity represented among faculty and staff and at all levels of administration?

Expanding Your Horizons: Additional Journal Readings and Books

KEEFE, J. W. (1990). "Learning style: Where are we going?" *Momentum, 21(1)*, 44–48. Keefe, an expert on learning styles, answers several key questions about cognition, and explains the NASSP Learning Style Inventory.

LINTON, T. E., & FOSTER, M. (1990). " 'Powerful environments' for underclass youth." *The Education Digest, 55(7)*, 27–31. Linton and Foster maintain that schools should provide underclass youth with needed "powerful environments" that would teach content material, interpersonal skills, and how to meet high expectations.

MANNING, M. L., & LUCKING, R. (1990). "Ability grouping: Realities and alternatives." *Childhood Education, 66*, 254–258. Manning and Lucking paint a gloomy (yet realistic) picture of ability grouping, and suggest that this form of organization can lead to segregation.

MANNING, M. L., & LUCKING, R. (1991). "The what, why, and how of cooperative learning." *The Clearing House, 64*, 152–156. Manning and Lucking explore the cooperative learning movement, various methods of collaboration, and also, show the effects of cooperative learning on intergroup and multiethnic relations.

STEWART, W. J. (1990). "Learning-style-appropriate instruction: Planning, implementing, evaluating." *The Clearing House, 63*, 371–374. After defining learning styles and showing their value to instruction, Stewart uses a question-answer format to show how learning styles can be used a basis for instruction.

TIEDT, P. L., & TIEDT, I. M. (1990). *Multicultural teaching: A handbook of activities, information, and resources* (3rd. ed.). Boston: Allyn and Bacon. As the title implies, Tiedt and Tiedt provide a wealth of activities which can be helpful in multicultural education programs.

TYLER, R. W. (1989). "Educating children from minority families." *Educational Horizons, 67(4)*, 114–118. Tyler draws from his 68 years of teaching experience and gives practical advice for teachers of culturally diverse students. Examples of Tyler's emphasis include moving from theory into practice, focusing on the home, and resolving personal learning problems.

9

Individual and Cultural Differences

Understanding the material and activities in this chapter will help the reader to:

1. List individual and cultural differences and similarities, and explain their influence on learning and achievement.

2. Develop positive orientations toward "cultural deficiencies" and "cultural differences" perspectives, and understand the importance of providing educational experiences based on the "differences" perspective.

3. List at least six individual differences (i.e., self-concept, gender, development, motivation, social class, and exceptionalities) which affect learning and achievement.

4. List several dangers associated with labeling exceptional learners (and, in fact, *all* children and adolescents), and demonstrate how their exceptionalities affect learning and achievement.

5. Describe an educational program (i.e., bilingual education and teaching English as a Second Language) that effectively addresses the needs of language-minority learners.

6. List several cultural differences, and explain their influence on learning and achievement.

7. Define learning styles, explain the complex relationship between culture and learning styles, and suggest inventories designed to assess learners' styles.

8. Recognize the need for a celebration of cultural diversity, and how elementary and secondary school programs can be enriched by diversity among learners.

9. Understand the importance of positive cultural identities, and suggest methods of building positive identities among learners.

OVERVIEW

Educators' positive responses to elementary and secondary learners' differences are crucial to celebrating cultural, ethnic, and racial diversity among Native-, African-, Asian-, and Hispanic-Americans. Whether individual, cultural, or both, differences can provide an effective framework for teaching and learning experiences, and can enrich and contribute to individual teaching/learning situations and to the total school program. This chapter looks at individual and cultural diversities, and examines their influence on student learning and overall development.

The Culture Quiz: Individual and Cultural Diversity

Directions: Match the following terms and definitions.

_____ 1. Gender

_____ 2. Learning Style

_____ 3. Bilingual Education

_____ 4. Self-concept

_____ 5. Assessment

_____ 6. Cognitive processes

a. develops competence in English and is taught through the subject areas

b. differences which include any kind of difference, i.e., cultural, social class, handicapped conditions, or giftedness

c. requires tremendous caution to avoid misplacing learners

d. using two languages as media of instruction

e. thoughts, feelings, and behaviors may be identified (very carefully!) as male or female

f. an individual's perception of self has immense potential for enhancing or

				destroying a learner's chance of success
_____	7.	Socioeconomic	g.	consistent patterns of behavior—cognitive, affective and physiological
_____	8.	Labeling	h.	may include language development, thinking strategies, hypothesizing, and skills at applying concepts
_____	9.	ESL Programs	i.	determining learning levels and progress
_____	10.	Exceptionalities	j.	parents' wealth determines learners' experiences

Answers: 1. e   2. g   3. d   4. f   5. i   6. h   7. j   8. c   9. a   10. b

---

THE REALITY OF INDIVIDUAL AND CULTURAL DIVERSITY

Recognizing and Responding to the Influence of Diversity on Teaching and Learning

All too often educators, whether classroom teachers, special services personnel, or administrators, assume too much homogeneity among learners' abilities, backgrounds, and interests. Apparently, learners are assumed to be so alike that individual and cultural differences either do not exist, or do not affect the learning process. Another reason may be that some educators still subscribe to the belief that a purpose of the school is to homogenize students (similar to the melting pot idea), and to eradicate or "remediate" differences. Regardless of the reasons for homogeneity among learners, the reality is that learners have many differences which affect their perceptions of learning and achievement, their ways of learning and knowing, and their overall learning and school achievement.

Educational institutions, regardless of grade or academic level, have the responsibility for recognizing individual and cultural differences, and planning appropriate educational experiences for all learners, regardless of individual and cultural backgrounds. Differences such as poverty, home and family conditions, and some exceptionalities, may appear difficult to overcome; nevertheless, students deserve an affirmative response to their differences and learning needs. During the 1990s and beyond, it will no longer suffice to plan educational experiences only for middle- or upper-class Anglo learners, and then expect students of other social classes and cultures to change perspectives on motivation and competition, to change their learning styles, and to change attitudes and values instilled by the home and the family.

Developing Positive Orientations Toward Diversity

As discussed in Chapter 1, for centuries, and still to some extent, differences among people were and are considered to be "deficits." The common belief was that differences which varied from middle-class norms or expectations were wrong or inferior, and should be remediated. Today, differences among children and adolescents are increasingly considered entities to be appreciated, and on which educational experiences can be built. Children's and adolescents' attitudes, customs, and sacred values should be recognized and respected, and a positive perspective toward these differences can form the basis for curricular decisions and intructional practices.

RECOGNIZING INDIVIDUAL AND CULTURAL DIFFERENCES AND THEIR INFLUENCE ON LEARNING

It is impossible to list children's and adolescents' many individual differences, yet every difference, whether of intellectual, developmental, or gender origin, affects learners' academic achievement and overall school success, and their perceptions of school achievement and success. While this section does not in any manner attempt to discuss comprehensively the many differences and their influence on learning, it does try to provide representative examples. For too many years, educators have planned for the "learner in the middle" (i.e., whether the learner is Anglo, middle-class, nonhandicapped, male, normally developing, etc.) and have expected other learners to learn and to use similar cognitive strategies to process information. Schools in the 1990s and beyond will be challenged to take a more enlightened or multicultural approach, and to recognize the multitude of differences among learners.

Achievement, Intelligence, and Cognitive Processes

The learner's achievement level can be defined as previously-acquired knowledge that relates to what is being taught. Any seasoned educator can attest to the fact that what students already know affects their present and future achievement (Bennett, 1986). The question should always be asked, "To what extent, and how, can previous learning contribute to new learning?" The learner who already knows numbers, who is fascinated with science, or who is interested in geography, will have a headstart over learners without special areas of expertise or interests.

A learner's degree of intelligence affects what will be learned; however, one must proceed carefully with the concept of intelligence, especially since intelligence can be defined in more than one way. Still, overall intelligence, abilities, or special expertise contribute to the degree to which learners process information.

Learners organize their perceptions and experiences of the school and physical world into their cognitive structures. While there is still much to be learned about the cognitive process, it is known that cognitive development is an active process in which learners assimilate information into their existing cognitive categories, and adapt their previous categories to accommodate new information. These functions of assimilation and accommodation cause the change and growth in learners' thinking that constitutes cognitive development. Educators who work with culturally diverse students should plan educational experiences that recognize the developmental capabilities and needs of children, and also involve them in the active process of constructing knowledge (Ramsey, 1987).

The learners' cognitive development is of particular importance in multicultural situations, because teachers cannot assume that all learners process information in the same manner. Norton (1985) argued that children's language, thinking strategies, abilities at making comparisons and hypotheses, and skills at applying concepts and information depends on their overall cognitive development—which is grounded in their cultural backgrounds. Rather than assuming too much homogeneity among learners, educators have to consider cultural orientations toward achievement, cultural diversity among learning styles, and the degree of active participation on the learner's part. IMPLEMENTING RESEARCH 9-1 examines the impact of culture on the cognitive processes.

IMPLEMENTING RESEARCH 9-1: Culture and Cognition

Distressed over the lack of academic achievement by many minority groups, Brown attempted to address the problem by examining the impact of culture on cognition, and by offering possible solutions. Brown's theories include lack of motivation to achieve and parental encouragement, single-parent households, teen pregnancies, low self-concepts, and truancy. Brown maintained that the cognitive processes are affected by learners' cultural backgrounds.

IMPLEMENTING THE RESEARCH:

_____ 1. Educators need to realize that most students can learn, but they may learn for different reasons.

_____ 2. Educators should use what students already know in helping them acquire new skills and abilities.

_____ 3. Educators should understand that values are neither right nor wrong, and that differences should be affirmed rather than merely tolerated.

Source: Brown, T.J. (1990). "The impact of culture." *The Clearing House, 63,* 305–309.

Self-Concept

The importance of the learner's self-concept and its effects on academic achievement have been mentioned repeatedly throughout this text. However, it is worth mentioning again that the self-concept is an individual difference with immense potential to enhance or destroy a learner's chances at school success. How learners perceive themselves, however, takes on special significance for culturally diverse learners. The culturally diverse learner who feels that others perceive him or her as inferior, deficient in some manner, or in stereotypical terms, may begin to feel less than adequate, or unable to cope with the United States school system. Both one's individual self-concept and the value placed on one's cultural heritage and background can plummet to a point where success in school, and in other areas of life, is in jeopardy.

Gender

Gender is a term that describes masculine and feminine differences—the thoughts, feelings, and behaviors that are identified as being either male or female. While few physical or psychological differences exist between male and female, their culturally-determined behavior can differ significantly. For example, a boy demonstrating feminine traits might be called a "sissy" (Gollnick & Chinn, 1990).

Activity:

Make a list of commonly-held stereotypical beliefs about boys and girls (For example: "Boys should not cry" or "Girls giggle a lot"). Then, observe the girls and boys in your class to test the validity of your list. Next, have the boys and girls make a list, and have a discussion of the differences between girls and boys. How might an educator's expectation of girls or boys affect actual teaching situations?

Educational experiences and outcomes continue to differ for males and females:

> At ages nine, 14, and 17, girls perform higher on assessments of reading achievement, but by ages 21 to 25, males perform at the same level as females in reading and literary proficiency (Mullis, 1987).
>
> On all subsections of the SAT and ACT, males score higher than females (Dauber, 1987).
>
> Females receive 36% of the National Merit Scholarships (PEER, 1987).

How can educators address gender differences? How can females be provided with an education which shows feminist perspectives? First, women's studies should include consciousness-raising efforts, and attempt to create a more enlightened view of women and their unique perspectives. Second, education should be as nonsexist as possible. All instructional materials should be scrutinized for sexist connotations and feminine learning styles, and cognitive strategies should be understood and considered whenever possible. Third, Title IX of the 1972 Education Amendment addresses the differing stereotyped, discriminatory treatment of students based on their sex. Title IX states that "no person shall, on the basis of sex, be excluded from participation in, be denied the benefits of, or be subjected to, discrimination under any education program or activity receiving federal financial assistance" (Gollnick & Chinn, 1990).

Developmental Levels and Cognitive Readiness

The learner's developmental stage is perhaps the most significant individual difference affecting learning. Learners functioning at one developmental level simply cannot comprehend material that requires the thinking and cognitive skills of the next higher developmental level. Rather than assuming that learners can succeed by trying harder or doing more homework, educators should understand that development and readiness, not effort alone, affects what youngsters can learn. A youngster at the concrete operations stage cannot master intellectual challenges that demand formal, abstract thinking abilities. Although some memorization might occur, learners will be unable to learn information that is beyond their cognitive ability at any given age. To assume that all learners can perform functions and master content at a level attained by a few precocious and intellectually-advanced students ignores individual differences, and what is known about cognitive readiness (Toepfer, 1988).

The challenge for educators is to determine developmental and readiness levels, and to plan and implement appropriate instruction. Some questions might be raised concerning theories of growth and development as cross-culturally valid. However, "development" as an individual difference affects learning, and crosses cultural boundaries. Regardless of cultural backgrounds and when developmental stages are reached, learners cannot master material for which they are not developmentally ready to learn. The challenge for educators is to diagnose the learner's developmental stage, and then provide developmentally appropriate curricular experiences and instructional practices.

Beliefs, Attitudes, and Values

Understanding culturally diverse children and adolescents requires knowing their beliefs, attitudes, values. These idiosyncrasies are based in each learner's culture, and influence all aspects of his or her life, whether in motivation, competition, perspectives toward the family, or perceptions of racism and its effects. Numerous illustrations provide evidence of the effects of attitudes: The Asian-American student who is taught to revere teachers; the African-American child who can listen, yet not look the speaker in the eye; the Native-American learner who values cooperation and sharing as being more worthy than competition; or the Hispanic-American adolescent who believes he or she should not stand out among peers.

Activity:

On a sheet with four columns (Native-, African-, Asian- and Hispanic-American), make a list of respective beliefs, attitudes, and values. Seek your students' input. Next, list school policies, practices, and expectations that might need to be reconsidered for their cultural implications (or lack of cultural implications).

Perceptive educators recognize the cultural baggage (prejudices, myths, and stereotypes) that children and adolescents bring to school, baggage that affects attitudes toward school, toward other learners, and toward actual learning achievement. The educator's challenge is to understand and to respect these personal aspects, and, whenever possible, to provide school experiences that are culturally compatible. Curricular practices and instructional methods that are genuinely multicultural in both theory and practice reflect the values, attitudes, and beliefs of culturally diverse learners, and do not require learners to participate in actions that contradict their cultural beliefs.

IMPLEMENTING RESEARCH 9-2 shows how educators should consider the distinctive traits of culturally diverse learners.

IMPLEMENTING RESEARCH 9-2: Teaching to Distinctive Traits

It is not uncommon to find teachers, both minority- and majority-culture, who are unable to identify with the distinctive cultural traits that affect the outcome of instructional strategies. Hispanic-American students feel that bearing the family name is an important responsibility, and that their behavior reflects upon the family. African-American students are more person-centered than majority-culture children, who are more object-centered. Native-American students learn from the general to the particular, and have more of a deductive or holistic approach to learning. Vasquez maintained that educators should understand cultural characteristics, and plan appropriate instructional strategies.

IMPLEMENTING THE RESEARCH:

_____ 1. Educators should use praise effectively. For example, the teacher might say to an Anglo child, "Good work,

Mary. You must be proud of yourself" (p. 301), but the teacher speaking to a Hispanic child might want to include a reference to the family.

_____ 2. Educators should first understand the learners' cultural characteristics, and then plan appropriate instructional strategies; i.e., while some learners might prefer learning alone, others might prefer working cooperatively.

_____ 3. Educators should also consider the content to be taught, and the physical and psychological environments in which teaching and learning occur.

Source: Vasquez, J.A. (1990). "Teaching to the distinctive traits of minority students." *The Clearing House, 63,* 299–303.

Motivation

It is important for educators in multicultural situations to understand motivation, both as an individual difference affecting academic achievement, and from its cultural perspective. Rather than perceiving motivation through middle-class Anglo eyes, educators need to understand the complex relationship between motivation and cultural diversity. For example, middle-class Anglo-Americans might be motivated by competition, by an outstanding achievement that sets the individual apart from peers, or by the desire to work independently. However, culturally diverse learners might appear unmotivated when they do not want to stand out among their peers, do not want to excel at the expense of others, or when they choose to work in cooperative learning situations so expertises can be shared.

Activity:

In a group or individual setting (in whatever setting culturally diverse students will be more likely to share personal information), talk with learners to see what motivates them. Are they motivated by competing with peers? Are they motivated by their parents' expectations? Does the teacher play a significant role in motivation?

Closely related to learners' motivation and willingness to employ cognitive abilities is their expectation of success or failure. Beliefs related to the likelihood of success, to judgments about one's ability, and to emotional reactions of pride and hopelessness, all contribute to the extent one is willing to use cognitive strategies. Over time, learners who believe that failure is caused by a lack of ability are likely to feel a sense of helplessness (Ames,

1990). This theory of the relationship between motivation, feelings of self-worth, and the willingness to use cognitive strategies, might be especially valid for educators who work with culturally diverse learners during periods when perceptions of individual abilities and cultural identities are being influenced daily.

Educators should focus on the particular motivational problems of individual students. School learning requires active effort, and children are not likely to put forth the active effort if they do not see that their schoolwork helps them to achieve their own purposes, or to satisfy their own interests. They may respond to their parents' or teachers' pressures, but unless students see a personal motivation for completing school assignments, motivation will be difficult to maintain. Educators need to understand motivation from its cultural perspective, and then attempt to help learners understand qualities in their assignments that are either interesting or useful (Tyler, 1989).

CASE STUDY 9-1 shows how 13-year-old Carl's motivation is misunderstood, and suggests that teachers should not view culturally diverse children and adolescents with middle-class Anglo perspectives.

CASE STUDY 9-1: Motivation and Cultural Considerations

Carl, a 13-year-old Native-American middle school student, shows a lack of motivation, initiative, and competition. He does not demonstrate any desire to set himself apart from, or rise above, others in his class. His teachers see him as "different": while most of the Anglos in this school strive for success and good grades, Carl does his work, yet shows no desire for anything more. The teachers who work together in Carl's unit wonder what to do and how to motivate him.

While this has often been typical of Native-Americans in this school, Mrs. Westerly, the Special Education teacher, recognizes a crucial aspect of this situation that others either have not seen or do not want to admit. Rather than the teachers looking at Carl from an Anglo perspective, Mrs. Westerly suggested understanding the Native-American perspective. Perhaps, from Carl's cultural perspective, he is motivated. His family has transmitted a cultural heritage that does not emphasize competition, motivation, or achievement that would set him apart from his peers. He does not value competing with other learners because it seems far more logical to share ideas and to work cooperatively and in harmony.

The teachers began to realize that they had evaluated Carl's motivation through a middle-class Anglo lens. (Their degree of acceptance is another issue.) In fact, they were expecting Carl to conform to expectations and behaviors that were completely alien to his cultural heritage and background.

Socioeconomic Class

The social class differential which exists in the United States includes the family's absolute income, educational background, occupational prestige, place of residence, lifestyle, and relative autonomy and power. It is worth remembering, however, than wealth and material success may be relative, i.e., while one family might consider a swimming pool as a sign of success, another family might perceive the addition of a porch to the mobile home as an indicator of success (Ramsey, 1987). In any event, a family's socioeconomic class and income level determine children's and adolescents' experiences, as do other factors (i.e., conditions of the home, books and other reading materials, computers, and trips with educational significance) that have positive effects on educational progress.

A troubling fact facing culturally diverse learners and their educators is that significant percentages (although certainly not all) of culturally diverse youngsters are growing up in conditions of poverty. For example, 28.2% of African-American families, and 23.7% of Hispanic-American families, fall below the poverty line. To further complicate the situation for children and adolescents (and their educators), the percentages of persons 16 and under living in poverty include 45.4% of African-Americans and 38.9% of Hispanic-Americans. The seriousness of the situation for culturally diverse youngsters is further illustrated when seen in perspective of the Anglo population: 7.9% for families below the poverty line, and 15.1% for children and adolescents under 16 (U. S. Bureau of the Census, 1990).

The implications for educators are clear:

1. Recognize poverty and its effects on educational achievement and learner motivation.
2. Provide appropriate educational experiences that recognize cultural diversity and socioeconomic status, and which build upon the experiences that children and adolescents bring to school.
3. Learn though seminars, course work, and first-hand experiences, how to respond most effectively to learners from lower socioeconomic backgrounds.
4. Recognize the relationship between socioeconomic status and such factors as motivation, perceptions of life, and acceptance of other socioeconomic groups.
5. Recognize the hurdles that poverty oftens creates for many students, but also realize that associating poverty with school failure can have serious consequences.

It is important to remember that learners and their families *must* be considered individually. It is a serious mistake, and an injustice to learners, to make assumptions of wealth and social class based on culture, race, or ethnicity. Conversely, a learner's educational potential should never be predicted on the basis of socioeconomic levels. Just as many higher socioeconomic class learners often fail to respond to efforts of their educators, students from lower-class homes and neighborhoods have demonstrated extraordinary educational successes.

Exceptionalities

The Dangers of Labeling and Erroneous Placement

Labeling learners has such potentially harmful effects that educators who assign labels may be placing children and adolescents at great risk. Although such educators probably have the learner's interest and educational welfare at stake, labeling learners as "handicapped", "slow", or "disabled" can sometimes cause irreparable harm, not only during school programs, but throughout entire lives. Educators should be cognizant of the disadvantages of labeling, and should know when the practice is or is not in the learner's best interest.

Several disadavantages of labeling children and adolescents are included below:

> Learners who are labeled as handicapped or exceptional may be permanently stigmatized, rejected, or denied opportunities for full development.

> Learners labeled as mentally retarded (or the equivalent) may be assigned to inferior educational programs in schools, or placed in institutions without the benefit of legal protection.

> Large numbers of culturally diverse learners are inaccurately classified as mentally handicapped on the basis of scores earned on inappropriate tests (Biehler & Snowman, 1990).

CASE STUDY 9-2 illustrates the dangers of labeling learners, and also shows how both students' and teachers' perceptions can be affected by placing learners in categories.

CASE STUDY 9-2: The Dangers of Labeling

Dr. Strobecker, principal of Cedarwood Elementary School, was looking through students' permanent records when several labels caught her eye: "behaviorally maladjusted," "slow learner," "retarded," "below average," "gifted," "trouble-maker," "unmotivated," "emotionally disturbed," and other labels which educators can imagine. She realized the dangers of labeling: Teachers sometimes expect too little, sometimes too much; learners are often placed in the wrong group; and learners' entire lives might be affected by labels placed upon them in the elementary school. Further, such labeling had the potential for being both unprofessional and unethical. She admitted to herself that, while labeling learners had the potential for helping, the practice should be limited to only those cases where learners were clearly helped.

Dr. Strobecker knew that as principal, she had the professional responsibility for addressing the situation. There were several things she might do: First, teachers should be made aware of the dangers of labeling; second, she would encourage teachers to read professional articles that dealt with labeling and alternatives; three, teachers would be encouraged to diagnose learners by using the most objective and reliable means; and fourth, teachers should assign a label only when the diagnosis was accurate and in the learner's best interest.

While the disadvantages of labeling mentioned above are sufficient to cause alarm, yet another problem may result from labeling: the overt segregation of learners. It had been suggested that learners have been racially segregated through grouping and placement practices (Sendor, 1989). Using subjective means or teacher recommendations, labeling or placement policies can contribute (either intentionally or unintentionally) to the segregation of students along racial and ethnic lines. Such policies are both unethical and unprofessional, and can condemn learners to slow groups, or inferior materials and methods. Such situations may occur because educators want learners segregated, or because educators erroneously equate race or ethnicity with achievement and ability. IMPLEMENTING RESEARCH 9-3 examines the possibility of racial bais during placement situations.

IMPLEMENTING RESEARCH 9-3: Rooting Out Racial Bias in Student Placement

Sendor reported on the *Montgomery v. Starkville Municipal Separate School District* case, which grappled with the thorny issue of grouping students by achievement. The policy grouped elementary and secondary students into classes within each grade level according to achievement, and kept the students in these groups for the entire school day. The National Association for the Advancement of Colored People (N.A.A.C.P.) filed a complaint with the Office of Civil Rights (O.C.R.), saying that the school officials were using student grouping as a subtle technique to maintain racially-segregated schools. While the O.C.R. did not order an end to achievement grouping, it did recommend four changes: (1) Only objective data should be used for placing students; (2) students should be re-tested frequently; (3) the curriculum should help lower-achieving students to improve performance; and (4) teachers should receive training in the remedial instruction necessary to help low-achieving learners.

IMPLEMENTING THE RESEARCH:

_____ 1. Educators should review all placement procedures that might lead to racial disparities.

_____ 2. Educators should test and re-test students frequently, and move students freely from group to group for the most effective placement.

_____ 3. Educators should view the racial disparities in tracking systems as vestiges of past discrimination, and should root out all racial bias in student placement.

Source: Sendor, B. (1989). "Root out racial bias in student placement." _American School Board Journal, 176(3)_, 24–25.

Then when, if ever, should learners be labeled? Students should be given a label when, and only when, placing a label on the learner is in the student's best interest, and when the learner's condition can be professionally documented with substantial objective data. The label should serve a meaningful purpose, and should provide a basis for assisting the learner's overall educational progress. Even when this is the case, educators have a moral, ethical, and professional responsibility to assess learners periodically, to diagnose accurately, to follow all due-process procedures, and to ensure that learners are placed in other groups or classes if the handicapped or exceptional conditions change.

Handicapped Conditions

Theoretically, culturally diverse children and adolescents can experience any handicap that other children or adolescents experience: behavior disorders, mental handicaps, visual impairments, communication disorders, and hearing and visual impairments, to name a few representative examples. However, one of the crucial issues to be considered is whether the decision-making process and diagnostic tests accurately reflect the strengths and weaknesses of culturally diverse, handicapped youngsters. When working with handicapped learners, the concept of behavior and its role in determining eligibility for special programs must be identified. Most importantly, professionals who make eligibility decisions should be sensitive to what is educationally best for the student (Patton & Polloway, 1990).

Gifted and Talented

The juxtaposition of "cultural diversity" and "gifted" continues to produce a dissonance in the minds of some people. Words and phrases like "underprivileged," "culturally deprived," or "disadvantaged" have a more comfortable ring when people think of culturally diverse populations. It has been difficult for some people to understand that a child or adolescent may be verbally gifted (albeit in a language other than English), that learners have higher-order cognitive processes in survival techniques (but not in taking standardized tests), and that culturally different does not imply culturally inferior (Bernal, 1979).

While much has been written to urge educators to be sensitive to the special characteristics of culturally diverse populations, most programs for gifted learners continue to use traditional methods of identification that rely on popular notions of gifted characteristics (Yarborough & Johnson, 1983). Identifying culturally different, gifted learners might pose a difficult situation because of the complexity of the learners' characteristics. Culturally different learners might have been raised in an environment that rewards certain types of behavior that are not consonant with conventional notions of giftedness. For example, in some Hispanic-Americans, there may be less reinforcement of highly verbal behavior. These children, upon entering school, may be somewhat reticent, and might be overlooked in screening for giftedness (Yarborough & Johnson, 1983).

Gifted children may be found in every socioeconomic and cultural group. However, educators have been less successful in identifying culturally diverse learners, perhaps because they are more difficult to recognize and teach. Several factors have contributed to an increased emphasis on identifying culturally diverse, gifted learners: First, broader definitions of giftedness and intellectual ability are contributing to more learners being identified; and second, there is a new willingness among educators to use a variety of screening and evaluating techniques and instruments (Wolf, 1990).

What instruments and techniques, then, do experts recommend for identifying culturally diverse, gifted learners (Wolf, 1990)?

1. Research indicates that the culturally diverse gifted are likely to score higher on the K-ABC Instrument (McCollum, Karnes, & Edwards, 1984) than on the Stanford-Binet or Wechsler Scales which depend more on verbal skills.

2. A study has attempted to identify and to test for specific types of giftedness using Guilford's Structure of Intellect Model. This is an important step, because it relates traditional intelligence measures to nontraditional structure of the intellect.

3. The subcultural Indices of Academic Potential is a test that requires students to assess their reactions to everyday situations. This test produces a profile of preferences, learning styles, and ways of approaching tasks (Renzull, 1973).

4. The Kranz Talent Identification Instrument is designed to raise awareness of the multiple criteria of giftedness, and to assist teachers in screening for talented learners in the classrooms (Kranz, 1982).

After educators have identified culturally different, gifted learners, their first need is to select programs that match the needs of culturally diverse, gifted youngsters. Rather than programs that are designed for Anglo learners and their cognitive styles, these programs should be designed and implemented with a consideration of the culturally diverse learner's psychological, cultural, and linguistic characteristics. Simply integrating culturally diverse learners into an established gifted curriculum may not be successful, since it requires learners to accommodate themselves to the school program, rather than having the program meet the needs of individual learners. While such programs might appear to be successful, they might inadvertently result in more acculturated learners, learners who have lost much of their ethnic talent or unique expertise (Bernal, 1979).

Successful programs for culturally diverse, gifted learners appear to have two major characteristics: They provide children with the opportunity to learn not only receptively, but also productively. These programs encourage learners to study, and to venture, risk, dream, reflect, and become involved in meaningful projects (Bernal, 1979).

Language-Minority Learners

The linguistic diversity in the United States has become a source of divisiveness among its citizens, and has contributed to the failure of schools to provide an adequate education for culturally diverse learners. In many school systems, the number of languages and dialects spoken by children and their families is staggering, as the languages of Central and South America, Africa, and Asia combine with the various American dialects. Across America, language-minority learners are not learning the essential lessons of schools, and are not fully participating in the economic, social, and political life of the United States. The problem for language-minority children and their educators will grow even more serious over the next decade or two as language-minority children and adolescents become the majority in the public schools (Bowman, 1989). This section will examine briefly the two-fold issue which is at stake: The dialectical differences among learners residing in the United States, and the learners who are actually learning English as a second language.

Dialectical Differences.   Dialect, and the issue of whether to require a standard American English dialect in the schools, is both a sensitive and controversial subject. Since there is a close relationship between ethnic, culturally diverse groups, and dialects that are often considered nonstandard, this issue also has civil rights implications. To require that standard English be spoken in the schools is considered discriminatory by some, who think that such a requirement places an additional educational burden on the nonstandard-English-speaking students. Further, the insistence on standard English may hinder the acquisition of other educational skills, making it difficult for these students to succeed. It can be argued that such a practice denies the nonstandard-English-speaking students the same educational opportunities as others, and thus morally, if not legally, denies them their civil rights (Gollnick & Chinn, 1990).

Bilingual Education and English as a Second Language.   The language diversity which exists in the United States extends itself into the schools, and in large urban and metropolitan school districts there may be nearly a hundred different languages spoken. While some students are bilingual in English and their native language, others either do not speak English at all, or have limited English-speaking skills. Furthermore, indications are that the number of students with limited English-speaking skills will continue to increase (Gollnick & Chinn, 1990). Some culturally diverse learners are quite competent in English; however, others may speak only Spanish, the second most common language in the United States; one of the many Asian languages; or a less common language such as Arabic or Tongian (Haring, 1990). This section looks at efforts such as Bilingual Education and English as a Second Language programs, which attempt to address the needs of culturally diverse learners.

Some confusion exists concerning bilingual education and ESL programs, which are often assumed to be synonymous. In the United States, the teaching of English is an integral aspect of bilingual programs; however, the teaching of English in and by itself (ESL) does not constitute a bilingual program. Both programs promote English proficiency for limited-English-speaking students (Hernandez, 1990). Bilingual education is generally defined as "the use of two languages as media of instruction" (Baca & Cervantes, 1989, p. 24). Bilingual education has been supported by federal funds that were provided by the Bilingual Education Act of 1968, and reauthorized in 1974, 1978, and 1984 (Gollnick & Chinn, 1990). Alatis (1976) defined *English as a Second Language* (ESL) as "the field of teaching English to speakers of other languages" (p. 5).

Bilingual education reinforces the student's home language and culture, while simultaneously teaching the ability to function in another language. Instruction in both skills and content is usually provided in the student's home language, and in English. The most important legal action related to bilingual education was the 1974 *Lau v. Nichols* decision, which pointed to the need for some type of special instructional program for students with limited English-speaking ability.

English as a Second Language programs rely exclusively on English for teaching and learning. ESL programs are used extensively in the United States as the primary means of assimilating limited-English-speaking students into the linguistic mainstream as quickly as possible. The main feature of the program is that educators place less emphasis on the maintenance of home language and culture than on English language acquisition (Hernandez, 1990). Chart 9-1 provides an overview of English as a Second Language.

The emphasis of the ESL program is concentrated in three major areas (TESOL, 1976):

1. Culture: Integrating students' cultural experiences and background into meaningful language learning.

Chart 9-1   Questions and Answers About English as a Second Language

What is English as a second language?

English as a Second Language (ESL) is intensive English language instruction by teachers trained in recognizing and working with language differences. The ESL program is required by state law in school districts with students who have limited English language skills.

What is an ESL program?

–An ESL program is structured language instruction designed to teach English to students whose English language skills are limited.

–ESL instruction considers the student's learning experiences and cultural backgrounds.

–ESL is taught through second language methods that are applied to teaching mathematics, science, and social studies.

What is the purpose of an ESL program?

–An ESL program develops competence in English.

–English language skills are taught through listening, speaking, reading, writing, and grammar.

–A student's instructional program is modified to make it easier to learn English.

Who should be enrolled in an ESL program?

–Students in pre-kindergarten through grade 12 who speak or hear a language other than English in their home, and who have difficulty in English, are eligible.

Who is responsible for teaching in an ESL program?

–Teachers who are specially trained, tested, and certified to teach in ESL programs that meet the special language needs of these students.

Source: *English as a second language program: Benefits for your child.* (1987). Austin, TX: Texas Education Agency.

2. Language Development: Teaching structures and vocabulary relevant to students' learning experiences.
3. Content Area Instruction: Applying techniques from second language learning to subject matter presented in English.

CELEBRATING AND RESPONDING TO CULTURAL DIVERSITIES

Recognizing the Effects of Cultural Diversities

Educators usually do not question the supposition that culture plays a major role in a learner's overall achievement and attitudes toward school. The ultimate challenge, however, is to recognize cultural diversities as strengths on which to build a solid education. The first step in achieving such a goal is to realize the effects of diversity, and to respond with a sense of positiveness, rather than viewing diversity as a hurdle to be overcome.

One example of diversity among groups is the variety of formal and informal rules governing interaction between individuals. When classroom interactional patterns are not consistent or compatible with those that children and adolescents experience in their homes and community, such variations may cause problems. For example, variations in what, how, and when something is said by the teacher (although perhaps unnoticed by the teacher) may interfere with learning, and damage attitudes toward school (Gollnick & Chinn, 1990). Hymes (1981) observed that the differences commonly recognized by the school and community are the most visible aspects of the culture, perhaps the very ones which are stereotypically expected. At the same time, the less visible aspects of the culture associated with everyday etiquette and interaction, as well as with the expressiveness of rights, obligations, values, and aspirations, are often overlooked.

An excellent example of how cultural backgrounds affect learning is the manner in which teaching/learning environments are structured according to rules that are not shared by the students and their community. Several differences may surface: How students and teachers interact; how teachers control and monitor behavior; what kinds of behaviors are used to intervene; what kinds of organization patterns exist; and whether learners are expected to participate by interrupting another speaker for a chance to voice an opinion. For example, Native-American learners might perceive instructional demands as strange, or as being contradictory to cultural expectations. Native-American learners who are expected to respond competitively or individualistically might feel that such instructional expectations violate their desire for cooperation and group efforts (Hernandez, 1990).

An equitable response to differences among learners includes: (1) Encouraging students to build and maintain a positive self-concept; (2) using the ethnic backgrounds of students to teach effectively; (3) helping students overcome their prejudices; (4) expanding the knowledge and appreciation of the historical, economic, political, and social experiences of ethnic and national groups; and (5) assisting students in understanding that the world's knowledge and culture have been, and continue to be, created from the contributions of all cultural groups and nations. A response should also include the provision of environments in which students can learn to participate in the dominant society while maintaining distinct cultural differences. Educators can work toward such responses by demonstrating respect and support for differences, by reflecting diversity in the curriculum, and by using positive differences to teach and interact with learners (Hernandez, 1990).

Building Cultural Identities

An individual's cultural identity is based upon a number of traits and values that are related to national or ethnic origin, family, religion, gender, age, occupation, socioeconomic level, language, geographic region, and exceptionality (Gollnick & Chinn, 1990). The identity is determined to a large degree by the interaction among these factors, and the degree to which individuals identify with different subcultures or cultural groups that share political and social institutions, and other distinctive cultural elements (Hernandez, 1990). Rather than allowing "different is wrong" perceptions to prevail, and to lower learners' opinions of cultural identities, perceptive educators recognize learners' cultural identities, and assist learners in developing positive, healthy, cultural identities.

James P. Comer, a prominent African-American psychiatrist and a co-author of *Black Child Care*, proposes that children of all cultures have the need to establish a positive racial identity. Comer suggests that children of all racial groups should be able to develop positive feelings about themselves and their cultural group. Negative or ambivalent feelings may result in adverse social and psychological consequences (Comer, 1988).

CASE STUDY 9-3 suggests that cultural identities can be improved through affirmative approaches such as activities that promote the understanding of cultural diversity, and assessment of the overall teaching/learning environment.

CASE STUDY 9-3: Enhancing Cultural Identities

Ms. Stepp, well-known for her plans and activities designed to enhance students' self-concepts and cultural identities, was asked by her principal to do an in-service presentation on working with culturally diverse children and adolescents. Due to the steadily increasing cultural diversity of the school, the administrative staff recognized these areas as crucial to the overall success of learners.

Ms. Stepp wondered what ideas, suggestions, activities, and materials she would be able to share. As she planned a rough outline, several broad topics came to mind: the needs of student activities (especially designed for each cultural group), informal assessments, and the overall teaching/learning climate. Teachers' attitudes and behaviors would also need to be mentioned.

The presentation would need to include teaching and encouraging respect for home, family, self, traditions, heritages, customs, and anything

> that accentuated the positive in the learner's culture. A last point would also need to be made: Teachers must have appropriate attitudes, and must value and respect cultural diversity, if attempts to improve cultural diversity are to be successful.

Educators who celebrate the richness that cultural diversity brings to the classroom readily recognize the need to build or enhance the learners' cultural identity. Family and cultural ties are so important to every learner that teachers should give these aspects prime consideration in teaching/learning experiences. Learners' earliest experiences are of home and family, and their language is an important part of this background. Teachers should remember the importance of respecting learners' cultural backgrounds, and at all times they should avoid abusing or dishonoring cultural backgrounds. A first step to building learners' cultural identity is for educators to understand learners' heritages, their values and traditions, and their languages. While efforts to ensure positive self-concepts and cultural identities should be an on-going process, educators should also work toward helping learners to have positive attitudes toward school and its practices (Petty, Petty, & Salzer, 1989).

Learning Styles

An increasing body of research suggests that equating learning styles and teaching/learning activities contributes to meeting each individual's unique needs (Stewart, 1990). Learning styles have been defined in several ways: First, Cornett (1983) believed that learning styles are consistent patterns of behavior defined in terms of cognitive, affective, and physiological dimensions. To some degree, learning styles are indicators of how individuals process information and respond to the affective, sensory, and environmental dimensions of the instruction process. A second definition came from the NASSP (1979): Learning styles are characteristic cognitive, affective, and physiological behaviors that serve as relatively stable indicators of how learners perceive, interact with, and respond to, the learning environment. The implications of learning styles, however, extend beyond mere definitions. Style characteristics derive from genetic coding, personality, development, motivation, and cultural and environmental influences. These are relatively persistent qualities in the behavior of individual learners (Keefe, 1990). It is important for educators to know how all students learn, to recognize that culturally diverse students have unique learning styles, and to determine the most appropriate instructional approaches and techniques.

Cultural Considerations

Although the relationship between culture and learning style is not fully understood, it is important to the teaching/learning process. Cultural and cognitive factors, and socialization practices influence cognitive and affective preferences, and are manifested in incentives and motivation, interpersonal relationships, and patterns of intellectual abilities (Ramirez & Castaneda,

1974: Hernandez, 1989). It is important for all educators to know how all students learn. However, educators who work in multicultural situations are in a particularly challenging position, since they must recognize that culturally diverse students have their unique learning styles, and determine the most appropriate instructional approaches and techniques.

Educators who recognize cultural differences should remember the dangers of generalizing group findings to individuals. The growing numbers of culturally diverse learners, and the increased recognition of culturally diverse learners, have resulted in research that focuses on the intricate relationships between cultural diversity and learning styles. IMPLEMENTING RESEARCH 9-4 looks at one such study, designed to study the learning styles of four ethnic groups.

IMPLEMENTING RESEARCH 9-4: Cross-Cultural Differences in Learning Styles of Students from Four Ethnic Backgrounds

Dunn and her colleagues provided a comprehensive look at learning styles of African-, Chinese-, Mexican-, and Greek-American elementary students. The students (fourth, fifth, and sixth graders) were assessed with the Learning Style Inventory (LSI) (Dunn, Dunn, and Price, 1986), and the Group Embedded Figures Test (GEFT) (Oltman, Raskin, and Witkin, 1971). After they had identified the problem of understanding the learning styles of culturally diverse learners, the authors summarized the related research findings, and explained their method and results. Through an impressive array of graphs and tables, the authors showed the difference in learning styles.

IMPLEMENTING THE RESEARCH:

_____ 1. Classrooms should be varied, and provide both quiet areas and sections for student interaction; well- and softly-illuminated areas; and a conventional, versus an informal, seating arrangement.

_____ 2. If they respond differently to established school temperatures, students should be permitted to wear sweaters or open-necked blouses and shirts.

_____ 3. Students should be permitted to work alone, in pairs, in small groups, or with the teacher.

_____ 4. Some students, like the Chinese-Americans in this study, require a variety of instructional approaches, while others feel most comfortable with patterns and routines, as indicated by the responses of the African-American students.

Source: Dunn, R. et al. (1990). "Cross-cultural differences in learning styles of elementary-age students from four ethnic backgrounds." _Journal of Multicultural Counseling and Development, 18,_ 68–93.

The speculation surrounding the relationship of learning styles and cultural diversity notwithstanding, what does the evidence indicate or suggest? Although reliable research on the learning styles of all culturally diverse groups is not available, Table 9-1 provides a cursory look at several representative findings. IMPLEMENTING RESEARCH 9-5 shows how learning styles differ, and looks especially at African-American learners.

Table 9-1   Cultural Diversity and Learning Styles: Representative Examples

Mexican-Americans. In this sample, Mexican-Americans were more motivated to learn than were students in the general population; the boys were the most authority-oriented students in the group; the boys were far more parent-motivated than students in the general population; the students were far more peer-oriented, and were more likely to succeed in small group learning situations (Dunn & Dunn, 1978).

African-Americans. Hilliard (1976) and Shade (1982) concluded that African-Americans have the following tendencies: They view things in their environment in entirety, rather than in isolated parts; they prefer intuitive, rather than deductive or inductive, reasoning; they approximate concepts of space, number, and time, rather than aiming at exactness or accuracy; and they rely on both nonverbal and verbal communication.

Native-Americans. More (1987) reports that many Native-Americans show strengths in visual/spatial/perceptual information, and that given a choice, they prefer these modes to verbal modes; they frequently and effectively use coding with imagery to remember concepts and words (mental associations assist in remembering); they are more reflective than impulsive, and watch-*then*-do rather than trial-and-error; they are more likely to participate in global processing on both verbal and nonverbal tasks, e.g., students might process using the whole and the relationships between the parts, rather than emphasizing the parts to build the whole.

IMPLEMENTING RESEARCH 9-5: Learning Styles of African-American Learners

Jacobs studied 150 high, average, and low African-American seventh grade students from three middle schools in a Louisiana school district. The learners' socioeconomic classes ranged from lower middle-class to middle-class. To determine student achievement in basic skills, the Achievement Series of the Comprehensive Assessment Program (CAP) was administered. The results indicated differences in learning styles between African-American students of varying academic levels. High achievers were teacher-motivated. Average achievers preferred to learn in the late mornings. Low achievers were more persistent, and preferred nonparental authority figures present while learning.

IMPLEMENTING THE RESEARCH

_____ 1. Educators should assess students' learning styles to determine appropriate instructional strategies and environmental conditions.

_____ 2. Educators should remember that while culturally diverse learners (in this case, African-Americans) share common cultural experiences, they also have many unique differences that must be considered.

_____ 3. Educators should plan instructional strategies that recognize that high, average, and low students use different learning styles.

Source: Jacobs, R.L. (1990). "Learning styles of Black high, average, and low achievers." _The Clearing House, 63_, 253–254.

Assessment

Understanding what learning styles are, and recognizing that culturally diverse learners differ from Anglo-American students, will undoubtedly be vital to the educational success of learners during the 1990s and beyond. Although the research on cultural diversity and lifestyles provides valuable information, educators need to be able to assess an individual student's learning style. Several assessment instruments provide elementary and secondary educators with a means of determining specific domains of styles, while other instruments assess overall styles. Readers who want a more detailed examination are referred to Appendix A, which provides a more comprehensive bibliography of learning style assessment instruments.

SUMMING UP

Educators who base educational experiences on the individual and cultural characteristics of culturally diverse children and adolescents should:

1. Recognize the various models, orientations, and models of diversity, and adopt the Culturally Different Model as the basis for instruction and personal interaction.
2. Recognize that both the learning styles and cognitive processes of culturally different learners may differ from the dominant population.
3. Provide carefully planned experiences for culturally diverse children and adolescents with exceptionalities.
4. Recognize the importance of positive self-concepts and cultural identities.

5. Plan activities that teach learners from both culturally different and the majority population the importance of cultural diversity, and the many contributions of culturally diverse people.

6. Plan special experiences for learners from language-minority backgrounds, and recognize the differences between Bilingual Education and English as a Second Language Programs.

7. Understand that attitudes, values, and beliefs of culturally different children and adolescents differ from the majority culture, and that these learners should not be expected to forsake their personal entities to achieve school "success".

8. Recognize gender as a varible that affects children and adolescents, and the complex relationship between gender and culture.

SUGGESTED LEARNING ACTIVITIES

1. Visit several schools to determine how, or on what basis, learners are grouped or placed in special classes. Does it appear that racial segregation occurs as a result of grouping or placement? To what extent are students "labeled"? What efforts are being made to reduce the negative effects of labeling?

2. List several ways to improve culturally diverse learners' self-concepts and cultural identities. What factors might educators consider to improve self-concepts? How might teachers determine the level of a learner's self-concept and cultural identity?

3. Respond to the language dilemma faced by many culturally diverse learners: Many cannot speak English well enough to understand educators, or to cope in a predominantly English-speaking society. What are the roles of administrators, classroom teachers, speech correctionists, and language specialists? What suggestions can you offer for helping learners with limited English-speaking skills?

4. Survey several programs designed to address the needs of culturally diverse, gifted learners. What instruments or techniques are used to determine eligibility? To what extent do the instruments measure the unique abilities and talents of culturally diverse learners? Do the programs expect culturally diverse learners to change to meet the demands of the program, or do programs reflect knowledge of cultural diversity?

Expanding Your Horizons: Additional Journal Readings and Books

BERNAL, E. M. (1979). "The education of the culturally different gifted." In A. H. Passow (Ed.), *The Gifted and Talented: Their Education and Development* (The '78 Yearbook of the National Society for the Study of Education) (pp. 395–400). Chicago: The University of Chicago Press.

BROWN, T. J. (1990). "The impact of culture." *The Clearing House, 63(7)*, 305–309. After summarizing the factors that are usually thought to be the reasons for the underachievement of culturally diverse students, Brown suggests that the cognition of learners should be considered.

COMER, J. P. (1988). "Establishing a positive racial identity." *Parents, 63(3)*, 167. Comer, a prominent African-American psychiatrist, explains the need for children to develop positive racial and cultural identities.

HILLIARD, A. G. III. (1989). "Teachers and cultural styles in a pluralistic society." *National Education Association, 7(6)*, 65–69. Hilliard examines culture, race, and class, and suggests that teaching styles and learning styles should be matched with these individual and cultural characteristics.

KEEFE, J. W. (1990). "Learning style: Where are we going?" *Momentum, 21(1)*, 44–48. Keefe, an expert on learning styles, answers several key questions about cognition, and explains the NASSP Learning Style Inventory.

STEWART, W. J. (1990). "Learning-style-appropriate instruction: Planning, implementing, evaluating." *The Clearing House, 63*, 371–374. After defining learning styles and showing their value to instruction, Stewart uses a question-and-answer format to show how learning styles can be used as a basis for instruction.

WOLF, J. S. (1990). "The gifted and the talented." In N. G. Haring, & L. McCormick (Eds.), *Exceptional children and youth* (pp. 447–489). Columbus: Merrill. Wolf examines appropriate methods of identifying culturally different gifted learners.

10

Culturally Diverse Parents and Families

Understanding the material and activities in this chapter will help the reader to:

1. State several reasons for including culturally diverse parents and families in parent involvement programs in elementary and secondary schools.

2. Understand that both immediate *and* extended families should be included in schools, especially since Native-, African-, Asian-, and Hispanic-Americans place considerable value on the extended family concept.

3. State at least five reasons for culturally diverse parents and families resisting teachers' efforts.

4. Understand that considerable diversity (including intracultural, generational, and socioeconomic differences) results in difficulty as teachers plan for "typical" or "prototype" families.

5. List the essential elements of effective parent involvement programs.

6. Explain procedures and factors to be considered during parent/teacher conferences.

7. Explain essential aspects and considerations to remember when

forming a parent advisory committee designed to address the needs and concerns of culturally diverse families.

8. Understand the importance of parent and family education, and explain how such programs can assist culturally diverse families.

OVERVIEW

For years, educators have recognized the importance of involving parents in children's education. Whether through involving, conferencing, or educating, efforts to include parents in the educational process have paid rich dividends. Until the past decade or so, however, educators mainly worked with middle- and upper-class Anglo-Americans, and ignored other races, cultures, and ethnic groups, probably because educators lacked knowledge of culturally diverse parents' and families' unique backgrounds and special needs. As schools increasingly reflect the cultural diversity that characterizes the nation, educators will be challenged to involve, educate, and conference with culturally diverse parents and families. This chapter focuses attention on parent involvement and conferences, and suggests that educators should implement parent education programs designed to acquaint culturally diverse families with United States school systems.

The Culture Quiz: Diversity Among Parents and Families

Directions: Mark the following as True or False.

_____ 1. The tremendous diversity among culturally different families prohibits educators from describing or assuming a "typical" or "prototype" family.

_____ 2. Educators who work with large numbers of culturally diverse students face a serious challenge because, realistically speaking, many minority families either do not have time for, or do not care about, their children's education.

_____ 3. Educators must recognize the "extended family concept", and understand the importance of including both immediate and extended family members in school experiences.

_____ 4. Evidence has suggested that the Asian's great respect for teachers can actually pose a barrier, because parents might be reluctant to communicate with teachers.

_____ 5. The parents' social class plays little role in the learner's academic achievement, and should receive only token consideration as the teacher plans learning experiences.

_____ 6. First-hand contact with culturally diverse families is probably the least effective means of learning about learners' home backgrounds, because it is time-consuming, and because most culturally diverse families maintain secrecy.

_____ 7. In some cases, learners who have attended United States schools might speak better English than their parents or families, and this might result in the latter being embarrassed, or feeling unable to cope or deal with educators.

_____ 8. It is best to address culturally diverse parents by their first names to communicate a sense of familiarity and personal understanding.

_____ 9. Parent education programs for culturally diverse parents should include efforts designed to transmit child-rearing values, skills, and techniques.

_____ 10. Culturally diverse parents and families should not be expected to serve on committees and advisory councils, since they might not understand expectations of United States school systems.

Answers: 1. T   2. F   3. T   4. T   5. F   6. F   7. T   8. F   9. T   10. F

INVOLVING AND EDUCATING PARENTS OF CULTURALLY DIVERSE LEARNERS

Defining the Issue

The positive effects of parent involvement on student achievement and overall school progress suggest a need to involve parents in their children's education. However, there may be an even more acute need to seek the involvement and participation of parents of culturally diverse learners: These parents may not understand the United States school system, its expectations, and its predominantly middle-class Anglo educators, and consequently, they may feel uncomfortable conversing with educators, and participating in school-sponsored events. The task facing educators is to involve parents of all cultural, ethnic, racial, and social class groups, rather than only the middle- and upper-class Anglo-American parents.

However, the issue is more complex than simply convincing parents to visit the school, and includes conscientious efforts in several areas: Explaining the school's function, making parents feel welcome and valued, educating parents about their children and adolescents, and involving parents in their children's and adolescent's education whenever possible. Only with the involvement and participation of *all* parents can schools genuinely reflect multiculturalism, and address the needs and concerns of culturally diverse learners and parents.

Reasons for Parent Involvement and Education

The reasons for, and advantages of, parents and teachers working as partners, and for teachers to provide appropriate educational experiences for parents, have been well-documented. There is a strong positive relationship between parent involvement and school achievement, increased student attendance, positive parent-child communication, improved student attitudes and behavior, and more parent-community support of the schools (Hoover-Dempsey, Bassler, & Brissie, 1987; Chavkin 1989). Although children of all backgrounds are special, and deserve the full consideration of teachers and parents, culturally diverse children and their parents might be in even greater need. Many culturally diverse parents and families do not understand school expectations (West, 1983). Some expect high achievement in all areas from their children and adolescents (Yao, 1988); they may have difficulties communicating with the school (West, 1983); and there are probably a plethora of other reasons. There is much to be gained, in terms of improved overall school achievement, and improved cultural and interpersonal relationships between parents, teachers, and students, when educators accept the challenge of building upon the rich cultural diversity of the United States and its schools. IMPLEMENTING RESEARCH 10-1 attempts to debunk the myth that minority parents do not care about their children's education.

IMPLEMENTING RESEARCH 10-1: Debunking the Myth About Minority Parents

Chavkin maintains that the belief that minority parents do not care about their children's education is a myth. The myth is reinforced as teachers see minority parents not attending and participating in traditional school/parent activities. If educators believe that minority parents are unconcerned, it becomes easy for educators to give up trying to involve parents in children's education. In fact, it may only be that educators misunderstand minority parents' attitudes. Chavkin offers several other findings: A positive relationship exists between parent involvement and student achievement (Kagan, 1984; Walberg, 1984); minority parents are sometimes imtimidated by the school staff; minority parents often are not invited to participate in the planning of involvement activities; and 95% of minority parents indicated that they wanted to make sure homework was done, and that they wanted to spend time helping their children get the best education.

IMPLEMENTING THE RESEARCH:

_____ 1. Educators should examine the myth that minority parents do not care, and should plan appropriate parent involvement activities.

_____ 2. Educators should involve minority parents in school decisions, such as evaluating children's progress, choosing classroom management methods, deciding upon the amount of homework, and setting school rules.

_____ 3. Educators should be involve minority parents in the planning of involvement activities, and the types, location, and scheduling of events.

_____ 4. Educators (many of whom may have had little under-graduate training in parent involvement techniques) should learn appropriate parent involvement techniques, and should focus efforts towarding involving all parents, especially minority parents who may hesitate to join in.

Source: Chavkin, N. F. (1989). "Debunking the myth about minority parents." *Educational Horizons, 67(4),* 119–123.

Understanding Both Immediate and Extended Families

Another important aspect of the parent involvement issue is to recognize the differences between Anglo-American and culturally diverse families' beliefs toward the family. While Anglo-Americans tend to demonstrate greater respect to immediate family members, culturally diverse families extend similar allegiance and respect to extended family members, such as grandparents, aunts, uncles, and cousins (Lum, 1986). The implications of such customs or traditions are readily apparent. Rather than educators conferencing, educating, or involving only the mother and father, there should be conscientious attempts to change traditional Anglo family expectations to a perspective which recognizes both immediate *and* extended families.

Reasons Parents Might Resist Teachers' Efforts

For any number of reasons, some parents have resisted teachers' efforts to involve them in the educational process, whether these efforts included conferences, involvement activities, or serving on committees. Although the reasons for lack of involvement of the general population are not being downplayed, this section looks only at the lack of participation by culturally diverse families.

Activity:

Prepare a survey to determine the reasons for parents resisting educators' efforts. Using the results, write a plan in which your goal is to obtain the culturally diverse family's participation and involvement in the school's efforts.

Why might culturally diverse parents and extended family members resist teachers' efforts? First, some cultures might harbor distrust and negative feelings toward Anglo-American professionals. For example, some Hispanic-American parents teach their children early that Anglo-Americans cannot be trusted, and should be looked upon with fear and hostility. Both parents and children who harbor such attitudes have difficulty believing that Anglo-Americans professionals have their best interests at heart (Vontress, 1976). Parents with such powerful feelings of distrust will, in all likelihood, shun a teacher's efforts to build a working relationship with the school.

Second, family members often fear disclosing personal problems or familial matters that might reflect negatively on the individual, the family, or on the father's ability to manage home affairs. To reveal difficulties with family members may arouse feelings of shame, and the perception that one has failed the family (Hartman & Askounis, 1989).

Third (and closely related to the above), some culturally diverse groups view the child's failure in either school achievement or behavior to be a negative reflection upon them and their parenting skills. West (1983) tells the story of a teacher who felt that she was not "reaching" a Vietnamese student. Although he was not disruptive, he was not participating fully in class. When she requested a parent/teacher conference, the father came to school full of dismay, and feeling his son had done something terrible. The teacher repeatedly explained that she liked the student, and was only trying to improve communication.

Fourth, language differences between parents' language and the language spoken in the school can contribute to parents resisting educators' efforts. Olsen (1988) reported several instances: Immigrant children who had to translate and explain school events and bulletins sent home to parents by the schools; a Mexican mother in San Francisco who did not understand repeated notices, written in English, that her daughter was failing to attend school; and one Chinese father who understood that the grading system began with A and progressed downward. When the daughter received S for "satisfactory", the father became confused and beat his daughter for her bad grades. To further complicate the situation, when he called the school, he could not understand the secretary, and repeatedly hung up the telephone (Olsen, 1988).

Activity:

Consult with the communications disorders specialist in the school, and also the Social Service agencies in the community, to learn how to work with and assist parents and family members whose language poses a barrier to effective communication. Make a list of publications, resource people, and special programs that help culturally diverse parents and families.

CASE STUDY 10-1 looks at how teachers might misunderstand culturally diverse parents and families.

CASE STUDY 10-1: Differing Expectations

The teachers at Park Street Elementary School, an urban school with a significant Asian-American population, did not understand what had happened. The Asian-American parents and families who had come to the PTA meeting the previous night were quiet, even subdued, and offered very little input and few suggestions during the discussion times. "Why did they even come?" one teacher asked. "During individual conferences, they just sat there and listened—they were not any help."

A teacher who had more enlightened knowledge, and more first-hand contact with Asian-Americans, overheard the conversation and recognized the need to clarify several points.

First, she explained that Asian-Americans often place teachers on a pedestal, and, generally speaking, consider teachers as worthy of honor and respect. Giving advice or suggestions to teachers is often considered to be speaking against an authority figure. Teachers know what is best, and to question their decisions can be construed as a personal attack.

Second, she explained that the Asian-American concept of family resulted in a reluctance to reveal information, because problems might be considered a negative reflection upon the family. Determining the source or factors contributing to a problem must not be construed as prying, or as a personal criticism of the family.

Third, she explained that the extended family concept resulted in other family members coming to the PTA meeting. Not only do the parents feel a responsibility for a learner's progress; other relatives also feel a sense of duty, and take pride or shame in the learner's behavior.

In effect, the teachers did not understand Asian-American parent and family members, nor their expectation of schools and teachers. A more enlightened perspective will allow the teachers to understand that the visitors were interested. Such understandings might also lead to more productive parent conferences in the future.

Fifth, culturally diverse parents often do not understand the United States school system and its expectations. For example, major differences exist between American teachers and Indochinese teachers: Indochinese teachers are accorded higher levels of respect than teachers in the United States; teachers are often awarded honorific titles; students are expected to bow and avoid eye contact; and students do not ask questions. Also, since Indochinese parents in their native land do not take active roles in schools, they have difficulty understanding PTA and other parent involvement programs; the teacher is viewed as the expert, and parents feel that making suggestions to teachers about the education of children is inappropriate. Likewise, immigrant parents are often baffled by group activities, independent projects, and library research, because in their cultures, the lecture method is considered the most effective means of teaching (West, 1983).

Sixth, culturally diverse parents have indicated that they were intimidated by the staff and institutional structure of the school. They have felt awkward about approaching school personnel, particularly if they had previous negative contacts with the school (Chavkin, 1989).

IMPLEMENTING RESEARCH 10-2 provides a study which suggests that parent involvement with Southeast Asians can be a reality.

IMPLEMENTING RESEARCH 10-2: Making Southeast-Asian Parental Involvement a Reality

Morrow maintains that ''schools are experiencing an influx of Southeast-Asian children, who along with their parents, often have values and behaviors that are considerably different from most Americans'' (p. 289). Several differences become evident as educators work with Asian people: communicational patterns, expectations of schools, cultural values, and general behavior. Morrow feels that parent involvement will be affected by factors such as literacy level, pre-arrival education, size of refugees's native community, and perceptions of parent involvement. Although Morrow wrote his article primarily for counselors, several of his implications are relevant to all educators:

IMPLEMENTING THE RESEARCH:

_____ 1. Educators should review the parents' backgrounds in order to have an accurate perception of cultural and ethnic backgrounds, literacy levels, rural or urban orientation, and overall education levels.

_____ 2. Educators should learn the cultural differences among Southeast Asians because Vietnamese, Laotian, Cambodian, and Hmong differ significantly.

_____ 3. Educators should develop a sense of trust, especially since most Southeast Asians revere education and rarely question educators' decisions.

_____ 4. Educators should respect the ''Pride and Shame'' principle by being careful to refer to the child or adolescent in such a way as not to bring shame and embarrassment on the family.

_____ 5. Educators should learn how parents feel about school, since Southeast Asians have reported that teachers' opinions are more important than parents', and most have reported that schools should teach basics and morals.

Source: Morrow, R. D. (1989). "Southeast-Asian parent involvement: Can it be a reality?" *Elementary School Guidance and Counseling, 23,* 289–297.

Speaking only of Asian-American immigrant parents, Yao (1988) maintained than Asian's great respect for teachers and the learning process can actually pose a potential barrier. These parents are often reluctant to challenge the teacher's authority, and sometimes feel that communicating with teachers may be perceived as disrespectful. Although these parents are usually attentive listeners, they seldom initiate contact with teachers and administrators, rarely ask questions, and seldom offer comments.

Cultural conflicts over child-rearing expectations and differing value systems also disturb many Asian families. As they reach child-rearing decisions on such issues as diet preference, sex education, dating patterns, and obedience to parents, these families are often torn between eastern and western manners and expectations, moral standards, and traditions, (Yao, 1988).

Understanding Cultural Diversity: Native-, African-, Asian-, and Hispanic-American

Educators can readily see the reasons for understanding cultural diversity among families. However, it might be more difficult to reduce the myths, stereotypes, and other baggage that educators (and other professionals in the United States society) have about culturally diverse parents and families. The following activity provides educators with an opportunity to question their beliefs and attitudes toward culturally diverse families:

Activity: Examining Perceptions

_____ 1. Are my opinions of culturally diverse parents and families based on myths and stereotypes, or on accurate and objective perceptions?

_____ 2. Have my experiences included positive, first-hand contact with culturally diverse people?

_____ 3. What means have I employed to learn about the customs, traditions, values, and beliefs of culturally diverse people?

_____ 4. Do I understand the "extended family concept", or

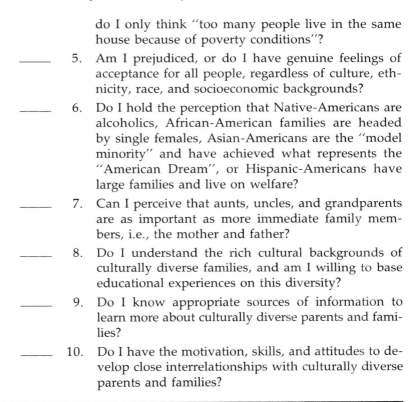

do I only think "too many people live in the same house because of poverty conditions"?

_____ 5. Am I prejudiced, or do I have genuine feelings of acceptance for all people, regardless of culture, ethnicity, race, and socioeconomic backgrounds?

_____ 6. Do I hold the perception that Native-Americans are alcoholics, African-American families are headed by single females, Asian-Americans are the "model minority" and have achieved what represents the "American Dream", or Hispanic-Americans have large families and live on welfare?

_____ 7. Can I perceive that aunts, uncles, and grandparents are as important as more immediate family members, i.e., the mother and father?

_____ 8. Do I understand the rich cultural backgrounds of culturally diverse families, and am I willing to base educational experiences on this diversity?

_____ 9. Do I know appropriate sources of information to learn more about culturally diverse parents and families?

_____ 10. Do I have the motivation, skills, and attitudes to develop close interrelationships with culturally diverse parents and families?

When reaching decisions about families, the need for objectivity cannot be overemphasized. Decisions concerning whether, and to what extent, to involve parents and families cannot be reached objectively when educators believe such statements as, "These parents just don't care," "The father is an alcoholic," "The father never lets his wife speak," or "Neither the mother nor the father has any ambition; they are satisfied to live off welfare." Educators who label parents with such stereotypes will probably do little to get to know and involve culturally diverse parents and families in their individual classrooms, and certainly not in the overall school program.

Differences in Parents, Families, and Homes

It will not suffice to think one knows the prototypic "Native-American family", "African-American family", or any other "family". For example, the African-American family is so diverse that some believe that the prototypic African-American family does not exist (Ho, 1987). Maintaining that this diversity among African-American families is a complex interplay of factors, Ho (1987) suggests the family should be viewed as a social system interacting with a number of other systems, and also suggests that the historical significance of the family should be understood. Just as educators recognize that Anglo-American families differ in many ways, conscientious attempts to understand the differences among culturally diverse families are also necessary.

Although the many differences among parents and families are too numerous to list, the intracultural, generational, and socioeconomic differences contribute further to the tremendous diversity that sets parents and families apart from one another. This section looks briefly at each of these differences.

Acquiring an objective picture of culturally diverse parents requires a determined attempt to understand both the culture, and the individuals within the culture. It is not any more reasonable to group all African-Americans into one cultural group than it is reasonable to assume all Anglo-American women are alike. One may assume that parents with black skin share cultural characteristics with other African-Americans, but intracultural or individual differences must also be recognized. Intracultural differences include clients' individuality, educational backgrounds, socioeconomic status, acculturation, and urban or rural backgrounds.

Social class differences also play a significant role in determining how a person acts, lives, thinks, and relates to others. Low wages, unemployment, underemployment, little property ownership, no savings, lack of food reserves, and having to meet the most basic needs on a day-to-day basis easily lead to feelings of helplessness, dependence, and inferiority (Sue, 1981). Differences in values, attitudes, behaviors, and beliefs among the various socioeconomic groups warrant the professional's consideration, especially since some minority groups' members come from the lower socioeconomic classes (Atkinson, Morten, & Sue, 1989).

Regrettably, a person's social class is sometimes thought to indicate his or her ambitions or motivation to achieve. However, it is a serious mistake to stereotype people according to social class, i.e., that the lower classes lack ambition, do not want to work, or do not want to improve their education status. It is not unreasonable to suggest that people of the lower socioeconomic classes, whether Native-, African-, Asian-, or Hispanic-American, want to improve their social status in life, but that they meet with considerable frustration when faced with low education, high unemployment, conditions associated with poverty, and the racism and discrimination all-too-often prevalent in the American society.

Generational differences within a particular culture result in varying beliefs and values, and represent another reason not to assume homogeneity within a culture. Older generations may be more prone to retain old world values and traditions because they tend to live in close proximity to people of similar language, traditions, and customs. Through public schooling and a tendency (or requirement) to adopt middle-class Anglo-American values, younger generations are more likely to accept values different from those of their elders (Osako & Liu, 1986).

Several examples illustrate generational differences among people. One difference may result from the level of the individual's ability to speak the English language. While older generations may have lived in cultural enclaves with others who speak their native languages, or who speak English at similar levels of fluency, younger generations who can communicate effectively in English are better able to cope in a predominantly English-speaking society. Another example includes Asian-American elderly people, who are often concerned about the acculturation of younger-generation Asian-Americans, e.g., changing opinions concerning the extent to which younger generations should visit and care for older generations (Osako & Liu, 1986).

PARENT AND FAMILY INVOLVEMENT

Essentials Elements of Effective Parent Involvement Programs

The Southwest Educational Development Laboratory (SEDL) identified and described characteristics of promising parent involvement programs. While some of the selected programs were affiliated with resources such as the National Educational Association or the National School Volunteer Program, others resulted from the efforts of local schools. The programs shared seven essential elements:

1. *Written policies* legitimized the importance of parent involvement, and helped frame the context for program activities.
2. *Administrative support* included a main budget for implementing programs, material/product resources, and people with designated responsibilities.
3. Promising *training programs* were initiated for both staff and parents.
4. Promising programs made the *partnership approach* their essence.
5. *Two-way communication* between the home and the school occurred frequently, and on a regular basis.
6. *Networking* served to identify additional resources, and encouraged people to share information, resources, and technical expertise.
7. Regular *evaluation*, during key stages and at the end of the cycle or phase of the program, provided indicators of progress and outcomes (Williams & Chavkin, 1989).

In some cases, children and adolescents who have attended United States schools might speak better English than their parents or families, and this might result in the latter being embarrassed, or feeling unable to cope or deal with teachers and other educators. It is imperative to consider these language differences and limitations when planning and implementing parent involvement programs with multicultural groups. Culturally diverse parents and families (especially first generations, or perhaps other people who live in language enclaves) might be unable to speak English with the proficiency necessary for effective communciation.

IMPLEMENTING RESEARCH 10-3 looks at a publication that focuses specifically on involving the Asian-American parent.

IMPLEMENTING RESEARCH 10-3: Working Effectively With Asian Immigrant Parents

Yao (1988) reports that more than 1.2 million Asians have legally immigrated to the United States since 1981. Defying cultural stereotypes, these recent Asian immigrants are diverse in terms of race, religion, language, national background, and economic status. Yao contends that the importance of schools' working closely with parents has been well-documented for all children, but that schools must employ special strategies to accommodate the unique cultural characteristics of Asian immigrant parents. Yao generalizes about Asian parents: Often depicted as quiet, submissive, and cooperative; often lack knowledge about American society and customs, which results in insecurities and confusion; often have problems with language that hamper smooth communication between parents and schools; often set high goals for their children and pressure them to meet high expectations, which can be detrimental to emotional and social development.

IMPLEMENTING THE RESEARCH:

_____ 1. Educators should work to understand Asian-American families, and how families and their beliefs influence the educational process.

_____ 2. Educators should minimize the barriers to effective communication, both verbal and nonverbal.

_____ 3. Educators should understand the role superstition plays in most Asian cultures, e.g., the owl stands for death in the Vietnamese culture.

_____ 4. Educators should encourage Asian parents and families (who may be hesitant to get involved or volunteer comments) to participate in Parent Advisory Committees, and other parent groups that focus on the needs of culturally diverse learners.

_____ 5. Educators should examine their opinions, expectations, and preconceived notions about Asian-American parents and families.

Source: Yao, E.L. (1988). "Working effectively with Asian immigrants." *Phi Delta Kappan, 70,* 223–225.

To lessen the problems associated with communication, both written and oral, the parent involvement program at Emerson School in Rosemead, California, sent letters in four languages to parents and conducted meetings in six languages. The program also included encouraging parents to offer, in their native languages, their input and opinions about school services. The school then translated their responses, and reported back in parents' native languages (Davis, 1989).

Five Major Types of Parent Involvement

Parent involvement programs can be basically divided into five types, each having different outcomes. Table 10-1 provides a summary of programs so educators can, first, distinguish between the types and, second, reach more informed decisions concerning which type is the most feasible for the goals they wish to meet. Regardless of the program or type selected, educators should remember the just-mentioned, seven essential elements of all parent

Table 10-1: Five Major Types of Parent Involvement Programs

Type 1: The *basic obligations of parents* refers to the responsibilities of families for ensuring children's health and safety; to the parenting and child-rearing skills needed to prepare children for school; to the continual need to supervise, discipline, and guide children at each age level; and to the need to build positive home conditions that support school learning and behavior appropriate for each grade level.

Type 2: The *basic obligations of schools* refers to the communications from school to home about school programs and children's progress. Schools vary the form and frequency of communications (such as memos, notices, report cards, and conferences), and this greatly affects whether the information about school programs and children's progress can be understood by all parents.

Type 3: *Parent involvement at school* refers to parent volunteers who assist teachers, administrators, and children in classrooms, or in other areas of the school. It also refers to parents who come to school to support student performances, sports, or other events, or to attend workshops or other programs for their own education or training.

Type 4: *Parent involvement in learning activities at home* refers to parent-initiated activities, or child-initiated requests for help, and ideas or instructions from teachers to parents that can help parents monitor or assist their own children at home with learning activities that are coordinated with the children's classwork.

Type 5: *Parent involvement in goverance and advocacy* refers to parents' taking decision-making roles in the PTA/PTO, advisory councils, or other committees or groups at the school, district, or state level. It also refers to parent and community activists in independent advocacy groups that monitor the schools, and work for school improvement.

Source: Brandt, R. (1989). "On parents and schools: A conversation with Joyce Epstein." *Educational Leadership, 47(2),* 24–27.

involvement programs (Williams & Chavkin, 1988). Educators should also consider local conditions and situations, culturally different parents and families in their community, and the specific goals and objectives for the individual school. In determining the type, content, and procedures for the school's parent involvement program, one of the first steps will be to learn as much as possible about the parents and families.

Understanding Culturally Diverse Parents

A prerequisite to understanding cultural diverse parents and families is to gain accurate and objective knowledge about expectations, needs, and challenges facing culturally diverse people. Without doubt, educators can improve their understanding by reading books and journals, taking courses, and attending professional conferences. Although these means can provide considerable insight into cultural diversity, and should be an integral part of the educator's learning agenda, first-hand contact with culturally diverse individuals continues to be one of the most effective means of gaining an accurate perspective of cultural diversity. First-hand contact has an advantage that other means cannot always provide: directly learning about "people", and their individual attitudes, values, and beliefs. With understanding and knowledge, it is hoped that genuine feelings of caring and empathy will be developed between people of differing races, cultures, and ethnic backgrounds.

CASE STUDY 10-2 illustrates how Mr. Johnson encourages teachers to have first-hand contact with culturally diverse people.

CASE STUDY 10-2: First-Hand Contact

Mr. Johnson, principal at Central Middle School, encourages teachers in his school to have first-hand contact with culturally diverse people. He praises teachers who take courses focusing on cultural diversity, attend seminars and conferences, and read professional books and journals. These are all excellent sources, he thinks, but he still wants teachers to have first-hand contact. This is imperative if genuine knowledge and respect are to develop.

Mr. Johnson encourages this first-hand contact in several ways. First, teachers are expected and encouraged to be integral members of the community, and to participate in as many social and cultural activities as possible. Second, culturally diverse parents and families are encouraged to visit the school any time, not just for parent conferences. During these impromptu visits, teachers are encouraged to meet parents and families, and to discuss items of interest. Third, he encourages home visits, which are scheduled at times convenient for the parents. These visits provide a means for teachers to get to know family members on a more personal basis. While teachers are required to record their observations and perceptions, the purpose of the visits is neither to judge nor condemn.

> Mr. Johnson's expectations are based firmly on the belief that teachers must understand learner's immediate parents, extended families, and home conditions for teaching/learning experiences to be more effective. He believes that knowledge of cultural diversity contributes to improved attitudes toward people with differences, regardless of degree or type.

Although there is probably no adequate substitute for first-hand experiences with culturally diverse parents and families, it is possible to gain information through a parent survey. Without doubt, the most effective means would be to use a parent survey in addition to first-hand contact. It is important for the educators who design the survey to remember that some questions may be culturally sensitive, e.g., questions that might not be offensive to Anglo-American populations might be construed as an invasion of privacy by culturally diverse parents and families. Examples of culturally sensitive questions might include those on child-rearing techniques, sex education, dating patterns, and parents' authority. While the questions below might be included on a parent survey, any final determination should depend upon the degree of cultural diversity, and the specific information sought.

Depending on the English proficiency of the parents, educators may decide to develop the parent survey in the parent's native language, rather than risk that the survey will not be completed, or that problems will result from poor communication. Generally speaking, parent surveys should be clear and short, require only a brief amount of time to complete, and avoid conveying middle-class Anglo-American perspectives.

Activity: Examples of Parent Survey Questions

_____ 1. To what extent do you feel educators in your child's or adolescent's school understand and meet the overall needs and concerns of its culturally diverse population?

_____ 2. To what extent do you feel school policies recognize that culturally diverse children and adolescents differ from the Anglo-American population?

_____ 3. To what extent does the media center (children's and adolescents' books, films, and other visual material) reflect the cultural diversity of the school?

_____ 4. To what extent has the school succeeded in employing a faculty/staff (administrators, teachers, special personnel, speech therapists, guidance counselors, psychologists, school nurses) that reflects the cultural diversity of the student body?

_____ 5. To what extent do you feel school expectations (competition, motivation, achievements, aspirations) reflect the values and expectations of culturally diverse learners?

_____ 6. To what extent do you feel extracurricular activities in the school reflect the needs and interests of culturally diverse children and adolescents?

_____ 7. To what extent do you feel teaching methods and strategies (lecture format, small group, cooperative learning, ability grouping) reflect a concern for the educational well-being of culturally diverse learners?

_____ 8. To what extent do you feel the school has provided opportunities to offer opinions, input, advice, and suggestions concerning improvement of the school program, or changing an aspect you would like to see changed?

_____ 9. To what extent do you feel your child or adolescent is "progressing" or "succeeding" toward goals that you feel are important?

_____ 10. To what extent do you feel the school provides information and assistance concerning social service organizations?

_____ 11. What comments or suggestions do you want to offer concerning your child or adolescent in school?

Readers are reminded that these are sample questions; they are not intended to be all-inclusive, nor are they designed for a specific culturally diverse group. Educators with a large percentages of one culturally diverse population might want specific questions designed to pinpoint certain areas.

Visiting the Parent and Family in the Home

Visiting in the home may be one of the most effective ways of getting to know learners, their immediate and extended families, and their home environment and culture. Too many middle- or upper-class Anglo-American professionals probably believe that their homes and families are representative of most learners. However, in many cases, especially with culturally diverse families or lower-class families, what teachers believe to be representative or prototypic might not be the case. This is certainly not to imply that all culturally diverse families are lower-class, living on welfare, and struggling to make financial ends meet. Nevertheless, culturally diverse families often perceive family roles differently, have differing expectations of the schools, and expect older family members to play significantly greater child-rearing roles than Anglo-Americans might expect.

While the home visit can result in valuable information about learners and their homes, there is perhaps an even greater benefit: Learners and their families see that educators care, and are interested in all children and adolescents. Culturally diverse parents may also feel more at ease in their own surroundings than they would in the (perhaps) strange and sterile school environment.

Prior to the home visit, educators should call or send a note to the parents, and to establish a time convenient for both the teacher and the parent. At the beginning of the visit, the teacher should talk informally with the parents and the child for a few minutes to establish a friendly tone, and to reduce the anxiety of the parents. At all times, teachers should remember that they are visitors, and should avoid judging situations and conditions in the home. Parents will have greater confidence in the teacher if they think the discussion will be held in confidence (Shea & Bauer, 1985). Teachers should dress properly, and should conduct themselves with dignity during the home visit. Many culturally diverse families view teachers as extremely important people in the community, people who deserve honor and respect unless they prove otherwise (Marion, 1979).

Communication

Mutually respectful and effective communication is imperative during any type of parent/teacher contact, and it may be even more essential when working with culturally diverse parents. Humans communicate at several levels simultaneously: Through verbal expression, or what they say; through body language or nonverbal expression, or how they behave; and through emotional responses, or how they show what they feel. The more congruent these levels of expression, the more meaningful or understanding the communication becomes to others (Shea & Bauer, 1985). One can easily recognize the importance of understanding the various types of communication with culturally diverse families.

Whether communicating through speaking directly, telephoning, or writing to parents, educators are responsible for not allowing language or communication differences, verbal or non-verbal, to interfere with overall communication. Several factors warrant consideration: First, as mentioned previously, the parents' English skills might not allow effective communication. Second, nonverbal communication might pose a problem: The Anglo-American who looks the Native-American directly in the eye while communicating might be considered rude, while the educator might think a Native-American glancing away to be a sign of disinterest or irritation. Another example of problems that can result from nonverbal communication includes Asian-American parents and families who are especially sensitive to nonverbal messages, and who may construe a teacher's folded arms or other casual gestures as indicative of an indifferent attitude (Chavkin, 1989). Third, educators should avoid jargon with which the culturally different parent might be unfamiliar: PET, assertive discipline, critical thinking, cooperative learning, mastery learning, percentiles, or terms associated with computers or technology, for example.

Telephoning represents another means of communicating with parents, and demonstrates the teacher's personal interest in both the learner and the parents. Positive telephone contacts can significantly affect a child's school performance, and, conversely, negative calls can have a negative effect. As with other forms of communication, teachers must use caution in using the telephone as a means of communicating with parents. Telephoning provides an excellent means of encouraging parents to attend meetings, conferences, and other school events (Shea & Bauer, 1985).

A telephone call from the teacher can be extremely threatening to culturally diverse parents and families, because they have come to expect bad news whenever a representative of the school calls. Marion (1979), writing specifically of telephoning culturally diverse parents, proposed guidelines for minimizing parent/teacher misunderstandings:

1. Address parents as Mr. or Mrs., because culturally diverse parents often do not receive the same respect and courtesy as other people.
2. Use a tone of voice that expresses respect and courtesy, because a call from school often raises anxiety levels.
3. Discuss the child's or adolescent's positive points prior to discussing the problem needing to be solved.
4. Use language the parent understands, and in a tone that does not sound condescending.
5. Respond with empathy if the parent has difficulty understanding unfamiliar educational concepts (Marion, 1979).

Educators can also write notes and letters to keep parents informed of children's progress, and of administrative and record-keeping problems and concerns, schedule changes, special events, holidays, workshops, field trips, and other items of interest. Effective notes are clear, concise, and positive, and may speak to parents and family members in their primary language. Unless used systematically, however, notes and letters have limited value in reinforcing the child's academic performance or social/emotional behavior, and are best used as one component of the overall parent/teacher communication (Shea & Bauer, 1985).

Urging caution in writing culturally diverse parents, Marion (1979) suggests the following guidelines:

1. Determine the parents' educational level before sending written communications.
2. Use Mr./Mrs. in all communications.
3. Be positive, and highlight the learner's positive attributes before discussing problems.

4. Guard against a superior tone, and eliminate educational jargon.
5. Be brief, clear, and precise.
6. Offer reasons for requesting a visit to the school, because parents often resent losing time from work or home tasks.
7. If appropriate, include a sign-off portion for the parents to provide a feedback mechanism (Marion, 1979).

Involving Parents and Families as Volunteers

Parent volunteers can contribute significantly to the quality of the services offered to learners in the school (Shea & Bauer, 1985). The National School Volunteer Program cited four reasons for using volunteers in the classroom and school:

1. Relieving the professional staff of nonteaching duties.
2. Providing needed services to individual children to supplement the work of the classroom teacher.
3. Enriching the experiences of children beyond that normally available in school.
4. Building a better understanding of school problems among citizens, and stimulating widespread citizen support for public education.

Although parents are the most frequent volunteers, siblings, relatives, older elementary and secondary students, college students, senior citizens, business and professional groups, and other members of the community can volunteer to participate in school activities (Shea & Bauer, 1985).

Although Shea and Bauer (1985) were referring to volunteers working with handicapped children, many of their recommendations and suggestions also apply to culturally diverse parents and family members who volunteer to assist. Volunteers should participate in a brief pre-service training program and an on-the-job training program. Pre-service training programs should introduce volunteers to school procedures and expectations, and spell out their roles and functions. This training should emphasize the importance of confidentiality and attendance, and should offer an opportunity to discuss the program with experienced volunteers, and to visit with the teacher in the actual classroom setting. On-the-job training is a continuous process in which volunteers learn the specific activities for which they will be responsible (Shea & Bauer, 1985).

Culturally diverse parents and extended family members have numerous talents and skills to share with children and adolescents. However, culturally diverse groups often consider educators and schools as being both authoritarian, and worthy of honor and praise. Therefore, some culturally diverse people might be hesitant to "interfere" with school routines, or feel that their talents are not "worthy" to be shared with the school. The administrator's and teacher's role in this situation is to encourage and convince people that schools are open to new ideas, and that their talents are worthy of sharing. To accomplish such a goal, educators should send home, at the beginning of the school year, a parent involvement questionnaire designed to determine skills, talents, and areas of interest.

Serving on committees is another means of involving parents and extended family members in classrooms and school. Through committee work, parents contribute to the classroom and school, and learn about program development, operation, staffing, and evaluation. Parents also develop an appreciation for staffing concerns, curriculum development, fiscal exigencies, materials and equipment needs, and other demands of the instructional program (Shea & Bauer, 1985).

As with other forms of involvement, culturally diverse parents and families might not understand the purpose of committees and how they function. It is important that educators work toward making the composition of the committee representative of the diversity of the student body. Pasanella and Volkmor (1977) offered several guidelines for parents working on school committees. Those particularly appropriate for culturally diverse volunteers include:

1. Remember the committee's purpose and objectives.
2. Be confident of the committee's ability to accomplish the assigned task.
3. Begin small, and take one step at a time.
4. Function within the school, and become an integral part of the classroom or school.
5. Seek financial, administrative, informational, and other assistance when necessary.

Rather than encouraging culturally diverse parents to serve only on committees that deal with multicultural concerns, these parents may serve on any committee in which they have an interest. Committees might include: Curriculum, discipline and related problems, teacher evaluation, student/teacher relations, home study and work habits, extracurricular activities, student assessment and test results, career education, student dropouts, or any other aspect of the school (Berger, 1981; Shea & Bauer, 1985).

PARENT/TEACHER CONFERENCES

The parent/teacher conference presents an opportunity for parents and teachers to exchange information about the child's school and home activities, and provides an occasion to involve parents in planning and implementing their child's educational program. When teachers contact parents to schedule progress report conferences, they should explain the purpose of the conference. In attempting to lessen the parent's anxiety about the conference, teachers might provide parents with a written agenda. Educators should also remember that the purpose of the conference centers on the child and school progress, not on the teacher's or parent's personal, social, emotional, or marital problems. While these issues may affect the learner's overall school progress, educators should direct the focus of the conference toward areas of school functioning (Shea & Bauer, 1985).

Activity:

Make a list of possible concerns and barriers that might interfere with the success of the parent/teacher conference. How will you motivate parents and families (who might feel that speaking forthrightly to the teacher is disrespectful) to speak, voice concerns, and make suggestions?

The agenda for the parent/teacher conference might include discussion by the teacher and the parent of the learner's test scores or assessment results. Although most parents, regardless of cultural backgrounds, might benefit from an explanation of the terms normally associated with measurement and evaluation, culturally diverse parents might need even more detailed information. Test results are often a concern for parents of culturally diverse children, and parents may react strongly to results that indicate their child or adolescent is functioning at a lower level than most learners. Educators should ask culturally diverse parents to state their understanding of the information, and make sure parents understand the results and conclusions. Also, teachers should make a sincere effort to alleviate any anxiety expressed by parents over possible misuse of test results (Marion, 1981; Shea & Bauer, 1985).

PARENT ADVISORY COUNCILS

CASE STUDY 10-3, and IMPLEMENTING RESEARCH 10-4, provide a brief look at who should be included on parent advisory councils, how councils should be organized, the importance of diversity, and the reasons for having a constitution that provides a description of purposes. However, educators in multicultural settings have additional challenges, because the parent advisory council can be an excellent means of providing culturally diverse parents and families with an opportunity to voice opinions, and generally influence the overall operation of the school. By having a council composition that reflects the cultural diversity of the student body, council representatives (or parents who make suggestions and comments through selected representatives) can make specific suggestions for making the school curriculum and the teaching/learning environment more multicultural in nature. Although an exhaustive list of topics is impossible to provide, council members might want to discuss the cultural diversity of the administrative and teaching staff, how the curriculum and teaching/learning process reflect diversity, policies that might not be understood by culturally diverse groups, methods of making the school more multicultural in nature, or any topic which might seem relevant at the time.

CASE STUDY 10-3 examines how Dr. Suarez carefully planned for cultural diversity on the parent advisory council

---

CASE STUDY 10-3: Parent Advisory Councils

Dr. Suarez, principal at Westview High School, carefully planned his Parent Advisory Council. The composition was all-important this academic year—the State Department of Education had mandated increasingly stringent academic rules that would threaten slower students' academic standards; the number of culturally diverse students was increasing; several acts of racism had plagued the previous school year; and his faculty was almost all middle-class Anglo. He thought parents could play a significant role this year, especially if he could convince leaders of the culturally diverse communities to participate.

He wondered what issues might be raised as the Council progressed with its work. His list grew: Grades, racism, evaluation, his district's inability (or lack of initiative, he thought) to employ culturally diverse faculty and staff members, language programs, school policies, curricular materials, instructional practices—the list seemed endless. "This will certainly be a challenging year," he thought. He wanted a Council with a proportional cultural diversity that equalled the diversity of the student body. What problems might this diversity on the Council bring? Again, his list grew: Differing expectations of schools and teachers, misunderstandings about United States school systems, language and communication problems, reluctance to take an active role, and not understanding the role of the Council.

He planned an additional meeting for the culturally diverse members to provide an opportunity to answer questions, resolve concerns, and become better acquainted. Even with the pressing issues and the challenges of involving culturally diverse members on the Council, Dr. Suarez perceived this as a positive time—a time when his school's role in helping culturally diverse learners could be defined more accurately, and a time of enhanced acceptance and understanding.

An advisory council can serve as a liaison between school and classroom, and home and community, and function as a permanent parent-to-parent communications committee to announce meetings, special events, personnel changes, and other notices of interest. The advisory committee can also assume responsibility for organizing and directing ad hoc or temporary committees (Shea & Bauer, 1985).

Orientation sessions might be in order, especially for culturally diverse parents and families, who might not understand the purpose of the council, might feel that parents would be meddling in schools' business, or might not understand procedures by which meetings work. An orientation meeting can help council members feel better prepared, and feel more comfortable about future meetings. Suggested topics to be addressed during an orientation session include: council role and authority, purpose, district organization, value and functions of committees, decision-making procedures (perhaps including a brief session on Robert's *Rules of Order*), how to disagree and the value of expressing a different view, and expectations of members (Jennings, 1989).

IMPLEMENTING RESEARCH 10-4 looks at parent advisory councils, and provides several suggestions for educators planning and organizing councils.

IMPLEMENTING RESEARCH 10-4: Organizing Parent Advisory Committees

Jennings suggests that school staff, parents, other community members, and students, working together on site councils, can create better schools. Aspects mentioned in the report include the importance of membership that represents diversity, an orientation session to make roles and functions clear, a constitution that spells out the council's purpose, and a commitment to work together and to participate in shared decision-making. Jennings has prepared a "how-to" article that provides practical advice and suggestions for educators.

IMPLEMENTING THE RESEARCH:

_____ 1. Educators should ensure that the membership of the council represents the diversity of the student body.

_____ 2. Educators should show equal respect for all participants, show the importance of their opinions and input, and show appreciation for their involvement.

_____ 3. Educators should form a council of nine to 18 members. Fewer than nine members can result in too few to represent a range of opinion; more than eighteen becomes expensive or unwieldly.

_____ 4. Educators should remember that *all* parents want a good education for their children and adolescents.

Source: Jennings, W. B. (1989). "How to organize successful parent advisory committees." *Educational Leadership, 47(2),* 42–45.

PARENT AND FAMILY EDUCATION

Defining Parent Education

The concept of parent education dates back to the 1800s, and carries differing definitions and perceptions that have resulted in a variety of forms and emphases. A wide array of activities continues to be considered appropriate for parent education programs. These range from family and cultural transmission of child-rearing values, skills, and techniques, to more specific parenting behaviors. Specifically, however, the term "parent education" has evolved to denote "organized activities that have been developed in order to further parents' abilities to raise their children successfully" (Mitzel, 1982, p. 1379).

Although schools should develop parent education programs specifically for individual learners and their parents, programs have been developed that help parents with special needs, further knowledge of family life, teach techniques for changing attitudes and behaviors, help parents change their own negative behaviors, provide health and sex education information, and teach parents how to help with the education process (Mitzel, 1982).

The need for parent education has been documented: Parents become more involved, and develop more positive attitudes toward school activities; parents often dread the changes in their child's or adolescent's development; parents sometimes absolve themselves of responsibility; and parents often need assistance in understanding curricular areas such as moral judgment, sex education, and family survival (Mann, 1983). Also, the need results from the heightened concern about pressures related to more working mothers, the effects of geographic mobility, divorce rates and economic uncertainties (Powell, 1986), and from parents needing relevant information related to children's social, physical, emotional, and intellectual development (Roehl, Herr, & Applehaus, 1985).

The realities, however, pose a dilemma that demands educators' understanding. Although parent education programs have become routine aspects of many early childhood programs, evidence indicates that many middle and secondary school educators have not developed parent education programs. Early childhood education appears to have made substantial progress in planning and implementing parent education programs (Powell, 1986), and has provided the framework in both theory and practice for schools of other levels.

Rationale for Parent Education Programs

Two reasons speak to the importance of parent education: understanding the various developmental periods, and responding appropriately to children's and adolescents' behavior. Although each reason will be addressed separately, close and intricate relationships between the two areas warrant parental recognition and understanding.

Effective parent education programs provide experiences that show a developmental basis for children's and adolescents' behavior. Rather than allowing parents to assume that they have failed in parenting roles, or allowing parents to absolve themselves of responsibility for behavior, programs can help parents understand the developmental changes, and the contemporary world of children and adolescents.

Specifically, parents need to understand the cause-and-effect relationship between development and behavior, and that the cause of behavior may result from children's and adolescents' quest for independence, and from being challenged by peers to experiment with alcohol, drugs, sex, and other challenges to authority.

Basically, educators should provide programs that convince parents that their children are not necessarily "going bad" or "turning into hoodlums", and that while understanding changes in behavioral patterns may be difficult for parents, children and adolescents need to feel accepted and understood. Parents need to understand that feeling guilty, or absolving themselves of responsibility, may result in even worse attention-getting, or even delinquent, behaviors. Parents need to understand the effects of one-parent homes on development and behavior; at the same time, educators should emphasize that not all behavior results from family disruption.

Understanding Special Needs of Culturally Diverse Parents and Families

Planning parent education programs for culturally diverse parents and families requires that educators look at issues, topics, and formats from the perspective of these parents and families. Prepackaged programs, or programs used with Anglo-Americans in middle- or upper-class suburban schools, might not suffice for culturally diverse parents and families, regardless of social class.

Although special needs vary with culture, social class, and geographic area, what specific needs might culturally diverse parents and families need addressed? Educators, after an objective and accurate needs assessment, might find that culturally diverse parents need educational assistance understanding such areas as: school expectations, parent's roles in the school, tests and assessment scores, children's and adolescents' development, appropriate social services agencies and organizations which can provide assistance, homework and how to get assistance, school committees and parent advisory councils, and other involvement activities. While this list provides only a few representative examples, it suffices to show that parent education programs should be designed for a specific culturally diverse group, and not rely on a program that parents may not understand or feel is not culturally relevant.

Methods and activities selected for the parent education program determine the success of the effort. Programs for culturally diverse parents should not rely too heavily on reading material (unless participants are clearly proficient in English), should not expect culturally diverse parents to take active vocal roles in the beginning stages, and should not expect or require parents to reveal situations or information which may be considered personal, or a negative reflection upon the family or the home.

Formats of Parent Education Programs

A decision must be reached concerning whether to employ a prepackaged parenting program which may lead to a loosely organized discussion group, or whether to develop a program that addresses parental needs for a particular school. Although prepackaged programs have several advantages, such as requiring less preparatory time and being unlikely to require major revision, these programs may be specific only to the community for which they were developed (Huhn & Zimpfer, 1984).

Developing a parent education program based on specific family and community needs might prove effective, and might be received more enthusiastically by parents. The format of the program can take several directions, and should reflect the needs and interests of individual schools and parents. Regardless of the format selected, first, prior to planning sessions, an assessment or needs inventory should be conducted to determine preferred methods and content. Parent education modes may include: lectures, discussion groups, computer programs, videotapes, cassettes, films, and slide presentations. Parent education goals may also be reached by parent educators working as resource people (Roehl, Herr, & Applehaus, 1985). Parents may schedule appointments with available parent educators to discuss the confidential and personal matters of their children and adolescents that might not be revealed in large group settings.

Parent education sessions will undoubtedly stimulate questions, comments, and other discussion. Therefore, rather than relying on a lecture format with a large group, the leader of the session should allow time for parents to speak or meet in small groups. Sometimes, one of the leader's most effective approaches may be to let parents know that other parents experience similar problems.

Helping Parents Understand Child and Adolescent Development

An agenda for the parent education program should include helping parents to understand the various developmental periods, and to recognize that children's and adolescents' behavior may be related to the developmental period.

Critical observers may question the cross-cultural validity of theories of human growth and development. Research directed toward development of multicultural populations has not reached definitive conclusions. Regarding culturally diverse children's development, for example, research efforts have focused on issues such as cultural conceptions of child development (Gutierrez & Sameroff, 1990), eating habits of obese Mexican-American children (Olvera-Ezzell, Power, & Cousins, 1990), extended family structures among African-American families (Pearson, Hunter, Ensminger, & Kellam, 1990), and social expectations for children among cultures (Rotheram-Borus & Phinney, 1990). As these studies suggest, research efforts directed at studying the specific question of whether human growth and development theories are valid cross-culturally do not appear to be at the forefront of interest. Although readers who plan parent education programs should be careful when generalizing about developmental theories, several studies have indicated that culturally diverse children and adolescents progress through similar development stages, and experience similar developmental tasks:

Werner (1979), in her text on cross-cultural child development, concluded that children from all cultures have the potential for advancing through Piaget's stages of intellectual development.

Tucker and Huerta (1987) studied developmental tasks in young adult Mexican-American females (age 18–34 years), and concluded that these women experienced the developmental stages suggested by Havighurst (1972).

In the development of his developmental theories, Erikson worked directly with the Oglala Sioux Indians of South Dakota, the Yurok tribes of Northern California, and the people of India, as well as other minority groups (Maier, 1969; Elkind, 1984).

Although the authors recognize that such evidence cannot be considered conclusive, it does suggest that developmental theories are valid cross-culturally, especially since research is not available to disprove present developmental theories.

Table 10-2 offers a look at developmental characteristics which parent educators should convey to parents and families.

Parents should be informed in an introductory session that the early adolescent developmental period has been recognized as a legitimate developmental period between the later childhood years and adolescence. Workshops or group sessions can then focus on selected developmental characteristics of 10- to 14-year-olds. Table 10-3 briefly examines the developmental characteristics of early adolescents.

Table 10-4 provides a summary of the physical, psychosocial, and intellectual characteristics of adolescents. Readers are reminded that Table 10-4 presents a general picture of adolescent development, and generally includes ages 14 through 18 years.

Educators should emphasize to parents that adolescents vary from culture to culture, and what might be a norm for one culture might be a serious breach of trust for another. For example, many Anglo-American adolescents feel a strong need to conform to peer pressure, while the Asian-American adolescent might feel that loyalty to one's parents is more important than to one's peers. In the same sense, the "machismo" (see Chapter 5 for a

Table 10-2   Children's Development (Approximate Ages – Birth through 9)

Physical Development

1. Children are extremely active, and often participate in pursuits such as fingernail biting, hair twirling, and general fidgeting.

2. Children need rest periods, since they become easily fatigued by physical and mental exertion.

3. Many children have difficulty focusing on small print, while quite a few may be far-sighted due to the shallow shape of the eye.

Psychosocial Development

4. Children often like organized games in small groups, but may be overly concerned with rules, or get carried away by team spirit.

5. Quarrels are still frequent, but words are more prevalent than physical aggression.

6. Most children place increasing value on their teachers' expectations than on their friends' expectations.

Intellectual Development

7. Generally speaking, children in this age range are eager to learn.

8. They like to talk, and have much more facility in language than in writing; differences in cognitive styles become apparent.

9. Because of their literal interpretation of rules, primary-grade children may tend to be tattletales (Biehler & Snowman, 1990).

more detailed discussion of "machismo") that influences the behavior of many Hispanic-Americans will be less important to both Anglo-Americans and Asian-Americans.

Helping Parents Understand School Expectations and Parents' Roles

A major role of parent education programs should be to help culturally diverse parents understand the school's expectations, and the parent's role in the teaching-learning process. Designing such a program requires educators to assess the needs and concerns of the specific culture. For example, although Native-American parents and Asian-American parents might share similarities, other substantial dissimilarities undoubtedly create the need for a program designed specifically for one culture or the other.

First, educators need to recognize that culturally diverse parents and families, especially the more recent generations, might not understand United States school expectations and perspectives, which place emphasis on individual achievement, competition, and responsibility for one's own

Table 10-3   Early Adolescent's Development (Approximate Ages – 10–14)

Physical Development

1. Rapid physical development includes increases in height, weight, stamina, and overall strength.

2. Considerable diversity exists among all students, especially slow and late maturers.

3. Sexual maturation occurs as the body continues its development toward adolescence.

Psychosocial Development

4. Peers become significant, and often set the standard of behavior for early adolescents.

5. The quest for independence and autonomy reaches a new high as early adolescents try to gain greater control over their lives.

6. Friendship formation during early adolescence is crucial to social development, and includes a shift from family members to same-sex and cross-sex friendships.

Intellectual Development

7. Early adolescents may exhibit intellectual behavior that reflects developing cognitive skills.

8. Early adolescents shift from concrete thinking to formal operations thinking.

9. Early adolescents begin to think rules should be considered in terms of circumstances, rather than all rules being unchangeable (Bondi & Wiles, 1981).

possessions. This is not to imply that culturally diverse parents and families should encourage their children and adolescents to adopt middle- or upper-class Anglo perspectives. Instead, educators can explain to parents the differing cultural expectations (group versus individual achievement; competition versus working together; sharing versus ownership) between culturally diverse groups. Educators should also explain the school's expectations in other areas, such as curricular matters, instructional strategies, classroom management and discipline, homework and extracurricular activities, and other aspects of the school with which parents and families may need assistance in understanding.

Activity:

Discuss with a group of culturally diverse parents their expectations of the United States school systems. After listening to their expectations, begin thinking about expectations in need of clarification, and also of ways to respond to the needs of culturally diverse children, adolescents, and their parents. How

Table 10-4 Adolescent's Development (Approximate Ages – 14 or 15 – 18)

Physical Development

1. There is likely to be a certain amount of adolescent awkwardness—probably due as much to self-consciousness as to sudden growth—and a great deal of concern about appearance.

2. Although this age period is marked by generally good health, the diet and sleeping habits of many adolescents are poor.

3. Many adolescents' sexual development and reproductive capabilities result in confusion regarding sexual relationships. This confusion leads to increased sexual activity, which in turn has led to high rates of illegitimate births and sexually-transmitted diseases.

Psychosocial Development

4. Students are greatly concerned about what others think of them.

5. Parents are likely to influence long-range plans, while peers are likely to influence immediate status.

6. The most common type of emotional disorder during adolescence is depression. If depression is severe, suicide may be contemplated.

Intellectual Development

7. There is a transition period between concrete operational and formal thought.

8. This is a transition period between the moralities of constraint and cooperation.

9. Beginning formal thinkers may engage in unrestrained theorizing, be threatened by awareness of possibilities, and be subject to adolescent egocentrism (Biehler & Snowman, 1990).

do their expectations differ from those of Anglo-Americans? How can schools convey their expectations to parents and families?

Second, educators should make clear the parent's role and responsibilities in their child's or adolescent's education. Sometimes, culturally diverse people may think they do not know enough about United States school systems to make a contribution, or they may perceive the school as an authoritarian institution which does not appreciate input and suggestions. The educator's role is to change misperceptions of the schools, and show that learners' academic achievement and overall school progress can be enhanced when parents take an active stance in their children's or adolescents' school. In meeting this goal, educators need to show culturally diverse parents and families that:

They are responsible for encouraging and helping their children and adolescents in all phases of the teaching-learning process;

they are encouraged to visit the school and voice their input, recommendations, and suggestions; and

they are encouraged to participate in conferences, involvement activities, parent education sessions, and parent advisory councils.

SUMMING UP

Educators who want to involve culturally diverse parents and families should:

1. Understand the "extended family concept", and should involve and plan educational experiences for both immediate and extended family members when working with culturally diverse groups.

2. Understand that culturally diverse parents and families may resist teachers' efforts to involve them in school activities.

3. Understand culturally diverse parents as individuals with intracultural, socioeconomic, and generational differences.

4. Learn as much as possible about culturally diverse parents and families though first-hand contact, parent surveys, and any other means that provide accurate and objective information.

5. Visit the homes of their culturally diverse students to gain a better understanding of family backgrounds, values, customs, and traditions.

6. Ensure that communication between the school and family reflect a genuine understanding of the problems that might result from language and communication differences, both verbal and nonverbal.

7. Plan and conduct parent/teacher conferences so parents will understand the purposes and procedures of the conference process.

8. Ensure that parent advisory councils have a composition that represents the cultural, ethnic, and racial composition of the student body, and that the councils address the specific needs and concerns of culturally diverse parents and families.

9. Understand that parent education programs are especially important for culturally diverse parents, who might not understand the school's roles and expectations, and who may need assistance with their child or adolescent in a predominantly Anglo-American school and society.

SUGGESTED LEARNING ACTIVITIES

1. Prepare a parent survey designed to obtain information from culturally different parents and families. List questions that will provide specific information on: What parents and families expect from schools, how teachers can help children and adolescents, and how parents and families can contribute to the educational process. In preparing this survey, what are some precautions you might want to consider?

2. Design the procedures needed for an effective parent advisory committee, with the purpose of involving culturally diverse parents and families. Your design should include: Means of selecting culturally diverse participants; overall goals of the committee; means of reporting to the general school population; a sample agenda (for an individual meeting, and for the school year); accommodations for participants who are not proficient in English; and any special factors that should be considered when dealing with minority populations.

3. Prepare a list of booklets or pamphlets that are designed to educate culturally diverse parents and families about children and adolescents, or the United States school system and its goals. Whenever possible, offer suggestions written in the parents' native language (unless the parent is proficient in English). Examples include: *Sida o Aids* (available from Network Publications, P. O. Box 1830, Santa Cruz, CA 95061-1830) or the many fine publications written in Cantonese, Korean, Spanish, and Vietnamese. A catalog is available from the California State Department of Education, 721 Capitol Mall, P.O. 944272, Sacramento, CA 94244-2720.

4. Design a parent involvement program that builds upon the strengths of cultural diversity. How might you capitalize on the knowledge and experiences of parents and extended family members? Specifically, how could you determine their strengths, and convince them to participate and share areas of expertise in parent involvement programs? How might you deal with problems resulting from language difficulties?

Expanding Your Horizons: Additional Journal Readings and Books

CHAVKIN, N. F. (1989). "Debunking the myth about minority parents." *Education Horizons,* *67(4),* 119–123. Chavkin provides credible evidence that minority parents care about their children's education, and also provides a discussion of promising parent involvement programs.

JENNINGS, W. B. (1989). "How to organize successful parent advisory committees." *Educational Leadership,* *47(2),* 42–45. Jennings looks at several aspects of parent advisory programs: Shared decision making, membership, orientation, constitution, and working together.

McCORMICK, L. (1990). "Cultural diversity and exceptionality." In N. G Haring, & L. McCormick (Eds.), *Exceptional children and youth* (pp. 47–75). Columbus, OH: Merrill. McCormick examines relevant issues such as racism, language differences, and making culturally diverse parents partners in their children's education.

MORROW, R. D. (1989). "Southeast-Asian parent involvement: Can it be a reality?" *Elementary School Guidance and Counseling, 23,* 289–297. Morrow reports on factors that affect parent involvement, and provides implications for professionals who want to make parental involvement a reality.

WILLIAMS, D. L., & CHAVIN, N. F. (1989). "Essential elements of strong parent involvement programs." *Educational Leadership, 47(2),* 18–20. Williams and Chavin examine successful parent involvement programs in a five-state area and conclude that seven essential elements characterize the programs.

YAO, E.L. (1988). "Working effectively with Asian immigrants." *Phi Delta Kappan, 70,* 223–225. Yao suggests that educators should employ special strategies to accommodate the unique cultural characteristics of Asian immigrant parents.

11

Administrators and Special School Personnel

Understanding the material and activities in this chapter will help the reader to:

1. Offer a sound rationale for administrators, faculty, and staff being culturally representative of the student population.

2. List several roles of administrators, special educators, librarians/media specialists, counselors, and communication disorders specialists in a school that promotes multiculturalism at all levels.

3. List several ways administrators can lead all school personnel in efforts to promote multiculturalism.

4. Explain the special challenges that face special educators in diagnosing and remediating culturally different learners.

5. Explain how the librarian/media specialist can select appropriate print and non-print materials that accurately portray culturally different children and adolescents.

6. Explain how the school counselor can understand culturally different children and adolescents, select culturally appropriate counseling techniques, and select culturally appropriate testing instruments.

7. Explain how the communication disorder specialist can accurately

distinguish between communicative disorders and communicative variations.

8. Explain from the teacher's perspective how these professionals can work together, and how the teacher can most effectively utilize the various areas of expertise for the benefit of culturally diverse learners.

OVERVIEW

Genuine multicultural education efforts include more than lofty goals and school philosophies. The school's effort to recognize and celebrate cultural diversity should demonstrate total school involvement by including the efforts of all school personnel. A commitment to multicultural education also includes an administration, faculty, and staff that reflects the cultural diversity of the student body. Employing culturally diverse school personnel at all levels shows respect for diversity; however, educators still need to work together, within their individual areas of expertise, to provide learners with educational experiences which address both individual and cultural needs. This chapter shows, from the classroom teacher's perspective, how administrators and special school personnel can contribute to the overall multicultural education program.

The Culture Quiz: Administrators and Special School Personnel

Directions: Mark the following as True or False.

_____ 1. The multicultural education program should include the efforts of all professional faculty and staff members, rather than only the isolated efforts of the classroom education.

_____ 2. Current levels of teacher education result in teachers qualified to deal with multiculturalism. Therefore, staff development programs within schools are not necessary.

_____ 3. Perhaps the best measure of a school's commitment to cultural diversity can be seen in the actual cultural, ethnic, and racial composition of the administration, faculty, and staff.

_____ 4. Community members sometimes view the multicultural education program as a frill, or a program that takes away from academic programs.

_____ 5. Special educators often use the Black Test of Bicultural Homogeneity to determine the intelligence of individuals, because the instrument is based on the African-American culture.

_____ 6. PL 94-142 was legislation designed primarily to ensure that culturally diverse learners had instruction in their native languages.

_____ 7. In the past, classes for educable mentally retarded (EMR) and emotionally handicapped (EH) learners were over-populated by children who were poor, bilingual, culturally different, or severely frustrated with school.

_____ 8. Socio-linguistics refers to the study of how language varies with social situation and culture, e.g., differences between home and school language.

_____ 9. The librarian/media specialist should ensure that print and non-print media reflect diversity, and should also work with classroom educators to provide apppropriate multicultural experiences to all learners.

_____ 10. A major role of the communication disorder specialist is to work with culturally different learners, and to eradicate dialectical differences whenever possible.

Answers: 1. T   2. F   3. T   4. T   5. F   6. F   7. T   8. T   9. T   10. F

ADMINISTRATORS, FACULTY, AND STAFF: TOWARD TOTAL SCHOOL EFFORTS

While multicultural education programs and curricula may have lofty goal statements, perhaps the best measure of a school's commitment to cultural diversity can be seen in the actual cultural, ethnic, and racial composition of the administration, faculty, and staff. Specifically, do school personnel reflect the cultural diversity of the student population? If school personnel are predominantly from one background, one might justifiably ask whether the goals of the multicultural education program are being translated into actual practice. Culturally diverse learners who hear the rhetoric of multiculturalism, but see members of culturally diverse groups only in custodian positions, might question the school's commitment to equal opportunity.

Defending the goal of employing culturally diverse school personnel is not difficult. First, having diverse school personnel shows students a commitment to include all people, regardless of cultural, ethnic, and racial backgrounds; second, such a policy shows a respect for the legal mandates that ensure equal opportunity for all people, regardless of cultural diversity. Having the school staff reflect the diversity of the student body is undoubtedly a fundamental goal, and a prerequisite to showing respect for cultural diversity and for equal opportunity under the law. Reaching the goal of a culturally diverse faculty and staff can be achieved by deliberate recruitment programs aimed at employing culturally diverse professionals.

Responsive multicultural education programs include a commitment by professionals at all levels to multiculturalism, and an acceptance of all learners regardless of diversity. While classroom teachers might have the most influence because of being in close proximity to largest numbers of learners, administrators have a major responsibility for ensuring that multicultural procedures are implemented. Similarly, special educators and communication disorders specialists must project equal dedication, enthusiasm, and commitment to the overall school goals of acceptance and respect. The following sections examine the roles of administrators and special school personnel; show how classroom educators can most effectively work with these professionals for the benefit of learners; and suggest a means of evaluating professional efforts.

ADMINISTRATORS

Roles in the Multicultural Education Program

The administrator's primary responsibilities include ensuring that multicultural education programs are carefully and methodically planned, and that procedures are implemented to meet specific goals and objectives. Administrators function in a capacity that requires the ability and motivation to challenge and to lead school personnel toward responsive efforts. While their participation might not include extensive first-hand efforts with culturally diverse youngsters, their commitment and leadership remain crucial to the success of the overall school program, and to generating other professionals' enthusiasm toward multicultural efforts. Administrators' efforts, and the zeal that they bring to the task, undoubtedly determine the degree of success of the multicultural education effort.

A major role of administrators is to provide learners with a faculty and staff that reflects the cultural diversity of the student body and the community. The recent push for increased teacher certification standards might challenge principals who seek culturally diverse teachers. Most states have initiated minimum competency tests for all beginning teachers. While some claim that these tests measure teaching effectiveness, an unintended result is that the number of minority teachers is rapidly declining. The principal's job grows even more complicated when one considers that at the present rate of decline, African-Americans will make up less than 5% of the United States public school teaching force by the year 2000 (McKenna, 1988; Lomotey, 1989). Through affirmative action programs, and deliberate recruitment attempts designed to attract qualified culturally diverse applicants, administrators can locate faculty and staff members with whom culturally diverse learners can identify. Administrators above the principal's level have significant responsibilities in these recruitment and employment areas; however, school administrators are in a prime position to employ culturally diverse personnel, and must accept responsibility for the degree of diversity among their schools' faculty and staff.

A second challenge is to provide appropriate leadership efforts for an all-school approach to multicultural education. Teachers often base their dedication or enthusiasm for educational programs on the administrator's apparent commitment. Because of this tendency, and their professional responsibilities, educators should demonstrate leadership toward specific objectives, should convey a genuine respect for cultural diversity, and should demonstrate a willingness to show first-hand involvement with efforts. These efforts may be among the most important, because the administrator is a major influence in the overall effectiveness of the programs, and can lead faculty and staff members toward excellence in all professional endeavors.

A third challenge is for principals to deal affirmatively with the racial attitudes of their staffs. For many teachers and other staff members, joining the school ranks is their first sustained contact with members of another culture, and they may enter the situation not only lacking in knowledge, but also fearful of confronting the issue of race. Such feelings can lead to an uneasiness that will not only hurt work performance but can also do further harm to racial relations. Principals, teachers, and other staff members in this situation should confront their own fears, and learn to discuss race and racial issues openly. This, however, represents only a beginning. They also need to acquire information and perspectives that have not been a part of their education. They also need to plan and implement strategies that will reduce both racism and discrimination (Sleeter, 1990).

IMPLEMENTING RESEARCH 11-1 examines how staff development can contribute to positive relations in desegregated schools.

IMPLEMENTING RESEARCH 11-1: Staff Development

Sleeter maintains that the body of literature on staff development is relatively small, that many staff development programs are ineffective, that some programs mislead educators into thinking problems are solved, and that some programs may be harmful because they foster a backlash. This article reviews the nature of staff development, discusses the limitations of the way staff development is conducted, and looks at several issues for staff development in the 1990s. Sleeter looks at "doing it right in the 1990s" (p. 36), and suggests promising alternatives to the present state of staff development.

IMPLEMENTING THE RESEARCH

_____ 1. Educators must realize that the problems resulting from desegregation continue to exist, and that they deserve an appropriate response.

_____ 2. Educators need staff development programs that are based on a needs assessment focused on those school processes which contribute to inequality.

_____ 3. Educators should have staff development programs

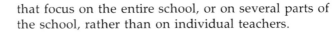

that focus on the entire school, or on several parts of the school, rather than on individual teachers.

_____ 4. Educators need to offer a commitment to do more than pay lip service to issues of race, gender, and social class.

Source: Sleeter, C.E. (1990). "Staff development for desegregated schooling." *Phi Delta Kappan*, 72, 33–40.

Another role in which administrators can offer significant contributions is communicating with, and involving, parents and community leaders. The administrator is in a position to assume the role of communicating the purposes of the multicultural education program to parents, both culturally diverse parents and parents of the majority culture. Parents and other community members may erroneously view the multicultural education program as a frill, or as a program that takes much-needed resources away from curricular areas or other school activities. Parents may be skeptical of programs that were not integral parts of their educational experience, and of which they might have little knowledge. Programs that are misunderstood will likely receive little support from the general public. Such a situation requires a skilled and competent administrator who is able to garner the support of parents and other community members.

Referring specifically to African-Americans, Lomotey (1989) suggested that principals who work in effective schools demonstrate confidence in students' ability to learn, a commitment to ensure students' success, and an understanding of students and their communities. Research about school climate, principal leadership, school culture, and effective schools indicates that principals should:

1. Believe that all their students can learn, and reflect this belief in their goals;
2. be concerned with the least successful students in their schools, rather than being satisfied that some students are doing above average work;
3. broaden the base of recognized achievement by acknowledging non-traditional accomplishments, particularly with minority students;
4. acknowledge students who have exceptionally good attendance or punctuality records (Lomotey, 1989).

Other implications for principals include believing that all students can learn; having confidence in their students; involving parents in their children's education; reflecting on the impact of the reform movement; and pushing for appropriate role models for culturally diverse learners (Lomotey, 1989).

From the Perspective of Classroom Educators: Working With Administrators

Classroom educators are often faced with getting administrators' attention and support, rather than each working in isolation, and perhaps moving toward different goals. Administrative support, however, is imperative, since teachers are somewhat limited in terms of resources, and basically can influence only their individual class.

Activity:

Ask one or more principals and assistant principals for a description of their multicultural education program, and their specific roles in the program. Specifically, seek information on school philosophies, library materials, efforts to celebrate cultural diversity, programs for non-English-proficiency and limited-English-proficiency students, and cultural diversity among their faculty and staffs.

What, then, can educators do as they work with, and seek assistance from, administrators? Classroom educators who have direct contact with culturally diverse learners are in a better position to determine learner needs, and are in a prime position to convey these needs to administrators. It will be necessary for educators to realize the many demands placed on administrators; however, it is also imperative that educators make concerns known, and insist on changes. While presenting the problem or concern will be the first step, working with (suggesting, providing input, and offering recommendations) the principal is the second step. Realistically speaking, the classroom educator may have a more accurate perspective of the problem than the administrator, and is responsible for explaining the problem in accurate and objective terms. Once the problem has been explained and classified, the classroom educator's responsibility continues while appropriate plans and strategies are developed.

Case Study 11-1 looks at a teacher who seeks the administrator's support for the betterment of the seventh grade students.

Case Study 11-1: Culturally-Relevant Educational Experiences

Mrs. Miller, a seventh grade teacher at Evergreen Middle School, had 28 students in her class: 12 Anglo-Americans, 11 African-Americans, 3 Hispanic-Americans, and 2 Asian-Americans. While less than half were Anglo-Americans, Mrs. Miller recognized that the school, its policies, and its teaching/learning practices were predominantly Anglo and middle-class in perspective. The culturally diverse students were expected to obey rules they did not understand, demonstrate expectations and levels of motivation compatible with Anglo perspectives, and learn using cognitive styles similar to those of middle-class Anglo learners. Mrs. Miller recognized the need for change, but also realized her limited time, resources, and expertise. For her students' welfare, she decided to seek the principal's assistance.

Mrs. Johnson, the principal, listened attentively to Mrs. Miller's concerns. She agreed not only that the 16 culturally different students needed culturally-relevant educational experiences, but also that the 12 Anglos needed a better understanding of the culturally different learners. Mrs. Johnson talked with Mrs. Miller, and decided to form a committee to address the learners' needs. The committee consisted of Mrs. Johnson, Mrs. Miller, another seventh grade teacher, one Anglo parent who expressed an interest, and three culturally different parents (one from each group represented).

Mrs. Johnson made a list of her and the committee's recommendations:

1. An administrator/faculty/parent commitment was in order, rather than Mrs. Miller tackling the task alone.
2. Both majority-culture and culturally different parents should be notified (and their advice sought) of the effort to meet learner's needs, and to provide multicultural experiences for all learners.
3. Textbooks and other curricular materials should be examined for bias, stereotypes, and cultural relevance.
4. Teaching/learning practices and the school environment should be examined from an administrative perspective.

Mrs. Johnson thought these steps served as a good starting point and thought that, from an administrative perspective, it was a manageable agenda. Viewing this agenda as only a first phase, Mrs. Johnson started to consider how the efforts could become a total school effort.

Evaluation of the Administrator's Efforts and Commitment

The administrators' effort and commitment to multicultural education need to be evaluated, just as educators' teaching effectiveness and learner's academic achievement are evaluated. The following checklist provides examples of items to evaluate in determining administrators' effectiveness.

Evaluation Checklist

_____ 1. The principal demonstrates and models respect for all forms of diversity among students and their parents and families.

_____ 2. The principal seeks to employ a culturally diverse faculty and staff.

_____ 3. The principal seeks to provide financial resources and other less tangible forms of support for the multicultural education program.

_____ 4. The principal works cooperatively with the school faculty and staff to provide effective multicultural educational experiences.

_____ 5. The principal supports a total school program (curriculum, instruction and environment) rather than the occasional teaching unit approach.

_____ 6. The principal accepts responsibility for acting as a catalyst and for providing significant leadership for the multicultural education program.

_____ 7. The principal arranges for convenient sessions for culturally diverse parents and families to voice concerns and suggestions.

_____ 8. The principal recognizes cultural differences among people as traits to be valued rather than in need of elimination or remediation.

_____ 9. The principal evaluates the efforts of faculty and staff and offers constructive and positive suggestions in areas needing improvement.

_____ 10. The principal coordinates efforts of faculty and staff members toward a common goal of recognizing and building upon cultural differences.

SPECIAL EDUCATORS

Roles in the Multicultural Education Program

Special education personnel can play significant roles in the multicultural education program, and are often challenged to distinguish between differences and deficits. Tasks confronting special educators include the cultural considerations surrounding testing and assessment, the legal perspectives related to educating handicapped children, the psychosocial variables affecting the teaching/learning process, and how efforts can be coordinated most effectively between special educators and regular classroom teachers.

The concern has been raised that culturally diverse students are overly-represented in special education classes. In the past, classes for the educable mentally retarded (EMR) and the emotionally handicapped (EH) became over populated by children who were poor, bilingual, culturally different, or severely frustrated with school (Amos & Landers, 1984). During the 1990s and beyond, special educators' roles will include responding to the increasing cultural diversity among learners by using assessment devices and making placement decisions that reflect an understanding of cultural differences.

Testing and Assessment

Special educators, like all educators, should carefully avoid labeling culturally different learners as handicapped, with differences construed as weaknesses to be remediated, and placement decisions based on faulty evidence or culturally-biased assessment instruments. Learners should not be considered intellectually inferior due to poor performance on standardized tests. Scores on standardized tests too often influence the teacher's expectations of the learner's academic performance in the classroom. Such a situation should be avoided at all costs, especially since teachers must maintain high expectations for all learners, regardless of cultural backgrounds. A standardized test score can provide an indication of a student's degree of assimilation, but provide little evidence of an individual's intelligence (Gollnick & Chinn, 1990).

In developing tests, and in using the results of standardized tests, special educators, as well as all educators, should recognize the inherent cultural bias that favors students of the majority culture. In fact, few tests have been developed from the perspective of a culturally diverse group. One such test is the Black Test of Bicultural Homogeneity (BITCH) (Williams, 1973), which is based on urban African-American culture, and includes language and terms familiar to this culture. Although African-Americans consistently score higher on this test than do members of the majority culture, this test is rarely used to determine intelligence of individuals or groups (Gollnick & Chinn, 1990).

Special educators should be constantly aware of the cultural biases among tests, and remind themselves not to rely on test scores as the only indication of students' intelligence. Like all educators, special educators should employ a number of culturally-appropriate assessments and other sources of information to avoid basing placement decisions and judgments of intelligence on faulty data.

Legal Perspectives

The legislative and legal perspectives that demand special educators' attention are far too numerous to explicate in a few pages. However, it is imperative that educators understand the increasingly prominent role of the federal government in special education.

More has been done in recent years to promote the education rights of the handicapped than in the entire previous history of the nation. During this period, legislation has been notable for an affirmation of handicapped students' education rights, addressing the problems of handicapped and limited-English-proficient students, and provisions for nondiscriminatory assessment, parental involvement, and expanded instructional services (Baca & Cervantes, 1984; Hernandez, 1989).

From the teacher's perspective, the Education for All Handicapped Students Act of 1975 (better known as PL 94-142) was a landmark law addressed to handicapped students in general, and to culturally and linguistically different populations in particular. Among the most important provisions of PL 94-142 are those addressing the right to due process; protection against discriminatory testing during assessment; placement in the least restrictive education environment; and individualized education programs (MacMillan et al., 1986; Hernandez, 1989). In essence, PL 94-142 addresses the basic rights and equal protection issues with respect to the evaluation, identification, and placement of handicapped learners, and under this law, assessment should serve to identify handicapped learners, and to guide instructional planning based upon established educational goals (Hernandez, 1989).

Litigation, as well as PL 94-142, has also dramatically affected the educational system. Court cases have examined the legality of assessment, classification, and placement of low-achieving children (*Diana v. State Board of Education, 1970; Larry P. v. Wilson Riles*, 1972), and the right of severely handicapped learners to a free and public education (*Pennsylvania Association for Retarded Children v. the Commonwealth of Pennsylvania*). These cases and other, similar, litigation led to the establishment of the following legal standards:

1. Assessment of intellectual capabilities using measures in English is inappropriate for limited-English-proficient students.

2. Identification of children as mildly mentally retarded requires consideration of factors such as adaptive behavior, sociocultural group, and motivational systems, in addition to measures of intelligence.

3. The degree to which culturally different groups have been overrepresented in special education classes for the educable mentally retarded is sufficient to constitute bias. Causes of the overrepresentation have included (a) failure to consider linguistic and cultural factors, (b) failure to identify appropriately, and to determine the eligibility of, handicapped students, and to provide proper procedures and special services, and (c) excessive reliance on IQ test results as placement criteria.

4. Factors such as item bias on measure of IQ and discriminatory

instruments alone does not suffice to account for misplacements and disportionate representation of culturally different learners in special education classes (Manni, Winikur, & Keller, 1984; Hernandez, 1989).

In summary, from classroom educators' perspectives, the placement procedures employed by special educators must be in accordance with PL 94-142, and the litigation addressing the rights of the handicapped. Classroom teachers are responsible for helping special educators understand culturally different learners, and the role of psychocultural factors on learning and assessment.

Psychocultural Variables and the Teaching/Learning Process

Special educators who work in multicultural situations should understand four psychosocial variables: social organization, sociolinguistics, cognition, and motivation. Table 11-1 looks at the four psychocultural variables, and provides an example of each.

Table 11-1 Psychocultural Variables and Teaching/Learning Processes

Social Organization refers to the organization of learners and educational experiences during the teaching/learning processes.

> Example: Rank-and-file seating and teacher-led, whole-group instruction, followed by individual practice and assessment procedures, produce a low level of attention and high levels of attention-seeking among Hawaiian learners.

Sociolinguistics refers to the study of how language varies with social situation and culture, e.g., functions and differences between home and school language.

> Example: African-American learners are sometimes considered below grade level and unresponsive, yet they speak and behave with complexity and competence in home settings.

Cognition refers to the schools' expectation that students will follow a certain pattern of cognitive functioning, e.g., verbal/analytic thinking, rather than visual/wholistic thinking.

> Example: Japanese-American and Chinese-American learners apparently have a cognitive function pattern congruent with school expectations.

Motivation refers to the basic reasons and cultural differences that influence what students want to learn, or their reasons for participating in learning activities.

> Example: Asian-American learners might demonstrate high levels of motivation due to family expectations, while children and adolescents of immigrant families might be motivated to avoid being withdrawn from school and put to work in the fields.

Source: Compiled from Tharp (1989) and McCormick (1990b).

IMPLEMENTING RESEARCH 11-2 looks specifically at Tharp's (1989) research and provides implementation suggestions for educators.

IMPLEMENTING RESEARCH 11-2: Psychocultural Variables and the Teaching/Learning Process

Tharp argued that several psychocultural teaching and learning processes, actually developed in the culture of the home and community, are related to the teaching and learning processes associated with schooling. At least four variables affect the teaching and learning process: social organization, sociolinguistics, cognition, and motivation. These vary by culture in ways that are differentially compatible with the expectations and routines of schools. Upon examining the school success of various cultural groups, Tharp explained his cultural compatibility hypothesis, which held that improvements in learning, including basic skills, can be expected when instruction is compatible with one's natal culture.

IMPLEMENTING THE RESEARCH:

_____ 1. Educators in multicultural situations should consider the relationships between organization patterns and instructional designs.

_____ 2. Educators should strive for sociolinguistic school/home compatibility, because learners are more comfortable, participate, and display abilities more effectively.

_____ 3. Educators should plan instructional practices that are culturally congruent with students' patterns of cognitive function.

_____ 4. Educators should understand that motivation varies among cultures, and plan educational experiences based on the individual's cultural perceptions of motivation.

Source: Tharp, R. G. (1989). "Psychocultural variables and constants." *American Psychologist, 44,* 349–359.

While the areas discussed in Tharp's study are complex and multifaceted in nature, this section offers only a brief examination, and only attempts to show readers the relationship between psychosocial variables, and teaching and learning.

From the Perspective of Classroom Educators: Working With Special Educators

From the perspective of the classroom educator, the special educator should be considered a major instructional resource. Although teacher accreditation requirements mandate that all teachers have at least a basic knowledge of handicapped conditions, most regular classroom teachers lack expert knowledge in the techniques of working with handicapped children, especially those who are culturally diverse. Rather than working toward individual goals, when students needs can be addressed in the regular classroom, classroom educators should seek help from special educators. Similarly, regular educators should rely on qualified special educators to handle students who, by law, cannot benefit from an education in a regular classroom setting.

Activity:

Through joint efforts with special educators, devise a plan for making culturally diverse, handicapped learners feel more a part of the whole school. List at least four or five specific ways to involve these learners in the mainstream of the school.

Special educators' responsibilities include responding to the classroom educator's request to assess students in need, providing culturally appropriate testing and assessment, working with regular classroom teachers to provide culturally diverse, handicapped students with appropriate educational experiences, and understanding the effects of cultural factors on the teaching/learning process. The classroom teacher should perceive special education personnel as valuable resources whose training and expertise can contribute to nearly any exceptional (or so-called normal) learner.

Classroom educators' responsibilities includes using appropriate procedures for referring students to special educators, working with special educators for the betterment of children and adolescents, helping special educators understand learners' cultural diversity, and providing follow-up as recommended by the special educators. It is important to note that regular classroom teachers should view special educators as partners, and not as people on whom to "dump" unwanted students. Special educators can provide educational assistance with both handicapped and nonhandicapped learners; however, in many cases, the organization of the school, and the legalities of the referral process result in regular classroom teachers being required to take the initial steps.

Case Study 11-2 shows how a secondary social studies teacher sought the professional assistance of the special educator.

CASE STUDY 11-2: Seeking the Special Educator's Help

Mrs. Heath, a tenth grade social studies teacher, noticed that four or five of her Native-American students seemed disinterested. She wondered whether the students were really unmotivated, whether they had reading problems and attention deficits, or whether the curricula topics were uninteresting. Fully realizing the consequences of making judgments based on erroneous beliefs, Mrs. Heath took her concern to the special educator in the school.

Mrs. Blackmon listened carefully to Mrs. Heath's concerns, and tried to avoid making judgments without accurate and objective data. Mrs. Blackmon first decided to test the students' reading abilities to determine their reading vocabulary and comprehension skills. Second, she explained to Mrs. Heath that Native-Americans could listen without looking a person in the eye, and that "looking interested" might be more of an "Anglo perspective", and one which might not cross cultural boundaries.

Mrs. Blackmon felt that, although the students' reading abilities were below grade level, they basically could read. She offered several suggestions to help Mrs. Heath and the students. First, she would work with the students two or three times a week to improve their reading comprehension. Second, she would help Mrs. Heath to provide some culturally-relevant materials. Third, she would help Mrs. Heath to develop a better understanding of Native-American learners.

Without labeling or making unjustified placements, both teachers realized the importance of working as a team to help the Native-American learners. Each recognized that providing learning experiences without regard to the efforts of the other would not result in the most effective educational experiences for the learners. A coordinated effort, with each teacher reinforcing and building upon the effects of the other, would best address the needs of the Native-American learners.

Evaluation of the Special Educator's Efforts and Commitment

The following checklist provides special educators with a means of self-evaluation to determine strengths, weaknesses, and overall commitment to promoting cultural diversity.

Evaluation Checklist

_____ 1. The special educator values and respects cultural diversity in all forms and degrees.

_____ 2. The special educator recognizes differences between handicapping conditions and cultural diversity rather than perceiving differences as liabilities or deficiencies in need of remediation.

_____ 3. The special educator coordinates the efforts of administrators, faculty and staff in the provision of the least restrictive environment for culturally diverse handicapped learners.

_____ 4. The special educator supports a racially and culturally diverse faculty and staff for all handicapped youngsters.

_____ 5. The special educator insists that screening and placement procedures recognize cultural diversity but also be in accordance with the legal mandates and guidelines for providing special education experiences.

_____ 6. The special educator works with parents and families on a regular basis, helps parents and families understand programs for the handicapped, and makes referrals to appropriate social service agencies.

_____ 7. The special educator provides screening with testing and assessment instruments with the least racial, cultural, and social class bias.

_____ 8. The special educator provides opportunities for culturally diverse handicapped youngsters to be mainstreamed or integrated with nonhandicapped learners of all cultural backgrounds whenever possible.

_____ 9. The special educator plans learning experiences which recognize differences in language and dialectical backgrounds.

_____ 10. The special educator supports community recognition and efforts to provide appropriate educational experiences for culturally diverse handicapped learners.

LIBRARIANS/MEDIA SPECIALISTS

Roles in the Multicultural Education Program

The librarian or media specialist in multicultural settings has the usual responsibilities of any professional serving in this capacity. However, working with culturally diverse children and adolescents requires an understanding of cultural diversity, and also includes building a library and media collection that shows positive portrayals of culturally diverse groups. Another role of library or media specialists is to work with classroom educators in positive, constructive ways that demonstrate a respect and commitment for providing appropriate multicultural education experiences.

Selecting Culturally-Appropriate Print and Non-Print Media
School librarians today have discovered that there have been radical changes in the cultural and ethnic backgrounds of the children and adolescents attending their schools (Nauman, 1987). Chapter 7 pointed out the importance of having positive portrayal of culturally diverse children and

adolescents, and also the necessity of addressing problems of sexism, racism, stereotyping, and outright omissions. Libraries are responsible for ensuring that books, magazines, audio-visual materials, computer software, and all library and media materials have positive and realistic culturally diverse characters with whom learners can relate. For example, culturally diverse children and adolescents should be shown in accurate and objective terms, not in stereotypical images. One of the better and more pragmatic solutions to librarians' and teachers' problems has been offered by the Council on Interracial Books for Children, which regularly evaluates children's materials, trade books, textbooks, and other educational resources (Nauman, 1987). Also, sections of this text, such as "Using Children's Literature" and the "Suggested Children's Books" listed in Chapters 2, 3, 4, and 5, provide examples of accurate descriptions of culturally diverse children and adolescents. Librarians with solid training in children's and adolescents' literature can serve as resource professionals as educators select appropriate books for classroom use.

Activity:

How might educators and librarians coordinate efforts to most effectively serve culturally diverse children and adolescents? Consider efforts such as books, poems, speakers, films, plays, skits, computer software, and times to celebrate diversity.

In a world of children's and adolescents' books and textbooks that continues to grow daily, librarians can refer to Table 7-3 (the Checklist for Racism and Sexism in Children's Books), and to the following guidelines suggested for professionals (Nauman, 1987):

1. Books and other library materials should reflect authentic cultural and ethnic perspectives.
2. Books and other library materials should reflect differences in lifestyle, socioeconomic levels, interests, and abilities.
3. Books and other library materials should portray characters who represent positions in society apart from, and uninfluenced by, their ethnic heritage.
4. Books and other library materials should reflect a variety of geographic locations of culturally diverse groups.
5. Books and other library materials should use language that shows the richness of the culture portrayed, with dialect used only as a positive, differentiating mechanism.
6. Books and other library materials should accurately depict history, and include opportunities to see differing viewpoints.

7. Books and other library materials should provide accurate illustrations that show truthfully the ethnic qualities of the characters, and which avoid stereotypes, tokenism, and demeaning implications (Nauman, 1987).

Coordinating Efforts With Classroom Educators

Like other professionals working in elementary and secondary schools, it is important that librarians and classroom educators work together for the welfare of children and adolescents. Librarians can be a valuable resource for regular classroom teachers, and can supplement learning experiences, or use a literature-based approach that bases instruction entirely on children's literature. Since the posssibility exists that some classroom teachers received training in teacher education before experiences in multicultural education were required by accrediting associations, librarians can be especially valuable in pointing out the problem of the many children's books that portray characteristics from middle-class Anglo perspectives, and can be helpful in suggesting culturally appropriate books for all children.

From the Perspective of Classroom Educators: Working With Librarians/Media Specialists

In what is hoped are isolated cases, classroom educators' and school librarians' professional paths cross all too seldom. Teachers bring, or allow, learners to visit the library during a specified time, during which the librarian might or might not have an activity planned. Teachers sometimes remain with the students during the library period, and make suggestions or encourage students' interest in books and reading. In other situations, teachers leave the students and work elsewhere.

From the perspective of classroom educators, the librarian or media specialist should be considered a prime resource professional who can teach learners about the library, and about books and magazines that provide positive images of culturally diverse groups. It is important that teachers and librarians share the perspective of working together as a team to provide the most effective educational experiences for learners.

The librarian's roles in supporting the multicultural education program include stocking the library and media center with books, magazines, and other materials that accurately portray culturally diverse children and adolescents; assisting classroom educators to choose and use these books; ensuring that library collections have works by non-Anglo authors and illustrators; ensuring that library holdings and materials are accessible to all students, regardless of social class and cultural backgrounds; and assisting students as they search for reading materials.

The classroom educator's responsibilities include working with the librarian (suggesting acquisitions, and completing book request forms) to secure a multicultural library; encouraging students of all cultures to read books that provide accurate portrayals of culturally diverse learners;

encouraging learners to read books written by qualified authors; and working with the librarian to plan activities that feature well-written reading materials.

Case Study 11-3 shows how one teacher improved her knowledge of multicultural books by seeking help from the school librarian.

Case Study 11-3

Mrs. D'Micio, the sixth grade teacher, and Mrs. Benton, the librarian, discussed cultural diversity and children's books with some intensity:

"Children's literature just has not kept pace with the cultural diversity in our society," Mrs. D'Micio said.

Mrs. Benton responded, "Perhaps not to the extent it should have, but there are some very good children's and adolescents' books which do include culturally diverse people."

Mrs. D'Micio looked at her class rolls and thought, "Well, it has been about ten years since I took a children's literature course—maybe there are some good books around now." She asked, "Can you help me find some books for my students? They are sixth graders, you know?"

Mrs. Benton responded in the affirmative, and began thinking of the sources she could consult: *Books in Print*, Charlotte Huck's *Children's Literature in the Elementary School*, Donna Norton's *Through the Eyes of a Child*, *The Hornbook Magazine*, and trade book publishers who specialize in multicultural books, such as Children's Book Press (1461 Ninth Avenue, San Francisco, CA 94122).

Mrs. Benton thought her responsibilities were more encompassing than just giving Mrs. D'Micio a list of books. Therefore, she began collecting books that provided acccurate portrayals of culturally diverse children and adolescents.

She also wondered whether other teachers in the school would like such books to supplement their instruction, or to suggest to their students. She decided to begin a program designed to increase the library's holdings of multicultural books, and decided to make all teachers in the school aware of the books and appropriate uses.

Evaluation of the Librarian/Media Specialist's Efforts and Commitment

As with other discussions of other professionals and their responsibilities, this section provides examples of evaluation items to be considered when determining the librarian's effectiveness.

Evaluation Checklist

_____ 1. The librarian or media specialist works to acquire a collection of print and non-print media that provide positive and accurate examples of culturally different children and adolescents.

_____ 2. The librarian or media specialist has an overall library program that contributes to the multicultural education program.

_____ 3. The librarian or media specialist works with teachers and other educators in planning appropriate multicultural experiences for all learners.

_____ 4. The librarian or media specialist has a system whereby library materials are accessible to all learners, regardless of cultural and socioeconomic backgrounds.

_____ 5. The librarian or media specialist plans developmentally- and culturally-appropriate teaching and learning activities for culturally diverse learners.

_____ 6. The librarian or media specialist has multicultural materials that are appropriate for varying reading, interest, and developmental levels.

_____ 7. The librarian or media specialist has established and approved criteria for evaluating the appropriateness (cultural, gender, socioeconomic, etc.) of print and non-print media.

_____ 8. The librarian or media specialist seeks input and suggestions for library purchases from teachers, organizations promoting cultural diversity, and interested parents.

_____ 9. The librarian or media specialist has acquired a professional library (both print and non-print materials) for educators who want to improve their professional knowledge of cultural diversity.

COUNSELORS

Roles in the Multicultural Education Program

Counselors' roles include understanding culturally different children and adolescents, counseling culturally different learners, understanding testing and assessment issues, and working with classroom teachers for the welfare of the learners.

Understanding and Counseling

Cultural, intracultural, ethnic, and racial differences deserve understanding and consideration when counseling children and adolescents in multicultural situations. Rather than being a homogeneous population, learners have many differences that vary according to individuals, individual cultures, gender, generation, and socioeconomic status. Examples with cultural and intracultural relevance include children as being basically *now* oriented and viewing their world, their cultures, their peers, their language, and their morality from a child's perspective. Similarly, adolescents are functioning developmentally in a stage between childhood and adulthood, and are developing self-concepts and cultural identities that will affect their entire adult lives.

Native-Americans. Herring (1989) describes the dismal state of many Native-American children, and suggests that guidance and counseling are the best vehicles for helping these children. Herring's suggestions include:

1. Counseling intervention should be highly individualized.
2. Assessment should have minimal socioeconomic or cultural bias.
3. Counselors should recognize learning styles and life purposes.
4. The child's culture should not be devalued.
5. Methodologies should place high value on self-worth.
6. The school counselor should help the school staff become sensitive to needs of Native-Americans.

African-American. School counselors should consider African-American's learners' cultural heritages and special needs, rather than assuming too much cultural homogeneity, or approaching counseling situations from Anglo perspectives. Specifically, school counselors can conduct self-awareness groups that emphasize self-appreciation through cultural heritages; explore the nature and importance of positive interpersonal relationships; conduct social behavior guidance groups; conduct motivation sessions; and conduct guidance workshops in areas such as academic planning, study skills and time management, "testwiseness," and remediation (Lee, 1982).

Asian-Americans. Reminding counselors of the tremendous cultural and individual diversity among Asian-Americans, Hartman and Askounis (1989) suggested:

1. Determining individual strengths and weaknesses, and assessing cultural backgrounds.
2. Understanding the learner's degree of acculturation.
3. Understanding the Asian-American's difficulty in exhibiting openness, i.e., restraint is a sign of emotional maturity, admitting problems is thought to reflect upon the entire family, and having emotional difficulties may bring shame upon the entire family.
4. Understanding that overly confrontational, emotionally intense ap-

proaches may cause additional problems and turmoil for Asian-American learners.

5. Learning about individuals and their respective cultures; asking about the culture, accepting the learner's world, developing cultural and ethnic sensitivity and consciousness, and avoiding stereotypical labels.

Hispanic-Americans. For the most effective multicultural intervention, Nieves and Valle (1982) offered several counseling suggestions:

1. Use active counseling approaches that are concrete, specific, and focus on the student's behalf.
2. Develop an awareness of the Puerto Rican culture.
3. Use approaches that take the client's frame of reference as a vehicle for growth.
4. Examine prejudices and attitudes toward Puerto Ricans.
5. Make home visits if possible, and make reference to the family during sessions.
6. Call students by their correct names. In Puerto Rico, people are given two last names: The first name is that of the family, the second is from the mother. Using the wrong name is an insult, and may raise identity questions.
7. Accept the role of expert; however, work to relinquish the role of authority. Clients must accept responsibility for their lives.

Testing and Assessment.

The counselor's goal in assessment is to minimize ethnocentrism, and maximize culturally appropriate information. Assessment in counseling and psychotherapy includes interviewing, observing, testing, and analyzing documents. Basic questions revolve around the issue of the extent to which cultural diversity affects assessment. Will a characteristic indigenous to a specific culture be mistakenly perceived and assessed using Anglo-American middle-class standards? Two important issues in multicultural assessment include (1) whether psychological constructs or concepts are universally valid; and (2) the effects of diagnosing and placing false labels. Other questions related to multicultural assessment include:

1. What level and type of assessment is indicated?
2. Which tests are most useful and why?
3. What are the ethical and legal responsibilities associated with multicultural assessment?

Source: (Lonner & Sundberg, 1985)

Are multicultural groups being assessed with instruments actually designed for middle-class Anglo clients? Lonner and Ibrahim (1989) maintained that without appropriate assessment strategies, counseling professionals are unable to diagnose problems, unable to develop appropriate goals, and unable to assess the outcomes of intervention. Specific assessment issues include initial client assessment, clinical judgments, standardized and non-standardized assessment, and the outcomes of counseling evaluation (Lonner & Ibrahim, 1989).

From the Perspective of Classroom Educators: Working With Counselors

Counselors may work with individuals, small groups, and large classes. The first contact between a school counselor and a troubled student may be initiated by the classroom educator, who has daily contact with learners, and who may be the first professional to detect a potential problem. Individual teachers, then, are in a prime position to either ask the counselor for direct assistance, or to refer students with problems to the counselor. It is wise for both the teacher and the counselor to determine the best means of referring students, of coordinating and scheduling large group counseling, and of determining the correct needs of the culturally diverse learners.

Activity:

Through "thinking sessions" with the counselor, plan several large-group topics that are designed to address subjects of concern to culturally diverse children and adolescents. Have two lists, because topics will vary according to developmental differences.

Children	*Adolescents*
1. Making friends across cultures	1. Friends versus family expectations
2. Feeling accepted regardless of cultural diversity	2. Expanding socialization in a predominantly Anglo world

---

Counselors may provide several forms of assistance to classroom teachers and their students. Considering the many demands on the counselor's time and expertise, however, the teacher might have to initiate contact, or inform the counselor of special areas of concern. Generally speaking, the counselor can assist with:

1. Determining and providing joint efforts of administrators and other educators to improve the adolescent's self-concepts and cultural identities.

2. Providing assistance in suggesting culturally appropriate instruments, and in interpreting test scores of of culturally diverse learners.

3. Working with culturally diverse families (both immediate and extended) in parent education endeavors.

4. Offering parents meaningful roles in school governance, and offering families opportunities to support the teaching and learning process at home and at school.

5. Providing individual and small-group counseling in areas of concern to culturally diverse learners, i.e., peer acceptance and approval.

6. Providing large-group counseling sessions in areas such as involvement meetings, rules meetings, thinking meetings, values clarification meetings, and group councils (Thompson & Rudolph, 1988).

7. Suggesting culturally-relevant materials for helping all children and adolescents to better understand one another's culture.

8. Working with older students in career planning, and suggesting appropriate subjects needed to pursue career plans.

9. Helping learners deal with concern over body development, the desire for social acceptance, and the conflicts between adult expectations and peer expectations of culturally-appropriate behaviors.

10. Designing special programs for at-risk, culturally diverse learners.

Classroom educators should view their roles, and the counselor's roles, as complementary, rather than as two professionals working alone. Since classroom educators have the most daily contact with culturally diverse learners, they are usually in the best position to detect learners with problems, make referrals, and to follow up on the counselor's efforts. Likewise, the classroom teacher and the counselor should always know each others' purposes and strategies, and whenever possible, should provide joint efforts for the benefit of the learners.

Case Study 11-4 looks at how a third grade teacher sought the counselor's assistance.

Case Study 11-4: The Importance of Friendships

Mr. Scott, a third grade teacher, recognized that several of his Hispanic-American students appeared bothered about not being asked to play with the Anglo children. He was unsure whether the Hispanic-American children lacked the social or linguistic skills to participate, or whether they felt unwanted. Either way, Mr. Scott decided to seek the counselor's help with the situation.

Mr. Scott and the counselor, Miss Wilkie, discussed the options, and decided on a joint effort with three main purposes: (1) Help the Hispanic-

American students to feel better about themselves and their cultural heritages; (2) help the Anglo-American students to gain a better understanding of the Hispanic cultures; and (3) develop situations where both cultures could play or learn together in cooperative efforts.

Miss Wilkie decided on several small-group sessions with the Hispanics, and several large-group counseling sessions with the entire class. In the small-group sessions, she tried to help the Hispanic-American children better understand themselves, and, overall, experience feelings of acceptance toward themselves and their culture. The large-groups sessions with the entire class focused on accepting cultural diversity, and understanding and accepting peers.

Working as an integral part of the team, Mr. Scott planned play and learning activities that required learners of both cultures to work together. Also, with suggestions and materials provided by Miss Wilkie, Mr. Scott continued the effort to improve the Hispanic-American learners' self-concepts and cultural identities. He also provided follow-up efforts that stressed the importance of friendships, and making all people feel comfortable and accepted in both learning and play situations.

Evaluation of the Counselor's Efforts and Commitment

As with all professionals, the counselor's efforts and commitment to promoting cultural diversity, and to working with classroom educators should be evaluated periodically. The following evaluation scale can serve as a means of self-evaluation, or as a means for other professionals' evaluating the counselor.

1. The counselor recognizes that culturally diverse children and adolescents differ from their Anglo-American counterparts.

2. The counselor plans culturally-appropriate counseling strategies for culturally diverse learners.

3. The counselor recognizes that traditional tests and assessment devices designed from Anglo perspectives may not measure the abilities and talents of culturally diverse learners.

4. The counselor recognizes that culturally diverse families differ (i.e., sex roles, expectations, and child-rearing techniques) from Anglo-American expectations.

5. The counselor works with classroom educators for the overall welfare of culturally different learners.

6. The counselor is able to suggest special services agencies and resources that respond to the needs of culturally diverse learners and their families.

7. The counselor recognizes the dangers of racial bias and cultural stereotypes, and works to overcome these limitations.
8. The counselor recognizes the richness that cultural diversity adds to both elementary and secondary schools.
9. The counselor recognizes the need for *all* students to experience appropriate multicultural education experiences.
10. The counselor recognizes the need to use resources (i.e., films and other materials) that portray positive images of culturally diverse children and adolescents.

COMMUNICATIONS DISORDER SPECIALISTS

While several titles have been used to designate the professionals working with speech-handicapped learners—"speech-language clinician", "speech correctionist", "speech clinician", and "speech therapist"—the authors of this text have selected the term, "Communications Disorder Specialist", because the term is sufficiently broad in nature to include communication problems of culturally diverse children and adolescents. The communications disorder specialist who works in multicultural settings has a broad knowledge of communication, and understands the unique communication situations of culturally diverse learners: dialects, bilingualism, and TOESL, as well as the differences between home and school language, and the various assessment challenges.

Roles in the Multicultural Education Program

Since communication is such a vital human aspect to learners of all cultural and ethnic backgrounds, communications disorder specialists play an important role in helping educators distinguish between disorders and variations. They can also help learners who are experiencing differences with communication, regardless of the reason. There is a need for all communications disorder specialists to become sensitive to cultural diversity, and to develop cross-cultural communication competencies as they work with children classified as non-English-proficiency (NEP), and limited-English-proficiency (LEP) (Cheng, 1987).

A primary role of the communications disorder specialist is to distinguish between communicative disorders and communicative variations, and to convey to classroom educators the differences between the two. Communication disorders include speech disorders (an impairment of voice, articulation of speech sounds, and/or fluency), and language disorders (the impairment, or deviant development, of comprehension, and/or a spoken or written symbol system). Communicative variations include communicative differences or dialects (a variation of a symbol system used by a group of individuals that reflects and is determined by shared regional, social, cultural/ethnic factors), and argumentative communication (systems used to supplement communication skills, such as prosthetic devices) (McCormick, 1990). It is imperative that communications disorder specialists in multicultural situations distinguish between disorders and variations. Culturally different learners who use a particular dialect or regional accent should not be labeled as having a "disorder" in need of elimination.

A second, closely related role of the communications disorder specialist is to understand, and to help classroom educators to understand, the difference between school language and home language. A learner may appear so "quiet" and "withdrawn" that the educator wonders if the child or adolescent has physical or emotional problems. However, the child or adolescent at home and in the community shows considered verbal proficiency. When there are substantial differences between language use and conversational use in the home and in the classroom, children and adolescents often appear to have low verbal ability. Despite being verbal in nonschool settings, these learners may talk very little in the classroom, and even then using only simple words and sentences (McCormick, 1990b). In such a situation, the communications disorder specialist might have to convince the classroom educator that the child or adolescent is not speech-handicapped, and is not in need of remediation or therapy.

Another goal of the communications disorder specialist is to understand dialectical differences of many culturally diverse learners, and learners of the majority culture. Understanding and responding appropriately to the dialect of the learner within a classroom can be a complex and sensitive issue. First, it should be recognized that dialects are not communicative disorders, and should not be treated as such by the teacher or the communications disorder specialist. The American Speech and Hearing Association (ASHA, 1983) has taken a strong position that dialectical varieties do not constitute speech or language disorders. It should be noted, however, that a dialect and a communicative disorder can exist at the same time. For example, if a learner with a Spanish- or African-American dialect also has defective articulation, or stutters, the classroom educator should refer the learner to the communications disorder specialist. The situation grows complex if a teacher is not thoroughly familiar with the features of the dialect. However, both the teacher and the communications disorder specialist should learn to distinguish accurately between linguistic diversity and disorders. Dialects should not be considered "less than", but only "different from", that which is recognized as standard English. A teacher is in a strategic position to promote understanding and acceptance of a child who has a dialectical difference (Oyer, Crowe, & Haas, 1987).

Activity:

How can educators and communication disorders specialists best distinguish between communication disorders and communication variations? List several ways variations can be best addressed.

Disorders	Response	Variations	Response
Articulation	Specific work on pronunciation of letters and patterns of letters	Dialects	To what extent does the dialect interfere with communication? Accept as part of cultural heritage.

From the Perspective of Classroom Educators: Working With the Communications Disorder Specialist

The classroom educator should view the communications disorder specialist as a valuable resource person, especially since this professional has such a wide range of expertise and abilities in dealing with communicative disorders. Working in a complementary fashion for the welfare of learners, the communications disorder specialist can assist the classroom educator in determining whether communication problems are to be remediated, or whether variations are to be accepted and appreciated.

Considerable interaction should occur between classroom educators and communications disorder specialists. First, the communications disorder specialist and the teacher need to consult with each other about their goals for a learner, how they expect to accomplish these goals, and what success has been achieved. Such interaction can be formal, informal, or by the communications disorder specialist providing the teacher with copies of written therapy progress reports sent home to parents. Second, the teacher in the classroom has more contact with parents and spends more school hours with a learners, who may talk about their feelings, wants, and life at home. Some information that a teacher receives from learners or their parents may be important to the communications disorder specialist. Third, the teacher is also in an ideal position to provide the communications disorder specialist with information regarding a learner's speech and language functioning within the classroom and in informal situations, such as in the hallway, the lunchroom, or on the playground. The teacher may also be able to provide reminders to the child during the habit-forming stages of therapy, when the child can best produce the targeted speech behaviors, but still must make them a habit in all communicative situations. Fourth, the communications disorder specialist will need the teacher's input with regard to referrals, and in establishing whether or not there is an adverse effect on education due to communicative problem (Oyer, Crowe, & Haas, 1987).

The communication disorders specialist's responsibilities include appropriate assessment, therapy, scheduling, and consultation with teachers and parents (Oyer, Crowe, & Haas, 1987). Other responsibilities in multicultural situations include understanding the communication problems of culturally different children and adolescents, being able to convey to teachers an assessment of disorders and variations, and providing a climate of understanding and acceptance for all learners.

The classroom teacher plays a major role in the lives of learners by serving as an important role model, a major force in shaping ideas, and an influence on emotional development (McFarlane, Fujiki, & Britton, 1984). The classroom educator's responsibilities include being a good speech model; creating a classroom atmosphere conducive to communication; accepting learners, and encouraging classmates to accept learners, with communicative problems; consulting with the communications disorder specialists; detecting possible communicative disorders and making referrals; reinforcing the goals of the communications disorder specialist; and helping the learner catch up on what was missed during therapy (Oyer, Crowe, & Haas, 1987). Other responsibilities include giving full participation when a decision has been reached to place the child in a limited- or non-English-proficient program.

Case Study 11-5 shows how disorders and variations can be confused, and how the communication disorders specialist can work with classroom teachers.

Case Study 11-5: Responding to Communication Differences

Miss Tyler, a ninth grade reading teacher in an inner-city school, felt somewhat overwhelmed as she took her concerns to the communications disorder specialist, Mrs. Clyburn. She said, "I have four—perhaps five—African-American students who I have difficultly understanding, two Hispanic-American students who have tremendous difficulty with English and intersperse Spanish with English, and one bilingual Japanese-American. What do I do, Mrs. Clyburn? There is such a wide variety of communication disorders in my class."

Mrs. Clyburn said, "Let's talk about your situation first; then, I will meet with the students individually to decide whether the apparent problems really are disorders."

About a week later after Mrs. Clyburn met with the students, she met with Miss Tyler concerning the students. First, the African-American students had dialectical differences or variations, rather than outright disorders to be "corrected"; second, she would recommend the Hispanic-American students for the limited-English-proficiency program so they could receive individual or small-group instruction; and third, the Japanese-American student should basically be allowed to speak both Japanese and English as long as speaking two languages did not interfere with communication.

Miss Tyler and Mrs. Clyburn agreed to meet again later in the month to see whether the former could better understand African-American dialects, and to discuss the Hispanic-Americans' progress in the LEP program. Miss Tyler felt better. She understood her students better, and she knew what should be accepted, and what should be remediated. "I will continue working with Mrs. Clyburn," she thought.

Evaluation of the Communications Disorder Specialist's Efforts and Commitment

A major point continually emphasized throughout this chapter has been that evaluation plays a central role. Rather than being perceived as a punitive or threatening device, the evaluation process should be a means to help professionals understand their responsibilities, and work as a team for the welfare of the learner. The following checklist provides a means of evaluating the communication disorders specialist's effort and commitment to the multicultural education program.

Evaluation Checklist

_____ 1. The communication disorders specialist realizes the need to recognize and to accept all culturally diverse learners, regardless of cultural, ethnic, or social class backgrounds.

_____ 2. The communication disorders specialist recognizes how the increasing cultural diversity in the United States school systems affects the roles and responsibilities of the speech professional.

_____ 3. The communication disorders specialist distinguishes between communicative disorders and communicative variations.

_____ 4. The communication disorders specialist understands dialects as "differences", and not as "disorders".

_____ 5. The communication disorders specialist plans appropriate communication for NEP or LEP students, or seeks the appropriate professionals to help these students.

_____ 6. The communication disorders specialist works with professionals responsible for bilingual students, and assists as needed.

_____ 7. The communication disorders specialist works with classroom teachers and other school personnel in joint efforts to help culturally diverse children and adolescents with communicative disorders.

_____ 8. The communication disorders specialist understands the various speech and language disorders, and is able to assist culturally diverse learners with communicative handicaps.

SUMMING UP

Educators who are working toward the involvement of the entire school professional staff in the multicultural education program should:

1. Encourage all administrators and special school personnel to offer whole-hearted commitment and support to the multicultural education program, rather than perceiving efforts as someone else's responsibility.

2. Convey to administrators, special educators, counselors, librarians, and the communications disorder specialist the importance of a total school effort in the multicultural education program.

3. Emphasize the necessity for having cultural diversity among the administration, faculty, and special school personnel that reflects the composition of the school and community.

4. Encourage administrators, special educators, librarians, counselors, and communications disorder specialists to recognize and respond appropriately to their unique roles in the multicultural education program.

5. Encourage administrators and special school personnel to work with regular classroom educators.

6. Convey the importance of evaluating *all* professionals (whether self-, peer- or administrator-evaluation) for the purpose of learning ways to contribute to the overall multicultural program.

SUGGESTED LEARNING ACTIVITIES

1. Visit an elementary or secondary school to learn how administrators and special school personnel contribute to the multicultural education program. Are roles clearly defined, or are they "assumed", whereby professionals simply do whatever appears to benefit the learner? How might administrators and special school personnel better address the needs of culturally diverse learners?

2. Some professionals and the general public feel that culturally diverse learners are over-represented in special education classes. Meet with a special education teacher to discuss the concern of over-representation. What legal mandates and placement procedures are in place to avoid or reduce the likelihood of a culturally diverse learner being placed in a special education class on the basis of being different from the mainstream learner?

3. Visit an elementary or secondary school counselor in a multicultural setting to determine factors such as:

    a. Differences in assessing and counseling culturally diverse children or adolescents;

    b. best methods of working and coordinating efforts with classroom teachers;

    c. interaction settings, i.e., individual, small-group, and large-group, and which mode appears most effective with culturally diverse learners;

d. ways counselors can best help the classroom educators who work daily with culturally diverse learners.

4. Prepare an evaluation scale that determines how print and non-print media portray culturally different children and adolescents. Pinpoint such factors as objectivity, accuracy, stereotyping, gender values, actual numbers of culturally different people (and what they are doing), and their contributions to an increasingly multi-cultural world. With the help of a librarian or media specialist, prepare a list of print and nonprint media that provides an honest portrayal of culturally different populations.

Expanding Your Horizons: Additional Journal Readings and Books

LOMOTEY, K. (1989). "Cultural diversity in the school: Implications for principals." *NASSP Bulletin*, 73, 81–88. Lomotey looks at the increasing cultural diversity in the schools, and offers both general implications and specific implications for principals.

NAUMAN, A.K. (1987). "School librarians and cultural pluralism." *The Reading Teacher, 41(2)*, 201–205. The growing diversity in students' ethnic backgrounds challenges librarians to provide material that meets children's individual needs. Nauman provides an excellent list of books for the multicultural library.

SLADE, J.C., & CONOLEY, C.W. (1989). "Multicultural experiences for special educators." *Teaching Exceptional Children, 22(1)*, 60–64. The authors look at the goals and objectives, strategies, and evaluation of multicultural education from special educator's perspectives. Readers will benefit from the family interview technique provided in the article.

12

Issues for the Twenty-First Century

Understanding the material and activities in this chapter will help the reader to:

1. Describe multicultural education as an issue challenging educators, its differing definitions, and the difference between ideal and practice.

2. Explain how racism continues to affect the United States, although considerable progress has been made.

3. Explain how victims are often blamed for the conditions affecting their lives, rather than more plausible causes being sought.

4. List the arguments supportive and critical of standardized testing, and explain how culture affects testing.

5. Describe how the issue of language and communication affects both individuals and social institutions.

6. List the responsibilities of professional educators in multicultural education programs.

7. Describe how various contemporary issues affect the progress and success of multicultural education programs.

OVERVIEW

While multicultural education has made considerable progress as a means of explaining diversity and teaching acceptance of all people, several issues are yet to be resolved as the twenty-first century nears. Educators should do whatever they can to at least reduce the impact of each issue; however, not all issues can be solved by educators. A societal response is needed to combat racism and discrimination, the tendency to blame the victims for their plight, and the issue of testing and assessing culturally different learners. Chapter 12 looks at several issues, not as a means of making educators feel guilty or negligent, but as a means of showing obstacles to the progress of multicultural education, and as a way to show where present and future challenges lie.

The Culture Quiz: Issues in Multilcultural Education

Directions: Mark the following as True of False.

_____ 1. All too often, victims are blamed for their conditions, rather than more plausible causes being sought.

_____ 2. Realistically speaking, multicultural education has never been totally accepted in the education community.

_____ 3. Multicultural education should address cultural differences only. Other programs should focus on ethnic, racial, gender, and handicapped conditions.

_____ 4. While racism has been (and still is) evident in United States schools, another form, institutional racism, is less blatant and just as dangerous.

_____ 5. Research indicates that IQ and other tests of mental ability have been replaced in an attempt to define abilities of learners with respect to their individual cultures.

_____ 6. English is the primary language of the United States; however, many dialects are spoken throughout the country.

_____ 7. The gap between stated ideals and actual practice in multicultural education programs has, surprisingly, been closed.

_____ 8. Progress toward equal treatment has been made; however, there is still room for tremendous improvement in reducing racism and discrimination, and in providing a just and equal society for all people.

_____ 9. Multicultual education efforts began during the early years of the twentieth century, and has met most of its goals and objectives.

_____ 10. Examples of nonverbal communication include learners appearing unattentive, and the tendency to avoid looking the speaker in the eye.

Answers: 1. T   2. T   3. F   4. T   5. F   6. T   7. F   8. T   9. F   10. T

ISSUE: MULTICULTURAL EDUCATION AS A CONCEPT

Several issues that have challenged multicultural education from the beginning will probably continue to test educators' commitment into the twenty-first century. As it progresses in its third decade, multicultural education has varied in definitions, and has not received wholehearted endorsement in all circles. Multicultural education, like the United States society as a whole, also suffers from a disturbing gap between stated ideals and actual practice. In addition, while multicultural education appears to be the most effective means of teaching acceptance of cultural diversity, several other approaches serve as a means of addressing racial, gender, and socioeconomic class differences.

Differing Definitions of Multicultural Education

Questions that linger around multicultural education include: Does multicultural education include only ethnic, cultural, and racial differences? Should multicultural education address gender and class differences? Should multicultural educators use unit approaches, or adopt total school approaches? Although educators will have to respond to these questions, the authors of *Multicultural Education for Children and Adolescents* have proposed a comprehensive approach to respond to diversity, and have elected to adopt the comprehensive NCATE definition, which recognizes and addresses a broad range of diversity: culture, race, gender and sex, ethnic, socioeconomic, and exceptionalities in the education process (NCATE, 1986, p. 47).

Multicultural Education's Lack of Acceptance

A related aspect is the lack of acceptance facing multicultural education, and uncertainty regarding the degree to which efforts should extend. Gay (1983) wrote that multicultural education must weather new priorities, such as vocationalism, technology, and insistence on quantifiable criteria of success. Gay (1983) wrote:

> Even under the best of circumstances, multiethnic education has never been totally accepted, nor has its legitimacy gone unquestioned in the education community (p. 562–563).

Fiscal allocations have always been minimal, and have usually fallen into the categories of "soft" money and "discretionary funds." Multicultural education programs tend to be among the first casualties when program reductions result from fiscal constraints. As educational practices go, Gay (1983) considered multiethnic education as still relatively new, and still to be fully absorbed into the mainstream of United States education.

Differences Between Stated Ideals and Practice

Realistically speaking, public schools in the United States have exhibited a pattern of inconsistency between stated ideals and actual practice. Concerned educators do not have to look for disturbing examples: The denigration of culturally different children's language differences, the outright denial of the use of any language except English, segregation practices, the labeling of culturally different learners as inferior or culturally disadvantaged, and the over-representation of culturally different learners in classes for the handicapped (McCormick, 1984).

It should not come as a surprise to readers that a difference often exists between what is intended, and what actually happens in school. CASE STUDY 12-1 looks at a situation where a high school principal recognizes that her school is not really meeting its goals and philosophical statements.

CASE STUDY 12-1: Differences Between Goals and Practice

Dr. MacDonald, a high school principal, looked objectively at her school's lofty goals, objectives, and philosophical statements, which spoke eloquently of valuing, recognizing, accepting, and respecting all people, regardless of differences. She compared these statements with what was actually happening in the school. Couldn't the students see that much of what was being done was only rhetoric, and lacked real substance?

Without being overly pessimistic or cynical, she asked herself several questions concerning the extent to which diversity was actually being respected and addressed:

Do school policies reflect an understanding of cultural diversity?

Do instructional practices recognize the differing learning styles of culturally different learners?

Is there an understanding of motivation and competition as related to culturally different learners?

Are there efforts to promote social interaction between learners of all cultures?

Is there genuine respect for all people?

Are testing and assessment differences among cultures recognized and addressed?

Do language programs assist limited-English-proficiency students?

Are the teachers and other school personnel professionally trained, and competent to deal with and teach the culturally different?

> Dr. MacDonald decided that an affirmative action plan was needed to address these, and other, issues and concerns. Such an effort would take a large-scale approach, and would include discussion groups, committees, in-service programs and activities, speakers, and an improved professional library.

Approaches to Race, Class, and Gender

Diversity may be addressed with approaches other than multicultural education: Teaching the exceptional and the culturally different, human relations, single-group studies, and education that is multicultural and social v reconstructionist. Rather than outlining the advantages and disadvantages of each approach, it suffices to state that each has expressed purposes, goals, and directions. However, from an issues perspective, each in some ways takes away from, or competes for, resources for other programs. While the authors do not in any way discredit other approaches to addressing diversity, it does appear that multicultural education provides a broad and comprehensive approach to addressing diversity of all kinds and degrees.

ISSUE: RACISM, DISCRIMINATION, AND INJUSTICE

Progress

Without doubt, people in the 1990s are more aware of racism, discrimination, and injustices. Even during times of racist acts, evidence suggests that notable progress has been made: More culturally diverse people are joining the work force in positions other than manual laborers and custodian positions; opportunities in housing (although admittedly not equal) have improved; doors to higher education have been opened to the culturally diverse; and federal legislation has been passed that guarantees equal rights for all people.

Asian and Hispanic groups encouraged a Disney-owned television station to cancel a 13-week cartoon series because two characters were considered ethnic stereotypes (*Disney cancels . . .* , 1990). While this is only one example, the removal shows a sensitivity to the concerns of culturally diverse groups, and a recognition that stereotypes can have harmful effects. These examples of progress, and the improved relationships between majority cultures and culturally diverse people, can be looked on with pride, but one must be careful not to assume that "all is well," and that there is not room for improvement in reducing racism and discrimination, and in providing a just and equal society for all people.

Lingering Racism and Discrimination

Although most people would probably agree that there has been progress toward reducing racism and discrimination, most would also concur with the hypothesis that the United States society as a whole still has hurdles to overcome. Nearly 40 years after *Brown v. Board of Education* and almost 30 years after the Civil Rights Act of 1964, racism and discrimination continue to impede the progress of many people. Evidence documenting this assertion includes a well-known Ku Klux Klan leader who ran for the United States Senate; a reputable professional African-American golfer who played in a PGA Tournament on a golf course that openly refused to admit African-Americans to its membership; acts of violence toward people of all races and cultures; increasing racial violence on college campuses; and the increasing number of "skinheads" or Neo-Nazi groups.

IMPLEMENTING RESEARCH 12-1 looks at the targets of racism, and shows areas on which educators should focus attention.

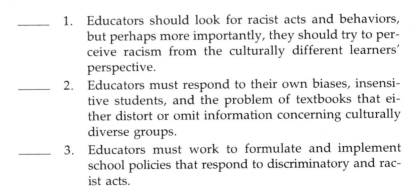

IMPLEMENTING RESEARCH 12-1: Targets of Racism

Murray and Clark maintain that culturally different children in schools today probably see or perceive racism that educators do not recognize. While various publications and speakers have brought many examples of racism to the public's attention, children may perceive racism in still other ways. Therefore, educators need to be more concerned with children's perceptions of racism than their own. Racism affects children in various ways; however, Murray and Clark believe that racism contributes to lower achievement and self-image, a poor perception of others, and apathy. Three main sources of racism suggested as harming children are insensitive students, biased teachers, and skewed textbooks. To combat the problem of racism and its effects, Murray and Clark suggest that teachers avoid omitting culturally different students' perspectives, and that teachers should take an affirmative stand to implement policies that reduce racism.

IMPLEMENTING THE RESEARCH:

_____ 1. Educators should look for racist acts and behaviors, but perhaps more importantly, they should try to perceive racism from the culturally different learners' perspective.

_____ 2. Educators must respond to their own biases, insensitive students, and the problem of textbooks that either distort or omit information concerning culturally diverse groups.

_____ 3. Educators must work to formulate and implement school policies that respond to discriminatory and racist acts.

Blatant, crude, and overt racism has come out of the closet again, and has surfaced in our schools. Public slurs, threats, racist slogans, physical assaults, and racial conflicts occur in schools in every part of the country. Schools, which should be a civilizing influence in our society, instead appear to be incubators of racial intolerance (Pine & Hilliard, 1990).

While *Brown v. Board of Education* ruled against legal segregation, de facto segregation (or segregation by the fact, e.g., no African-Americans living near a predominantly Anglo school may attend that school, or vice versa), continues to exist, as can be seen in all-Black or all-White schools and neighborhoods. Similarly, even with the Civil Rights Act, notable gaps in income and level of position continue to exist between racial groups, and in some cases, differences are becoming more acute.

Many children in the United States are affected by institutional racism. Although such issues as equal opportunity, desegregation, and inequities in educational achievement have been vocalized during recent years, very few schools have developed deliberate and systematic programs to reduce prejudice. The attitude appears to be that society has done away with racism through legislative and special programs, but overt racism and institutional racism can continue to occur. While educators should be on guard against racism of all forms, institutional racism, which is less blatant and therefore more dangerous, continues to hurt the aspirations and talents of culturally diverse learners (Pine & Hilliard, 1990).

Equally disturbing as the various open forms of racism are the more subtle and covert forms of racism, in which members of culturally diverse groups suffer a form of social prejudice, such as being neglected as potential friends, and "overlooked" in employment promotions and in special recognition in employment situations.

Goals for the United States Society

The issue of continuing racism, discrimination, and injustice continues to plague the United States and its progress in dealing with its history of racism and discrimination. People of all cultures, both majority cultures and the culturally diverse, should work independently and in concerted efforts toward the achievement of several broad goals for the United States society:

1. Unconditional acceptance of all people regardless of cultural, ethnic, racial, gender, or socioeconomic backgrounds.
2. Equal social, economic, and educational opportunities for all people.
3. Acquiring objective information about culturally diverse individuals and groups in an attempt to dispel or reduce stereotypes, myths, and misconceptions.

While these goals may appear to be broad, lofty, and perhaps idealistic to some, they continue to be goals that can make the United States a more humane, caring, and respecting nation.

ISSUE: BLAMING THE VICTIM

Responsibility of Being a Victim

An issue facing culturally different learners and their educators is where to place the blame for the minority person's plight. In essence, should the victim or the society be held accountable? For example, should lower-class African-Americans blame themselves for their high unemployment rates and poverty, or should the blame be placed on a racist society that allows discrimination? Must Native-Americans blame themselves for their high school dropout rates and high levels of alcoholism? Should Hispanic and Asian learners be blamed for their poor English skills? Responsive educators recognize that such questions are examples of the "blaming the victim" issue, and realize that children and adolescents are often victims of racism and discrimination, and all too often cannot change the conditions surrounding their lives.

In *Blaming the Victim*, Ryan (1971) maintained that victims are often blamed for their plight. In researching this problem, Ryan examined the consequences of blaming the victim, rather than looking for actual causes. Examples of blaming the victim are too numerous to name: The boy in an elementary school who cannot read; the old and the ill; people from lower classes who must struggle to survive financially; the pregnant, unmarried, teenage girl; the handicapped; even illegitimate children.

As CASE STUDY 12-2 shows, it is possible to adopt the blaming the victim attitude, and perhaps fail to realize its dangers.

CASE STUDY 12-2: Blaming the Victim

Mrs. Smith said despairingly, "I don't know what to do! Why don't they try to better themselves, improve their grades? They just sit there all day and do nothing. They didn't know today what I taught yesterday. How do they expect to make something of their lives? I will never understand those people."

The assistant principal, Mr. Allen, overheard this classic "blaming the victim" statement, and thought that this tendency represented an easy answer that failed to recognize the real problem. All too often, victims, especially culturally diverse people, are blamed for being uneducated, slow learners, poor, and unable to find employment, just to name a few, representative, examples.

Mr. Allen thought of the consequences of such thinking, and of considering all people from a middle-class, Anglo perspective. He thought there must be a serious effort to look for more valid social, economic, or educational causes. The implications of "blaming the victim" can be widespread, and can influence educational decisions such as grouping, questioning, curricular issues, and teaching/learning activities. Yet the problem extends even further: students are being blamed for not wanting to learn when they really do, and considered too unmotivated to change when, actually, significant change is difficult, or sometimes impossible, to achieve.

There are two orientations toward victims. First, people who hold a person-centered orientation emphasize the individual's motivation, values, feelings, and goals. A person's success or failure is attributed to individual skills or inadequacies, and many people correlate ability and effort with success in society. Second, the system-blame view holds that success or failure is generally dependent upon the social and economic system rather than on personal attributes. The Western world tends to hold individuals responsible for their problems, and often labels minorities as deviant in both thought and behavior (Sue, 1981).

For some people, it is easier to blame victims for their condition than to look for more specific societal and economic causes. However, the consequences of blaming the victim often extend further than just thinking that people deserve blame for their shortcomings. The practice of blaming learners for their conditions has been used to excuse or justify many unjust actions: Poorer-quality educational programs in areas with "victims"; outdated and worn-out textbooks and curricular materials; teachers who give "victims" less wait-time during questioning sessions; believing that poorer or different students cannot learn; and a plethora of other reactions that appear to be appropriate if children and adolescents are to blame for their lives.

More Humanistic Perspectives

An adequate response to the "blaming the victim" issue requires that educators make several commitments: First, educators should recognize the fact that victims are often blamed for their predicaments. Second, educators should use caution not to allow their middle-class backgrounds (if this is indeed their background) to serve as a basis for blaming the victim for not taking a more assertive stand in changing life events. Third, educators should offer a personal and professional commitment to victims, to understanding how children and adolescents become victims, and the difficulty involved in victims changing their lives. Fourth, on a larger scale, educators should do their part in working to reduce the racism, poverty, despair, injustice, and discrimination that contribute to the victimization of people.

ISSUE: TESTING AND ASSESSMENT

Even after several decades of knowing that standardized testing instruments are prepared from Anglo, middle-class perspectives, culturally different children and adolescents are still being tested with instruments that do not satisfactorily measure their intelligence. The issue is, why do educators and testing specialists administer these assessment devices, especially when it has been concluded that learning styles and cognitive strategies differ?

The assumption that IQ, and other tests of mental ability, can accurately measure innate abilities continues to be rampant within the schools. Even after assessment devices have been questioned, students are still being assigned to academic tracks based on their performance in tests of mental ability, and on other factors such as teacher recommendations and grades. Such assessment and placement policies are often unquestioned, and result in a disproportionate number of lower-class and culturally different students being relegated to lower-ability groups (Banks, 1988).

Educators who work with culturally different learners have the professional responsibility for recognizing the relationship between culture and testing, and the arguments for and against standardized testing. They must remember the danger of labeling, and placing culturally different learners in lower groups based upon scores that might not be valid.

Arguments that support standardized testing include their widespread public and professional acceptance; their relative cost-efficiency in administration and reporting; their usefulness in accountability; their usefulness in placing students in special programs and ability groupings; and their role in the making of curricular decisions (Miller-Jones, 1989).

Arguments critical of standardized testing question how well tests address the following questions:

1. Is the knowledge domain understood well enough to be adequately represented in a sample of items?
2. Are test items biased, or can they be written in a manner that does not favor a particular sociocultural experience?
3. Are test items, especially for achievement devices, fair? That is, do the test items reflect the kind of subject matter likely to be encountered by most students (Miller-Jones, 1989)?

While the testing and assessment issue will continue to be fought in theory and research, it appears that the implications for educators in multicultural situations are fairly clear. IMPLEMENTING RESEARCH 12-2 examines the effect of cultural differences on testing, and offers several implications and implementation suggestions for educators.

IMPLEMENTING RESEARCH 12-2: Culture and Testing

Miller-Jones examined research and theory related to the assessment of cognitive abilities on culturally different populations, particularly African-Americans. The author discussed the issue of validity in test content and procedures, and reviewed the cross-cultural research that shows the interconnectedness of competencies and interpersonal events. Specifically, the study examined arguments supportive and critical of standardized tests, culture and assessment of cognitive abilities, and recommendations for assessment of culturally different populations.

IMPLEMENTING THE RESEARCH:

_____ 1.   Educators should recognize how culture affects learners' testing and scores on assessment devices administered in schools.

_____ 2.   Educators should use multiple tasks, with a variety of different materials, and not assume a generality from a single measure.

_____ 3.   Educators should assess by using tasks with which a particular culture can relate.

_____ 4.   Educators should assess by using instruments that allow, or provide an understanding of, the reasoning behind a child's response to an item.

Source: Miller-Jones, D. (1989). "Culture and testing." *American Psychologist, 44,* 360–366.

ISSUE: LANGUAGE AND COMMUNICATION

Language and communication have both been sensitive and controversial issues, and have far-reaching implications for learners and educators. While one argument holds that English should be the primary language and used by all, others feel that one's native language is a personal and precious aspect of one's cultural heritage. The issue extends further, however. Should students be allowed to learn in their native language? What should educators do about dialects? Should learners actually become bilingual? This section looks at dialects, bilingual education, English as a Second Language, and nonverbal communication.

Dialects

Although English is the primary language of the United States, numerous English dialects are used throughout the country. Dialects are any given variation of language that is shared by groups of speakers. This variation typically corresponds to other differences between groups, such as ethnicity, religion, culture, geographic location, and social class (Wolfram & Christian, 1979; Gollnick & Chinn, 1990). It is important to emphasize that all people speak in a dialect of their native language.

Dialect is a popular term, yet it also carries a negative connotation. It is sometimes used to refer to a particular variety of English that may have a social or geographic basis, and which differs from what is usually considered "standard" English. Dialects may include such variations as Black English,

Hawaiian Pidgin English, and rural Appalachian English (Gollnick & Chinn, 1990).

The issue facing multicultural educators centers on what to do about dialects. One group has suggested that students be allowed to learn in their own dialects, and that to do otherwise only further handicaps the learner. Others have argued that the school has the responsibility for teaching each student standard English to better cope with the demands of society. There is little doubt that the inability to speak standard English can be a decided disadvantage to an individual in certain situations, such as seeking employment (Gollnick & Chinn, 1990).

There are several alternatives for handling dialect in the educational setting. The first would be to accommodate all dialects, based on the assumption that they are all equal. The second would be to insist that only a standard dialect be allowed in the schools. This alternative would allow for the position that functional ability in such a dialect is necessary for success in personal, as well as vocational, pursuits. A third alternative is a position between the two extremes, and it is the alternative most often followed. Native dialects are accepted for certain uses, but standard English is encouraged and insisted upon in other circumstances. Students in such a school setting may be required to read and write in standard English, since this is the primary written language they will encounter in this nation. They would not be required to eliminate their natural dialect. Such a compromise allows the student to use two or more dialects in the school. It acknowledges the legitimacy of all dialects, while it recognizes the social and vocational implications of being able to function in standard English (Gollnick & Chinn, 1990).

Bilingual Education

Bilingualism, as applied to both individuals and social institutions, has been surrounded by considerable controversy. On the individual level, debate has centered around the possible costs and benefits of bilingualism in learners. On the larger societal level, arguments have focused on the wisdom of bilingual education, and the official support of languages other than English (Hakuta & Garcia, 1989).

Proponents of bilingual education have recommended aggressive development of the native language before the introduction of English. This argument is based on the belief that competencies in the native language provide important cognitive foundations for second-language acquisitions, and for academic learning in general. The ease of transfering skills acquired in the native language to English is an important component of this belief (Hakuta & Garcia, 1989).

The other side of the debate recommends introduction of the English curriculum from the very beginning of the student's schooling experience, with only a minimal use of the native language. This approach is typically combined with an English as a Second Language (ESL) component. One appeal of the English-only method is its consistency with on-task arguments.

These suggest that spending more time being exposed to English should aid students in their acquisition of English (Rossel & Ross, 1986; Hakuta & Garcia, 1989).

IMPLEMENTING RESEARCH 12-3 looks at the concept of bilingualism, and the controversies surrounding the concept.

IMPLEMENTING RESEARCH 12-3: Bilingualism and Education

Hakuta and Garcia claim that bilingualism has been used to describe an attribute of individual children, and a social institution. At the outset, the authors point out that both aspects have been surrounded by controversy and debate. On the individual level, debate has focused on the costs of bilingualism in children. On the social level, the argument has centered on bilingual education, and the official support of languages other than English, in public institutions. Issues examined in the article include the bilingual child, the various aspects of bilingualism, and areas in need of additional research.

IMPLEMENTING THE RESEARCH:

_____ 1. Educators need to recognize that the controversy surrounding bilingualism is magnified by the rapidly changing population of the United States.

_____ 2. Educators need to understand that in the process of second language acquisition, the use of the native language does not interfere in any significant way with the development of a second language.

_____ 3. Educators should be careful not to over-attribute the causes of culturally diverse learners' problems to language problems or deficiencies.

Source: Hakuta, K., & Garcia, E. E. (1989). "Bilingualism and education." *American Psychologist*, 44, 374–379.

English as a Second Language

English as a Second Language (ESL) is a program often confused with bilingual education. In the United States, the learning of English is an integral part of bilingual programs. However, the teaching of English as a second language, in and by itself, does not constitute a bilingual program. Both bilingual education and ESL programs promote English proficiency for limited-English-proficiency students. The approach to instruction distinguishes the differences between the two programs. Bilingual education accepts and develops native language and culture in the instructional process. Bilingual education may use both the native language and English as the medium of instruction. However, ESL instruction relies exclusively on English as the medium to assimilate LEP children into the linguistic mainstream as quickly as possible. Hence, some educators place less emphasis on the maintenance of home language and culture than on English-language acquisition, and they view ESL programs as viable means of achieving these goals (Gollnick & Chinn, 1990).

Nonverbal Communication.

The issue of nonverbal differences and misunderstandings can be frustrating for both students and educators. To reduce the difficulty often associated with this form of communication, educators must work to analyze particular nonverbal communications when students do not respond as educators expect. Miscommunication may result from several nonverbal behaviors: Appearing unattentive even when the student is listening; the tendency of the student to look away from the teacher when being called upon or addressed; and interruption by the student at times that may appear inappropriate to educators.

It is easy to jump to the conclusion that the student is not showing respect, when actually she or he is simply not following the informal rules of the classroom. In most school settings, the culturally diverse learner is expected to become bicultural, and to adopt the nonverbal communication of the majority culture of the school. The ill effects of the issue are reduced when educators also learn to operate biculturally in the classroom (Gollnick & Chinn, 1990).

ISSUE: ACCEPTING PROFESSIONAL RESPONSIBILITIES

For Being Professionally Qualified and Committed.

First and foremost, educators must accept responsibility for being trained to work with culturally diverse students. Regardless of the multicultural education program and its goals, efforts will succeed only when educators are trained in cultural diversity, understand the effects of culture on learning, and convey genuine feelings of acceptance and respect for all people. Professional education for all educators, not just those planning to teach in multicultural areas, should include content methodologies courses that show the relationship between culture and learning, and how to address this relationship in teaching situations; first-hand practica and clinical experiences in working with culturally diverse learners of various grade levels and socioeconomic classes; and appropriate experiences in interpersonal skills. The point should be reemphasized that professional responsibilities include a broad expertise in content, instructional techniques, and the ability to work with culturally diverse learners. Yet, responsibilities extend even further. Having knowledge of culturally diverse people, but holding on to racist attitudes and the belief that ''different is wrong'', will not provide responsive multicultural education. Knowing that a relationship exists between cultures and education is a prerequisite to effective teaching, but continuing to teach with styles and strategies appropriate only for middle-class Anglo learners fails to meet the needs of culturally diverse children and adolescents.

CASE STUDY 12-3 looks at Dr. Thomas' thoughts concerning professional competencies of teachers who work in multicultural situations.

CASE STUDY 12-3: Professional Competence

As Dr. Thomas, a Staff Development Specialist, looked at his district's guidelines for determining professional competence, he wondered what specific attributes or characteristics teachers should have, especially regarding cultural diversity. Although he considered his efforts to be only brainstorming at this point, he basically placed items into several categories:

    A. Overall Comptencies
        1. Knowledge
        2. Attitudes
        3. Skills

    B. Educational Competencies
        4. Curricular practices
        5. Instructional techniques
        6. Classroom rules and policies
        7. Language considerations
        8. Testing and assessment

Dr. Thomas knew his thinking represented only a beginning point, but he did realize that teachers working with culturally diverse learners need an understanding of how culture affects learning and achievement. He also realized that in all likelihood the teachers in his district needed appropriate in-service training, and activities to make them more effective with culturally diverse learners.

For Ensuring Cultural Diversity in all Curricular Materials

A major responsibility, one which educators must accept, is the commitment to ensure cultural diversity in all curricular materials. Educators play a significant role as they scrutinize all print and non-print materials for bias and racism. It is important to note that this issue includes both omissions and distortions. Educators are responsible for being on the lookout for material that places culturally diverse people in a derogatory light or in demeaning situations, and that show these characters in stereotypical images. Only two decades ago, families were portrayed as two-parent and Anglo, and usually lived in white houses with a picket fence. Educators in most situations can readily perceive that most culturally diverse learners would be unable to understand or relate to such images in stories. While considerable progress has been made, educators continue to be responsible for insisting on materials that include culturally diverse characters shown only in positive, fulfilling roles. Without doubt, educators' responsibilities include adopting only textbooks that portray culturally diverse learners and their families in a favorable light.

For Ensuring that Multicultural Emphasis Permeates All Curricular Areas and the School Environment

Another major responsibility of educators is that of working toward multiculturalism in all areas of the curriculum and school environment. A basic assumption of this text has been that multicultural education should be a broad-based effort that has the full cooperation and support of all school personnel, rather than a half-hearted effort.

Since they are representative of our culturally pluralistic society, schools must plan appropriate learning experiences for different children: Native-, African-, Asian-, Hispanic-American, and other cultures and ethnic groups, as well as children and adolescents from differing economic, social, and religious backgrounds. Many questions must be answered: What (or perhaps whose) religious holidays will be observed? How will cultural differences affect testing and assessment? What special problems will culturally diverse learners bring to school? How will learning styles differ?

These and other questions raise the overall question of what, specifically, should educators do? First, a one-shot, Multicultural Week or unit featuring African-American History, tacos, and oriental dresses and customs will not suffice. Such approaches have not worked and will not work, because being aware of diversity does not necessarily result in acceptance and respect of individuals within the cultural group. The curriculum, learning environment, and the mindset of learners and faculty/staff must become multicultural in nature, and must reflect the cultural diversity of the school. Second, well-meaning multicultural education programs may serve only cosmetic purposes if students and school personnel harbor long-held cultural biases and stereotypes. Rather than schools' presupposing learners' ability and behavior based upon stereotypes and myth, the school curriculum must genuinely respect cultural diversity and regard all learners objectively.

For Involving Parents, Family, and the Community in Multicultural Efforts

Educators' recognition of the role of parents, the family, and the community in the multicultural education effort is prerequisite to the multicultural education program's success. Actually, two aspects are at stake, and both play a significant role in determining the success of the multicultural education program. First, including both immediate and extended families, and community members, demonstrates concrete evidence that educators are serious about accepting and promoting multiculturalism outside the school boundaries. When educators show that their efforts do not stop at the schoolhouse gate, such a commitment adds credence to the multicultural education program's efforts. Second, culturally diverse parents, families, and community members can play significant roles when they come to visit schools and offer their participation. Educators may have to deal with parents' language differences, misunderstandings associated with United States school systems, and the reluctance of some parents to share strengths. While overcoming these challenges requires both time and energy, the benefits outweigh the efforts expended.

The fact that Chapter 10 is devoted entirely to including culturally diverse parents and families shows the major importance and emphasis the authors place on the role of parents and families in education. The issue at stake is the extent to which educators genuinely want to effect multiculturalism. Children and adolescents who see only Anglo parents in schools could easily arrive at the conclusion that cultural diversity is not as valued as educators suggest. While educators usually find it is easier to gain the attention of middle- and upper-class Anglo parents, perceptive educators recognize the need to involve culturally diverse parents and families.

SUMMING UP

Educators who understand the issues facing multicultural education, and the challenges that such programs will face in the future should:

1. Understand that several issues affect the social and educational progress of culturally diverse children and adolescents, and contribute to the degree of support the multicultural education receives.

2. Remember that while multicultural education may have several definitions, its overall rationale is to assist all learners to gain a better understanding and acceptance of others' cultural, ethnic, racial, and socioeconomic backgrounds.

3. Understand the futility of "blaming the victim" for life conditions, develop more enlightened perspectives of the reasons for people being victims, and recognize the difficulty in overcoming "victim" conditions.

4. Understand that a relationship exists between culture and testing, and that culturally diverse learners' cultural backgrounds can significantly affect standardized test scores.

5. Remember that the language issue includes dialectical differences,

bilingual education, and TOESL, and that all educators need to address learners' language differences and needs.

6. Accept that educators have professional responsibilities that are prerequisites if responsive multicultural education programs are to become a reality.

7. Remember that the ultimate success of any multicultural education program depends on each teacher's commitment to the program, and to the acceptance and respect for all people, regardless of differences or backgrounds.

SUGGESTED LEARNING ACTIVITIES

1. In a study of racism, look at specific examples of racist acts during the latter half of the twentieth century. Begin with the integration of America's schools during the 1950s and 1960s, and the accompanying racial violence. Then examine the more current acts of racism occurring in the United States. What programs do schools have to teach the dangers of racism, and to reduce racism and its effects on children and adolescents?

2. Discuss with several educators ways in which teachers may, knowingly or unknowingly, blame the victim for learning problems, socioeconomic conditions, or language problems. List several consequences of blaming the victim. Rather than blaming victims for particular conditions, how can educators gain a better, or more objective, perspective of learners' conditions?

3. Make a list of assessment instruments (and the addresses of publishers) that claim to reduce cultural bias in their test items. Provide two or three examples of culturally biased test items. How might educators determine cultural bias in assessment instruments?

4. Survey a number of schools in an urban area with a significant percentage of culturally diverse populations. What programs do these schools have to address language differences? Do language-minority youngsters receive equal opportunities, or are learners sometimes expected to learn and deal with language problems simultaneously? Looking at your survey, what language programs or approaches appear to be more likely to meet the needs of language-minority learners?

Expanding Your Horizons: Suggested Journal Readings and Books

BACA, L., & AMATO, C. (1989). "Bilingual special education: Training issues." *Exceptional Children, 56,* 168–173. Baca and Amato examine the issue of training programs for teachers of students with both limited-English-proficiency and disabilities.

HAKUTA, K., & GARCIA, I.E. (1989). "Bilingualism and education." *American Psychologist, 44,*

374–379. The authors discuss the concept of bilingualism as applied to individual children and adolescents.

MILLER-JONES, D. (1989). "Culture and testing." *American Psychologist, 44,* 360–366. Miller-Jones provides readers with a detailed discussion of culture and testing, and looks at the arguments for and against standardized testing.

MOLNAR, A. (1989). "Racism in America: A continuing dilemma." *Educational Leadership, 47(2),* 71–72. Molnar examines racism, which continues to pose a serious problem for both society and schools, although in a different form from that of the 1960s.

Epilogue
The Future: A Time for Responsive Action

What will be the future of multicultural education? Will multicultural efforts take a back seat to accountability, technology, and the contemporary push for academic achievements? Will multicultural education programs, as a major education effort, grow more acceptable, or will some people still view them as a frill or an education fad? How can educators continue to learn about the effects of culture on learning styles, motivation, testing, cognitive strategies, and behavior? This epilogue looks at these questions, presents evidence that suggests an increasing culturally diverse society, and projects how multicultural efforts might be most effective both now and in the future.

A CHANGING U.S. SOCIETY

Increasing Cultural Diversity

All population data suggest that the United States will continue to grow in diversity. The *Statistic Abstracts* of the U.S. Census Bureau (1990) show the Hispanic population (ages 5–17) growing by 28.6% between 1990 and 2000. The African-American population (ages 5–17) will increase by 10.1% during the same time. Due to the large influx of Asian-Americans during the 1980s, census information cannot predict percentage increases at this time, but sizable gains are a certainty.

The United States has always opened its doors to people from other lands. It appears that the future will see this nation continue to grow in diversity, due to high birthrates and immigrants fleeing to a land of better opportunity.

Increasing Knowledge Base of Cultural Diversity

Accompanying the growth of these population has been an increased knowledge base of culturally diverse children and adolescents. An improved knowledge base of culturally different people has enlightened people to a point where it is not necessary to be suspicious, to fail to understand others' customs and traditions, or to question culturally diverse people's "worth" as human beings.

How can an improved knowledge base help educators of the future? First, learning about culturally diverse people can show that, amidst a myriad of differences, people have similarities: We all need to experience feelings of love, trust, respect, accomplishment, and security, just to name a few. Second, by increasing our knowledge, we become more understanding of differences. Rather than differences being wrong, inferior, or something to be remediated, differences are viewed as having the potential to enrich both the schools and the nation, and are addressed by educators just as other differences (learning strengths, special talents, the gifted) deserve to be addressed. Third, an improved knowledge base can provide educators with a better understanding of culturally diverse children's and adolescents' learning strengths and weaknesses, such specific areas as motivation, learning styles, and cognitive strategies.

Even with our improved knowledge of culture and culturally diverse individuals, acts of racism, injustice, and discrimination during the 1990s provide evidence that knowledge of people and their cultural backgrounds has not always been accompanied by acceptance and respect.

Increasing Need for Awareness and Acceptance of Cultural Diversity

As we move toward the twenty-first century, there is a great need for awareness and acceptance of cultural diversity. The knowledge of culturally diverse people has improved our understanding, and this has led to greater acceptance. However, to suggest that the United States is an accepting society would require overlooking all-to-common acts of racism and discrimination.

Although the authors continue to hope that the twenty-first century will bring greater acceptance and recognition of cultural diversity, they must report that discrimination, racism, and bigotry continue in the United States. For instance, racial incidents have occurred at 250 colleges since the fall of 1986 (*Lessons from Bigotry 101 . . .* , 1989). Whether overt racism, such as the Ku Klux Klan's acts of violence and hatred, or the more covert forms of racism and discrimination often found in employment and housing, African-Americans and other culturally diverse people continue to experience inequities and inequalities. Although the overt acts and John Crow attitudes are not as visible as they were several decades ago, racial injustices continue to affect culturally different people's progress and well-being.

To say that the 1990s and the twenty-first century will be times of responsive action is an understatement. While elementary and secondary schools should not be expected to accept total responsibility for making the United States society more equitable and just, schools will be expected to take a major role in teaching recognition, awareness, acceptance, and ultimately, respect for all people, regardless of differences and backgrounds.

MULTICULTURAL EDUCATION

A Rationale

It is relatively easy to offer a rationale for multicultural education: To learn about culturally diverse people; to understand ourselves and our cultural backgrounds; to reach greater levels of acceptance and respect; and to understand race, culture, ethnicity, socioeconomic, and gender differences. The increasing numbers of culturally diverse learners just discussed, and the benefits acquired from an improved knowledge base, provide other, justifiable reasons for children and adolescents' needing multicultural education programs. The authors base their faith in a more accepting and respecting United States society on the assumption that knowledge can lead to understanding, which in turn leads to acceptance and respect. Even with the acts of racism that scar our nation, it is believed that multicultural education can be one (and a major) means of teaching acceptance and respect for all people.

Lingering Questions

Even with this powerful rationale for effective multicultural education programs, lingering questions continue in the minds of some people. Whether due to vestiges of racism, ignorance, or a belief that all culturally diverse people should assimilate (Alas! The continued belief that the melting pot *should* work, and that differences are to be eradicated.), questions and doubts continue to slow the progress of multicultural education. Questions and concerns that must be satisfactorily answered include whether multicultural education takes away from more-academic subject areas; how programs compete for the resources of money and people's efforts; whether learning about people and their cultural backgrounds should be a part of schools' curriculum; how educators can be held accountable; whether efforts should be unit approaches or a total curricular effort; and whether emphasis should be on one culture, or on a cross-section perspective of a number of cultures.

While these questions deserve answers, they do not cause serious doubts for the authors, especially in light of the increasing cultural diversity of the United States, and the critical need for awareness and acceptance of all people.

Growing Acceptance: Present and Future

Lingering questions and doubts notwithstanding, evidence exists that multicultural education is progressing, and that it will continue to grow in popularity. First, Banks (1988) reported that multicultural education was one of the most frequently-used sources available to teach about culture and ethnicity. Second, more school districts are seeing the need to allocate funds for multicultural education. At one time, there was a belief that multicultural education was not "needed" if a district did not have racial problems, or had only a small percentage of culturally diverse learners. However, a more enlightened perception holds that Anglo learners (and learners of other cultures) need to learn about cultural diversity. Third, NCATE and state teacher education accreditation associations have taken a strong stand in favor of multicultural education standards for all prospective teachers. Fourth, several excellent textbooks (James Banks' *Multiethnic Education*, Hilda Hernandez's (1989) *Multicultural Education: A Teachers Guide to Content and Practice*, and Donna Gollnick's and Philip Chinn's (1990) *Multicultural Education in a Pluralistic Society*) show an interest in preparing teachers to understand, and work with, culturally diverse populations.

The future looks bright for multicultural education even when one considers the push for academic subjects, the emphasis on technology, and the contemporary emphasis on accountability. Several factors working in conjunction will promote multicultural education, both as a concept, and as a humanistic goal worth pursuing: A growing population of culturally diverse children and adolescents, a rapidly expanding knowledge base of culture and its effects on learning, more effective and demanding teacher preparation, and, the authors hope, a deeper and more genuine respect for all people and their cultural backgrounds.

What can educators do to promote multicultural education and respect for all people? First, educators themselves must learn about cultural diversity, and develop a genuine respect for all people. Second, educators can work with their administrators and other school personnel to develop a multicultural education program that permeates curricular areas, instructional methodology, and the overall school environments. Third, educators can "sell" the multicultural education program to parents and the community by debunking the myth that these programs are "frills" or "fads", and by promoting the idea that the increasing cultural diversity of our nation makes such programs a necessity. Fourth, educators must work to build or promote a society—admittedly somewhat idealized—that demonstrates respect and acceptance for all people.

THE FUTURE

It is indeed difficult to predict the future, especially during rapidly changing demographic, educational, and societal times. Without the benefit of a crystal ball or the ability to see future events, one can only rely on "what has been" and "what is presently happening" to build a case for "what will be".

Professionally Trained Educators

The present emphasis on schools playing significant roles in teaching about culture, and the accompanying acceptance and respect for culturally diverse people, leads one to believe that teacher-education accrediting agencies will continue their emphasis on multicultural education standards. The NCATE and state accrediting standards already provide evidence that this movement is well underway. Rather than offering an add-on component or making a superficial effort to meet standards, teacher education programs will offer prospective teachers significant classroom and first-hand experience and contact with culturally different learners. Prospective teachers will learn about (and be able to respond appropriately to) such issues as culture and education, cultural bias in testing, and the influence of culture on learning styles and cognitive strategies. Instead of teaching from Anglo perceptions of how students learn, or perhaps how middle-class learners process information, teacher education institutions will prepare teachers to plan effective and appropriate educational experiences for all children and adolescents, regardless of backgrounds.

Comprehensive Multicultural Education Programs

A second prerequisite to responding effectively to the needs of culturally different learners is to provide comprehensive multicultural education programs. It is an understatement to say that a multicultural week will not suffice. Learners should experience a truly multicultural curriculum and environment—not just a few days a semester or even occasional experiences during a semester.

Comprehensive multicultural education programs must have sufficient planning; lead time for implementation; administrative support and leadership; parent and community involvement; teacher preparation for planning educational experiences for culturally diverse learners; school policies and practices that have been carefully examined; materials checked for cultural bias; testing programs that have been fully studied; provisions for appropriate extracurricular activities; training for proficiency in interpersonal relationships; and commitment of all school personnel to the program. Multicultural education programs need assessment mechanisms that evaluate program effectiveness in all aspects. Evaluation efforts should be just as comprehensive as the program itself, and evaluations should be done by all participants, including students and parents.

Appropriate curricular materials, an aspect only briefly mentioned earlier, will continue to be a basic requirement of any responsive multicultural education program. Curricular materials, both print and non-print media, must recognize cultural diversity, and must include culturally diverse people in positive, meaningful roles. Accomplishments of culturally diverse people, both historical and contemporary, must be presented in such a way that learners will not be led to believe that people in their culture function only in subservient roles. Educators have a responsibility for examining all material for any hint of bias or racism, and for selecting only materials that contribute positively to the overall multicultural education program.

Curricular materials, and the evaluation used to evaluate them, have improved during the past decade or so, and the authors hope the future will bring additional recognition of culturally diverse people in meaningful roles.

Personal and Professional Commitments

Another major prerequisite to the occurrence of responsive action is the personal and professional commitment of all educators, regardless of their roles in the schools. It is not sufficient for educators merely to know about cultural diversity, and be aware of the instructional methodology that reflects the relationship between culture and education. There must be both a personal and a professional commitment to understand, relate to, and teach culturally diverse learners. Educators' commitment must extend to the inclusion of a teaching/learning environment that respects *all* learners, regardless of their cultural backgrounds.

To what extent have educators offered personal and professional commitments? As with professional training in comprehensive multicultural education programs, the authors feel that great strides have been made: Learners, and the relationship between culture and learning, are being better understood. Educators, we hope by choice, are offering a more enlightened response to culturally diverse learners. Without doubt, there is room for improvement. The racist acts of the 1990s, and the low educational achievement and high dropout rates of some culturally diverse learners, provide indicators that educators still have challenges to meet. The future, however, looks bright. There is a better understanding of cultural diversity, and there appears to be an affirmative response toward the cultural diversity of the United States society and its schools.

SUMMING UP

The 1990s and the twenty-first century undoubtedly will be times for responsive action. The steadily increasing cultural diversity of the United

States, multicultural education programs moving beyond the infancy stages, and trained and committed educators, provide evidence that cultural diversity is becoming increasingly recognized, and will be addressed more responsively in future years. Responsive multicultural education begins with individual educators who demonstrate genuine acceptance and respect for all people. This commitment requires effort, yet the United States as a nation will benefit from educators' daily interactions with culturally different children and adolescents.

Appendix A

A selected bibliography of learning style assessment instruments.

The Learning Style Inventory (LSI) [Source: Dunn, R., Dunn, K. & Price, G. E. (1986). *Learning style inventory manual.* Lawrence, KS: Price Systems]. LSI is a widely-used assessment instrument in elementary and secondary schools, and incorporates many useful affective and physiological elements of learning style, but only touches on the cognitive (in the area of perceptual modalities). The Dunns and Price define learning style in terms of four pervasive learning conditions and 18 elements. Students complete a 104-item self-report questionnaire that identifies learning preferences about immediate environmental conditions, and emotional, sociological, and physical needs.

The NASSP Learning Style Profile (LSP) [Source: Keefe, J.W. (1987). *Learning Style—Theory and Practice.* Reston, VA: National Association of Secondary School Principals]. LSP is a second-generation instrument for the diagnosis of student cognitive styles, perceptual responses, and study and instructional preferences. The Learning Style Profile contains 23 scales representing four higher-order factors: cognitive styles, perceptual responses, and study and instructional preferences (the affective and physiological elements). The LSP scales are as follows:

- Analytic Skill
- Spatial Skill
- Discrimination Skill
- Categorizing Skill
- Sequential Processing Skill
- Memory Skill
- Perceptual Response: Visual
- Perceptual Response: Auditory
- Perceptual Response: Emotive
- Persistence Orientation
- Verbal Risk Orientation
- Verbal-Spatial Preference
- Manipulative Preference
- Study Time Preference: Early Morning
- Study Time Preference: Late Morning
- Study Time Preference: Afternoon
- Study Time Preference: Evening
- Grouping Preference
- Posture Preference
- Mobility Preference
- Sound Preference
- Lighting Preference
- Temperature Preference

Learning Style Identification Scale* by Paul Malcom, William Lutz, Mary Gerken, and Gary Hoeltke. Publishers Test Service (CTB/McGraw-Hill), 2500 Garden Road, Monterey, Calif. 93940, 1981. A short (24-item), self-scored rating scale based on the concept of learning style as the "method students use to solve any problem that they encounter in their educational experiences." Five styles are identified, based on classification of information reception and use, cognitive development, and self-concept.

Learning Styles Inventory* by Joseph Renzulli and Linda Smith; Mansfield Center, Conn.: Creative Learning Press, 1978. Both teacher and student forms are available for this 65-item instrument designed to measure attitude toward nine modes of instruction. Students and teachers indicate their reasons, using a Likert scale ranging from very unpleasant to very pleasant. Forms are computer-scored. Requires 30 minutes to administer, and can be used in grades four through twelve.

Learning Style Inventory: Primary Version* by Janet Perrin. Jamaica, New York: St. John's University, 1981. Based on the Learning Style Inventory of Dunn, Dunn, and Price and designed for young children, this questionnaire consists of 12 charts, each containing a series of pictures and questions that assess a different element of learning style. The inventory is individually administered in about 20 minutes and scored on a student profile form.

Learning Styles Inventory* by Albert A. Canfield and Judith S. Canfield. Humanics Media, (Liberty Drawer) 7970, Ann Arbor, Mich. 48107, 1976. Self-report instrument based on a rank ordering of choices for each of 30 questions. For use with junior high and higher, and takes about 15 minutes.

Short Inventory of Approaches to Studying* by [Source: Entwistle, N. (1981). *Styles of learning and teaching*. New York: John Wiley and Sons]. A 30-item test, using a Likert scale, in which students respond to statements concerning their achieving orientation, reproducing orientation, meaning dimension, comprehension style, operation style, and versatile approach. An index of learning pathologies can be obtained by summing three subscales. There is also a prediction of success score. Appropriate for junior high and higher, and takes about 30 minutes.

Cognitive Profiles* [Source: Letteri, C. A. (1980) *Cognitive profile: basic determinant of academic achievement*. Burlington, Vt.: Center for Cognitive Studies]. Seven tests of cognitive style that, in combination, predict student achievement as measured by standardized achievement test scores. The seven dimensions are: (1) Field Independence/Dependence, (2) Scanning/Focusing, (3) Breadth of Categorization, (4) Cognitive Complexity/Simplicity, (5) Reflectiveness/Impulsiveness, (6) Leveling/Sharpening, and (7) Tolerant/Intolerant.

Concrete-Operational Reasoning Test and Logical Reasoning Test*. [Sund, R. (1976). *Piaget for educators*. Columbus, Ohio: Charles E. Merrill]. Two paper-and-pencil, group-administered, multiple-choice tests designed to reveal formal or concrete operational reasoning.

Inventory of Learning Processes* [Source: Schmeck, R. R., Ribich, F., & Ramanaiah, N. (1977). Development of a self-report inventory for assessing individual difference in learning processes. *Applied Psychological Measurement, 1,* 413–431]. A 62-item, true-false, self-report inventory grouped by factor analysis into synthesis/analysis, study methods, fact retention, and elaborative processing, reflecting a continuum of student information-processing preferences from deep and elaborative to shallow and repetitive. Approximate administration time is 20 minutes.

Learning Style Inventory* by David Kolb. [Source: Kolb, D. (1981) Disciplinary inquiry norms and student learning styles: Diverse pathways for growth. In A. Chickering (Ed.), *The modern American college*. San Francisco: Jossey-Bass]. A five- to ten-minute self-report based on a rank ordering of four words in each of nine different sets. Each word represents one of four learning modes: feeling (Concrete Experience), watching (Reflective Observation), thinking (Abstract Conceptualization), and doing (Active Experimentation). For use with upper-grade students, with an approximate administration time of ten minutes.

Your Style of Learning and Thinking* Forms A & B [Source: Torrance, E. P., Reynolds, C. R., Riegel, T. R., & Ball. O. E. (1977). *Gifted Child Quarterly, 2,* 563–573]. A 36-item, self-report, multiple-choice questionnaire that classifies subjects according to right hemisphere, left hemisphere, and integrated information processing. Each item presents three choices for the three modes, based on an analysis of the research on brain hemispheric functioning. Approximate administration time is 20 minutes. Can be used with upper-grade students and adults.

Student Motivation Information Form* by Raymond J. Wlodkowski. University of Wisconsin, Milwaukee, 1978 (Available from NEA.) A 35-item, incomplete sentences test that elicits information about what motivates the person, i.e., intrinsic or extrinsic rewards. Could be administered orally to younger children.

Swassing-Barbe Modality Index* by Walter Barbe and Raymond Swassing. Columbus, Ohio: Zaner-Bloser, 1979. This is a series of tasks involving visual, auditory, and kinesthetic-tactile processing of the order of geometric shapes. It can be used with learners of any age, but must be individually administered. Results tell the percentage of the time each mode is used successfully. Kit includes a textbook on modality instruction, and a filmstrip and tape.

"Finding Your Modality Strengths"* [Source: Walter B. W. (1980) *Instructor, 89(6),* 44–47]. This is a series of ten incomplete sentences that are supposed to give "a rough idea of the relative strength of each of your modalities." Can be used by teachers and older students.

Learning Methods Test by Robert Mills. Available from The Mills School, 1512 E. Broward Blvd., Ft. Lauderdale, Fla. 1955. Individually administered, the LMT determines the "students' abilities to learn new words under different teaching procedures." The tasks involve visual, kinesthetic, phonic, and combination presentations of words. Since immediate and delayed recall is assessed, the test takes four days, 15 minutes each day.

SRI Student Perceiver Interview Guide. Selection Research, Incorporated, 2546 South 48th Plaza, P.O. Box 6438, Lincoln, Neb. 68506, 1978. A structured interview process designed to elicit student perceptions, grouped under 16 themes that are predominantly affective in nature. Institutes leading to trained certification are held regularly in designated cities. Administration time is approximately 45 minutes. Can be used with intermediate students and up.

*Adapted from: Cornett, C. C. (1983). "What you should know about teaching and learning styles." (PDK Fastback 191). Bloomington, IN: *Phi Delta Kappan*, pp 32–37.

References

Ada, A. F. (1987). "Hispanic-American classic and best loved books for children." *Journal of Reading, 30,* 195–202.

Alatis, J. E. (1976). "The compatibility of TESOL and bilingual education." In J. E. Alatis, & K. Twaddell (Eds.), *English as a second language in bilingual education* (pp. 5–14). Washington, DC: Teachers of English to Speakers of Other Languages.

Ames, C. A. (1990). "Motivation: What teachers need to know." *Teachers College Record, 91,* 409–421.

America's first . . . (1989). *Census and you, 24(3),* 1.

Amos, O. E., & Landers, M. F. (1984). "Special education and multicultural education: A compatiable marriage." *Theory Into Practice, 23,* 144–150.

Appleton, N. (1983). *Cultural pluralism in America.* New York: Longman.

Aronson, E., Blaney, N., Stephan, C., Sikes, J. & Snapp, M. (1978). *The jigsaw classroom.* Beverly Hills: Sage.

ASHA Committee on the Status of Racial Minorities. (1983). "Social dialects." *ASHA, 25(9),* 23–24.

Asian and Pacific islander data: 80 census goldmine . . . (1988). *Census and You, 23,* 3.

Association of American Publishers. (1984). Statement on bias-free materials (rev. ed.). Brochure available from School Division, AAP, 220 E. 23rd St. New York, NY 10010.

Atkinson, D. R., Morten, G., & Sue, D. W. (1989). *Counseling American minorities: A cross-cultural perspective* (3rd ed.). Dubuque, IA: Wm. C. Brown.

Au, K. Hu-Pei, & Jordan, C. (1981). "Teaching reading to Hawaiian children: Finding a culturally appropriate solution." In H. T. Trueba, G. P. Guthrie, & K. Hu-Pei Au (Eds.), *Culture and the bilingual classroom* (pp. 139–152). Rowley, MA: Newbury House.

Axelson, J. A. (1985). *Counseling and development in a multicultural society.* Monterey, CA: Brooks/Cole.

Baca, L. M., & Amato, C. (1989). "Bilingual special education: Training issues." *Exceptional Children, 56,* 168–173.

Baca, L. M., & Cervantes, H. T. (1984). *The bilingual special education interface.* St. Louis: Times Mirror/Mosby.

Baker, G. C. (1983). *Planning and organizing for multicultural education.* Reading, MA: Addison-Wesley.

Baker, G. C. (1979). "Policy issues in multicultural education in the United States." *Journal of Negro Education, 48,* 253–266.

Banks, J. A. (1988). *Multiethnic education: Theory and practice* (2nd ed). Boston: Allyn and Bacon.

Banks, J. A. (1987). *Teaching strategies for ethnic studies* (4th ed.). Boston, MA: Allyn and Bacon.

Banks, J. A. (1981). *Education in the 80's: Multiethnic education.* Washington, DC: National Education Association.

Bell-Scott, P. & McKenry, P. C. (1986). "Black adolescents and their families." In

G. K. Leigh, & G. W. Peterson (Eds.) *Adolescents in Families* (pp. 410–432). Cincinnati, Oh: South-Western.

Bennett, C. I. (1986). *Comprehensive multicultural education: Theory and Practice.* Boston: Allyn and Bacon.

Bernal, E. M. (1979). "The education of the culturally different gifted." In A. H. Passow (Ed.), *The gifted and talented: Their education and development* (The Seventy-eight Yearbook of the National Society for the Study of Education) (pp. 395–400). Chicago: The University of Chicago Press.

Berger, E. H. (1981). *Parents as partners in education: The school and the home working together.* St. Louis: C. V. Mosby.

Bernson, M. H., & Lindquist, T. L. (1989). "What's in a name? Galloping toward cultural insights—appreciating cultural diversity in the upper grades." *Social Studies and the Young Learner, 1(4),* 13–16.

Biehler, R. F., & Snowman, J. (1990). *Psychology as applied to teaching* (6th ed.). Boston: Houghton-Mifflin.

Billingsley, A. (1968). *Black families in white America.* Englewood Cliffs: Prentice-Hall.

Black population is growing . . . (1988, June). *Census and you, 23(6),* 3–4.

Bond, M. H., & Shiraishi, N. (1974). "The effect of body lean and status of an interviewer on the nonverbal behavior of Japanese interviewees." *International Journal of Psychology, 9(2).* New York: Springer.

Bondi, J., & Wiles, J. (1981). *The essential middle school.* Columbus, OH: Merrill.

Bowman, B. T. (1989). "Educating language-minority children: Challenges and opportunities." *Phi Delta Kappan,* 71, 118–120.

Boykin, A. W. (1982). "Task variability and the performance of black and white schoolchildren." *Journal of Black Studies,* 12, 469–485.

Brandt, R. (1989). "On parents and schools: A conversation with Joyce Epstein." *Educational Leadership, 47(2),* 24–27.

Brislin, R. W. (1981). *Cross-cultural encounters.* New York: Pergamon.

Brown, T. J. (1990). "The impact of culture." *The Clearing House,* 63, 305–309.

Brown, V. S. (1988). "Dimensions of Black history." *Teaching K-8, 18(5),* 46–48.

Bruneau, O. (1985). "Self-concept: A comparison of Native-American and Anglo preschoolers." *Psychology in the Schools,* 22, 378–379.

Bruner, J. W. (1966). *Studies in cognitive growth.* New York: John Wiley.

Bryde, J. F. (1971). *Modern Indian psychology* (rev. ed.). Vermillion, SD: Institute of Indian Studies, University of South Dakota.

California State Department of Education. (1979). *Planning for multicultural education as a part of school improvement.* Sacramento, CA: State Department of Education.

Casas, J. M., & Vasquez, M. J. T. (1989). "Counseling the Hispanic client: A theoretical and applied perspective." In P. B. Pedersen, J. G. Draguns, J. Lonner, & J. E. Trimble (Eds.). *Counseling across cultures.* (3rd ed.) (pp. 153–175) Honolulu: University of Hawaii Press.

Chaika, E. (1982). *Language: The social mirror.* Rowley, MA: Newbury House.

Chavkin, N. F. (1989). "Debunking the myth about minority parents." *Educational Horizons, 67(4),* 119–123.

Chen, S. (1987, April 6). "Suicide and depression identified as serious problems for Asian youth." *East-West News,* 9, 3–4.

Cheng, L. L. (1987). "Cross-cultural and linguistic considerations in working with Asian populations." *American Speech and Hearing Association, 29(6),* 33–36.

Christensen, E. W. (1989). "Counseling Puerto Ricans: Some cultural considerations." In D. R. Atkinson, G. Morten, & D. W. Sue (Eds.) *Counseling American minorities: A Cross-cultural perspective* (3rd ed.) (pp. 205–212). Dubuque, IA: W. C. Brown.

Clark-Johnson, G. (1988). "Black children." *Teaching Exceptional Children,* 20, 46–47.

"Closing the educational gap for Hispanics: State aims to forestall a divided society." (1987, September 16). *The Chronicle of Higher Education*, p. 1.

Coladarci, T. (1983). "High-school dropout among Native-Americans." *Journal of American Indian Education, 23*, 15–21.

Colburn, D., & Melillo, W. (1987, June 16). "Hispanics: A forgotten health population." *Washington Post*, p. 16.

Collier, J. L., & Collier, C. (1981). *Jump ship to freedom*. New York: Dell.

Collier, C., & Hoover, J. J., (1987). *Cognitive strategies for minority handicapped students*. Lindale, TX: Hamilton Publications.

Comer, J. P. (1988). Establishing a positive racial identity. *Parents, 63(3)*, 167.

Conger, J. J. (1977). *Adolescence and youth: Psychological development in a changing world*. New York: Harper & Row.

Cordova, I. R., & Love, R. (1987). "Multicultural education: Issues, concerns, and commitments." *The North Central Association Quarterly, 61*, 391–398.

Cornett, C. E. (1983). *What you should know about teaching and learning styles* (Fastback 191). Bloomington, IN: Phi Delta Kappa.

Cuban, L. (1984). *How teachers taught*. New York: Longman.

Dauber, S. (1987). "Sex differences on the SAT-M, SAT-V, TWSE, and ACT among college-bound high school students." Paper presented at the annual meeting of the American Educational Research Association, Washington, DC.

Davis, B. C. (1989). "A successful parent involvement program." *Educational Leadership, 47(2)*, 21–23.

Dawson, M. M. (1987). "Beyond ability grouping: A review of the effectiveness of ability grouping and its alternatives." *School Psychology Review, 16*, 348–369.

DeCosta, S. B. (1984). "Not all children are Anglo and middle class: A practical beginning for the elementary teacher." *Theory Into Practice, 22*, 155–162.

Deyhle, D. (1985). "Testing among Navajo and Anglo students: Another consideration of cultural bias." *Journal of Educational Equity and Leadership, 5*, 119–131.

DeVries, D. L., & Slavin, R. E. (1978). "Teams-games-tournament (TGT): Review of ten classroom experiments." *Journal of Research and Development in Education, 12*, 28–38.

Dillard, J. L. (1972). *Black English: Its history and usage in the United States*. New York: Random House.

"Disney cancels cartoon because of stereotypes." (1990, July 9). *The State Newspaper* (Columbia, SC), p. 8-A.

Divoky, D. (1988). "The model minority goes to school." *Phi Delta Kappan, 70*, 219–222.

Dorris, M. A. (1981). "The grass still grow, the rivers still flow: Contemporary Native-Americans." *Daedalus, 110(2)*, 43–69.

Draguns, J. G. (1989). "Dilemmas and choices in cross-cultural counseling: The universal versus the culturally distinctive." In P. D. Pedersen, J. G. Draguns, J. Lonner, & J. E. Trimble (Eds.), *Counseling across cultures*. (3rd ed.) (pp. 1–21). Honolulu: University of Hawaii Press.

Dunn, R., Beaudry, J.S., & Klavis, A. (1989). "Survey of research on learning styles." *Educational Leadership, 46*, 50–58.

Dunn, R., Dunn, K. & Price, G. E. (1986). *Learning style inventory manual*. Lawrence, KS: Price Systems.

Dunn, R.S., & Dunn, K.J. (1979). "Learning styles/teaching styles: Should they . . . can they . . . be matched?" *Educational Leadership, 36*, 238–244.

Dunn, R., & Dunn, K. (1978). *Teaching students through their individual learning styles: A practical approach*. Reston, VA: Reston Publishing Co., Division of Prentice-Hall.

Dunn, R., Gemake, J., Jalali, F., & Zenhausern, R. (1990). "Cross-cultural differences in learning styles of elementary-age children from four ethnic backgrounds." *Journal of Multicultural Counseling and Development, 18,* 68–93.

Edelman, M. W. (1989). "Black children in America." In J. Dewart (ed.), *The state of Black America* (pp. 63–76). New York: The National Urban League.

Elkind, D. (1984). "Erik Erikson's eight stages of man." In H. E. Fitzgerald, & M. G. Walveren (Eds.), *Human development* (pp. 11–18). Guilford, CT: The Dushkin Publishing Group.

Elkind, D. (1972). "Piaget and science education." *Science and Children, 10,* 9–12.

English as a second language program: Benefits for your child. (1987). Austin, TX: Texas Education Agency.

Erikson, E.E. (1963). *Childhood and society.* New York: W. W. Norton.

First, J. M. (1988). "Immigrant students in the U.S. public schools: Challenges with solutions." *Phi Delta Kappan, 70,* 205–210.

Fitzpatrick, J.P. (1987). *Puerto Rican Americans* (2nd ed.) Englewood Cliffs, NJ: Prentice-Hall.

Fletcher, J. D. (1983). "What problems do American Indians have with English?" *Journal of American Indian Education, 23,* 1–12.

Gade, E., Hurlburt, G., & Fuqua, D. (1986). "Study habits and attitudes of American Indian students: Implications for counselors." *The School Counselor, 34,* 135–139.

Garcia, R. L. (1984). "Countering classroom discrimination." *Theory Into Practice, 22,* 104–109.

Garfinkel, P. (1983, September). "The best "Jewish mother" in the world." *Psychology Today,* pp. 56–60.

Gay, G. (1983). "Multiethnic education: Historical developments and future prospects." *Phi Delta Kappan, 64,* 560–563.

Gay, G. (1975). "Organizing and designing a culturally pluralistic curriculum." *Educational Leadership, 33,* 176–183.

Gibson, M. A. (1984). "Approaches to multicultural education in the United States: Some concepts and assumptions." *Anthropology and Education Quarterly, 15,* 94–119.

Gill, W. (1990). "African-American: What's in a name?" *Educational Leadership, 48(1),* 85.

Glazner, N. (1981). "Pluralism and the new immigrants." *Society, 19,* 31–36.

Glazer, N., & Moynihan, D. P. (1970). *Beyond the melting pot: The Negroes, Puerto Ricans, Jews, Italians, and Irish of New York City* (2nd ed.). Cambridge, MA: The M.I.T. Press.

Gonzales, R. (1967). *I am Joaquin.* New York: Bantam Books.

Gonzalez, E. (1989). "Hispanics bring "corazon" and "sensibilidad"." *Momentum, 20(1),* 10–13.

Goldenberg, C.N. (1987). "Low-income Hispanic parents' contributions to their first-grade children's word-recognition skills." *Anthropology & Education Quarterly, 18,* 149–179.

Gollnick, D. M., & Chinn, P. C. (1990). *Multicultural education in a pluralistic society* (3rd ed.). Columbus: Merrill.

Gollnick, D. M., Sadker, M. P., & Sadker, D. M. (1982). "Beyond the Dick and Jane syndrome: Confronting sex bias in instructional materials." In M. P. Sadker, & D. M. Sadker (eds.), *Sex equity handbook for schools.* New York: Longman.

Goodlad, J. I. (1984). *A place called school.* New York: McGraw-Hill.

Gordon, M. M. (1978). *Assimilation in American life.* New York: Oxford University.

Gordon, M. M. (1964). *Human nature, class, and ethnicity.* New York: Oxford University.

Grant, C. A., & Sleeter, C. E. (1986, April). "Race, class, and gender in educational research: An argument for integrative analysis." Paper presented at the meeting of the American Educational Research Association, San Francisco, CA.

Green. J. W. (1982). *Cultural awareness in the human services*. Englewood Cliffs, NJ: Prentice-Hall.

Gutierrez, J., & Sameroff, A. (1990). "Determinants of complexity in Mexican-American and Anglo-American mothers' conceptions of child development." *Child Development, 61*, 384–394.

Hakuta, K., & Garcia, E. E. (1989). "Bilingualism and education." *American Psychologist, 44*, 374–379.

Hale-Benson, J. E. (1986). *Black children. Their roots and their culture* (rev. ed.). Baltimore, MD: Johns Hopkins.

Hall, E.T. (1981). *Beyond culture*. Garden City, NY: Anchor.

Hall, S., & Reck, C. (1987). "What about the language program in teaching Hispanics?" *Momentum, 18*, 52–55.

Haring, N. G. (1990). "Overview of special education." In In N. G. Haring, & L. McCormick (Eds.), *Exceptional children and youth* (pp. 1–45). Columbus, OH: Merrill.

Hartman, J. S., & Askounis, A. C. (1989). "Asian-American students: Are they really a 'model minority'?" *The School Counselor, 37*, 109–111.

Harvey, K. D., Harjo, L. D., & Jackson, J. K. (1990). *Teaching about Native-Americans* (Bulletin no. 84). Washington, DC: National Council for the Social Studies.

Havighurst, R.J. (1972). *Developmental tasks and education* (3rd ed.). New York, NY: McKay.

Havighurst, R. J. (1976). "The relative importance of social class and ethnicity in human development." *Human Development, 19*, 56–64.

Hernandez, H. (1989). *Multicultural Education: A teacher's guide to content and process*. Columbus: Merrill.

Herring, R. D. (1989). "Counseling Native-American children: Implications for elementary school counselors." *Elementary School Guidance and Counseling, 23*, 272–281.

Heys, S. (1988, February 14). "Is Black English standing in the way of learning" *The State Newspaper* (Columbia, SC), 1B, 6.

Hilliard, A. G. (1989). "Teaching and cultural styles in a pluralistic society." *National Education Association, 7(6)*, 65–69.

Hilliard, A. (1976). *Alternatives to IQ testing: An approach to the identification of gifted minority children*. Final Report to the California State Department of Education, Sacramento, CA.

Ho, M. K. (1987). *Family therapy with ethnic minorities*. Newbury Park: Sage.

Hodge, J. L., Struckmann, D. K., & Trost, L. D. (1975). *Cultural bases of racism and group oppression*. Berkeley, CA: Two Riders.

Holland, S. H. (1987). "Positive primary education for young Black males." *The Education Digest, 53(3)*, 56–58.

Hoover-Dempsey, K. V., Bassler, O. C. & Brissie, J. S. (1987). "Parent involvement: Contributions of teacher efficacy, school socioeconomic status, and other school characteristics." *American Education Research Journal, 24*, 417–435.

Huang, L. J. (1976). "The Chinese-American family." In C. H. Mindel, & W. Haberstein (Eds.), *Ethnic families in America: Patterns and variations* (pp. 124–147). New York: Elsevier.

Huhn, R., & Zimpfer, D. G. (1984). "The role of middle and junior high school counselors in parent education." *The School Counselor, 31(4)*, 357–365.

Hurmence, B. (1982). *A girl called boy*. Boston: Houghton Mifflin.

Hymes, D. (1981). "Ethnographic monitoring." In H. T. Trueba, G. P. Guthrie, & K. Hu-Pei Au (Eds.), *Culture and the bilingual classroom* (pp. 56–68). Rowley, MA: Newbury.

"Indian tribes, Incorporated." (1988, December 5). *Newsweek,* pp. 40–41.

Ishii, S. (1973). "Characteristics of Japanese nonverbal communicative behavior." *Journal of the Communication Assoiciation of the Pacific, 2 & 3.*

Jackson, G., & Corsca, C. (1974). "The inequality of educational opportunity in the Southwest: An observational study of ethnically mixed classrooms." *American Educational Research Journal, 11,* 219–229.

Jacobs, R. L. (1990). "Learning styles of Black high, average, and low achievers." *The Clearing House, 63,* 253–254.

Jarolimek, J., & Foster, C. D. (1989). *Teaching and learning in the elementary school* (4th ed.). New York: Macmillan.

Jaynes, G. D., & Williams, R. M. (1989). *A common destiny: Blacks and American society.* Washington, DC: National Academy Press.

Jenkins, A. H. (1982). *The psychology of the Afro-Americans: A humanistic approach.* Elmsford, NY: Pergamon Press.

Jennings, W. B. (1989). "How to organize successful parent involvement advisory committees." *Educational Leadership, 47(2),* 42–45.

Jensen, J. V. (1985). "Perspective on nonverbal intercultural communication." In L. A. Samovar, & R. E. Porter (Eds.), *Intercultural communication: A reader* (4th ed.) (pp. 256–272). Belmont, CA: Wadsworth.

Johnson, D. W., & Johnson, R. (1989/1990). "Social skills for successful group work." *Educational Leadership 47(4),* 29–33.

Johnson, D. W., & Johnson, R. (1987). *Learning together and alone: Cooperative, competitive, and individualistic learning.* Englewood Cliffs, NJ: Prentice-Hall.

Kagan, S. L. (1984). *Parent involvement research: A field in search of itself.* Boston: Institute for Responsive Education.

Keefe, J. W. (1990). "Learning style: Where are we going?" *Momentum, 21(1),* 44–48.

Keefe, J.W. (1987). *Learning style: Theory and practice.* Reston, VA: NASSP.

Keefe, J. W. & Monk. J. S. (1986). *Learning style profile examiners's manual.* Reston, VA: NASSP.

Kitano, H. H. L. (1989). "A model for counseling Asian Americans." In P. B. Pedersen, J. G. Draguns, W. J. Lonner, & J. E. Trimble (eds.), *Counseling across cultures* (pp. 139–151). Honolulu: University of Hawaii Press.

Klein, J. P. (1985). "Separation of church and state: The endless struggle." *Contemporary Education, 54(3),* 166–170.

Kostelnik, M. J., Stein, L. C., Whiren, A. P., & Soderman. A. K. (1988). *Guiding children's social development.* Cincinnati, OH: Brooks/Cole.

Kranz, B. (1982). *Kranz talent identification instrument.* Morehead, MN: University of Minnesota.

Lafrance, M., & Mayo, C. (1978). "Cultural aspects of nonverbal communication: A review essay." *International Journal of Intercultural Relations, 2,* 71–89.

Laosa, L. M. (1977). "Multicultural education—how psychology can contribute." *Journal of Teacher Education, 28(3),* 26–30.

Lee, C. C., & Lindsey, C. R. (1985). "Black consciousness development: A group counseling model for Black elementary school students." *Elementary School Guidance and Counseling, 19,* 228–236.

Lee, C. C. (1982). "The school counselor and the Black child: Critical roles and functions." *The Journal of Multicultural Counseling and Development* (formerly *The Journal of Non-White Concerns), 10,* 94–101.

Lee, E. S., & Rong, X. (1988). "The educational and economic achievement of Asian-Americans." *The Elementary School Journal, 88,* 545–560.

"Lessons from bigotry . . . " (1989). *Newsweek,* pp. 48–49.

Lester, J. (1968). *To be a slave.* New York: Scholastic.

Lewis, R. G., & Ho, M. K. (1983). "Social work with Native-Americans." In D. R.

Atkinson, G. Morten, & D. W. Sue (Eds.) *Counseling American minorities* (3rd ed.) (pp. 65–72). Dubuque, IA: Wm. C. Brown.

Light, H. K., & Martin, R. E. (1986). "American Indian families." *Journal of American Indian Education, 26(1),* 1–5.

Linton, T. E., & Foster, M. (1990). " 'Powerful environments' for underclass youth." *The Education Digest, 55(7),* 27–31.

Little Soldier, L. (1989). "Cooperative learning and the Native-American student." *Phi Delta Kappan, 71,* 161–163.

Little Soldier, L. (1985). "To soar with the eagles: Enculturation acculturation of Indian children." *Childhood Education, 61,* 185–191.

Locke, D. C. (1989). "Fostering the self-esteem of African-American children." *Elementary School Guidance and Counseling, 23,* 254–259.

Lomotey, K. (1989). "Cultural diversity in the school: Implications for principals." *NASSP Bulletin, 73,* 81–88.

Lonner, W. J., & Ibrahim, F. A. (1989). "Assessment in cross-cultural counseling." In P. B. Pedersen, J. G. Draguns, J. Lonner, & J. E. Trimble (Eds.) *Counseling across cultures.* (3rd ed.) (pp. 299–333). Honolulu: University of Hawaii Press.

Lonner, W. J., & Sundberg, N. D. (1985). "Assessment in cross-cultural counseling and therapy." In P. B. Pedersen (Ed.), *Handbook of cross-cultural counseling and therapy* (pp. 173–179). Westport, CT: Greenwood.

Luftig, R. L. (1983). "The effect of schooling on the self-concept of Native-American students." *The School Counselor, 30,* 251–260.

Lum, D. (1986). *Social work practice and people of color: A process-stage approach.* Monterey, CA: Brooks/Cole.

McCallum, R. S., Karnes, F. A., & Edwards, R. P. (1984). "The test of choice for assessment of gifted children: A comparison of the K-ABC, WISC-R, and Stanford-Binet." *Journal of Psychoeducational Assessment, 2,* 57–63.

McCormick, L. (1990). "Cultural diversity and exceptionality." In N. G. Haring, & L. McCormick (Eds.), *Exceptional children and youth* (pp. 47–75). Columbus, OH: Merrill.

McCormick, L. (1990b). "Communication disorders." In N. G. Haring, & L. McCormick (Eds.), *Exceptional children and youth* (pp. 327–363). Columbus, OH: Merrill.

McCormick, T. (1984). "Multiculturalism: Some principles and issues." *Theory Into Practice, 23,* 93–97.

McFarlane, S. C., Fujiki, M. & Britton, B. (1984). *Coping with communicative handicaps.* San Diego: College-Hill Press.

McKenna, G. (1988). "Our future demands Black teachers." *The Black Collegian, 18(4),* 118–123.

MacMillan, D. L., Keogh, B. K, & Jones, R. L. (1986). "Special education research on mildly handicapped learners." In M. C. Wittrock (Ed.), *Handbook of research on teaching* (3rd ed.) (pp. 686–724). New York: MacMillan.

Madden, N. A., Slavin, R. E., & Stevens, R. J. (1986). *Cooperative integrated reading and composition: Teacher's manual.* Baltimore: Johns Hopkins University, Center for Research on Elementary and Middle Schools.

Maier, H. W. (1969). *Three theories of child development* (rev.ed.). New York: Harper & Row.

Mann, S. R. (1983). "Adolescents, schools and parents: Support for success." *Educational Horizons, 61,* 201–204.

Manni, J. L., Winikur, D. W., & Keller, M. R. (1984). *Intelligence, mental retardation and the culturally different child.* Springfield, IL: Charles C. Thomas.

Manning, M. L. (1991). More than lipservice to multicultural education. *The Clearing House, 64,* 218.

Manning, M. L., & Lucking, R. (1991). The what, why, and how of cooperative learning. *The Clearing House, 64,* 152–156.

Manning, M. L., & Lucking, R. (1990). "Ability grouping: Realities and alternatives." *Childhood Education, 66,* 254–258.

Manning, M. L. (1989). "Multicultural education." *Middle School Journal, 21(1),* 14–16.

Marion, R. (1981). *Educators, parents and exceptional children.* Rockville, MD: Aspen Systems.

Marion, R. (1979). "Minority parent involvement in the IEP process: A systematic model approach." *Teaching Exceptional Children, 10(4),* 1–15.

Meltzer, M. (1984). *The Black Americans: A history in their own words.* New York: Crowell.

Mendelberg, H. E. (1986). "Identity conflict in Mexican-American adolescents." *Adolescence, 21,* 215–224.

Miller-Jones, D. (1989). "Culture and testing." *American Psychologist, 44,* 360–366.

Mindel, H. C., & Habenstein, R. W. (1981). "Family lifestyles of America's ethnic minorities: An introduction." In C. H. Mindel, & R. W. Habenstein (Eds.), *Ethnic families in America: Patterns and variations* (pp. 1–13). New York: Elsevier.

Minderman, L. (1990). "Literature and multicultural education." *Instructor, 99(7),* 22–23.

Mirandé, A. (1986). "Adolescence and Chicano families." In G.K. Leigh, & G.W. Peterson (Eds.), *Adolescents in families* (pp. 433–455). Cincinnati, OH: Southwestern.

Mitchum, N. T. (1989). "Increasing self-esteem in Native-American children." *Elementary School Guidance and Counseling, 23,* 266–271.

Mitzel, H. E. (1982). "Parent education." *Encyclopedia of Education Research* (5th ed., vol. 3, pp. 1379–1382). New York: The Free Press.

Molnar, A. (1989). "Racism in America: A continuing dilemma." *Educational Leadership, 47(2),* 71–72.

Molnar, J. P. (1972). *Graciela: A Mexican-American child tells her story.* New York: Franklin Watts.

Moll, L.C. (1988). "Some key issues in teaching Latino students." *Language Arts, 65,* 465–472.

Montagu, A. (1974). *Man's most dangerous myth: The fallacy of race.* New York: Oxford University Press.

Montano, M. (1979). "School and community: Boss-worker or partners?" In C. Grant (Ed.), *Community participation in education.* Boston: Allyn and Bacon.

More, A. J. (1987). "Native-American learning styles: A review for researchers and teachers." *Journal of American Indian Education, 27(1),* 17–29.

Morrow, R. D. (1989). "Southeast-Asian parent involvement: Can it become a reality?" *Elementary School Guidance and Counseling, 23,* 289–297.

Morrow, R. D. (1987). "Cultural differences—be aware!" *Academic Therapy, 23(2),* 143–149.

Mullis, I. (1987). "Trends in performance for women taking the NAEP reading and writing assessments." Paper presented at the annual meeting of the American Educational Research Association, Washington, DC.

Multicultural teaching strategies. (1990). (Technical Assistance Paper No. 9). Tallahassee: State Department of Education.

Murray, C. B., & Clark, R. M. (1990). "Targets of racism." *The American School Board Journal, 177(6),* 22–24.

NASSP. (1979). *Student learning styles—diagnosing and prescribing programs.* Reston, VA: NASSP.

National Council for Accreditation of Teacher Education. (1986). *Standards, proce-*

dures and policies for accreditation of professional teacher education units. Washington: NCATE.

Nauman, A. K. (1987). "School librarians and cultural pluralism." *The Reading Teacher, 41(2)*, 201–205.

Nieves, W., & Valle, M. (1982). "The Puerto Rican family: Conflicting roles for the Puerto Rican college student." *Journal of Non-White Concerns in Personnel and Guidance, 4*, 154–160.

Norton, D. E. (1990). "Teaching multicultural literature in the reading curriculum." *The Reading Teacher, 44(1)*, 28–40.

Olsen, L. (1988). "Crossing the schoolhouse border: Immigrant children in California." *Phi Delta Kappan, 70*, 211–218.

Oltman, P. K., Raskin, A. J. & Witkin, H. (1971). *Group embedded figures test (GEFT).* Palo Alto, CA: Consulting Psychologists Press.

Olvera-Ezzell, N., Power, T. G., & Cousins, J. H. (1990). "Maternal socialization of children's eating habits: Strategies used by obese Mexican-American mothers." *Child Development, 61*, 395–400.

Ornstein, A. C., & Levine, D. U. (1989). "Social class, race, and school achievement: Problems and prospects." *Journal of Teacher Education, 40(5)*, 17–23.

Osako, M. M., & Lui, W. T. (1986). "Intergenerational relations and the aged among Japanese-Americans." *Research on Aging, 8*, 128–155.

Ovando, C. J. (1990). "Intermediate and secondary school curricula: A multicultural and multilingual framework." *The Clearing House, 63*, 294–297.

Oyer, H. J., Crowe, B., & Haas, W. H. (1987). *Speech, language & hearing disorders.* Boston: Little, Brown and Company.

Padilla, A.M. (1981). "Pluralistic counseling and psychotherapy for Hispanic-Americans." In A. J. Marsella, & P. B. Pedersen (Eds.), *Cross-cultural counseling and psychotherapy* (pp. 195–227). New York, NY: Pergamon.

Pang, V. O. (1988). "Teaching about ethnic heritage." *Learning 88, 16(5)*, 56–57.

Papalia, D. E., & Olds, S. W. (1989). *Human development.* New York: McGraw-Hill.

Pasanella, A. L., & Volkmor, C. B. (1977). *To parents of children with special needs. A manual on parent involvement in educational programming.* Los Angeles: California Regional Resource Center, University of Southern California.

Patton, J. R., & Polloway, E. A. (1990). "Mild mental retardation." In N. G. Haring, & L. McCormick (Eds.), *Exceptional children and youth* (pp. 195–237). Columbus, OH: Merrill.

Payne, C. (1984). "Multicultural education and racism in American schools." *Theory Into Practice, 22*, 124–131.

Pearson, J. L., Hunter, A. G., Ensminger, M. E., & Kellam, S. G. (1990). "Black grandmothers in multigenerational households: Diversity in family structure and parenting involvement in the Woodlawn community." *Child Development, 61*, 434–442.

Pedersen P. (1988). *A handbook for developing multicultural awareness.* Alexandria, VA: American Association of Counseling and Development.

PEER (Project on Equal Educational Rights). (1987, May 29). *Equal education alert 7.*

Petty, W. T., Petty, D. C., & Salzer, R. T. (1989). *Experiences in language: Tools and techniques for language arts methods.* Boston: Allyn and Bacon.

Pine, G. J., & Hilliard, A. G. (1990). "Rx for racism: Imperatives for America's schools." *Phi Delta Kappan, 71*, 593–600.

Pinkney, A. (1975). *Black Americans.* Englewood Cliffs: Prentice-Hall.

Polakow-Suranksy, S., & Ulaby, N. (1990). "Students take action to combat racism." *Phi Delta Kappan, 71*, 601–606.

Pollard, D. S. (1989). "Reducing the impact of racism on students." *Educational Leadership, 47*, 73–75.

Powell, D. R. (1986). "Parent education and support programs." *Young Children, 41(3)*, 47–53.

Purkey, W.W., & Novak, J.M. (1984). *Inviting school success: A self concept approach to teaching and learning.* Belmont, CA: Wadsworth.

Pyle, W. (1976). "Sexism in children's literature." *Theory Into Practice, 15*, 116–119.

Ramiriz, M., & Castaneda, A. (1974). *Cultural democracy, bicognitive development and education.* New York: Academic Press.

Ramsey, P. G. (1987). *Teaching and learning in a diverse world.* NewYork: Teacher's College Press.

Raybon, P. (1989, October 2). "A case of 'severe bias'." *Newsweek*, p.11.

Religion in America, 1985. *The Gallup poll, 236*, 27.

Renzulli, J. S. (1973). "Talent potential in minority group students." *Exceptional Children, 39*, 437–444.

Richardson, E. H. (1981). "Cultural and historical perspectives in counseling Indians." In D. W. Sue (Ed.), *Counseling the culturally different* (pp. 216–255). New York: John Wiley.

Riccio, L. L. (1985). "Facts and issues about ability grouping." *Contemporary Education, 57*, 26–30.

Riessman, F. (1962). *The culturally deprived child.* New York: Harper & Row.

Rindone, P. (1988). "Achievement motivation and academic achievement in Native-American students." *Journal of American Indian Education, 28(1)*, 1–8.

Rist, R. C. (1979). *Desegregated schooling: Portraits of an American experiment.* New York: Academic Press.

Roehl, J. E., Herr, J., & Appplehaus, D. J. (1985). "Parenting education—Now more than ever." *Lifelong Learning, 9(3)*, 20–22, 27.

Rossel, C., & Ross, J. M. (1986). *The social science evidence on bilingual education.* Boston: Boston University Press.

Rotenberg, K. J., & Cranwell, F. R. (1989). "Self-concepts in American Indian and White children." *Journal of Cross-cultural Psychology 20(1)*, 39–53.

Rothermam-Borus, M. J., & Phinney, J. S. (1990). "Patterns of social expectations among Black and Mexican-American children." *Child Development, 61*, 542–556.

Rubin, R. H. (1977). *Family structure and peer-group affiliation as related to attitudes about male-female relations among Black youth.* San Francisco, CA: R & E Associates.

Ruiz, R.A. (1981). "Cultural and historical perspectives in counseling Hispanics." In D. W. Sue (Ed.) *Counseling the culturally different* (pp. 186–215). New York, NY: John Wiley.

Ryan, W. (1971). *Blaming the victim.* New York: Pantheon.

SACUS. *Multicultural Education: A Position Statement.* (1988). Little Rock: Southern Association for Children Under Six.

Sadker, M. P., & Sadker, D. M. (1982). "Between teacher and student: Overcoming sex bias in classroom interaction." In M. P. Sadker, & D. M. Sadker (Eds.), *Sex equity handbook for schools* (pp. 96–132). New York: Longman.

Sanders, D. (1987). "Cultural conflicts: An important factor in the academic failures of American Indian students." *Journal of Multicultural Counseling and Development, 15*, 81–90.

Santiestevan, H. (1986). "Hispanics and education." *Social Education, 50*, 396.

Santrock, J. W. (1990). *Life-span development (3rd ed.).* Dubuque, IA: Wm. C. Brown.

Sendor, B. (1989). "Root out racial bias in student placement." *American School Board Journal, 176(3)*, 24–25.

Shade, B. (1982). "Afro-American cognitive style: A variable in school success?" *Review of Educational Research, 52*, 219–244.

Sharan, Y., & Sharan, S. (1989/1990). "Group investigation expands cooperative learning." *Educational Leadership, 47(4),* 17–21.

Sharan, S. (1985). "Cooperative learning and the multiethnic classroom." In *Learning to cooperate, cooperating to learn,* edited by R. Slavin, S. Sharan, S. Kagan, R. Lazarowitz, C. Webb, and R. Schmuck, (pp. 255–276). New York: Plenum.

Shea, T. M., & Bauer, A. M. (1985). *Parents and teachers of exceptional children: A handbook for involvement.* Boston: Allyn and Bacon.

Simich-Dudgeon, C. (1987). "Involving limited-English-proficient parents as tutors in their children's education." *ERIC/CLL News Bulletin, 10(2),* 3–4, 7.

Slade, J. C., & Conoley, C. W. (1989). "Multicultural experiences for special educators." *Teaching Exceptional Children, 22(1),* 60–64.

Slavin, R. E. (1987). *Cooperative learning* (2nd ed.). Washington, DC: National Education Association.

Slavin, R. E. (1983). *An introduction to cooperative learning.* New York: Longman.

Slavin, R. E. (1978). "Student teams and achievement divisions." *Journal of Research in Education, 12,* 39–49.

Slavin, R. E., Leavy, M. B., & Madden, N. A. (1986). *Team accelerated instruction—Mathematics.* Watertown, MA: Mastery Education Corporation.

Sleeter, C. E. (1990). "Staff development for desegregated schooling." *Phi Delta Kappan, 72,* 33–40.

Sleeter, C. E., & Grant, C. A. (1988). *Making choices for multicultural education: Five approaches to race, class and gender.* Columbus: Merrill.

Smith, E. J. (1981). "Cultural and historical perspectives in counseling Blacks." In D. W. Sue (ed.), *Counseling the culturally different* (pp. 141–185). New York: John Wiley.

Smitherman, G. (1972). *Talkin' and testifyin'.* Boston: Houghton-Mifflin.

So, A.Y. (1987). "Hispanic teachers and the labeling of Hispanic students." *The High School Journal, 71,* 5–8.

Starr, J. (1989). "The great textbook war." In H. Holtz, I. Marcus, J. Dougherty, J. Michaels, & R. Peduzzi (Eds.). *Education and the American dream: Conservatives, liberals, and radicals debate the future of education* (pp. 96–109). Granby, MA: Bergin & Garvey.

Steinberg, L., Blinde, P.L., & Chan, K.S. (1984). "Dropping out among language minority youth." *Review of Educational Research, 54,* 113–132.

Stewart, W. J. (1990). "Learning-style-appropriate instruction: Planning, implementing evaluating." *The Clearing House, 63,* 371–374.

Stover, D. (1990). "The new racism." *The American School Board Journal, 177(6),* 14–18.

Sue, D. W. (1981). *Counseling the culturally different.* New York: John Wiley.

Sue, D. W., & Sue, S. (1983). "Counseling Chinese-Americans." In D. R. Atkinson, G. Morten, & D. W. Sue (Eds.). *Counseling American minorities: A cross-cultural perspective* (2nd ed.) (pp. 97–106). Dubuque, IA: Wm. C. Brown.

Sue, D. W., & Kirk, B. A. (1972). "Psychological characteristics of Chinese-American college students." *Journal of Counseling Psychology, 6,* 471–478.

Sue, D. W., & Sue, S. (1972). "Ethnic minorities: Resistance to being researched." *Professional Psychology, 2,* 11–17.

Swisher, K., & Deyhle, D. (1989, August). "The styles of learning are different, but the teaching is just the same: Suggestions for teachers of American Indian youth." *Journal of American Indian Education, Special Issue,* 1–11.

TESOL. (Teachers of English to Speakers of Other Languages) (1976). "Position paper on the role of English as a second language in bilingual education." Washington, DC: Author.

Tesconi, C. A. (1984). "Multicultural education: A valued but problematic ideal." *Theory Into Practice, 22,* 87–92.

Tharp, R. G. (1989). "Psychocultural variables and constants." *American Psychologist, 44*, 349–359.

"The Hispanic population of the United States: March 1988." (Advance Report) (1988). *Current population reports: Population characteristics.* Series P-20, No. 431. Washington, DC: U. S. Government Printing Office.

"The new whiz kids . . . : Why Asian-Americans are doing so well, and what it costs them." (1987, August 31). *Time,* pp, 42–51.

Tiedt, P.L., & Tiedt, I.M. (1990). *Multicultural teaching: A handbook of activities, information, and resources* (3rd ed.) Boston, MA: Allyn and Bacon.

Toepfer, C. F. (1988). "What to know about young adolescents." *Social Education, 52,* 110–112.

Trecker, J. L. (1977). "Women in U. S. history high-school textbooks." In J. Pottker, & A. Fishel (Eds.), *Sex bias in the schools: The research evidence* (pp. 146–161). Cranbury, NJ: Associated University Presses.

Trimble, J. E., & Fleming, C. M. (1989). "Providing counseling services for Native-American Indians: Client, counselor, and community characteristics." In P. B. Pedersen, J. G. Draguns, J. Lonner, & J. E. Trimble (eds.) *Counseling across cultures* (3rd ed.) (pp. 177–204). Honolulu: University of Hawaii Press.

Tucker, B., & Huerta, C. (1987). "A study of developmental tasks as perceived by young adult Mexican-American females." *Lifelong Learning: An Omnibus of Practice and Research, 10(4),* 4–7.

Turkovich, M., & Mueller, P. (1989). "The multicultural factor: A curriculum multiplier." *Social Studies and the Young Learner, 1(4),* 9–12.

Tyler, R. W. (1989). "Educating children from minority families." *Educational Horizons, 67(4),* 114–118.

U.S. Bureau of the Census. (1990). *Statistical abstracts of the United States* (110th ed.). Washington, DC: U. S. Government Printing Office.

U.S. Bureau of the Census. (1989). "Population estimates by race and Hispanic origin for states, metropolitan areas, and selected counties: 1980–1985." *Current population reports, Series P-25, No. 1040.* Washington, DC: U.S. Government Printing Office.

U.S. Bureau of the Census. (1988). *Statistical Abstracts of the United States: 1988* (108th ed.). Washington, DC: U. S. Government Printing Office.

U. S. Bureau of the Census. (1988b). *Statistical abstracts of the United States: 1988* (108th ed.). Washington, DC: U. S. Government Printing Office.

U. S. Bureau of the Census (1988c). "The Hispanic population in the United States: March 1988 (Advance Report)." *Current Population Reports, Series P-20, No. 431.* Washington, DC.: U. S. Government Printing Office.

U. S. Bureau of the Census. (1986). "Estimates of the population of the United States, by age, sex, and race: 1980–1985." Current population reports, Series P-25, no. 985. Washington, DC: U. S. Government Printing Office.

U. S. Bureau of the Census. (1980). *Census of the population, Vol. 1 General population characteristics PC 80-1-B.* Washington, DC: U. S. Government Printing Office.

U. S. Commission on Civil Rights. (1980). *Characters in textbooks.* Clearinghouse Publication 62. Washington, DC: U. S. Government Printing Office.

Uthe-Reyno, M. G., & MacKinnon, D. L. J. (1989). "Teacher's modeling encourages learning in Indian students." *Educational Horizons, 67(4),* 163–165.

Valdivieso, R. (1986). "Hispanics and schools: A new perspective." *Educational Horizons, 64,* 190–197.

Valero-Figueria, E. (1988). "Hispanic children." *Teaching Exceptional Children, 20,* 47–49.

Vander Zanden, J. W. (1989). *Human development* (4th ed.). New York: A. A. Knopf.

Vontress, C.E. (1976). "Counseling the racial and ethnic minorities." In G. S. Belkin

(Ed.), *Counseling: Directions in theory and practice*. (pp. 277–290). Belmont, CA: Wadsworth.

Walberg, H. J. (1984). "Increasing the productivity of America's schools." *Educational Leadership, 41(8)*, 19–27.

Walker, J. L. (1988). "Young American Indian children." *Teaching Exceptional Children, 20*, 50–51.

Walsh, C. (1987). "Language, meaning, and voice: Puerto Rican students' struggle for a speaking consciousness." *Language Arts, 64*, 196–206.

Watanabe, C. (1973). "Self-expression and the Asian-American experience." *Personnel and Guidance Journal, 32*, 273–282.

Wax, M. L. (1971). *American Indians: Unity and diversity*. Englewood Cliffs, NJ: Prentice-Hall.

Werner. E. E. (1979). *Cross-cultural child development: A view from the planet Earth*. Monterey, CA Brooks/Cole.

West, B. E. (1983). "The new arrivals from Southeast Asian." *Childhood Education, 60*, 84–89.

Whaley, K., & Swadener, E. B. (1990). "Multicultural education in infant and toddler settings." *Childhood Education, 66*, 238–240.

Williams, D. L., & Chavkin, N. F. (1989). "Essential elements of strong parent involvement programs." *Educational Leadership, 47(2)*, 18–20.

Williams, L. R. (1989). "Diverse gifts: Multicultural education in the kindergarten." *Childhood Education, 66*, 2–3.

Williams, R. L. (1973). *Black intelligence test of cultural homogeneity (BITCH)*. St. Louis: Williams and Associates.

Wilson, R. (1989). "Black higher education: Crisis and promise." In J. Dewart (Ed.), *The state of Black America 1989*. (pp. 121–135). New York: National Urban League.

Wolf, J. S. (1990). "The gifted and talented." In N. G. Haring, & L. McCormick (Eds.), *Exceptional children and youth*, (pp 447–489). Columbus, Merrill.

Wolfram, W., & Christian, D. (1979). *Exploring dialects*. Arlington, VA: Center for Applied Linguistics.

Yao, E. L. (1988). "Working effectively with Asian immigrant parents." *Phi Delta Kappan, 70*, 223–225.

Yao, E. L. (1985). "Adjustment needs of Asian immigrant children." *Elementary School Guidance and Counseling, 19*, 222–227.

Yarborough, B. H., & Johnson, R. A. (1983). "Identifying the gifted: A theory-practice gap." *Gifted Child Quarterly, 27*, 135–138.

Yee, L. Y. (1988). "Asian children." *Teaching Exceptional Children, 20(4)*, 49–50.

Yetman, N. R., & Steele, C. H. (Eds.). (1975). *Majority and minority: The dynamics of racial and ethnic relations* (2nd ed.). Boston: Allyn and Bacon.

Youngman G., & Sandongei, M. (1983). "Counseling the American Indian child." In D. R. Atkinson, G. Morten, & D. W. Sue (Eds.) *Counseling American minorities: A cross-cultural perspective (pp. 73–76)*. Dubuque, IA: Wm. C. Brown.

Zychowitz, M. J. (1975). *American Indian teachings as a philosophical base for counseling and psychotherapy*. Unpublished doctoral dissertation. Northern Illinois University.

INDEX

Academic achievement, 229–230
  African-American levels of, 73–75
  Asian-American family, role of, 101–102, 104, 108, 259–260
  Asian-American levels of, 102–104
  educator's perspective on, 219
  Hispanic-American levels of, 131
  Hispanic-American self-concept and, 139–140
  Native-American learner levels of, 47–48
  Native-American views of, 34–35
  parent influence on, 221
Administrators, role of, 288–294
  evaluation of, 293–294
  support of classroom educators, 292–293
Adolescents
  African-American, 82
  friendship patterns in early, 65–66
  Native-American, 36–37, 41
  problems of female Asian-American, 102
African-Americans, 58–86
  academic achievement of, 74–75
  children's literature, 59–60, 62, 64, 66, 69, 74, 86
  cultural characteristics of, 63–66
  demographics, 5–7, 60–62, 337
  educating males, 79–80
  families, 65, 68–70
  guidance and counseling of, 306
  language, 71, 76–78
  learning styles of, 78–79
  names, 7
  origins of, 59
  percentage of teaching force, 289
  religion, 70
  socioeconomic status of, 67, 220, 236
  stereotyping of, 62–63, 159, 182
  use of term, 6
American Indians. See Native-American
Anglo-American culture
  comparison with African-American, 72
  comparison with Asian-American, 100
  comparison with Native-American, 42–43, 44
  comparison with Hispanic-American, 128
Asian-Americans, 87–113
  academic achievement of, 101–104
  children's literature, 91, 113
  cultural characteristics of, 94–95, 101
  demographics, 8, 88–89

  families, 96–98, 108, 259–260
  guidance and counseling of, 306–307
  language, 98–100, 104–105
  learning style, 106
  origins of, 88
  refugee groups, 6
  religion, 98
  shame, concept of, 96, 98, 108
  socioeconomic status of, 95–96, 220
  stereotyping of, 91–94, 101, 107, 159, 182
Association of Hispanic Arts (AHA), 122
Athletic programs, 191

Biculturalism, 10
Bilingual education, 175, 242, 329–330
Black-Americans. See African-American
Black Intelligence Test of Cultural Homogeneity (BITCH), 81, 295
Blaming the victim, 16, 79, 325–326
Brown vs. Board of Education of Topeka, 199
Buddhism, 98

Catholicism
  among Asian-Americans, 98
  among Hispanic-Americans, 126
Chicano Family Center (CFC), 125
Chicanos. See Hispanic-American
Childrearing practices
  of Asian-American families, 96–98
  of Native-Americans, 39, 43
Children's literature
  about African-Americans, 59–60
  about Asian-Americans, 91, 113
  about Hispanic-Americans, 118, 120, 127, 140, 144
  librarian selection of, 301–303
  and multicultural education, 173
  about Native-Americans, 34
  sexism and racism in, 184–185
  written in Spanish, 140
Chinese Cultural Association, 89
Chinese Cultural Center, 89
Civil Rights, Office of (OCR), 238
Civil Rights Movement, 6, 24
Cognitive processes, 229–230, 232
Communications disorder specialists
  and classroom educators, 313–314
  evaluation of, 315

role of, 311–312
Community involvement, 189–191
Confucianism, 98
Cooperative integrated reading and compo-
    sition, 209
Cooperative learning, 206–210
Council for Indian Education, 35
Counselors
    and classroom educators, 308–310
    evaluation of, 310–311
    role of, 305–308
Court decisions, 23
    regarding curriculum materials, 184
    regarding handicapped children,
        296–297
Cross-cultural competency, 149
Cubans. See Hispanic-American
Cultural characteristics
    of African-Americans, 63–66
    of Asian-Americans, 94–95, 101
    of Hispanic-Americans, 120–122,
        136–137
    of Native-Americans, 33–37
Cultural deficit model, 15–16
Cultural diversity, 15, 150, 153, 228–229
    changing attitudes toward, 156, 169, 338
    educator's knowledge of, 154, 199–200
    effects of , 244–245
    guidelines for respecting, 178–180
    and motivation, 234, 235
Cultural identity
    of African-American learner, 81–84
    of Asian-American learner, 103, 108–110
    developing positive, 20–21, 157–159,
        245, 245–246
    of Hispanic-American learner, 127,
        139–142
    of Native-American learner, 33–37,
        51–54
    promoting in school, 216–217
Culturally different model, 17, 163
Cultural mismatch model, 16
Culture, characteristics of, 9–10
Curriculum, 167–195
    evaluating, 185
    guidelines for developing, 175–176
    needs assessment, 180–181
Curriculum materials, 181–185, 342
    educator's responsibilities for, 332–333
    and stereotyping, 172

Daycare. See Infant and toddler education
Demographics, 5–7
    African-American, 5–7, 60–62, 337
    Asian-American, 5, 6–7, 88–89
    Hispanic-American, 5, 6, 8–9, 116–117,
        337
    Native-American, 5–6
Developmental levels, 232
    of adolescent, 282

of child, 280
    helping parents understand, 278–280
    of preadolescent, 281
Developmental tasks, 130, 279
Developmental theory, 279
    and African-American learners, 73
    and Asian-American learners, 103
    and Hispanic-American learners, 130
    and Native-American learners, 47
Dialects. See Language
Dropout rate
    of African-American learners, 151
    of Hispanic-American learners, 151
    of Native-American learners, 48, 151,
        208

Ecological culture, 10
Education for All Handicapped Students
    Act, 296
Educator's responsibilities, 172, 199–204,
    217, 228, 331–334
Educator's roles in multicultural education,
    154–155, 342
Educators' roles in understanding
    African-American learners, 72
    all learners, 162–163
    Asian-American learners, 100–103,
        108–109
    Hispanic-American learners, 129–130
    Native-American learners, 43–46
Educator's skills and abilities, 155, 200–202
English as a Second Language (ESL), 134,
    241, 242–243, 330–331
Entitlement, 148
Ethnicity, 11–12
Ethnocentrism, 156–157, 172, 307
Extended family
    Hispanic-American, 124, 128
    involvement of, 222, 256, 271–272
    See also Kinship networks
Extracurricular activities, 191–192
Eye contact
    among African-Americans, 65, 72
    among Hispanic-Americans, 128
    among Native-Americans, 42

Family
    African-American, 65, 68–70
    Asian-American, 96–98, 108
    differences between, 261–263
    Hispanic-American, 124–125, 140
    involvement of, 252–285
    Native-American, 38–40
Family tree, use of, 141
Friendship patterns in early adolescence,
    65–66

Gender, 13–14, 231–232
    role of in Hispanic-American family, 125
Generational differences, 262

Gifted children, 239–241
Grouping
    by ability level, 172, 204, 205–206
    part of hidden curriculum, 178
Group investigation, 210
Guatemalans. *See* Hispanic-American
Guilford's Structure of Intellect Model, 240

Handicapped children, 239
    labeling of, 237
    rights of, 296
Head-touching, prohibition against, 95
Hidden curriculum, 177–178, 216
Hispanic-American, 114–144
    academic achievement of, 131–132
    Anglo-Americans, attitudes toward, 121,
        257
    children's literature, 118, 120, 127, 140,
        144
    cultural characteristics, 120–122,
        136–137
    demographics, 6, 8, 116–117, 337
    families, 124–125, 140
    guidance and counseling of, 307
    identity conflicts in, 21–22
    language, 119, 126–128, 132–135
    learning styles, 135–136
    origins, 8, 115
    races, 8, 115, 117
    religion, 126
    socioeconomic status of, 122–123, 220,
        236
    stereotyping of, 118–119, 132, 138, 159,
        182
    values, 120
Hispanic Institute for the Performing Arts
    (HIFPA), 122
Hispanic names, 135, 141, 233
Hispanic Policy Development Project, The,
    123
Holidays, 211, 215
Home visits, 268–269
Honor, concept of, 98, 107, 121

Indians. *See* Native-American
Indian Youth of America, 35
Indices of Academic Potential, 240
Individual differences, 15, 226–251
Infant and toddler education, 176–177
Instructional practices, 196–225
    activities, 211–214
Integral Education Model, 134
Intelligence, 229–230
Interaction, rules governing, 244
Interdisciplinary approaches, 152–153
Interracial marriage, 69

Jigsaw methods, 207, 209

K-ABC Instrument, 240

Kindergarten, 174
King, Martin Luther, Jr., 6, 60
Kinship networks, 68–69, 128
    See also Family
Kranz Talent Identification Instrument, 240

Labeling
    counselor's role in, 307
    dangers of, 237–243, 327
    of Hispanic-American learners, 138–139
    special educator's role in, 295
    See also Grouping
Language
    of African-Americans, 71, 76–78,
        328–329
    of Asian-Americans, 98–100, 104–105
    of the curriculum, 192–193, 210, 241
    differences of parents, 257, 263
    disorders, role of specialist, 311–312
    of Hispanic-Americans, 119, 126–128,
        132–135
    of Native-Americans, 41–42, 45, 48–49
    non-sexist, 175
Latin-American. *See* Hispanic-American
Learner evaluation, 222–223
Learning styles, 246–249
    of African-American learners, 78–79, 248
    of Asian-American learners, 106, 247
    of Hispanic-American learners, 135–136,
        248
    of Native-American learners, 46, 49–51,
        210, 233, 244, 248
    related literature, 136
Learning together method, 208
Librarians
    and classroom educators, 303, 303–304
    evaluation of, 304–305
    role of, 301–303
Limited English proficiency, 133, 221, 296
    role of communications disorder special-
        ist, 311

Machismo, 120, 121, 128, 137
Melting pot metaphor, 2, 228, 339
    and emergence of multicultural educa-
        tion, 22
Mexican-American. *See* Hispanic-American
Minority Caucus of Family Services
    America, 65
Model minority stereotype, 91–94, 102, 103
Modesty among Asian-American learners,
    101, 108
Multicultural education, 22–26, 145–166
    assumptions underlying, 147–148,
        150–151
    controversy in, 163–164, 320–321
    definitions of, 23–24, 25, 320
    emergence of, 22–24, 340
    goals of, 148–150, 339, 341

guidelines for developing curricula, 175–176
in infant and toddler settings, 176–177
in kindergarten, 174
policies and practices of, 24, 321
principles of, 152, 322
units, 185–189
Multicultural Pluralistic Assessment (SOMPA), 81

Name-calling, 119
National Association for the Advancement of Colored People (NAACP), 238
National Black Child Development Institute, 64–65
National Black Youth Leadership Council, 65
National culture, 10
Native-Americans, 29–54
achievement levels, 47–48
adolescents, 36–37, 41
children's literature, 34, 35, 56–57
concept of sharing, 36, 208
cultural characteristics of, 33–37
demographics, 5–6
families, 38–40
guidance and counseling of, 306
lands, 5, 31, 159
language, 41–42, 45, 48–49
learning styles of, 46, 49–51, 210
origins of, 30
religion, 40–41
socioeconomic status, 37–38, 220
stereotyping of, 32–33, 182
treaty rights, 30
tribes, 5, 35
Natural Indian Education Association, 35–36
Navajo Nation Reservation, 5
Negro. See African-American
Nonverbal communication, 331
of African-Americans, 71, 78
of Asian-Americans, 99–100
of Hispanic-Americans, 127–128
of Native-Americans, 41

OCR. See Civil Rights, Office of

Parent advisory councils, 273–275
Parent education, 276–283
formats of, 278
rationale for, 276–277
Parent involvement, 52, 80–81, 106, 189–191, 221–222, 252–285
administrative support for, 291
Asian-American, 264
educator's responsibilities for, 333–334
Hispanic-American, 125
programs, 263–266
reasons for, 255

and school expectations, 280–283
Parent survey, 267–268
Parent-teacher communication
language difficulties, 269
telephoning, 270
written, 270–271
Parent-teacher conferences, 272–273
Personalismo, 128, 137
Phases of multicultural education, 25–26
Physical contact, prohibitions against, 95
Population. See Demographics
Poverty. See Socioeconomic status
Powerful environments, 221
Principals. See Administrators
Protestantism among Asian-Americans, 98
Psychocultural variables, 297–298
Puerto Rican Family Institute (PRFI), 125
Puerto Ricans. See Hispanic-American

Race, 10–11
of Hispanic-Americans, 8
developing positive identity, 245–246
Racio-ethnic culture, 10
Racism, 18–19, 81, 159–160, 169, 322–324, 338
children's literature about, 59–60
in curriculum materials, 181–185
guidelines for analyzing in books, 184–185
responding to, 170–172, 322, 324
Regional culture, 10
Religion
of African-Americans, 70
of Asian-Americans, 98
of Hispanic-Americans, 126–128
of Native-Americans, 40–41
Remedial language programs
and Asian-Americans, 105
and Hispanic-Americans, 134
See also Bilingual education and ESL
Respect for teachers, 95, 100, 258–260

Salad bowl metaphor, 3
and emergence of multicultural education, 22
Salvadoran. See Hispanic-American
School environment, 214–218
School practices, 170
impeding African-American learners, 79–80
impeding Asian-American learners, 106–107
impeding Hispanic-American learners, 137
Segregation. See Grouping
Self-concept
of African-American learner, 81–84
of Asian-American learner, 108–110
and children's literature, 184

of Hispanic-American learner, 127,
139–142
importance of, 231
and names, 6
of Native-American learner, 51–54
promoting in schools, 216–217
Self-evaluation, 202–204
Sexism and sexist language, 175
in curriculum materials, 183
guidelines for analyzing, 184–185
See also Gender, Stereotyping
Shame, concept of, 96, 98, 259
Sharing, Native-American concept of, 36,
208
Slavery, 59
children's literature about, 59–60
Social class differences, 12–13
See also Socioeconomic status
Social expectations of African- and Hispanic-American children, 130–131
Socioeconomic status
of African-Americans, 67, 220, 236
of Asian-Americans, 95–96, 220
educator's perspective on, 218–221
effects on family, 262
effects on learner achievement, 236–237
of Hispanic-Americans, 122–123, 220,
236
of Native-Americans, 37–38, 220
SOMPA. *See* Multicultural Pluralistic
Assessment
Southeast Asian Center, 89
Spanish, 126
punishment for speaking, 137
See also Language
Spanish-American. *See* Hispanic-American
Special educators
and classroom educators, 298
evaluation of, 300
responsibilities of, 299–300
role of, 294–298
Speech therapists. *See* Communications disorder specialists
Staff development, 290–291
Staff diversity, 217–218, 288
Standardized achievement tests, 222, 295,
326–328

Stanford-Binet, 240
Stereotyping, 20, 160–162
of African-Americans, 62–63
of Asian-Americans, 91–94, 101
counteracting, 161
in curriculum materials, 182, 184
by gender, 13–14, 231–232
of Hispanic-Americans, 118–119, 132,
138
of Native-Americans, 32–33
by race, 18, 20
Student teams achievement divisions
(STAD), 209
Superstition, role of, 264

Taoism, 98
Teacher accreditation, 341
Team assisted individualization, 209
Teams-games-tournament (TGT), 209
Textbooks. *See* Curriculum materials
Themes of Black Awareness (TOBA), 81
Title IX, 232
Tokenism, 184
Total school curriculum, 150–151, **173–176**,
179, 333, 341–342
Toys, gender-stereotyped, 176
Tribes, 5

Unemployment
of Hispanic-Americans, 122
of Native-Americans, 38
Universal culture, 10

Values and beliefs, 232–234
of Asian-Americans, 94–95, 233
of Hispanic-Americans, 120
of Native-Americans, 34, 233
Verbal teaching style, 107
Volunteering
and the Asian-American learner, 107,
110
parental, 271–272

Wechsler Scales, 240
Word recognition skills, 125